STORYTELLING
THROUGH ANIMATION

STORYTELLING THROUGH ANIMATION

MIKE WELLINS

CHARLES RIVER MEDIA, INC.
Hingham, Massachusetts

Publisher: Jenifer Niles
Cover Design: The Printed Image
Front Cover Image: Mike Wellins
Back Cover Images: Mike Wellins, Gesine Kratzner, and Allan Steele

CHARLES RIVER MEDIA, INC.
10 Downer Avenue
Hingham, Massachusetts 02043
781-740-0400
781-740-8816 (FAX)
info@charlesriver.com
www.charlesriver.com

This book is printed on acid-free paper.

Mike Wellins. *Storytelling through Animation.*
ISBN: 1-58450-394-7

Library of Congress Cataloging-in-Publication Data
Wellins, Mike.
   Storytelling through animation / Mike Wellins.— 1st ed.
       p. cm.
   Includes bibliographical references and index.
   ISBN 1-58450-394-7 (pbk. with cd-rom : alk. paper)
   1. Computer animation. 2. Computer graphics. 3. Animated films—Technique. I. Title.
   TR897.7.W46 2005
   791.43'34—dc22
                                      2005000314

Printed in the United States of America
05 7 6 5 4 3 2 First Edition

With endless gratitude and appreciation,
this book is dedicated to everyone who ever
helped me make a movie.

CONTENTS

ACKNOWLEDGMENTS

I'd like to thank my friends and fellow filmmakers who helped on this book by supplying their incredible art and valuable insight. I also want to thank all the talented artists, animators, and filmmakers, both past and present, who have taught me so much about the craft of animation and film. It is on their shoulders that we all stand.

Thanks to Darrel Anderson for his amazing 3D animation and designs. Darrel is a talented illustrator and recently illustrated the Stephen King book *Savannah*. He also created most of the digital effects in the film *Johnny Mnemonic*.

Thanks to Colin Batty who has always been so generous with his amazing artwork over the years. Colin created many images throughout this book. Colin is a character designer, illustrator, and artist. He sculpted the original stop-motion puppets for the movie *Mars Attacks!*, and created the characters for the short films *The Sandman* and *The Periwig-Maker*. Colin also designed the characters on the animated television show *The PJs*.

Thanks to Barry Bruce who helped me become a better director and an animator. With true style and humor, Barry has always been generous with his knowledge. Barry has since retired from animation production and moved to Colorado to work on his own art.

Thanks also to Guy Burwell for his fantastic and unique art. Guy was a designer on numerous commercials and animations and is recognized as a fine artist and rock-poster creator.

Thanks to Laura DiTrapani for providing her diverse imagery. Laura is a busy independent filmmaker making very cool art and animation and continues to make films for *Sesame Street*.

Thanks to Don Flores for the use of his designs that were then modeled by Patrik Puhala. Don is now an intern at Vinton Studios.

Thanks to Andrew Gordon for his insight and input. Andrew is at the forefront of CG feature animation, and his experience is incredibly valid for modern animators.

Thanks to Paul Harrod for his insight and the imagery and experience as an art director.

Thanks to John Hazzard and Ben Neall for the images of their 3D characters and models.

Thanks to the legendary Glen Keane at Walt Disney Feature Animation for his incredible insight into the creative process, and being so giving and sharing when it comes to his incredible knowledge and experience.

Thanks to Gesine Krätzner for her stills from her film, *Rat Trap*. Gesine is a director at Vinton Studios.

Special thanks to Ira Latour, for his photographs and observations. Ira is perhaps the most prolific artist, filmmaker, and photographer I've ever known. He has always been a great source of encouragement, humor, and inspiration for a long time.

Thanks to Joanna Priestley for her truly unique imagery. Joanna is a prolific animator and filmmaker who has shown all over the world and garnered countless awards. She truly explores uncharted waters of animation and film.

Thanks to Tracy Prescott MacGregor who has always been so generous with her knowledge and art, and is always fun to work with. Tracy also designed the characters for Marilyn Zornado's *Insect Poetry*.

Patrik and Amila Puhala created the short CG film, *107.6 Degrees*, which is the temperature where the brain starts to go a bit funny in the heat. A truly talented couple, the Puhalas animated many scenes in *Shards of Death*, under the animation direction of another great animator and friend, Sean Burns. Partrik and Amila now work in Texas on *The Adventures of Jimmy Neutron: Boy Genius*.

Thanks to Chris Sanders for his candid conversations and interview and amazing perspective on directing and creating.

Thanks to Toni Smith for her awesome graphic designs and all her help over the years.

Thanks to Allan Steele for his imagery from his short film *The Lester Show*. Allan has animated on countless TV commercials, such as the M&Ms® and many others, as well as television pilots. Allan is now working on a new film of his own titled *Pancake Circus*.

Thanks to the legendary Will Vinton for his kind words and for giving me some major breaks and letting me in on some amazing projects.

Thanks to my talented brother Dean Wellins for all his help over the years, and for his amazing sound tracks and his insight into the monster that is the story, but more recently thanks for introducing me to the talented individuals at Walt Disney Feature Animation.

Thanks to Marilyn Zornado for being able to use images as well as her film *Insect Poetry*. Marilyn has been nothing but kind and generous and has always been a pleasure to work with.

Special thanks to Lisa Freeman for all her hard work; Christopher Murrie; everyone at the IMC at Chico State; Erik Vignau, Jamie Haggerty, and Happy Hour Entertainment; and artist Steve Wilson, Mark Noland, and The CSU Summer Arts. Most important, thanks to my Dad and family and friends for putting up with years of bad films, as I tried to figure all this stuff out.

FOREWORD

The author of *Storytelling Through Animation*, Mike Wellins, is one of those rare animation directors who is a true "filmmaker." Mike does it all and has literally made at least 100 films or more—only he knows. He explores the worlds of live action and animation as both an avid experimentalist and as a professional. Even rarer still, Mike is a genuine writer of comedy, drama, and now books. The fact that this book exists despite Mike never having written a book before is a testament to yet another of his strong filmmaker qualities—his energy and determination as a creator.

Mike joined the company I founded and built, Will Vinton Studios, in 1996 when it was still in its creative heyday. We had just shifted from doing the highly experimental and quite well-known *Claymation* work I had initiated, to following the pack into the digital animation world. From the beginning, I found in Mike a kindred spirit and a complete filmmaker. Together and between other directing jobs, Mike and I spent the better part of two years trying to get an animated sketch comedy show, *Klay's TV*, off the ground with the Fox™ network. While the project didn't go beyond the full pilot episode, the experience with Mike was a blast and an education. In addition to his easygoing manner, what I always enjoyed about Mike was his can-do, go-for-it attitude built on huge amounts of street smarts and a deep love of animation and filmmaking. When we worked together, it commonly felt like "guerilla filmmaking"— my favorite kind—where creativity and resourcefulness trump craft, and where everyone involved is a collaborator back in film school. During that period we (or at least I) learned more about comedy than if I had done two dozen big-budget, highly specialized "professional" comedic projects.

While Mike Wellins is not what you'd call "classically trained" (usually meaning steeped in 2D feature animation vernacular of the early and mid 20th century) like many animation masters, he possesses the gifts that the best animators possess: curiosity, keen observation of the world around him, and a deep love of the art form. He is a perpetual and permanent student of the craft of animation, with an exhaustive enthusiasm and energy to continue a lifetime of exploring every fascinating aspect of animation and of filmmaking in general. In Mike's case, this exploration goes on day and night as near as I can tell—perhaps even in his sleep. These are all qualities that I recommend readers embrace and nurture in their own pursuit of animation—they are the cornerstones to learning to become a real animation filmmaker.

I have used the word "filmmaker" several times. To me, it is a significant word. These days (and probably forever after) we are all involved in digital media and the digital/computer-based arts even if we are practicing hand-drawn or hand-sculpted forms of animation or other old animation technologies. The computer has forever changed many of the ways we do things. It tends to force people into being technicians or specialists and working in large teams out of necessity. But there are a great many skills and important aspects of filmmaking that have not changed and probably never will. Being a filmmaker to me means being mentally capable of doing it all—it means understanding the creative aspects of a project so well that if one had the technical ability, one could be the animator, the lighting/texturing artist, the editor, or the sound designer and always remain in the service of the story and capable of moving the production forward in the best possible way.

Storytelling Through Animation is a book for filmmakers and animators. It's a general overview of the whole process of conceiving and producing a media production—animated or live action—Flash, 3D, CG, or Mini-DV. Regardless of the specific process or the tools used, filmmakers know that all media projects must always be in the service of their stories and the characters through which the stories are told. Ad nauseum, every great filmmaker will tell you the same thing: "We are first and foremost storytellers. The story is the most important element of a production."

Since early man, the story was probably the first form of entertainment, told around a campfire. Perhaps even before language, stories were acted out, ultimately giving rise to and expanding language. Stories and tales of the hunt begot the first art—cave paintings. Today, those same paintings and the drama they depict can look and feel strikingly similar to characters and stories in a modern stylized animated film. Stories, fables, and tales have taught humans lessons for ages. Some tales have such a deep routed connection to everyone that arguably, modern man carries the basic form of these tales in his DNA.

Not much has changed in the last 30,000 years. People still enjoy a good story. Whether it's told around the campfire or in a blockbuster movie, a good story is what really grabs an audience. Fundamentally, the stories themselves haven't changed much either. There are still stories of good against evil, stories of love, and stories of betrayal. The basic stories are the same, but they can be told well or poorly in an infinite number of ways.

As a director and as a filmmaker (and being in business for longer than I care to admit), it's sometimes hard to watch a movie or a new animated film without thinking about the directing, the animation, and the whole business side of the film and digital media production. But those are the poorer films in my opinion, because their stories didn't succeed in sucking me in. That's the real judge of a good movie. When it gets me—when it really pulls me in—I stop looking at how it's made and instead get deeply drawn into the characters and their plight. That's the goal for the viewer and it should be the objective for the filmmaker as well.

Of course this is all more easily said than done. Admittedly, telling a compelling story and staying true to that story and its characters throughout a production is not easy. This is especially the case with all the other things that have to be dealt with when creating animation since it has a whole second level of challenges above basic filmmaking. Not only do animators have to know about filmmaking, but they must also have the mastery and control of animation software and technology. They usually must be able to work collaboratively with many kinds of experts with a variety of technical skills.

In the end, the animator, along with everyone else on an animation crew from the director and the editor to the lighting director and the surfacer, should have one objective that drives everything else—tell a good story by creating compelling performances. "Breathing life into a character" is the common goal of the animator and the animation team. This means to go so far beyond merely "moving" characters that they seem alive, and more importantly, that they perform and act deftly in the service of a story. Whether an epic or just a simple gag, animators must manipulate their characters to give meaningful, caricatured performances and not simply mimic random human movement.

That's a tall order, but it's a worthwhile pursuit that I wholeheartedly recommend. Beyond the general quality and success of their projects, in my experience, good animators are good and interesting people! Animators are fast, life-long learners. They often have a wonderful, sometimes offbeat, sense of humor. They are students of movement and of life. They try things and experiment freely, and they approach animation with passion. Your guide through this book, Mike Wellins, has these qualities. He has assembled here a general path designed to help make you a very special kind of filmmaker—one who loves to play God, breathing life into the inanimate. It is a filmmaker who, regardless of the countless hours and sometimes less than perfect results, still has fun.

Will Vinton
Freewill Entertainment
Portland, Oregon

PREFACE

Filmmaking, animation, and visual media are everywhere in modern society. They are used as major forms of information, dissemination, and entertainment the world over. Visual media are involved in every aspect of life. Between television, films, the Internet, and games, modern societies spend an incredible amount of time watching film and animation. If the 1940s and 1950s were considered the golden age of animation, by sheer volume, the current age must be the platinum age.

Film and animation are a complex amalgam of story, characters, writing, photography, music, lighting, and, most important, imagination. Animation incorporates even more potential elements than standard filmmaking. It can be more complex and elaborate because there are no rules and it is only limited by imagination, and now that digital tools are used, animation is more complex than ever. For animation, the process is always in flux, and the term "filmmaker" itself now applies to people who use a huge array of media that uses no film whatsoever. When it comes to computer animation and digital filmmaking, there are many new jobs and career paths that never existed before. From animators, surfacers, riggers, and compositors, the list goes on and on for new digital production jobs. Although these new jobs are very specific and technical, the people holding these jobs need to view their part of a project like a solo filmmaker.

For the filmmaker, all the separate elements are interesting in their own right. When all the elements come together to tell a good story, that is when the sum is greater than its parts. The grand unifying idea is to tell a good story. At its most distilled state, the story must create a personal and emotional connection that moves and changes an audience, and goes beyond simple entertainment. Some clichés are clichés because they are true—it's all about the story. There are countless examples of entertainment forms that are entertaining in their own right. However, anyone who watches film and animation can easily recognize when a film or a story rises above the rest to create an emotional connection with the audience that isn't soon forgotten, if ever.

Characters are the main tools a storyteller uses to create this important connection. Characters that move an audience and establish an emotional connection are the ones that grow from, and bring forth, a great story that viewers can make a serious emotional connection with, while being thoroughly entertained.

To that purpose, filmmakers and animators are storytellers as well as entertainers. When a story is compelling, unique, and interesting, it's entertaining by its very nature. Entertaining stories don't have to have the latest special effects and they don't even have to use cameras. All they need are a good storyteller and someone to listen.

Audiences love committing to a good story and welcome stories and characters that make them laugh, cry, or move them in some way. They also want stories to take them places they've never been or always wanted to see.

By its very nature, visual media takes a specific amount of time. Whether it's a feature movie or even a first-person video game, it's largely based on discovery, surprise, elements revealed, and situations unfolding before the viewers' eyes. Audiences suspend their disbelief from the moment they walk into the theater or sit down in front of a television. Acceptance of the medium is as important as the electricity that powers the projector or the television. Audiences want to be fooled, and in that sense, filmmakers and animators are illusionists. Audiences that have had a steady diet of film and television for decades still want to be fooled, but they are much more sophisticated. Their tastes are always evolving and changing.

The illusion filmmakers strive for is reality on the screen, so that their story is true in some form and their characters are alive. Filmmakers want to make the characters' problems, challenges, and lives interesting and relatable to the viewers' lives.

Film and animation, however, are unique. The two form a machine that can work even though some parts may be completely broken. Film and animation can function at a less interesting level, and still produce an average, mediocre, or even a good film. That ultimate emotional connection of the audience with the story can be complete, intermittent, or nonexistent, and yet the movie or animation still exists and is watched by large audiences. In many instances, lack of a story or lack of good storytelling doesn't doom a film's or animation's success or appeal. Modern professional productions always have all the other elements securely in place—action, special effects, one-liners, the works—as insurance policies in case the emotional connection is broken.

At the other end of the spectrum is the great story with great depth, complex characters, surprises, insights, and extraordinary scenes and visuals. This is the world of the greatest films and there is no arguing the importance and the compelling nature of the story. Whether the story comes out of the characters or the characters come out of the story is academic; the two cannot exist without each other.

Filmmaking and animation can be difficult and rewarding at the same time because it's always changing. How it evolves technically from day to day, project to project, character to character, and scene to scene is always different. What worked great on the previous project not only doesn't work, but is totally irrelevant.

Akira Kurosawa, the late great Japanese director and unarguably one of the greatest film directors of all time, received a lifetime achievement award near age 90. When he received the award, he said that he didn't understand why he was getting an award when he'd made so few films; he felt as if he was just starting to understand the process.

Of all the varied and talented artists, animators, and filmmakers who are included in this book, a single underlying idea joins them. Each and every one of them is keenly aware that there is no solving the visual storytelling puzzle once and for all. The puzzle pieces are always changing shape. Visual storytelling is an ongoing learning process and a development and evolution of imagination. For truly talented artistis of any kind, it is a life process of observation, study, and trial and error. This concept of forever adjusting, modifying, and learning is even more applicable to animators. Animation requires another huge level of knowledge and artistic understanding that can be more precise and involve more science and strict rules than filming alone.

Visual media are based on photography, and photography is based on the absolutes of science, chemistry, electronics, and physics. Unlike a painter who requires only a canvas, paints, and a subject before his creativity can begin, filmmakers and animators have a huge list of technical requirements that must be met before their creativity can even start. Because of these technical requirements and their complexity, the mechanics and challenges that make up the actual act of production often require all the effort, while the story becomes a distant second. The issue of the story being left behind because of technical and other issues is far too common. As a result, audiences constantly suffer.

An analogy to this idea would be a great sculpture that is going to be molded and cast in bronze; the molding process becomes so complex that the actual sculpture is forgotten in the process. All the compromises on the mold show up on the final bronze statue, and the sculptor considers it an artistic disaster. Film and animation, however, can still exist with a dead story, because of talented actors, visual effects, action, jokes, twists, and a whole host of techniques that can prove interesting and entertaining for audiences. Unfortunately, these elements can't create that abstract emotional connection. The bad bronze sculpture can be melted down, but films and animations with dead stories often wind up on DVD.

With so many factors involved in the process, from hard science to the most subjective feelings, it is obvious how challenging and rewarding the process can be. This process of learning and problem solving while being informed by the story is an ideal way to look at filmmaking, animation, and storytelling, regardless of the topic, budget, or production. All the artists and animators included in this book share this main idea, and whether talent comes from this continual learning or vice versa isn't important. The most talented filmmakers walk away from a scene not only solving and creating the best possible solution, but learning more about their craft, continually refining their critical eye, and pushing their imaginations.

The continual effort, both mechanically and creatively, of trying to find the best solution to the storytelling puzzle is in fact the solution. Whether a filmmaker or artist is a legend like Kurosawa or is just starting to explore visual storytelling, the goal isn't much different: tell the best story possible. For filmmakers, the rewards and the process keep them working on the giant illusion puzzle by making as many films as possible.

For the filmmaker, because films and animations can run over a given amount of time and go from scene to scene, they can have moments of perfection. They can have perfect sequences, perfect editing, and segments that the filmmaker feels work best just the way they are. The larger goal is to find the exact fit for all the pieces from the big picture to the last frame.

For many animators and filmmakers, in spite of all the technical hurdles, fuss, and problems, there is a basic thrill—the charge that comes from seeing animated characters come to life or seeing how scenes start to tell a story. When the characters are alive, can walk, talk, and do just about anything; they are ready to act out the story and the story is ready to come from the characters.

For the animator and filmmaker, there is an element of playing Dr. Frankenstein. It is the alchemist act of bringing an inanimate object to life to creating virtually anything imagined. The power of filmmaking and visual media carries tremendous weight in modern society. So many people get most of their news and entertainment watching countless hours of movies, television, games, and commercials with a common goal. Most viewers want an emotional connection from whatever it is they watch.

Animation's relationship to filmmaking is unique, a true hybrid of many art forms and techniques. In its simplest form it's a flipbook or a fixed security camera taking time-lapse images, but at the other end of the spectrum are the full blown films like *Fantasia, The Lord of the Rings, Blade Runner, Akira, Baraka,* and everything in between.

In reality, filmmaking and animation are expensive, laborious, and complicated and take mountains of work from start to finish. A clear testimony to how complex and difficult an animated or live-action movie can be is the many examples of competent filmmakers who often make movies that just aren't that good. They have all the latest tools, armies of talented people on the crews, and millions of dollars. Yet these movies that work technically don't work on the emotional level, tell the story right, or have the right story.

Before digital filmmaking emerged in all its different incarnations, flexible filmmaking was far more difficult and expensive. One talented person on a single desktop system can now do special effects that were completely impossible or prohibitively expensive. Overall, the digital production side of entertainment, from screenwriting software to special effects, sound design, and photo-real animation, has exploded and risen to a level of polish and "realism" that completely fools the human eye. Although the eye can be fooled, the emotional connection can't be fooled. It's far more complex, fickle, and critical. A movie empty of story and full of slick special effects is similar to an illusionist's job. Although he has plenty of flash, lasers, smoke, and moves, he doesn't really make anything magical happen.

The process of visual storytelling has infinite solutions. The good filmmaker is always searching for that combination of ideas and decisions that is unquestionably the best possible approach to telling the story. Filmmakers are fans by nature and many grew up watching movies, eager to be entertained.

With all its complexities and areas of subjectivity, it's fortunate that all of the great works are visible on the screen so we can study the story, performance, lighting, composition, pacing, etc. and learn from these great works. Centuries of talented artists have figured out techniques and developed processes and styles of every kind. The results of all that work are there to see and experience in the huge history of film, animation, and art.

Many true genius artists and masters created compelling art long before the invention of the camera. Many more artists and technical people have worked for years behind, in front of, and around the cameras. Many outstanding books, which go into incredible depth, have been written on every topic in this book. Therefore, this book's purpose is to identify and encapsulate the most important ideas, films, shorts, and books to provide clear examples that will help you tell better stories.

Examining each department that contributes to film and animation, from lighting to costuming, is enough material to spend an entire lifetime studying and perfecting. For the countless volumes that go into the specific details of every element of film and animation, this book will instead create a working overview. This overview will infuse the most important concepts and techniques for establishing a working system, so that the technical aspects can be managed and the telling of the story and the emotional connection can be the driving forces from the first idea to the final fade-out. In setting up a working, flexible system and by distilling complex ideas into basic concepts, it's possible to create a pattern of imaginative and critical thinking, evaluating, and problem solving.

There is also an energy and a momentum to filmmakers, especially new filmmakers who want to charge ahead to the "exciting" part of the process—the actual filming or animation. To the good filmmaker, however, every part of the process is exciting. From the first storyboards and designs to the layering of the most subtle sound effects, the good filmmaker is going to make something that connects, changes people, or does something new. He knows that although the filming and animation are important, making something special requires dissecting every level. He also sees every task as another opportunity to improve the overall project.

With the daily proliferation of visual media, the level of sophistication that audiences now expect is incredibly high. Audiences are hungry and ready for new and compelling ways of telling a story; they are ready to be thrilled, delighted, awed, frightened, and tickled. They expect a level of sophistication in performance, slick special effects, solid pacing, and brilliant acting. Even though digital technology has made many aspects of production simpler, cleaner, and faster, the final product still has to be that much better.

It is this lopsided process where it takes so much longer to make good stories than to watch them that causes the entertainment industry to always be searching frantically for the next great form.

In searching for new ways to tell stories, filmmakers have moved away from the standard story. The idea of reality, or mixes of reality with fantasy, along with the idea of turning the camera around have been added to the huge pool of entertainment options. This method has evolved into shows and movies that are aware of the camera and use it to affect the story. The new term "mockumentary" has been coined to describe films like *This is Spinal Tap* and *Waiting for Guffman*, which are presented as documentaries but are acted, planned, spoofs of the documentary genre. However, in this new age of camera awareness, the characters are still complex and rich and bring a new style of comedy that moves far away from the sitcom, which revolved around "one-liners." Instead, the new mockumentary style creates humor out of stories from the characters' actual lives.

There are certainly specific traits that all filmmakers have and some that they need to learn. Success is measured in many ways, but for a filmmaker or animator, success should be in telling a compelling story, whether it's a feature film, short, commercial, video, documentary, or even a cinematic video game. Film and animation can be extremely complex, and it becomes extremely important to be able to deal with, anticipate, and solve technical problems. Telling the story must be the focus of the effort, so that you create a truly emotional connection.

EMOTIONS IN MOTION

1

THE ILLUSION OF CINEMA AND ANIMATION

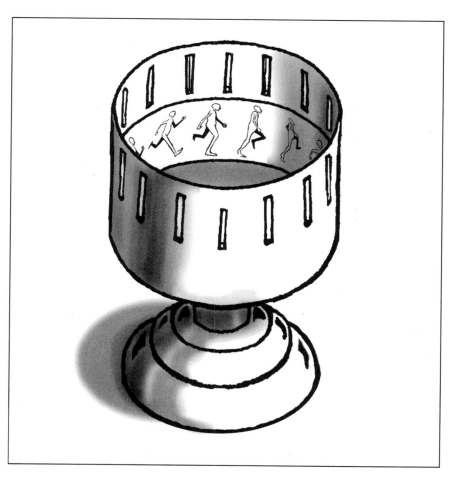

It's easy to make a film or animation without knowing the history of the medium, but the purpose of knowing the history is to know how things evolved and why. The driving force that helped develop film and animation was an ongoing attempt to develop more compelling stories and visuals. Film and animation are also tied to physical equipment, and knowing how the equipment works creates a foundation in understanding how devices, new and old, record light and motion.

People have been fascinated with motion and movement for a long time. From very early on, it was discovered that drawings and motion can create an illusion of movement; this illusion was the drawings coming to life. To the early discoverers it was mesmerizing, and that hasn't changed in hundreds of years. It's not possible to create a detailed history of the over 100 years of film animation in a single book, let alone a chapter. But even the brief history of the development of visual storytelling tools presented here will inform the animator and filmmaker about the ongoing struggle and desire to create more complex and engaging stories, many of which are anchored on technical innovations and countless creative individuals.

Flipbooks and the thaumatrope (see Figure 1.1) were probably the first tools used in animation. The technique is still largely the same: pictures shown in succession at a specific speed will appear as movement. People were in love with the novelty of animation, and inventors quickly came up with other versions of cycled animation in various toys and novelties. One of these novelties was the zoetrope (see Figure 1.2), a device that could make a strip of images move. The zoetrope was limited to a small number of frames, but the effect worked incredibly well. In the mid-1800s, a Belgian inventor invented the praxinoscope, a hybrid of the

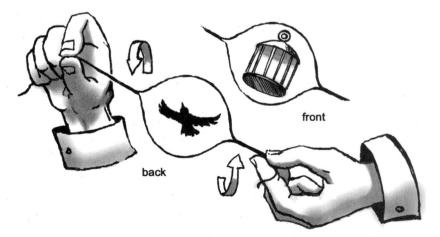

FIGURE 1.1   A thaumatrope is a two-sided card with two different images that creates a simple animation when flipped back forth.

zoetrope that incorporated simple projection. Inventors quickly came up with other versions of cycles of animations in various toys and novelties, all functioning like the original zoetrope. The zoetrope was a cylinder with a series of slits that the viewer looked through, while a sequence of animation on a strip of paper was set inside. Seeing the image through the slit allowed for a shutter effect, and the image became animated. Simple animations that looped, such as a horse galloping, a frog leaping, or other actions, became the elements of the simple animation.

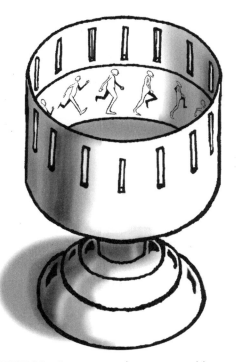

FIGURE 1.2   A zoetrope, when spun, could show a short cycle of animation drawn on a slip and viewed through slits that act like a shutter, creating animation.

Devices like the praxinoscope were hybrids of the zoetrope and used mirrors instead of slits to show the image. The later devices began to develop the basic traits of the modern projector and projected images through glass and could sequence a few more frames, making the animated sequence a bit longer, but the whole presentation was still very limited in the amount that could be shown. Over the years, many devices were created that looped animation, but it wasn't until the invention of acetate film that film and animation became more than just a novelty.

The first crude photographs were taken in the 1830s, and British mathematician and inventor William Henry Fox Talbot is credited with inventing the basic process that first recorded a true visual image of the real world. In the 1870s, Eadweard Muybridge began a comprehensive study of motion, which started as a wager and became a massive study that is still useful to artists, animators, and anyone curious about human and animal motion. In 1884, George Eastman was credited with creating photography as it is now understood, but in principal, between then and now, very little changed in the basic process until it became possible to record images without film via electronics, either digitally or on analog tape. Prolific inventors Thomas Alva Edison and William K.L. Dickson are credited with inventing the first motion-picture camera in 1891. Early pioneers like Georges Méliès and J. Steward Blackton are often credited with creating the first filmed animation in the early 1900s. Between the noted milestones like Edison and Eastman, countless other artists, engineers, inventors, photographers, chemists, and hobbyists all contributed to this growing novelty, science, and industry. Whether aware of the overall concept or not, early filmmakers' developments all worked toward a language that would use visuals to tell more complex and compelling stories [Llewellyn05].

The early filmmakers, including pioneer D.W. Griffith, created the film language. Foundations like the wide shot, close-up, match cut, and all the standard elements still used today can be traced to Griffith and his contemporaries in some form. In the final analysis, contributions by early filmmakers may have been closer to a discovery than an invention. There seems to be a mental format in the viewer's mind that filmmaking tries to service. For modern filmmakers, there are important lessons from early filmmakers that show the foundation of visual storytelling. The history of film and animation is a complex process of trying to fulfill what is expected and what the audience needs to see to get the key emotional connection, while creating engaging and unexpected images. Serious filmmakers can use the early films as a map for developing a true emotional connection by determining what works and what doesn't. Studying the history of film also transcends modern editing techniques or effects and strips down storytelling to camera placement and composition in relation to the all-important emotional connection.

Whether a discovery, an invention, or a combination of both, what stands out is that the fundamentals of filming have stood the test of time. Early filmmakers like Griffith experimented and made countless films to establish and develop a visual language that used techniques to record a story in a cohesive and comprehensive manner. The visual language, which can work from the patently simple to the profoundly complex, is the language of directors. In creating that visual language, directors are always trying to say it better, clearer, and with more impact. In fact, the entire point of all film study for filmmakers is simply that: create better, clearer, and more compelling film and animation, regardless of the genre. F.W. Murnau, in my opinion, is a standout contributor to visual storytelling. The German cinematographer, who is best known for his 1922 film *Nosferatu*, was one of the pioneers who furthered the language to start expressing complex ideas, stories, and emotions visually with the camera as the compelling element. His film *Sunrise: A Song of Two Humans* is considered by many to be one of the greatest silent films ever made. Murnau made a film that visually told a story with a camera and no dialogue cards, all with acting and ingenious camera use [Bohr03].

Using Murnau's techniques, the camera now moved and cut to unique and extreme angles. This helped set the tone of the story and focused on ideas and specifics, both real and ethereal. Murnau also included a shot of a person's point of view by walking through a revolving door. Taking a running camera through a revolving door isn't such a feat in the modern day film; one could take any camcorder or shoulder-mounted camera and walk through a door. However, back in the early 1900s, cameras were delicate and required a tremendous amount of light because of the film's lack of sensitivity. Finding unique shots like going through a revolving door was innovative enough, but the overall idea of the camera being used to enhance elements of the story by its very use was revolutionary.

The camera was no longer idle, akin to sitting in the front row of a play; it was now deeply involved in the story, often in complex ways. Filmmaking was no longer passive. It was a third player: the script, the acting, and the way the story was visually told.

This was new territory that Murnau was charting and he was keen to discover and create this new form of expression. Other innovations in *Sunrise* included a sequence where Murnau suspended a camera on a cable so that its movement could mimic the movement sounds coming out of a horn. As the invisible sound drifted upward and out, Murnau's camera flew high into the air, revealing the horn player below. This was another monumental new idea and a simple shot and solution. Murnau recognized a visual poetry and called these unique and new shooting ideas "dramatic angles" [Bohr03].

Murnau also recognized what Griffith had discovered and developed and coined a term that sounds more like it relates to music than film: "harmonious structure." He used this term to describe that innate feeling of the correct camera placement and editing and pacing. Harmonious structure is a truly appropriate term. It is a remarkable achievement in its own right, illustrating how such an early pioneer could accurately name something so intangible and subjective [Collier98].

Harmony isn't meant to be taken as jovial or always melodic like music; it instead describes a relationship between the story and the way it is visualized dependent on that story. Harmonious structure is more about emotion than frame counts. The story and the characters inform the visual. Suppose a story calls for abrupt cuts, flash frames or spinning cameras, and frenetic handheld shots. If the project is less without them, then that chaos is actually that project's unique harmonious structure. If the production calls for long shots locked off, with long dissolves and slow camera moves and the project is less without them, then that is that specific project's harmonious structure. Around 1908, Emile Cohl made his film *Fantasmagorie*, which is considered the first true animated film, although there were many proto-animation techniques prior to this film. In 1911, the famous cartoonist Winsor McCay created *Little Nemo*, but his film *Gertie the Dinosaur* was unique in that it created character animation and a character with a visible personality. Many legendary animators like Max Fleischer and Willis O'Brien began their careers in animation in the early 1900s. O'Brien, who would later make *King Kong*, made stop-motion shorts. World War II severely crippled the animation in Europe and allowed the United States to take the lead in animation production and development. Animators, like their filmmaker counterparts, were exploring the same ideas of developing stories that were unique and more engaging. However, animators were far more steeped in the technical aspects of filmmaking. Without realistic constraints they were able to explore more extreme forms of entertainment like Krazy Kat and other extreme characters with even more extreme personalities. From early on, animation and humor became tied together [McLaughlin01].

Large movie studios quickly came into existence and began producing movies all over the world, embracing a formulaic structure for most big-budget films. Synchronized sound partnered with films in the early 1920s, allowing far more complex acting and scripts. Synchronized sound also made it necessary to establish a uniform convention of speed so that film and sound were the same for each film print, projector, and theater. The rate that was developed was 24 frames per second, which closely mimicked what the human eye saw as far as visual speed. Color film had been around since the 1890s when films were tinted or hand painted with dyes, and many systems were developed with varying results. Color, like sound and angles, was simply another tool to try to create more compelling films and stories. Films became staples of entertainment and were wildly popular as escapism in the Great Depression, but films and their predecessor, stage plays, have always been about escapism. Films didn't require a stage or actors, but instead a screen, seats, and projector; the proliferation of story had found its massive outlet.

In 1920, Walt Disney and Ub Iwerks teamed up to begin making animated films. Walter Lantz also started his own studio four years later.

Disney's film *Skeleton Dance,* animated by Ub Iwerks, was one of the first films that had a tight synchronization with sound and created the process of animating to the prerecorded soundtrack that still is essential today. In the 1930s, Warner Brothers™ Studios introduced Merrie Melodies short films. In the production scheme, storyboards are essential, and it's believed that the use of storyboards was developed at the Fleischer studios in 1930. In 1932, Disney won its first Academy Award for *Flowers and Trees,* which was Disney's first film to use the Technicolor™ film process [McLaughlin01].

Animation came into its stride with animators like Bob Clampett, Chuck Jones, and Tex Avery, who began to develop comedic extremes. They pushed animation to a new and hilarious level, taking full advantage of the medium with *Looney Tunes* and characters like Porky Pig and Daffy Duck. Looney Tunes was a send-up of *Merrie Melodies,* which was in turn a send-up of Disney's *Silly Symphonies.* These send-ups were a running joke among animators that spoke to their ongoing development of types of cartoons. Carl Stalling began his animation career in 1937 by creating music for cartoons that would become the flavor of cartoon music. Stalling went on to compose music for over 600 films. In 1938, Disney released the feature-length animated film *Snow White and the Seven Dwarfs.* Disney reigned supreme in the feature animated film business with *Fantasia* and *Pinocchio* in 1940. The Disney studio created countless animation masterpieces over the next 60 years [McLaughlin01].

Animation's ability to tell stories and create characters was used as propaganda during World War II, with many studios jumping on the propaganda bandwagon. Films and animation have always been used to persuade through emotion, and creating and reinforcing morale during a war is no exception. In fact, many great films were created as war propaganda. Robert McKimson and Friz Freleng were among the other legends of animation who continued to develop animated films after World War II. The animation community was tiny and animators often left one studio to go work with another studio or teamed up with other animators to start their own. In the following years, countless animated characters were refined and created. Characters such as Bugs Bunny, Speedy Gonzales, Sylvester, Foghorn Leghorn, Mr. Magoo, and Tom and Jerry all became animated celebrities. Animation flourished all over the world with Japanese animation such as *Astroboy,* becoming the first animated Japanese television show. In 1961, Disney's *101 Dalmatians* made effective use of Xerox™ photocopies with the cel production. Characters were recognizable and animators and animation had become far more than a fascination; it was instead a true commodity and big business. From Yogi Bear to Scooby Doo and Johnny Quest to Speed Racer, animation went from a novelty to a true entertainment outlet to a standard fixture and even babysitter.

Animated films started out as entertainment for adults, but by the 1960s, animation and kids were forever locked together. No longer was there any guesswork in animation. It became a tried and true system that was easy to produce with overseas coloring and inbetweening. This relative ease resulted in a lot of poorly made animation that was created solely to entertain kids with the fixture of Saturday morning cartoons. Disney truly became the high-end feature animation company of the era. With the advent of truly refined special effects, animation got a huge blast of interest.

Animation had always been used as special effects and the first animations were mostly that, but the revolution of digital animation created a whole venue for animation that is now tied to the current blockbuster action movies and the special-effects epics. Although animation fueled the current mode of mainstream films such as *Star Wars, ET: The Extra-Terrestrial, Raiders of the Lost Ark,* and *Jurassic Park,* action movies have been a unwavering staple of cinema from their beginning. For example, the 1996 film *Titanic* was an epic driven by action and special effects. More recent films like *The Matrix* trilogy films are also example of films where the entire story is driven by special effects and digital animation.

The history of film and animation is about a fascination with illusion—the illusion of movement and the story. The characters on the screen aren't just a projection, but become people to whom the audience is emotionally connected. Animation's history is tied to filmmaking, but animation has had its own movement headed up by individual animators and studios for years. In fact, animation has slowly become a major revolution and fixture in modern society. Animators and filmmakers need to know the roots of their medium because the successes and the failures are there to be seen—at speed or one frame at a time. Art begets art, and inspiration and ideas have always been driven by what has and has not been done before.

ANIMATION, EXTREMES, AND ABSTRACTION

Animation is a study in extremes and abstraction. Visuals are far more extreme than a filmed live-action reality; color, design, composition, and movement are all different. Abstraction is the stylizing and manipulating of reality from a little tweaking of color or space to pure abstraction where nothing is familiar. The animated illusion is a foreign concept to the eye. Seeing drawings come to life is a unique experience. Compared to the world around us, animation is extreme in every aspect beyond just color, motion, and design; it is also extreme in the story, focus, and intent. It makes no promise to its own reality and instead basks in imagination; the viewers' expectations are limitless like the medium. Anything can happen in animation.

Abstraction is an extreme version of reality and a study of extremes. Disney characters have big eyes with huge irises and pupils, *The Simpsons'* characters have large bugged eyes, while other characters have eyes like pencil points—all abstractions of what normally is seen. This is not to say that there can't be calm and soothing animation, but by and large even pastoral pleasing scenes, such as the famous sequences from *Fantasia*, are still very extreme in their visual relationship to reality, color, and light. Such is the audience's connection with the graphical side of animation. Symbols from drawn comics can be incorporated and enhance rather than detract from the performance. For example, someone gets hit in the head and stars circle the wound, someone falls flat and is literally flattened, and someone cries and literally cries rivers.

Animation's relationship to the truly extreme—exaggerated characters and explosive animation—is unique. Similar to the educational film *Powers of Ten*, created by Charles and Ray Eames, which explained cosmological concepts so easily through animation, extreme animation has the ability to cycle through comedic gags and use jokes so quickly that it takes numerous viewings to catch them all; for this type of humor, nothing works better than extreme animation. In the 1951 Tex Avery classic *Symphony in Slang*, visuals move and jokes go off incredibly fast. The animation takes total advantage of the brain's ability to quickly recognize clean visuals, and then the film allows just enough time to actually get the visuals as well. Because a sight gag can be perceived in a split second, scenes can be loaded with visual cues and gags faster than anyone could ever read or try to act out physically or practically. *Symphony in Slang* and the other classic animated cartoons truly pushed exaggeration and stylizations not only in animation, but also in humor and in story; they are to cartoon comedy what *Power of Ten* is to science films. Almost anything can work in animation, and the simplest animated motion can have tremendous effect. However, the more challenging aspects of animation, when done right, can have the most impact. The illusion of movement and the illusion of living characters are equally as important as the illusion of the story. Good filmmakers and animators are keenly aware that they control everything that creates that illusion.

Filmmakers and animators must be able to look at the big picture of what they're trying to accomplish from an emotional standpoint. It does not matter whether a scene or shot is funny and slapstick-filled or somber and sad. Filmmakers cannot gloss over any element that has the ability to contribute to the overall emotional connection. From each frame, pose, and choice, the filmmaker who has distilled the ideas down to their key emotional connections and truly understands what connection he is trying to make overall will have that much more control and creative ammunition on every decision he makes.

Whether it's a 100-year-old film or the special-effects blockbuster of last week, filmmakers recognize that the harmonious structure that Murnau recognized is never the same for any two projects, but it is critically important in every one.

INTERVIEW WITH GLEN KEANE

Glen Keane is a director and legendary Disney animator. He has worked on such Disney classics as *Aladdin, Beauty and the Beast, The Rescuers, Tarzan, Mulan, The Lion King,* and many others. He is considered one of the best animators working today.

Wellins: *When you're developing a character, what informs you most about how you create that character? Its performance, the way it talks, looks, the driving force? How do you infuse the story, which is essential, into every little aspect of animation? How would somebody with a script or a story translate it the best possible way into an animation? The purpose of animation is to tell the story the best way, so I'm just wondering how you personally go about it. It's a huge question, but when you start out, what are the first things that you look at or pull apart when you start to develop a character?*

Keane: There's a couple different stages, for me. In some ways it's like meeting somebody. You first just have a first impression when you meet somebody. It's by the way they dress, it's the way they talk, and the circumstances that you meet them in and reading about the character on the script, or if it's even storyboarded ahead of time. You get a first impression and say, OK that's what it's like, but you can't animate from that. Just like you don't really know that person—it's just the first superficial information you get.

But then with that person that you've just met, you start to spend time with him and you start actually talking about your own experiences, and if they relate to you, like, "I like to play tennis. Oh, I like to play tennis too! Oh really, well, maybe let's go play tennis together!," then you go to the third thing where you're actually doing something together. And it feels to me like that's the same process for each of these characters. First I get to see, OK that their function is in the story: Tarzan has to become the king of the jungle. He's a man but he doesn't fit in with the gorillas. OK, that's basically the thing, but then how does he feel being in the jungle? That's really interesting to me. When I went to Africa then, and actually spent time in the jungle and hearing these noises at night out in the darkness around you, hear skittering and patter across the tent and I just thought, "Whoa, I would not want to be here without that guide and his gun." And yet, Tarzan is this little baby, grows up, completely left alone and raised by gorillas, so what kind of man could he possibly be? He's got to be incredible. I started to gain this respect for this person and became fascinated with him. Then when I'm starting to animate the character I can't just be fascinated. I have to actually feel like it's me. I don't know how this has always worked out, but somehow I can always be me in every character that I've done.

Wellins: *So you have to find something that relates to you personally or an aspect of that character that you identify with?*

Keane: Yeah, because that's the only way I could do what I'm doing here at Disney being able to put myself into those characters. It's never like, just an easy thing. It always comes to a certain point where it's kind of a soul-searching thing that I go through on a character. With Tarzan, because I was living in Paris and I was adapting to this whole living a French life, though I didn't speak French and I was learning to speak, I felt like I was Tarzan. And I was giving the lectures to

→

the animators there about flexibility. The only way that Tarzan can survive in the jungle is to be flexible. I was really talking about surviving in Paris, being flexible, just learning to adapt, and really drawing on my own experiences of being there and having fun with it. Being surprised and having fun with the challenges life was throwing us as a family and putting as much of that into knowing how Tarzan related. It really helped me. But then it was also drawing on moments like, where Tarzan was seeing Jane for the first time, and really relating that. When had I experienced that in my own life? And I remembered seeing Claire, our newborn daughter for the first time. In order to animate this moment, where Tarzan is seeing a human being, I realize this is like Adam and Eve. This is Adam thinking, "this is bone of my bones, flesh of my flesh." And when had I experienced that? I remember when Claire was born, holding her and looking at her and I could see my face. There was a little mirror of me in Claire, it was really weird. Even though she was just born, I remember trying to animate that moment, where Tarzan is looking at Jane and putting his hand on her hand.

When I was storyboarding it, I was thinking of that stuff as I was starting to board it. In the script those were just like maybe two little lines, you know, that Tarzan sees Jane. I forget what the lines were that came after; it was a very short little paragraph describing it, but it was all between the lines. It was investing your own life and putting it in there. There's always this little bit of a feeling like you're kind of embarrassed about exposing your life like that, that lets me know if I'm on the right track. If I'm feeling sort of, Oh gosh, should I do that? Everybody's going to think that's stupid. I'm saying so much about my own personal life here. Can I do that?

Wellins: *Really putting yourself out there then?*

Keane: Yeah, there's this uncomfortable feeling of like . . . I mean it takes courage to take that step and I feel like when I'm feeling awkward about stepping out with something so raw and real about me then I feel like I'm going into the right area in the story. And it can be comedy. It doesn't have to be just a very emotional moment too. It could be a dumb little thing: I think the first time it really clicked for me was animating *Mickey's Christmas Carol.* Willy the Giant kind of pushes the roof off of this house and he's stepping out and pulls this little street lamp off and he's going to go walking away with it as a lantern. But I remember when I was a kid I always just kind of just liked the click, click, click, turning the lantern on and off. And I'm thinking as I'm animating it, oh I should really have him kind of turn the thing on and off. And I started thinking, this is stupid. People are going to wonder, why are you doing that? You're wasting all this time. The scene is only this long, and now you've made it like that long. You can't do that! But I did it anyway because it was fun, and as soon as it was up everyone was going, "Oh, I love that whole thing with the little light where it's just click-click, and he goes walking."

Wellins: *That was so great. That was one of the most memorable scenes in that whole thing. I haven't seen that in 20 years and I remember that scene specifically!*

Keane: Yeah, because it was this real little moment that was entirely based on something I'd loved and did as a kid. And I almost didn't put it in because it was superfluous or not worth it or something. But it was also real. Right now, with this current character, I feel like I've been searching, walking around. You wanted to really feel like, I want to see that character get pulled into

$\rightarrow$

the story. I really want to know that about that character Which started me really thinking, "Why is this character acting this way?" I had this storyboard the very first time we see the character, and as I've been boarding this sequence, I feel like I'm circling around the character and I cannot just start boarding it yet. I've got to know something real about the character, and I keep circling and scribbling stuff and talking about it. It's weird; it's like this moving train you're trying to hop on to and get the right rhythm to leap on somehow, because you don't want to blow it. Yeah, you don't want to screw it up. You don't want to hop on the wrong car or something. There's a commitment that you make in a way. I want this to be the right character and I feel like I'm really getting very close to it right now, hoping that the voice talent who were recording tomorrow give another piece to it.

Wellins: *Is that because of the time commitment that it'll take for you to do all the work, that you kind of have to have that kind of connection to it? To have the steam to do the whole project so that you stay interested, you stay invested in the project? Is that part of that? Because obviously this takes a lot of time; it's tedious work.*

Keane: No, it's more like . . . it doesn't have anything to do with time. It has to do with whether I'm believing the character or not. Do I really know this character, because it feels like there's always this point where I know this character so well, and I know exactly the way The Beast [from *Beauty and the Beast*] would act if he came into the room right now? I've gotten to know him and at a certain point he's easy. It's like writing your name. Boarding a character that you know, it's very clear and strong, but if you don't know him it's painful, awful work.

Wellins: *That's funny because anybody watching* Beauty and the Beast *can see those big ideas of his personality, because you knew it so well and you were able to put it into every acting scene he did. The Beast comes off as volatile, impatient, unpredictable, all those things that just really set him off, and he's just so closed off to me. I can see in every scene that you capitalized on it every moment.*

Keane: To me he's also very frustrated . . .

Wellins: *All those made him unpredictable, which was really cool because you didn't know when he was going to go off, and it made it really interesting.*

Keane: Yeah, and I'm getting really close on this current project, but to me the way the door is actually open—this week anyway. Actually, it was Saturday and Sunday I just kind of, Wham! I did like about 200, maybe 300 drawings I must have done of the sequence. Just scribbling it out and it all kind of triggered with, just acting, drawing the character laying the first time we see it. And it was something about just the way it was evolving, just being itself. I just said to myself, "I like this character. There's something curious and interesting about" . . . and the character sort of pulled on the clothing, and as I was drawing it I knew the poses through the acting. There's something that's a mysterious thing for me that happens, that as you draw the performance starts revealing the character through drawing poses, thinking it through, suddenly it's more. I think it's because I just grew up as an animator here, that's how I approach story, really from acting it through and then everything else grows around there.

$\rightarrow$

Wellins: As the animator and as a storyboarder, I think the two are totally intertwined. I think it's interesting all the driving force comes from you. You don't worry about some viewer in Kansas or someplace. You're not thinking about the audience—what their reaction will be. I mean, you are the audience, It has to entertain you first; you have to be invested first. I think it's a mistake to go, "Now what is somebody in some theater someplace going to think?"

Keane: Well, I am always really conscious of whether what I'm doing, that it's something they're going to get. I'm always thinking of them, whether they're going to get it. But it's more . . . does what I have to say, is it valuable? Is it worth taking their time to do it? I can't be just gratuitous.

Wellins: Respect the audience?

Keane: I just know how it is for us. We don't have a lot of time to go see movies and if we're going to take somebody on this trip, this has got to be a real person. It can't be just this . . . the thing that I hate the most is doing something that feels formulaic. Doing something that feels like you done it before, you've seen it before. Why do it? This is our one chance here on earth to be an artist. For me this is my art, and I want it to be self-expressive and personal. Formulas are great for looking at why it communicates and analyzing the principles behind the clear staging, timing something in a way that's surprising. I really just don't like the Disney formulas that we kind of get trapped into any time we're into success, for a period. It feels like you've got to work really hard to get rid of all that stuff that made you successful. Chris Sanders was saying the other day, "Any time you're successful at something, success creates a rut and everything else kind of wants to fall into it. You've got to work really hard not to fall into that rut again."

Wellins: Kind of like with the automatic sequel? That one was successful. Hey, let's do another one.

Keane: At least sequels are blatant.

Wellins: They're not trying to pretend to be something else. This is the same thing—we're just going to do a different chapter. It's when you look at a movie and you go, This is just . . . You're just trying to hold people. This is just the same thing. You're just sticking in different animals and you're just sticking in different songs?

Keane: Yeah, it's like, [saying mockingly] I hope this will get me by, this sequence. I'll sell it to the director because it's supposed to be funny. This is where the gag happens and, OK, I did my job. I hope nobody notices. Why would you even want to do that, because that's what it is? It's really got to be a personal thing. That's what I like right now about this studio. There's a lot of angst going on in each of the projects because I think we're all suffering and struggling with trying to be who we are in our work. It's not easy to hand the scripts out to the other guys in the story [and] trust and see what comments come out of it. It's a little scary. You want people to like it, but at the same time if it's not working you want to hear that too. It's really . . . you're talking to me at a very formative stage of where I think I'm just about to get to know who this main character is that we're going to go on this whole journey with and I'm just reminded that I never see something clearly before I do it. Eric Larson was always saying to me, "You can't animate a scene unless you see it in your head." Well, I didn't see it. And he said, "Yes you do!" "No I don't." "Yes

→

you do. You see it because you can't draw it unless you see it." "But I . . . I really don't see it." I know what I feel, and when I start drawing it'll come out in some feeling and I find it that way. It's an internal compass . . . but I never approached animating that way, where I saw it all in advance, and I don't approach story that way either.

I feel like the characters exist before I start working on them. As I'm trying to find them, whether it's designing it or doing the story-boarding, there's something that feels right. Feels like, "Yeah, that's it, that's it," and you're getting closer and closer, or you know it's like a little witching rod and you're trying to find the water out on the land. Ping! It's right down here! And you get off track and nothing's happening. You can feel it.

Wellins: *And you kind of explore those feelings. Sounds like you spent all weekend drawing and you mostly just draw and that's sort of like the divining rod for you?*

Keane: Often I'll look in the dictionary too, for the key word. In this new character is the problem; it does not feel desirable. So I looked up the word *desire* and I wrote down definitions of desire and what is desire and what does desirable mean and what does it feel like to not be desirable. The words really kind of open it up for me. I really like words on a page, on the script too. Words mean a lot, and I like to sit and analyze it and write down my thoughts and explore it. Sometimes I'll write paragraphs and pages of just thoughts about a character and that kind of starts getting me focused on it.

Wellins: *So for you, it's really about feeling and discovering a connection through this kind of reaching and finding your way. Kind of like the sculptor who felt like he was freeing something that was trapped in the marble.*

Keane: Yeah, that is what it's like.

Wellins: *You're just chipping 'til you suddenly find this smooth . . . you reached in and you're kind of uncovering . . .*

Keane: Yeah, but you know the thing that really frustrates me is that the other element that's really important is pressure. The heat has to be turned up to get the impurities out of the iron ore or to get the gold out of the ore. That's the same thing with this: it never happens until there's like some big pressure. You gotta get this thing done! OK, now you're forced to make some choices and decisions and now it starts happening because you are committing to something. Committing to an idea is really important and because of this reluctance I have to commit to the wrong thing. I tend not to commit at all, until I'm forced to. Time is up. You're out of time. Right now I'm out of time. I gotta do this. You gotta do it. We're recording the voice talent tomorrow. Tomorrow, I gotta explain about the character, and I'm still not committed. Who is this character? It feels like you're out on the freeway, and there's . . . a dime is out there and you gotta pick it up for some reason. You gotta pick up this dime, but the traffic's coming and the faster you try to pick it up, the more you can't pick it up and you try to get it under your fingernails and the traffic is coming and . . . that's how it feels sometimes, the pressure of it.

→

Wellins: *Do you enjoy that process?*

Keane: No, I hate it! I really hate it, and my wife watches me go through this always, always.

Wellins: *Does that happen on pretty much every film?*

Keane: Every film. Every film.

Wellins: *What is the most satisfying part? What do you enjoy in the process? What's the most satisfying part of the process, besides seeing the movie all done and it's really good?*

Keane: Yeah, and actually that's not the most satisfying, seeing the movie all done. The most satisfying is whether it's storyboarding or animating something and it's still in pretty much its rawest form. These are my drawings that I've done and I'm presenting it to my peers. And when I get a response. Maybe it's not even that. It's when I've done it and it's on the page is when I feel like, "Yeah! Oh, that's it!" It never gets better than that, than actually sitting down and just doing it and I've done it. There it is. It actually worked. And then presenting it, having it proven out that, yeah, you're right and then nothing is ever perfect and you start changing it around and the enthusiasm, or the thrill starts to drop a little bit at that point when you present it because people now didn't get that idea that you though was so clear. But it's just so wonderful when you actually finally get it out and on paper. I love that. I remember on Tarzan, coming to here. And I flew back from Paris and I had to storyboard this sequence where Tarzan learns how to read, and Phil Collins had written the song *Strangers Like Me,* and it was all about him just discovering. We didn't really have any storyboards or anything and the script wasn't even—it was just the words to the song. And I had lots of little scribbles and little tiny thumbnails and just thoughts. And I had to present it to [the producer and director] that next morning. And I flew out and kind of exhausted. I spent the night, got up real, real early, like at 3 in the morning, and sitting out by the pool and thinking, "Actually I don't have any idea. They just paid me all this money to fly me out here and . . . what am I going to do, what am I going to do?" OK, well . . . and then I started looking at all the little pages and scraps and thoughts and I started fitting them together, and it was a little bit like *A Beautiful Mind,* where suddenly patterns started. OK, that actually goes there and, oh there it is, and, and it all just, Whoosh! Whoa, it came together and I presented it and, Oh that's great! Ha ha! That's fantastic! They liked it! And I was like, "Why is it this way for me?" I wish it was different and I should try to make it different but it never seems to be.

Wellins: *The pressure's just got to be turned up, I guess.*

Keane: Yeah, and I . . .

Wellins: *As long as it equals a good outcome, it's probably going to be like that every time.*

Keane: I guess so. Are you like that?

→

Wellins: Oh yeah, and it is still like that. It's so interesting that it's like that for you too, to hear how your process works. And interesting that someone who had done so much still has to really fight it out, with yourself. It's interesting that it's never gotten easy, and it's still not easy, after all these years for you. It's still like higher math. It still takes all your brainpower. For as masterful as you are, it's still a tough process to make that connection. I think that's really valuable. It's really hard to describe these kinds of nebulous ideas. It's really hard to convey that kind of ideas to people starting out.

Keane: It is this combination of real struggle, and not knowing what the heck you're doing, that actually is a scary thing, with true skills that you've developed over 30 years. There are things that I've developed that I couldn't just be passionate and really sincerely try and get there. There has to be also skills at the same time. For me, [it's] drawing skills. I'd spend a lot of time just learning the bones and muscles and anatomy. Rather than watching TV, sometimes I would just get a book on anatomy and study it, and just draw the hand, and ask myself, "Do I understand the ear? Do I understand an eye? What is the nose structure? How does the jaw work? What is the shoulder? How does that fit in with the scapula?" And just really learn it and draw and draw and draw and draw, and feeling like, "How am I going to animate if I don't get myself up to a level of draftsmanship?" The level that I aspire towards is, I look towards Michelangelo, or I look towards a lot of the classic artists, whether it's Rembrandt or Monet or Degas. I want to draw . . . I want the drawing to be really excellent. It's got to be excellent; that's what I want. You never get there. So I'm pushing it on that level, and there's also just learning about what communicates in a film, studying, learning from what failed and what worked in watching cartoons, seeing how an idea is presented really clearly, arcs, staging, anticipation, building suspense, surprise—all that stuff is really important. Composition, how you can create the direction, how you can direct somebody's eye to see just what you want them to see. All that stuff has to be there. But having all that stuff doesn't make anything work.

Wellins: No guarantees.

Keane: No, then it gets to this point where, what are you going to say with it? And is what you're saying have any value to . . . is this character real? Is anybody going to get it? Beforehand . . . it is like walking into a room trying to find the light switch and you're stumbling in the dark and feeling your way through and when you turn on the light finally, you look back and go, "Oh, that's easy. That was the path I took and here it is." It's always looking back. I always give this book to any of the animators and artists I work with. It's called *Art and Fear*. It's really on the perils of art making and how fear is such a part of that. It's kind of like a good sign when you don't know what you're doing and yet you're moving forward anyway. There's this part of me that always feels like I'm going to be found out that I really don't know what the heck I'm doing. I told Michael Eisner, "If you knew how much I don't know, you would not hire me." I really don't know what the heck I'm doing. I just keep at it until it actually seems to work. It's perseverance and persistence: drawing, getting better at drawing. To me the whole key has been about wanting to believe that the thing that I'm drawing is real. When I did drawings as a kid, I remember I didn't draw to do a drawing. I did a drawing because I wanted to live in that moment. And I would draw, like, dinosaurs or whatever, but it was like a time machine. So I could kind of, whoosh. There I was looking up at his jaws, of this tyrannosaurus rex, and suddenly if I wanted to be in

→

this battlefield, I'd draw it, so they were like time machines for me. And it's still the same thing now, animating is kind of like; you just want to whoosh go into the page. And I can sure feel it when I'm there. I can kind of get lost. And when I'm not, I'm working, working, working, 'til I find myself there again. I just keep searching, searching, and try to get people around you who also feel the same.

Wellins: *That's great.*

Keane: Yeah, I wish there was a really simple, clear . . .

Wellins: *One of the most discouraging things to me as a filmmaker, and in my own films, is when you watch a film that has everything going for it, good characters, good story—it's all put together—but yet, it still doesn't hit. It still doesn't . . . you think, why? When there's a problem and I can figure out what the problem is, it's like, "Oh, OK," but when I can't figure it out, it really proves how subjective and how difficult and how complex this whole process is whether it's a short film or a long film. There's still a real area that depends on people's moods and how it's made and, just so many elements, it's almost infinite, the details that could help or hurt.*

Keane: Yeah, and the things that you, as you're trying to figure out the complexities of a story and it seems like the problems are insurmountable and you're never going to figure it out, then a gift is given. I really do believe that the best stuff is a gift. Peter says that every good and perfect gift is from above, and I feel like that's true in my work. I come in and the idea is there. Where'd that come from? The answer was there, and it seems like it's always the right person comes in and they're part of this little creative spark that starts firing in you and just works. I guess that's why in this greater process, it takes a lot of faith. It takes a lot of faith to keep moving forward because you don't know if you're going to get there, but somewhere deep down trusting that the gifts are going to come. It's humbling because once you've actually done it, you realize all the really good stuff in here. I didn't come up with it. I just got the chance to recognize it. Like, 'Oh, that's good. I should pick that up. Oh, I like that.' I'm always standing on the shoulders of somebody else, style wise. Drawing after [John] Singer or Augustus John, [Gustav] Klimt, [Edgar] Degas, or [Amedeo] Modigliani, all these different people who I've been taught by. I've been taught by a lot of dead people. I like to take their art and look at it and then try to think like they thought to draw it and see what they were trying to do. I do that with the late, great animator Freddie Moore. I get his scenes out, put down certain drawings of, say, Mickey, and I try to guess what the next pose was, and I draw it. Then I'd pull out his drawing that he actually did and I'd look at it and go, "Aww gosh, yeah, it's so simple, and they're so clear and so beautiful." And I'd worked with that, and it was like he was standing over my shoulder teaching me. So I feel like I've really had the greatest teachers I could possibly have, and they don't even have to be living. You just want to keep learning and getting better.

Wellins: *So it seems like to plateau is really counter to how you work?*

Keane: I always plateau. I always kind of get to this very frustrated point of just, "Oh gosh, I hate the drawings. I don't like the ideas. I'm stuck in the mud." And thinking, "What am I doing? Why

→

am I doing this?" My wife has to listen to that over dinner a lot of times. "Everyone else is so good. Everyone else's ideas are better, those other guys are so great. I'm such a loser! What am I doing?" And she'll always remind me, "You always talk like this." "Yeah, but you know, this time I really mean it."

Wellins: *You eventually find that gem though?*

Keane: Yeah, it's a plateau though. You're frustrated with the level where you're at and that's really good because that means you're ready to grow. That's when I tend to know when I get past that point of, "Woe is me because I stink, then I kind of get rid of that and I go," OK, I don't care about deadlines. I don't care about anything, work, you know. If I get fired I get fired, but I'm leaving. I'm walking out of here. I'm going to the museum; I'm going to a bookstore. I'm going to watch a movie. I'm going to go sit in the park. "And I just start like," I'm on like a hunt and I don't know what I'm looking for. This always happens to me where I just go to a bookstore looking, picking up, could be a book of poetry, could be a book on some artist I've never seen or a photography book, and suddenly the spark is there. I say, "Oh! Oh man, I never . . . !" A couple of years ago I picked up a book on Rembrandt. I'd seen Rembrandt, but I'd never really looked at his drawings. Gosh, he's drawing . . . it's the same . . . he's animating in forces. These are like little slashes, like his little sketches of people. It's perfect bold gestures that he's drawing from. He would have been a perfect animator. I just consumed him. I just ate him up there for a while, trying to draw like him and trying to think like him. Suddenly I wasn't stuck in that plateau anymore. I was just trying to work toward where he was doing. That's what's fun. This is really a fun job if you're open to kind of learn and go out and pick out from other artists and filmmakers.

Wellins: *A famous sculptor once said that the best thing an artist can do is to set a goal that he can never ever reach. Just keep working towards it. You can dream about it but you can never possibly get to it your whole life. You just keep working. It's always been a goal in my mind.*

Keane: Like Joe Grant. He's great. He still comes in every day and he's 96 years old. If you see him stop him and ask him, 'So, what's your drawing for today?' Every day he's got another drawing. He's does tons of drawings every day, but there's one that he particularly likes and he colors it and he puts watercolor on it. And they're always just really fresh ideas. It could be birdhouses or bird feeders one day. He came up with like 50 different bird feeders. Some looked like little carousels, some were like spinning wheels, some are just odd little shapes. And he says, "Oh, I don't edit myself anymore." I just start to draw, and it just flows. I mean at 96 years old it's just flowing out. It's like this art teacher who used to teach adults figure drawing. And his little girl, seven years old said, "Daddy, where do you go all day?" He said, "Well honey, I go teach people how to draw," and she said, "You mean they forget?' And that's what you want to be. You want to just be like Joe Grant, where you never forget to think like a child and just to draw for the pleasure.

Wellins: *Strip all the rules away and just go for it.*

Keane: Yeah. That's something I really want to do. I really want to try to get there.

Wellins: *I think you're there.*

REFERENCES

[Bohr03] *The Way to Murnau,* directed by Alexander Bohr. Documentary short on *Tartuffe* DVD release. Kino International, 2003.

[Collier98] Collier, J.L. *From Wagner to Murnau (Studies in Cinema).* University of Rochester Press, Rochester, NY. 1998.

[Llewellyn05] Llewellyn, Richard. "Chronology of Animation." Available online at *www.public.iastate.edu/~rllew/chronint.html.* Copyright © 1998–2005.

[McLaughlin01] McLaughlin, Dan. "A Rather Incomplete But Still Fascinating History of Animation." Available online at *http://animation.filmtv.ucla.edu/program/anihist.html.* 2001.

THE STORY

THE NATURE OF STORY

Man has been telling stories for tens of thousands of years. Stories were told in countless forms: songs, plays, fables, and lessons told around the fire. The ancient Greeks prized their great tragedies, and the whole scope of literature featured hundreds of thousands of great authors in between. But in the 21st century, people have taken that idea of a play and immersed themselves in hours upon hours of story every day in the form of television, movies, and video games. Some have thin stories while others are complex, but ultimately there's no denying that people are enraptured with the story in all its forms. At its simplest, stories have a conflict at their basis whether overt, where one character conquers another, or the sublime, where a character whose conflict is with life in general. Obviously people can't get enough of it; from soap operas running for decades to musicals and reality shows, the story and the audience have a symbiotic relationship.

But a story, however thinly entwined or tenuous, is always present. Without it, a film or a play or an animation is just a series of incidents and events.

Joseph Campbell, a well-known mythologist, described the roots of stories and myth, with good over evil, and man overcoming obstacles; Campbell called this "the hero's journey." It is this simple theme that can be morphed into almost endless versions. It's easily recognizable, but when it's done right, people generally never tire of seeing it. *The Power of Myth* by Joseph Campbell is required reading for all artists and storytellers, because it establishes the roots of the story, conflict, and motivation from its earliest forms and identifies what is so engrossing about stories that viewers and audiences gravitate to. Like every other aspect of animation and filmmaking, knowing thefundamentals and principals that drive a specific subject is crucial to being able to create, manipulate, and control. Filmmakers can make a film without knowing anything about lighting, but knowing lighting and its fundamental rules makes it possible to use light as an effective emotional tool, instead of just a light lighting a scene. This couldn't be more true when it comes to creating a compelling story; knowing the fundamental human connections to a story, at their very basics, allows for maximum control and creation.

THE TOOLS OF STORY

All people tell stories. People are storytellers and telling a story can be a complex form of communication. For writers and filmmakers alike, the creator finds a story worthy of going beyond simply telling. Whether a writer or filmmaker is so moved by a story that he is compelled to recreate it, or whether a writer or filmmaker develops a story to create emotions, they both lead to the same end result. Telling stories is a sharing of experiences on a very simple level; shared experiences allow people to place themselves in their groups and judge and measure their lives and positions in the world. So strong is the need to tell stories and communicate that stories are now in every facet of our society.

Storytellers who want to write down stories, write plays, or make films go one step beyond the normal retelling of the day's events. Written and visual storytellers go to the next level where they move beyond the events and have something they want to point out or create an emotion from. In the process, the storyteller is going to try and tell the story in the most compelling way possible. Take the following example of a simple set of related events. A man named John comes home and tells his wife about his day: drivers driving like maniacs, cutting him off and almost causing a wreck. It gets worse with people pushing and shoving during his lunch and rude coworkers talking all day on the phone. Then he's panhandled on the way into the building, and finally in the apartment he finds a huge stack of bills that need to be paid.

In a series of potentially negative events , the story comes out of what happens next and the character reacts to the situation. In reaction to these events John isn't going to stand for it anymore, and the family is moving to the Yukon to work the land. In another scenario, John is going to continue to take what he perceives as abuse, but he'll never tell anyone, and it will continue to gnaw at him, make him sick, and ruin him.

What happens next? His wife rises to the challenge, supports him, and saves him; in another scenario she is disgusted and leaves him, or, like him, she does nothing and it eventually ruins her as well.

As filmmakers and storytellers, our goal is to develop what happens beyond the simple events into an interesting and compelling form that creates some type of emotional connection.

Think of movies and films as a string of light bulbs. The light bulbs are the scenes or events, and the wire where the actual electricity comes from is the story. The story is often the reason why the bulbs of the story are even connected at all. The story in the first scenario is a story about John, who has decided that there's more to life than the bustling city and is willing to sacrifice comfort for something potentially better. The second story is about John who is beaten down, but trapped for whatever reason. Then, here's another story to tell about why John reacts the way he does. As a child or young adult was he encouraged or abused, did he experience some trauma, or was his life normal and he just never had any conviction? The possibilities are endless as are the connections.

Similar to the production of film itself, the storyteller works two angles simultaneously, watching the global ideas of what the story is, while being able to focus on the actual actions and scenes, and being aware of how they pertain to, tell, or reinforce the story; the story can be plain and straightforward or convoluted, and often even allegorical. Edgar Allan

Poe said something to the effect that it's impossible to tell a story when nothing really happens. Many animals, mammals, and creatures play when they're young, and playing is a way of exploring without getting seriously hurt or killed. Through play, thinking creatures discover the world around them, learn lessons on ways to be comfortable and safe, and avoid pain and suffering on the simplest level. Stories are play for the mind, and were obviously one of the earliest forms of teaching. With words, stories move along supplying the brain with a carefully mixed series of descriptions that audiences turn into their own images. How characters appear and interact and what the characters do, say, and even think are all woven together in reaction to the story. For the filmmaker and the animator, the process is far more difficult because instead of allowing the audiences' imagination to create images, all the images have to be created for them. The results are cinematic masterpieces and masterful storytelling in both animated and live action. Classic films like *Raging Bull, Alien, Toy Story, Shrek, Akira, Citizen Kane, Casablanca, Star Wars, Dumbo, Annie Hall, Apocalypse Now*, and so many more credit their success to masterful filmmaking and masterful storytelling.

A story must not just tell events, it must be about some larger idea; how obvious or metaphorical that idea is will be left up to the writer and director. The simplest universal idea is that story is conflict: man versus nature, man versus man, or man versus himself. Whether readers and audiences can pick it out specifically or not, they are always keenly aware of the existence of the fundamental conflict in a story.

All storytelling is a constant retelling of those foundational ideas of conflict, and when they are combined, they are that much more interesting, such as a man against nature and himself is that much more dynamic. John, who hated the city, but did nothing about it, might be a rich character for a drama type film about man's personal struggles. On the other hand, John, who hated the city and dragged the family to the Yukon, is reacting simply and might be better suited for a family comedy about man versus nature. The complexity of the conflict often defines the story.

THE PLOT

The first step in developing your story is defining the plot. The plot is the main story or events that happen in a film. Another popular cliché that is often heard when someone is pitching a movie or project idea is the single line that describes the whole project—a line that sums up the very basic motives of the story. The line for *Gone with the Wind* might be, "A woman can't decide between two men, and gets no one in the end." Being able to encapsulate the plot or the main theme of a story is in fact a useful mental exercise, and can be helpful in understanding the project in its simplest form.

Even a very complicated movie with tons of characters, all with different motivations, can be summed up in its basic story. *The Lord of the Rings* trilogy has a complex plot and even with all its 12 hours and multitudes of characters and effects, it can still be described simply as a story of good versus evil; goodness prevails as usual.

The plot is the events that illustrate the story, and the good versus evil theme in *The Lord of the Rings* is pretty obvious and cut and dry. There are also many plot points in *The Lord of the Rings* that are complex and intertwined with the various journeys and battles. These plot points are the backdrop for all the basic conflicts the heroes must go through: betrayal, courage, fear, hunger, fatigue, danger, confusion, death threats, and romance, to name a few. Plot points are the events or obstacles that compel the characters to react and to exhibit whom the character really is. Plot points are often obstacles or intrusions in the story that can cause change. The plot is the basic conflict or points that cause the story to become something that will cause the characters to react. In *Star Wars,* the plot of the Evil Empire and the Dark Side of the force trying to quash the Rebellion sets the background for all the other plot points and creates the drama. *In Raiders of the Lost Ark*, the Germans' discovering the lost ark is the plot point that gets Indiana Jones involved and sets the entire story in motion, while the core conflict is good versus evil. The plot also sets up events that create motion, action, and ultimately some result of resolution. In *Star Wars*, the plot is resolved when the Evil Empire is crippled when Luke Skywalker destroys the Death Star. In *Raiders of the Lost Ark*, Indiana recovers the powerful ark, ensuring the Germans never use it as a weapon.

Many modern filmmakers have created truly unique ways of creating plots and stories, and often the filmmaker shifts the onus of what the story is about back on to the viewers to decide for themselves. Stories have been cut and dry for as long as they've been told, but as stories evolve, gray areas begin to emerge that mimic reality and plots or stories aren't as simple as good versus evil. In Stanley Kubrick's *Full Metal Jacket,* Mathew Modine's character seems to play the good guy, but in fact, perhaps because of the pressure of war, does bad things and is aware of doing these things as he does them. With this mixed motivation, Kubrick seems to hint at the complex nature of an intelligent man being asked to become a killer and the duality and conflict that creates.

MOTIVATION

Detectives out to solve a crime know that there are only a few basic types of motives that cover all human motivation. The most basic motive is to simply stay alive by obtaining the basic needs of food, water, shelter, and clothing. The basic motivation to not die or avoid pain is the next most simplistic. So important is the fear of pain and death that it permeates all the other motivations. Philosophers for ages have debated the significance of this motivation on every level.

Once the basic needs are met, then people and creatures have a lot more time to think and start to feel complex feelings, such as love, hate, jealousy, happiness, sadness, envy, greed, and boredom. They can also feel a whole host of negative feelings, such as depression, rage, and paranoia. Interesting characters have lives and stories that compel them to do things—often things that are beyond average behavior. Motivations for people and creatures don't change. Motivations can manifest themselves in countless ways with a modern spin, but stealing a fish from a neighboring villager or trying to take over a multinational corporation can still be the same simple motivation: greed. Why a character is greedy and steals or tries to get more and more personal wealth then becomes part of the story.

When one or more people are involved, emotions and motivations become exponentially more complicated. Desperation for acceptance or loneliness; experiencing one-sided love; showing admiration, adulation, and revenge; gaining power over others; caring for others; and being self-serving are all examples. Motivations are not always cut and dry, and combining motivations often makes characters more complex and real when driven by different or conflicting motivations.

A prehistoric man would feel the same motivations that modern people feel today. A primitive man is hungry and cold. A neighboring man has a warm cave and has caught a big fish. The motivation to attack him is simple, basic animal preservation, but there's a risk. The man with the fish is pretty good-sized, and there could be a real fight (to be injured was to be selected out). After all, there are other caves and other fish. There is motivation to attack, but there is motivation to go find something easier.

If the prehistoric man is joined by a woman, then he has several more layers of motivation. He must feed the woman and be the protector, and now his status is on the line, because the other male is perfectly suited to his female. The other male already has a cave and a fish, so he could potentially look appealing to the female. The first prehistoric man now is motivated to attack, but still he can walk away and go find other prospects.

The other male has motivations as well: he has food, shelter, and would like a mate, and one is now nearby. All he has to do is get rid of that other male. There may be a fight, and he may lose, but there are other caves and fish to be found. On the other hand, finding a mate is rare. The second male starts to move in, and now the first male must really retreat quickly with or without the woman or stand and fight. The root of this final fight or flight decision is really what makes people and creatures individuals and starts to define a specific character about a person or creature.

Is the prehistoric man afraid? Is he indifferent to the woman? At this level, an animal level, there is no right and wrong, but right and wrong and the perception of right and wrong can become a motive as strong or stronger than any others.

Right and wrong has been the debated topic of philosophers for millennia; libraries are filled with that fundamental debate on the nature of the human existence. Regardless of the reason, when characters feel that they are right in their cause or their convictions it's a powerful motivator; whether or not they're truly right is irrelevant. The Academy Award-winning movie *Gandhi* is the true story of a man who is motivated by what is fundamentally right and what is wrong. Gregory Peck in *To Kill a Mockingbird* does what is right, regardless of what his peers think of his defending an African American man. Believing one is right is a powerful motivator, especially when the audience agrees with what is right and wrong. As a motivator, being right can be subjective, and the audience can know that the character is wrong, but still be drawn into the story or character. Al Pacino in *Scarface* is a murdering drug lord, but believes whole heartedly that he's simply out to get the American dream.

Storytellers need only to recognize the motivations and aren't necessarily required to explain them. All behavior is controlled by some type of motivation, even if it's counter-motivation, or being unmotivated and bored. Even impulsive behavior is motivated by something: a trait in the personality, an event, a history. Characters often will act opposite to this motivation, which adds to their complexity, however, to do something unexpected, a bad thing, or things that are obviously bad for them, or irrational, only serves to add to this complexity. A man is motivated to pay his rent so he isn't living on the street, but when he gets paid he goes and buys something extravagant, spends his money on drinking and partying, or loses it all at the track. He's impulsive, in denial, an alcoholic, has a gambling problem or is self-destructive. Most people behave rationally, but doing bad things is interesting material for viewers because they can watch bad behavior, which perhaps they've considered, and see how it plays out.

Motive, which is often hidden many layers deep, is the element that is always necessary in solving a crime. From these basic conflicts come the motives that detectives know so well (revenge, greed, love, jealousy, and insanity), and to a lesser degree these motivations are the same when telling a story, but can also include compassion, justice, beauty, etc. A motive, whatever it is, is the single driving force for any and all characters.

This is not to say that every story has to have an overt motive simply and cleanly, and it certainly does not mean that the motives or the underlying story rings true to everyone. Many interesting stories are based on ideas that viewers find interesting because the subject is so foreign to them, but instead see their motivation as the complete opposite of themselves. Most people aren't criminals, yet crime television shows and movies are hugely popular. Aliens, vampires, and monsters of every kind go back far into mythology because of their extraordinary natures. In *Jaws*, the motive of the shark is simple: eat. In the simplicity of that motivation, a mindless eating machine is horrifying to people because there's no reasoning or bargaining with it. In fact, the shark only sees people as food, and that diminishing of a person, not to mention the horrific terror of being eaten, creates a horrifying story that has magnetic appeal. In *Jaws*, audiences are able to explore their darkest fears however briefly, and that exploration, that roller-coaster ride of emotion, made *Jaws* popular the world over, with the simplest of motivations and the simplest of plots.

In many instances it's the filmmaker who knows a character's motivation and then decides how much of that actual motivation will be represented on screen. The filmmaker might be able to describe his character at a base level; a character's goal is revenge for someone who has unjustly wronged him. How the revenge is shown could be overt. It can range from where the character announces, "I will get my revenge!," to saying something more subtle where the character pretends to be the man's friend, works his way into his life, and slowly destroys the man piece by piece. A boy is raised in a hostile environment, where horrible parents remind him daily of his lack of worth, but for his revenge he pays his way though school and becomes a prominent doctor solely for revenge on his parents. The examples are endless. The filmmaker, whether it's stated or not, needs to know what is driving the core of a character; the drive can change or waiver, but the storyteller knows the root because that motivation is drawn from the story and plot.

Story is grounded in conflict with a protagonist and an antagonist whether it's a person, an internal struggle, or a genuine struggle on a mountain side. It's a cliché that is used over and over in movies and television when the thespian asks the director, "What's my motivation?" It's a valid question that all real and animated characters are asking. Motivations can be simple. The short film *107.6 Degrees*, by Patrik and Amila Puhala, on the CD-ROM, **1076_degrees.mov**, illustrates the basic motivation of preservation: the story of characters simply trying to find shade and get out of the heat.

ON THE CD

In classic animations, classic characters have all been driven because of some powerful motivating factor. In Disney's *101 Dalmatians*, Cruella De Vil is motivated to make a coat out of the Dalmatian puppies because she is so thin and hates the way she looks; she will do anything to get the coat. Her own self loathing is turned outward toward the puppies. In *The Shawshank Redemption*, the main character, played by Tim Robbins, is motivated by his surroundings, a brutal prison, but more than that, he's fundamentally motivated to escape because he is innocent and wrongly convicted. As the plot develops, he includes payback at the evil warden and guards who abused him. The same is true in *The Fugitive*, where the main character is driven to prove his innocence at any cost. Greed and power are two huge motivators of action films, and the two themes are illustrated in films like *Die Hard, Heat,* and *The Grifters.* They are all basically stories of power over others and flat-out greed: wanting to be rich, desiring to steal something powerful. The point of films like *Heat* and *The Grifters* isn't as cut and dry, because the characters the audience roots for are bad, and are criminals, and yet the audience wants them to get away unhurt. They identify, by their actions, with what that character wants (e.g., money to go away and live on an island someplace, even if the character has to steal money to do it).

All of James Bond's adversaries wanted to rule the world or affect the world and steal a lot of money; Again, they're bad and James Bond is good. However, interesting characters don't have to be motivated by good to be interesting, and many memorable characters aren't good at all. Such is the power of characterization—an audience who knows right and wrong still can root for the bad guys willingly. Opposite of *The Shawshank Redemption,* the Clint Eastwood movie *Escape from Alcatraz* is a story chronicling the escape from the brutal island prison. Largely due to Clint Eastwood's persona, the lead character has some type of unflinching prison honor. Once the escape begins, the audience is clearly hoping that he does escape. The prison's conditions are appalling and the warden is a torturous megalomaniac, but the fact remains that the escapee is a real career criminal who is a public menace and belongs behind bars. Yet the audience is delighted when the warden is left empty-handed. *Dog Day Afternoon,* with Al Pacino, shows a bank robbery gone awry, and yet the audience can't help but love the flawed, yet well-meaning heart of the obvious criminal bank robbers.

Motivations Can Change

Motives can change; in fact, a motive change can be a crucial or interesting turning point in a story when a character changes their motives. In the first *Shrek* movie, at first the character Shrek only wants to be left alone and get everyone out of his swamp, but then his motivation turns to love. A hired killer is motivated by money, but then falls for his victim. Usually there's some epiphany associated with a major change like motivation: someone cruel becomes kind because someone was kind to him. In Charles Dickens' *A Christmas Carol,* the character Ebenezer Scrooge goes from being greedy and self-centered to humble and philanthropic, because he got a rare glimpse of his self-centered life, his happy youth, and his own death. In an abstract sense, the ghosts who visited him actually did him a favor and gave him a shot at redemption, even though they scared him nearly to death. What is the motivation of the ghosts of Christmas past, present, and future to want to help Ebenezer? Is it the ghost of his old partner Jacob Marley, who enlists the other ghosts, or is it all simply a nightmare in Scrooge's head?

Filmmakers and storytellers need to dissect the motivations of the characters and trim them down to the core motivations, for basic motivations can be used to inform everything a character does and says. Filmmakers need to take motivation beyond characters and examine and establish the motivation of the film and ultimately of themselves. What is it they're trying to do in creating a film or animation? Audiences are ready and willing to follow any story that is clear in its telling, regardless of how complex the story or plot as it long as it seems genuine and is interesting enough for them to invest emotions. Audiences are willing to be emotionally connected, but making emotional connections makes them feel vulnerable. To make strong connections, audiences need to trust the story to be truthful to its ideas and motivations.

In all cases, motivations are distilled down to the basics. Whether it's a simple 30-second spot and the character's motivation is a simple uncontrollable urge to eat cereal or whether a character is human and complex, directors and writers need to think like a detective and know what a motivation is and how it manifests itself. Moreover, animators, directors, and writers need to know when a simple motivation is enough, or when a story calls for a more complex motivation. Like a great detective who truly understands what is making his subject tick, at a base level, directors, animators, and writers need to know that as well. Knowing what is at the heart of a character's desires allows the director and the detective to accurately predict the character's next move.

THE POINT

When anyone tells a story or an anecdote, there's always a point. For example, a person tells a lengthy story about getting caught in a rainstorm, walking home without an umbrella, and being soaked to the bone. The point of the story may be vague or not that monumental: the unexpected rain surprised the person. The point also could be completely turned inward on the storyteller: the reason the person got all wet is because he has bad luck, always gets caught in situations like that, and getting caught again and soaked just proves how unfair life is to him.

Stories have a point, however trivial: traffic is bad, the store was more crowded than ever before, a man took a short weekend hike and had a good time. The point doesn't have to be earth-shattering, but instead, down at its simplest form, it's the point that is important. The point of a story is why the story was worth telling at all.

Without a point, talking just becomes rambling and events are simply events. They don't lead up to anything, because there is no ultimate point, no conclusion, and no meaning that is arrived at; there is nothing to really say. The point, or whatever it is that is being said, doesn't have to be cohesive. It can be very overt, with scenes laid out and narrated, or images and events can be strung together, with the point being shifted back to the audience to decide what the meaning of certain events is or what the story is trying to say. Whether the storyteller tells the story or sets up a scenario where the audience creates their own story and subsequent point, a story that says something, is still the point.

Even films that have random scenes stuck together where things just happen for no reason and people's lives mix by sheer randomness have a point, even if the point is that life has no point; the fact that life is random and things happen with no reason is in fact the point of the story.

When a person telling a story doesn't have a point, it quickly becomes obvious. The classic film scenario is the husband and wife who have been married for 30 years. One of them rambles on, goes off on tangents, and does not really have anything to say, other than just wanting to recite the day's events. Finally the annoyed spouse demands, "Get to the point!"

A point doesn't have to be uplifting or make some grand conclusion. Points can be banal and bitter. The point of a film can be that life is unfair to some people. The fact that life is sometimes rotten to good people, is an idea that is tragic to most people and often entertaining to watch.

The point of Shakespeare's *Romeo and Juliet* is tragic: true love can't last. Filmmakers and animators need to know the point they're trying to make, whether as an overall story point or the point of a specific scene. The storyteller needs to focus the story so it arrives at some type of point—something that hopefully leaves the viewer with something to think about or consider.

Point of View

In telling a story, the storyteller also takes a point of view. It's impossible to tell a visual story without a point of view, because choices are made on what is told and what is omitted. In a practical filming sense, the physical elements like lighting and camera position all inform that point or view.

Even the default point of view—the simple recording of events—creates a point of view. For instance, even if a camera was positioned in the audience to record a stage performance and it became locked in one position for the whole performance, this would still be a point of view, but a dull one. When a people watch a play, they move their eyes, focus their attention where the action is, jump, cringe, and laugh, all of which affect their point of view, both physically and emotionally. The editing takes place in their heads; people constantly edit and frame shots with their brain and eyes. Without a point of view, live or animated, the story tells like a policemen's report: this event happened, that event happened, and as a consequence, this becomes decidedly flat.

A point of view is the storyteller's attempt to reinforce whatever the underlying theme is, without having to come right out and say it. A point of view usually has a definite bias somehow linked to the point of the story. For writers or filmmakers, a point of view isn't just about low camera angles or stark lighting. A point of view should be a plan that picks and chooses events and the way they are told to solidify the emotion of the story. There is a practical and pragmatic point of view as well, a more mechanical idea, such as getting the shot so the audience can see it, but it is always tied to the point of view of what the story is.

For example, a young woman walks from her car carrying her wedding dress. She's spent a fortune on it, and just as she rounds the corner, a bus drives through a huge standing puddle of muddy water, which drenches her and the dress. There are many possible points of view to this story. The woman's point of view has inherent value. It's her dress, her money, and she has some serious problems. She is soaked, ruined, and has no dress for the wedding.

The woman and her reaction are basic ideas of her point of view, but there are potentially irrelevant points of view as well. The bus driver, busy and annoyed, has no idea what has happened. The passengers on the bus don't see it, so there's no connection. However, depending on the point of view, the bus can have significance. A bystander, in his own depression, sees the scene and starts a huge cathartic laughing fit that changes his mood and subsequent life.

The bus driver is in a bad mood and sees the dress and is out to ruin someone's day, or perhaps the bus driver is actually the woman's exboyfriend and seizes the opportunity of a lucky coincidence. There's also the removed point of view: the voice of a friend who hates the woman getting married and somehow causes her bad luck. Another removed point of view could be the voiceover of a sympathetic friend who wishes the world wasn't always out to get her friend.

The point of view can be totally different from the same event, and that idea has been the foundation for many stories and comedies. Two characters describe the same events, each heavily slanted to each other's version: "I spent so much money on that dress, and now it's ruined and I feel awful." A mean "friend" could take the other point of view: "Serves her right! She thinks she's so great. She stole her fiancé from me and now this little incident ruined the wedding and I couldn't be happier!"

Two different points of view can have two very different takes on the same scene. Like motivation, it can be dynamic to change a point in a film or animation. A point of view can be very subtle or obvious or common or unique. Point of view is always biased by the person taking that point of view, and the truth is frequently distorted. Even someone making a documentary, trying to record everything exactly truthful, will distort and bias the truth by simply showing one thing and not the other or by missing any elements out of control or range.

A point of view can be intertwined with motivation, but is not necessarily the same. A man's motive could be simple: not to get fired from a bad job, so he doesn't wind up on the street. His point of view might be that everyone else is the idiot, and he's just misunderstood. The Pulitzer Prize-winning book *A Confederacy of Dunces* is such an example.

When characters believe things to be the truth, they have justification to do just about anything. From conquering a country to something as trivial as relating a story about a unexpected rainstorm, takes a justification from the teller, who says, "That rain really was *truly* unexpected. That's unusual. I think I'll tell it, and it will be interesting."

John, the man who took his family to the Yukon from the city, believes moving is the best thing to do. The element of truth is that cities are big; although some people like it, others don't. Most viewers can relate whether they agree or not.

If John lived on a nice quiet farm and decided that it was too hustling and bustling, it wouldn't work because there's no truth behind his reasoning. He would need to change his motivation. He hates the farm and he wants to be completely alone, even away from his family; something must ring true, at some point.

A storyteller must find an element of truth in whatever the point of view is. The audience must recognize this truth. Whether they agree or not isn't always necessary, but they must at least recognize through the story that the storyteller believes the point of view he's taken. Even with an element of truth, the storyteller is still allowed to dismiss, trivialize, or omit elements that don't reinforce the point of view. Point of view is about slanting ideas to reinforce whatever point or truth the story is making.

In the brief scene, John uses his examples to bolster his point of view: the city is too crowded, moving too fast, and is faceless. He describes garbage in the streets, crowded subways, expensive restaurants, crime, and crazy drivers. Because John believes these things to be true, he makes his case that the city isn't worth living in anymore.

The listener to the story, a fellow city person, might hear the story and agree with the individual reason, but won't agree with John's point of view. The listener certainly believes that John is truly fed up with the city, but regardless of John's point of view, the friend still loves the city. The friend points out that John failed to mention the beautiful park only a few blocks away, the easy access to the beaches, the convenience of all the great restaurants, and all the exciting things happening all the time. These are two completely different points of views of a complex situation. Writer and filmmaker Woody Allen is one of those city lovers, and in many of his films makes reference to how much he dislikes nature, but people who love nature can still enjoy his films.

Truth is a slave to the story and it can change, and a person can have his ideas of what is true change. These changes often make great moments of awareness and direction change in the story. It's entertaining in a viewer's mind when they he has to rethink what was preconceived about a scene. It's also a fun brain exercise to ponder about what is true;

certain events can happen and can immediately switch to another truth. A character who doesn't believe in the paranormal sees a ghost and can't explain what he's seen. A character that does nothing but mean and bad things can do a grand-sweeping gesture, such as pushing a stranger out of the way of a bus and the character is killed himself. The audience forgives the badness and sees the character as ultimately good.

In another example, a man goes for a walk and is caught in the rain. If the man's point of the story is that the rain was unexpected, then his point of view would be of someone caught unaware: "I went outside, not a cloud in the sky, to take a quick walk, and suddenly, it's pouring and I'm instantly soaked. I've never seen a storm come up like that!" It's nothing personal. The man isn't that put off about getting wet; he's more surprised by the sudden appearance of the storm.

If the point of the story was that the man caught in the rain was incredibly unlucky, then his point of view would be more negative: "Stupid me, went out with out an umbrella, and even though it was cloudless, of course a storm roars in, and I'm soaked. This is typical of how things go for me." On the opposite side of the spectrum, a woman finds out that she's discovered a long-lost sister. Out of sheer joy, she runs outside and although it begins raining, she is jubilant and dances in the rain. The point of view of her story was that it was a happy and magical day. The woman says, "It was hot and balmy and I was asleep when the phone rang, and it was my long lost sister! We're going to meet next week! I was so happy that I ran outside, and like magic, just then a cool rain poured in, and I danced for joy, I know it was meant just for me."

In telling the story, an internal point of view can also work with or against an overall point of view. When a character has an opposing point of view that differs from the overall story, an interesting dynamic can be created.

In the story where the woman discovers her long-lost sister, a neighbor across the street has a very limited perspective of the situation, and sits inside reading the newspaper and glances out the window just in time to see the woman run out in the rain. The neighbor says, "I was just reading the paper, and then that crazy woman from across the street runs out and starts dancing in the rain. I think she has mental problems." His limited perspective gives him the point of view that the woman is crazy.

There are many approaches to telling a story: from first person, to third person, to omniscient, to a extremely restricted point of view. Deciding which approach will ultimately tell the clearest story with the most impact is up to the writer or filmmaker; it is relative to the story and relative to which angle will best create the story and an interesting point of view.

PACING

In most writing, pacing is merely described, and the burden of pacing is usually shifted to the reader. Specific types of prose and poetry create pacing, like haiku, but in creating stories for film and animation, pacing rests squarely on the shoulders of the director. The music analogy for pacing is again valid: pacing for music is like the tempo or the beat. Not to say that visual pacing should happen to the beat of a drum, but in music as well as in telling a visual story, there is a rhythm in which things happen. That rate is decided by the mood and the motivating elements. Beyond the practical pacing of allowing a character enough time to walk in the door or sit down, the rest of the story pacing is almost completely subjective. "Harmonious structure" was the term Murnau coined, and when developing the pacing both the structure and story have to be incredibly strong. There is a harmonious structure in the visual pacing of a scene, and that pacing is driven by the story and the mood that is being created.

The result of pacing that doesn't work is always apparent. In bad pacing, the viewers aren't set up properly for upcoming events; setups can take too long or become uninteresting and the audience then becomes bored, confused, and no longer engaged or entertained.

Setting the perfect pacing has to be one of the most intangible ideas to develop, but with modern tools it's easy to perfect. Other jobs of the storyteller can be fleshed out with processes. In filming, you can cover a scene with wide shots, medium shots and close-ups; use intercutting; follow the action; and then create a few unique shots to pepper throughout. However, how they fit together and how long they stay on screen can only be discovered by trial and error. To truly test this, the story must get glued to a fixed time that can be adjusted, and the ideal place for this is the editing of an animatic or story reel.

Like music, pacing can change; it can grow frenetic and hyper or it can switch to being slow and plodding. Pacing can be a driving force overall, and can also be a consideration from scene to scene. The material on animatics in Chapter 9 is practical for editing and creating a functioning product, but the filmmaker needs to also use the animatic first and foremost as a storytelling tool that is emotionally and story-driven and where overall pacing of how the story unfolds is truly defined. Time is a valuable tool in judging pacing, and being able to revisit works in progress even days later is incredibly useful.

STRUCTURE

The three-act structure has been the template for a vast number of movies, and the idea goes back to the earliest of human plays. In its simplest form, each act ends with a large change in the character, story, or the tone. At the end of the first act, the hero is in hot water. By the end of the second act, the hero has tried to get out of hot water, but has gotten in further. For the third act, the hero makes a huge comeback and saves the day. There are many forms of the three-act structure and some screen writing books actually recommend or demand that the solid three-act structure is a necessity for a good story. It's an ongoing debate, but obviously in certain films the acts are quiet clear. In others the lines are blurry to the point where the act structure and its changes aren't discernable; if it can't be perceived is it there at all? Audiences have gotten incredibly sophisticated. Many interesting films instead create a unique structure of their own. Again, the story carries the weight on deciding whether the structure should be traditional or something else.

Structure believers often go so far as to say that, in a feature film, a certain act be a certain number of pages, and the next be a certain number, and so forth. The idea of such a strict structure can be problematic, and in many instances, the three-act structure in its most obvious form seems overworked. Almost any action movie wears the three-act structure plainly. In the first act, the audience meets the hero and by the end, the act has arched from normalcy to the hero having to make a big decision and being in big trouble. In the second act, the hero gets involved, gets beat up, and saves the girl, but the bad guys kidnap the girl again, get the money, and tie up the good guy on a boat with a time bomb. In modern movies, the hero also undergoes physical abuse and punishment to the point of near death. In the third act, somehow the hero, motivated by his anger, revenge, or the torn picture of his daughter in his fist, finds the energy to come back to life. The hero, now wounded and battered, often with superhuman effort, frees himself, brutally dispatches his captors, narrowly escapes, frees the girl, and then has a showdown with the bad guy. The bad guy then dies in some exotic way, by falling on a sharp fountain, falling out of an airplane, or getting pulled into a jet engine. Many viewers enjoy the predictable ride, while others spend the time checking their watch.

Many of the action standards suffer from this structure failure most of the time. However, it's not just action movies either; romantic comedies nearly always follow the exact same structure. The three-act structure is actually inherent in telling a story; even a dull story will go through a three-act process.

For example, in the first act, a person goes out on a sunny day. In the second act, the rainstorm abruptly appears and drenches him. In the third act, he goes home, surprised at the sudden storm. The three-act structure works on the simplest story. Rick went to work, Rick was late, and nobody noticed. The three-act structure is out of pragmatism: set up the story, tell what happened, and tell how it turned out. The structure is very familiar to viewers and is often the perfect solution to telling a story, but exploring other structures can possibly work better and are always worth exploring, especially for short film projects where the three-act sturcture doesn't always work. Modern films like *Mystery Train, Adaptation, Memento,* and *13 Conversations About One Thing* have blurred the lines of strict structure.

Even though a good and compelling story is key to a true emotional connection, the story shouldn't be treated as if it were carved in stone. Words can change easier than a drawing or a scene. In animation, the story isn't king; the finished, well-made film that changes people is the king, and the story must fall in line, like everything else, to make the final project work. Translating written word to interesting and compelling visual media doesn't work by any formula. The idea that the story is never locked demands that the writer and director know and recognize the fundamental concepts and motivations behind the story; this is so that decisions can be made that keep the emotional connection intact, protect the story, and still be extremely flexible on almost everything else. Filmmaking is compromise, and animation is just that much more. A live-action film can be filmed, as mentioned previously, with a very specific, tried and tested system. It's not required to discover the true pulse of the pace until editing starts. Animation currently is too expensive and too laborious to be treated just like footage, but the day may come quickly when video-game systems are able to render incredible animation, and the art of acting out that animation will be as simple as a video game. This type of interface is now completely doable, but has yet to be seen.

Once a system like that exists, then it may be possible to remove huge areas of planning, and an improvised animation may exist. Until that day, quality character animation is still expensive and needs to be worked out not only because of economy, but because of the complex nature of all that goes into telling a story through animation and performance.

Like complex music, film and animation's structure can have several story threads going on simultaneously. Not only in separate story lines, but even characters and scenes that are motivated by more than a single motivation can exist and work well as complicated elements.

In music, audiences can listen to a three-piece jazz band or a huge symphony and follow many instruments, move their focus, and then bring all the pieces together as one harmonious sound. Likewise, all the elements of the story—simple, complex, and varied—all blend together to make the story cohesive.

By its very nature, anything that runs at a specific amount of time has a beginning, middle, and an end. So regardless of what a filmmaker does, these positions in the project will occur, whether they're acknowledged or not. The Guy Ritchie film *Lock, Stock and Two Smoking Barrels* ends before the audience gets to see what finally happened, and the film *The Rules of Attraction* ends in mid sentence. On the idea of a structured convention, formula story writing makes the case that the storyteller must carve out and establish these milestones. The nature of the good story almost always has these areas built in, how the story started, what happened, and how it finally ended.

Many films and stories are told with linear storytelling, where all the elements of story are built up and doled out by the storyteller. However, there are many forms of telling a story and there are antinarratives as well, where the audience doesn't get the story but instead gets the result of the story and is left to figure out what has happened to lead the characters up to the point the audience now sees. It's a type of removed mystery; storytellers are always looking for new ways to tell the same basic stories, and with infinite possibilities and as many stories, the possible combinations are endless.

ACTS AND RESOLUTIONS

Resolution, or resolving story points, is usually essential to conflict. There is usually some resolution or some definite change, and even if it's not the intended resolution, something should happen. A man goes up against nature and survives or a man goes up against nature and dies are both straightforward stories with legitimate endings. If, however, a man goes up against nature and the story ends before the audience knows if he lives or dies, the story would have to be really unique for such a vague ending to work.

Interesting stories can still have a feeling that is unresolved and leaves ultimate conclusions hanging. People like mysteries, and a sense of mystery can be infused when something is unresolved. Resolutions can happen in small fragments as a director works his way through a story or film. Minor problems can be solved or goals can be achieved toward a larger goal. For example, in a romance film's first act, the man tries to get the attention of the woman, and finally does, and she realizes he's not such a bad guy. There is a sense of resolution and there's a sense of an act coming full circle. The main character sets out after something and he achieves it. In the second act, the man neglects the girl, or does something stupid, and loses her. He then realizes what he's lost and must get her back: another resolution and another act. Resolutions and acts are structural anchors that are tried and true, but ultimately the story decides how long acts play out and what is resolved or not. Animation also often works in smaller shorts and segments, and many of those are single-act visual plays. Acts and structure and resolutions are to some screenwriters absolutes, but there's always creative ways to blur the lines with an interesting story.

The Monkey's Paw, a classic short story by W.W. Jacobs, is an example in which the resolution is subtle and buried below the actions. The end is unexpected, and adds another unique wrinkle, where the reader is left not sure what has happened.

In the story, a man is given a monkey's paw that grants three wishes, but the wishes aren't as they appear. Skeptical, the man wishes for $200, but nothing materializes. The next day, the man and his wife are informed that their son was killed accidentally in the machinery of a local mill, and the company will pay a restitution of $200. The couple is devastated, but the wife is sure it is the work of the monkey's paw and demands that the husband wish for the return of their dead son. Against his better judgment he does so, but is terrified. The son has been dead and buried two weeks, and the man realizes what condition his son would be in, just as a pounding begins on the their front door. The wife goes to open the door and let her son in, but the horrified man makes his last wish, the knocking ceases, and the woman opens the door to an empty cold night wind. Obviously the man wished it all undone, which in a vague way did happen. Was it all coincidence? Did the paw even work? The story twists and turns and leaves a big mysterious question and the readers must decide for themselves. Is it a horror story, a story of temptation and greed, or a mystery story, or a combination of all three? Working out a story that is simple and complex at the same time and speaks to basic human urges and flaws with such a sense of mystery is a true measure of story telling talent.

ON THE CD

In the short animated film *Shards of Death* (included on the CD-ROM as **Shards.mov**), the resolution is deliberately flat; nothing is really accomplished and the resolution only further depresses the already too sensitive monster. The film ultimately returns to the mundane, where the monster calls to his secretary for the next interview subject; the film's resolution ends with the monster going on with the idea of a dull life and more strange interviews. The intent is that the projected ongoing of the monster's job is humorous.

Subplots

A subplot is a storyline that can run simultaneously with another overall plot or story. A film can have one or many subplots or stories running simultaneously. Subplots can make a story or a film more dynamic and entertaining, or overloaded and confused. Classic screwball comedies, such as *It's a Mad, Mad, Mad, Mad World* intertwine all the stories and plots of all the characters under the main story: all the characters are trying to get rich. Characters benefit from subplots because they tell their stories, and subplots can be attached to the main plot and unattached as well. Subplots can also have a lot of impact and change the direction of the story completely.

In the sci-fi classic *Blade Runner*, Harrison Ford's character is out hunting down the replicates who have illegally returned to earth; the subplot that the replicates have returned to earth to try to extend their lives is an example of how a subplot forced the main plot into existence. Subplot by definition sounds like it's a minor plot point. A hypothetical story's plot is a romance, but a minimal subplot is that one of the love interests has been dishonest about their past. A large subplot is a romance set against World War II. When subplots are done right and interwoven, they can create truly effective stories that require much more thought on the viewer's side than just watching a single driven plot type story. For example, an old bank robber wants to rob the town bank, but also wants to settle a score with the sheriff who jailed his brother. Subplots can be simple or complex, reveal themselves at the beginning, be discovered, or be a level of secret motivation that is surprisingly revealed at the end of the story.

Story Arcs

A story arc is when a story is bigger than the segment being watched. It can be serialized, like a weekly return to the same story as in an old *Buck Rogers* serial; can be more like the *Lord of the Rings* trilogy with a massive story evolving over several films; or can be a standard series like *The Sopranos*. The television show *The Simpsons* doesn't have an arc specifically because the story is just unwanted stories of a family, and the subsequent episodes are not continuations of previous episodes. The characters in *The Simpsons* don't age, and they don't get wiser; Bart and Lisa never graduate to the next grade, so the arc is somewhat irrelevant. Sequels often have a story arc, but it isn't essential and the same characters in a sequel can do something completely different or take part in a whole different story ignoring any story arc from the first film.

Plot Twists

Plot twists are major story elements that often prove to be the opposite of what was being seen or expected. Twists go back far into history, and a twist is frequently ironic and is caused occasionally by happenstance. *The Gift of the Magi*, by O. Henry, is a classic example of a story that ends with a bitter twist. The story focuses on a very poor couple. The wife has beautiful long hair, and has admired a set of combs in a shop window, and the husband's one possession is a pocket watch. For Christmas, the wife cuts off her hair, sells it for money, and buys a chain for her husband's watch. The husband, in turn, has sold the watch to buy his wife the combs. It's a bitter ironic twist, but has a powerful impact; viewers can relate to the story, because things like that happen. *Romeo and Juliet* has the same bitter plot twist when Juliet awakens to find Romeo "dead" and then takes the real poison to kill herself.

In modern action and thriller films, twists have become essential and are almost verging on tired. In *Fight Club*, the big twist is that Edward Norton's character is actually two characters in the movie. In *The Sixth Sense*, Bruce Willis' character is actually dead, and similarly with *The Others*, the characters think they're being haunted by ghosts when in fact they are the ghosts. The twist of the plot is well-used and powerful when developing a story; radical twists aren't essential to films, but when done correctly they are truly shocking. In Alfred Hitchcock's classic *Psycho*, the illusion that Norman Bates's invalid mother was calling the shots, only to find out she'd been dead for years and he had been carrying on an insane relationship with his imaginary mother, was a truly powerful twist. Audiences walked away from *Psycho* rethinking the entire movie in the context of Bates' insanity. Modern Canadian director and writer Atom Egoyan's film *Exotica* is a film that is a complete twist from start to finish. The story is laid out in such a way that the audience draws conclusions about characters that are continually proven wrong. Not until the end of the film do all the motivations and story lines become clear. The delayed unfolding of the true story creates a brilliant ending, but it's incredibly difficult to hold back information and create misdirection and have it still ring true and be compelling. Egoyan does exactly this, relying on interesting characters and subplots that don't tip his hand to the actual truth.

Exceptions

Exceptions have a unique roll in telling a story, especially when it comes to film and animation. When things go against the rules, it's often very dynamic and magnetic and a good form of surprise. Exceptions should not be treated lightly because breaking too many rules can create a complete collapse, specifically when it comes to structure and motivations. Whether it's because of the massive history of story and visuals that the audience has lived with or just the evolution of the medium, exceptions and broken rules often work amazingly well.

The Cary Grant classic *Arsenic and Old Lace* is one of many great examples of the exception to the rule carrying a lot of weight. In the movie, two nice elderly women have been systematically poisoning men who come through their parlor. In modern society, old women are thought of a grandmothers or nice old aunts who aren't usually capable of harm, but the comedic and shocking exception in the film is that the women are serial killers.

Terry Gilliam's *Time Bandits* ends with the main character, a boy named Kevin, being left alone after his parents have just been killed in an explosion. Usually in big-action fantasies, the hero returns to something similar to how he was or better. Perhaps Kevin is better off without his dismal parents, but the ending scene of the child standing alone in front of his burned down house is an effective exception.

Narration

Narration has been used effectively from caption cards in silent films to voice narration in current modern films. Narration is another point of view that can be of the omniscient storyteller or the narrator describing the scene. Take the previous example when a woman learns about her long-lost sister. The narration for this story could be: "After 52 years, the long-lost sisters finally spoke and arranged to meet. The older sister, happier than she'd ever been, rushed outside and danced in a downpour. The neighbor across the street must have thought she was crazy." Narration isn't a strict genre and it can come in and out of a production be omniscient and describe events from a completely wrong point of view, such as the neighbor who thought the woman dancing in the rain was crazy.

The classic film noir movie *Sunset Boulevard* has the unique point of view of retrospect. The narration comes from the lead character who is already dead.

The film *Grime Shoed Diaries* on the CD-ROM, **Grime.mov**, is an homage to that style of narration which involves speaking from an impossible point of view. It recalls incidents that lead up to the character's death so that the character is speaking from beyond the grave.

Narration can be effective, but can also be overused. The attraction to narration is that ideas can be simply said, which can be an easier, quicker way to convey a lot of information. Narration also has the ability to reflect on a scene any place in time. Narration can speak of the day before, thousands of years ago, or even into the future. *The Shawshank Redemption* is a powerful and complete movie that is driven by a powerful narration track.

Surprise

Surprise is a basic and strong element in every form of story. Whether it's a comedy, horror, thriller, or drama, the revealing of some information is always pivotal to the story and gives the characters events to react to. A surprise is an event, action, or element that appears changes unexpectedly. It's a function of the mechanics of film or television that plays linearly, with one event coming after another, and is integral to the process. Surprise isn't always the turning on of the light and finding something totally strange. Surprise can be bitter; it can be what was expected, but there was always the possibility it wouldn't happen.

For example, a young boxer, who has always done what was right is asked to take a dive and throw a boxing match for a huge sum of money so that he can pay for an operation for his ailing younger brother. The fighter had done right all his life, but what will he do when faced with such a dilemma? Either way, it will be a surprise, but viewers learn more through the reveals in the film. Reveal is a function of film and visual media, as the camera or the edit reveals objects and scenes either by editing or physically moving around revealing themselves to the camera's angle of view. A lot of humor is also based on surprise, another action that works well with humor and animation, because it's possible to create huge surprises that are impossible in almost any other form.

An example is the familiar beginning to the original *Rocky and Bullwinkle* cartoon. During each intro segment, Bullwinkle would attempt to pull a rabbit out of a hat, and instead it would be a roaring lion's head. The impossibility of a lion being in the hat is a complete and absurd surprise. But surprise is very short lived, and usually only works once. The cartoon's writers knew this and switched it up, so that it wasn't always a lion; sometimes it was a gorilla or even a rabbit, creating a new surprise and a running gag.

Repetition

Visual stories use shots and scenes like words. Just as adjectives describe an object, specific shots help to describe a scene. Repetition of the same ideas seems technically repetitive, but instead it is continually reinforcing the ideas.

For example, take this fish-out-of-water story: A wild man who has lived all his life outdoors has dinner at a luxurious and extravagant palace. Shot after shot reinforces how opulent the surroundings are: famous paintings; well-dressed guests; lavish food; black-tie waiters; ice sculptures; a string quartet; and a dozen forks, knives, and spoons at every setting. All these shots, although different, repeat the idea that it is a very fancy party. When the filthy wild man, in his tattered clothes and rags full of sticks and leaves comes in, the contrast is amplified. Repetition shots then shift to the wild man: dirty clothes, bare filthy feet, overgrown fingernails, and matted hair. The repetition now reinforces what it is about the wild man that is so out of place. Repetition is important in establishing tones and bond, but it has to be created so that it reinforces ideas without seeming like it's saying the same thing over and over.

In *The Shawshank Redemption*, Tim Robbins' character helps almost everyone. He does people's taxes, starts a library, helps an illiterate prisoner learn to read, and proves through repetition how good he actually is. Even in a horrible prison under cruel conditions, he still helps others. Bad guys often do bad stuff over and over for the same reason. Repetition is part of establishing stories by reinforcing everything even beyond just the characters. Comedies like *Planes, Trains, and Automobiles* and *National*

Lampoon's Vacation are loaded with funny repetitive plot points where everything is repeatedly going wrong, pushing the characters to their breaking points.

Time

"A long time ago, in a galaxy far, far away," begins *Star Wars*. Time is as malleable for the storyteller as choosing words themselves, and time is an incredible tool that can be used in infinite ways—some overt and some covert. Time is a physical necessity of the medium, but for the storyteller, time doesn't have to be taken in the form that ticks in a linear fashion.

Storytellers can create a story that spans generations of lives, or a story can exist in a moment. The classic short story *An Occurrence at Owl Creek Bridge*, by Ambrose Bierce, makes incredible use of time. In the story, an innocent man is about to be hanged from a bridge for treason. Instead, the hanging goes awry and he miraculously escapes and swims to freedom into a beautiful and tranquil scene with his welcoming family. In reality, it's just a desperate fantasy in his mind, and in an instant he is actually hanged. *An Occurrence at Owl Creek Bridge* is an excellent short story that treats time very differently and surprises and fools the audience. A 28-minute, black-and-white French short film was also made of *An Occurrence at Owl Creek Bridge*, which is a faithful telling of the story.

Time can be used for effect like in the classic film *Little Big Man*, which spans Dustin Hoffman's character's entire adult life, from a young teenage boy to a 100-year-old man. Time can also be used to reinforce ideas like tragedy. The classic film *Dr. Zhivago* has unrequited love compounded by decades. At the end of the film, after what the audience has learned has been nearly a lifetime, it's wrenching irony when the main character dies just a few paces before seeing his true love.

In Stanley Kubrick's *The Shining*, time is used again to solidify an emotion. Near the end of the film, Shelley Duvall's character discovers that Jack Nicholson's character, who has been supposedly diligently writing a novel, has in fact only been actually typing, "All work and no play makes Jack a dull boy," over and over and over. It is the elapsed amount of time that makes this point in the story so shocking because so many shots prior to the discovery featured Jack Nicholson's character typing day after day, week after week. When the audience sees what he's actually been typing for all that perceived time, they are shocked. They too had been lead to believe that Jack was writing a novel, and now all that writing has been discovered to be pure, dangerous, and brooding insanity. The story deliberately misleads the audience to great effect, just as Hitchcock did in *Psycho*. The audience believed that the controlling mother was actually alive, when in reality, she'd been long dead, and Norman Bates had been mimicking her voice.

Time also expands beyond the story itself, and a history or future can go off in either direction beyond the actual filmed time. The Japanese animated classic *Akira* takes place after a huge nuclear event, and everything in the film is a result of that atomic blast that happened years before the actual film takes place. The audience is very accepting of these time jumps and repositions. Often a graphic in a film says it all. In the film, *Cast Away,* the words "four years later" send the audience reeling because Tom Hanks' character has been marooned for all that time. A graphic can also say something as simple as "the next morning." The animated feature *Ice Age* has a title card that reads, "20,000 years later."

Independent filmmaker Jim Jarmusch, in his film *Mystery Train,* tells the stories of separate groups of people one night in Memphis, Tennessee. Time loops in this film, and the audience only becomes aware of the loop when a gunshot goes off and a disc jockey on the radio says the same things and plays the same song, over and over. Jarmusch creates a woven timeline and builds it so that separate groups of people all hear the shot. The audience actually doesn't see the scene where the shot came from until the last looping of the film.

The film *Momento* pushes the edge and tells the story in complete reverse, The Disney feature *Holes* seamlessly made use of jumping back and forth in time from the Old West to the present day. The most obvious of time manipulation is the most overt—time travel—and is a major plot point in both *Back to the Future* and *Time After Time.*

Omnipresence

Being able to know what is going to happen to a character long before, or even just seconds before it happens, is a great tool for storytelling. Like the written story, omniscient means being able to use the best elements of story whether they're in a room or in someone's mind. Humor extensively uses the ability of being able to briefly glance ahead. Other filmmaking does as well, but there is inherent humor in the viewer being in on the joke, prior to the character's pulling the joke or gag. The woman carrying her wedding dress from her car and a quick shot of a bus approaching the puddle tells the audience that these two ideas are about to collide. A rake lies in the grass as a man walks out to grab his morning paper.

Omnipresence, or being in two or more places simultaneously, is a simple writing tool, simply sending the story back and forth between plot lines. The same is true about film, but it does it visually by either cutting back in forth or using split screens or superimposing one image onto the next. Modern directors have used a wide variety of omnipresence or unique points of view to tell a story, beyond the regular cut. The modern film *Timecode* features four simultaneously running split screen stories through the entire film.

DRAMA

Animation and drama can prove challenging because a fair amount of drama is based on subtly of expression, where real acting is very important, and being able to be subtle requires a level of detail that action and wacky humor don't necessarily require. The extra level of detail costs more on every level. From animator ability, to puppet design, rigging, expression studies, and pacing, everything is more complex when complicated ideas are communicated, and a lot of drama deals with complicated emotions and acting. Many modern feature animated movies, such as *The Iron Giant, Toy Story*, and *Dumbo*, combine drama and even tragedy and sadness with slapstick comedy as well as verbal and sophisticated humor, and the characters and animators have to be able to perform and act the spectrum.

Like comedy, drama can benefit from creating clean and often extreme and exaggerated poses to sell ideas. Animation has the luxury of emphasizing the poses and the emotions that sell the conflict of the drama, breezing over others that don't. In drama, like any other genre, from animation to art direction, everything should be geared to reinforce the underlying emotions of the story.

HUMOR

Humor has a very close relationship with animation as well as creating strong emotional connections. Comedy is a genre that relies on the viewer's sense of humor, more than any other genre of film. Certain things are universally sad (e.g., death, plague, horrible injustices) and certain things are universally scary (e.g., danger, death, serious pain or injury), but funny is in a class of its own. It doesn't use the same area of the brain like the others do. Animation and comedy have a unique bond based on extremes and exaggeration.

There's a Zen quote that says, "Humor is like a frog; dissect it and it dies." This is true; what actually makes someone laugh is intangible and as unique as a fingerprint. Humor is mysterious, but creating a setup where humor can grow isn't as ethereal. A person's view of the world, age, experience, and beliefs all factor in on a person's sense of humor. There are many forms of humor, but there are few that are universally funny. There's a good argument that silent-era actors like Buster Keaton, Charlie Chaplin, and Ben Turpin are probably universally funny to almost anyone possibly because they based their humor on universal themes: physical comedy, good versus evil, love, and the bully and the underdog. These are themes that are in every culture.

Obviously, not having language or a dialogue track to explain the story also requires the films to tell their story visually, a pantomime of story. Universal themes that could be acted, or physical comedy, was the inevitable form of story and of a nearly universal comedy. Slapstick is also another example, which goes back as far as drama and acting do. But it still works, and even today, certain actors and filmmakers like Jackie Chan and Roberto Benigni use the same universal conflicts and elaborately choreographed slapstick comedy. Even filmmakers who are considered more thoughtful or intellectual, such as Woody Allen, almost always have an element or scene of physical or slapstick comedy, especially Allen's early films. Slapstick physical comedy doesn't mean base or humor without intelligence. In fact, some slapstick often relies on a very intelligent premise. The French film *Delicatessen*, by Jean-Pierre Jeunet and Marc Caro, is an incredibly realized film in every respect with some of the most unusual and amazing slapstick comedy. Slapstick or physical comedy of course thrives in the land of animation, and because of the limitlessness of animation, slapstick comes into its own. The legendary director Tex Avery took full advantage of the limitless possibilities and pushed slapstick to a new level, with visual gags pushed to the point of absurdity and animation extremes following close behind. Another key element in humor is opposites; in action, size, and energy, comedic friction is often created by opposites.

Animation and humor have a very unique relationship because of the way they can be presented. This is in part because animation is capable of such surprise, extremes, and exaggerations. There's a saying that goes, "Humor is always at someone else's expense," and in that statement is a fair amount of truth. This statement also speaks to a dark side of humor that some people find hilarious while others find offensive. There is plenty of violent and mean-spirited humor, which a large fan base might enjoy but that the mainstream audience would find offensive and funny least of all. If an old woman slips on a banana peel it and gets up cursing and mad, it's funny; if she falls, breaks her hip, and never gets up again, it's tragic, but some still find that tragedy humorous. Live action and animation are different when it comes to violence, because animation isn't real. Blow up a cat in a cartoon, and that's normal, acceptable cartoon action. On the other hand, blow up a cat in a movie, even though it's not a real cat, and it reads as animal cruelty. For others, the offensiveness is what they find humorous, proving how elusive an answer to the question, "What is funny?" truly is.

Absurdity

Absurdity is unique in elements of humor because not everyone thinks absurdity is funny. Like the silent era films mentioned earlier, whether slapstick, surprise, opposites, or stupidity, most people can agree on its humor value at some level, but absurdity is intangible. The men of *Monty*

Python again were the masters of absurdity—a form of humor that appeals to certain types of viewers. Nonsequiturs are absurd turns where something that has no relation or bearing happens or appears. Absurd humor is often breaking the fourth wall, or winds up in completely madcap films as in *Airplane!*, the *Hot Shots!* movies, or *The Naked Gun* films. Daffy Duck and similar extreme characters rely on absurd props, costumes, locations, and actions as a true sign of their cartoon craziness. Monty Python's *Quest for the Holy Grail* features the classic absurd ending with King Arthur and his Knights of the roundtable being arrested by modern police.

Stupidity and Embarrassment

People find it amusing when they watch other people or characters act in a way that goes against common sense; they could be in love, trying to prove themselves, or could just be stupid. An often hilarious take is when the viewer or the audience knows the next logical and sensible move, and yet the character instead does something that is the opposite of common sense. The moment the character's face shows that he's going to make the wrong decision becomes the epicenter of the joke or humor. For example: A guy on an old, broken motorcycle sits at the top of a ramp and he watches three other guys, with much better motorcycles, attempt the stunt and crash into the ravine. He looks, thinks, and then goes for it anyway. That look, that moment of wrong decision is the key. That is the moment it becomes funny; that transitional moment is the opposite of what he should do. It's a surprise because logic tells any reasonable person that after what he's seen, he shouldn't attempt it. The idea of making the wrong decision can be humorous. Often, people who are crazy, or a little bit off, make good and interesting characters. However, when you start to go too far into that idea of mental illness it can become an issue of social rules and norms.

A character who is a bit crazy or eccentric, but still lucid, seems to be OK and is used extensively. However, if a person is truly mentally retarded or mentally ill, for most people it no longer is a source of humor. The *Monty Python's Flying Circus* television series and the subsequent movies had countless characters that were strange, bizarre, and often completely crazy. But they lampooned the craziness by making their characters fantastically crazy. They were never in wheelchairs or severely retarded, and their characters weren't the butt of the joke. Instead, they were just strange and often clever characters.

Misunderstandings and Confusion

The cartoon *Mr. Magoo* first debuted in 1949—an entire cartoon series based solely on misunderstandings and confusion. The character Mr.

Magoo also flirts with making fun of a true disability: blindness. For all practical purposes, Mr. Magoo was blind and wandered around mistaking things for other things. Because his actions were so extreme and he seemed to be happy (it also helped that he was also fabulously rich), it became an avenue of humor, although how funny it was is open to debate.

Behavior that is out of the ordinary is often humorous, and awkward situations and embarrassing situations are staples of comedy. But, embarrassing situations can become tired gags. The unusual or rowdy boyfriend who meets the stiff and humorless parents is a setup that goes back to *Romeo and Juliet*; has been done thousands of times in thousands of ways, but clever filmmakers can always find a new version that seems fresh. There's always a director or writer who thinks up a new way or, like *The Simpsons*, lampoons the reference.

Homage and Parody

Homage is the retelling of something familiar or recognizable with a new spin or twist; it's an almost reverent compliment, or it can be a total lift of someone else's idea. Parody is similar, but an homage can be once removed and instead mimic a style or a technique; a parody pokes fun at the recognizable or familiar event, technique, or style. *The Simpsons* is the grand master of homage and continuously transposes famous scenes in movies into the *Simpsons* style. Homage and parody go back a ways too, probably to the first person who dressed up as someone else and mimicked what someone said or acted out someone else's funny behavior.

For film and television, homage has become a standard form of humor unto itself. Examples include famous scenes like Cary Grant getting buzzed by the biplane in *North by Northwest,* scenes from the *The Godfather*, or footage from *Gone with the Wind*. It's obvious that people who watch visual entertainment will know and recognize other classic entertainment and enjoy a spoofing or lampooning of the scene.

Parody and homage in modern visual media is highly effective. Modern comedies like *Toy Story, Shrek,* and *Shrek 2* are loaded with homage and references to other movies and TV shows. Opposites are at work, on top of the homage as well. For example, the *Shrek* world is a fairy tale. Most people's perception of a fairy tale is very old world, almost medieval. However, the movie features a Starbucks® coffee shop, other well-known shops, and a "television show" via the magic mirror similar to the television show *Cops.*

It's absurd humor, and again absurdity is the theme. Comedies like *Airplane!* and *Young Frankenstein* are films built on other films, spoofs, and send-ups; these films work very well if they're clever. Homage goes back millennia. However, there's never been such a backlog of imagery and there's never been an audience that regularly watches so much imagery, so homage has evolved into a major form of humor and entertainment.

Using homage is naturally powerful when it connects to another movie or well-known show or figure. The audience knows the reference and feels in on the joke, even if it's an obvious one: The music from *Jaws* edited over any swimming pool scene automatically brings in the horror of a shark attack, but because there aren't sharks in swimming pools, it's absurd and comic. It's campy and it's instantly saying, "This is silliness and this is fun."

The Simpsons recreates the beginning of Indiana Jones in *Raiders of the Lost Ark* with Bart stealing Homer's coin jar and running down the stairs; the shots and the music are closely mirroring the scene as Indiana Jones tries to escape from the cave at the beginning of the film. To *The Simpson's* audience, a movie like *Raiders of the Lost Ark* is a given reference. Fans of the film enjoy a retelling, ready to see what the writers have added and how they've changed it to be more in line with the world of the show. It also doesn't hurt that visual homage is riding on the shoulders of great scenes by great filmmakers, animators, and writers. However, if taken too literally, homage can become copyright infringement.

Breaking the Fourth Wall

Breaking the fourth wall is a device where the story or the play references itself, or makes the viewer aware of the medium. The phrase describes the basic setup of a stage play and the audience watches the play through an invisible wall. When the play or actors draw attention to themselves as actors, then they've moved through that barrier of suspended disbelief. Breaking that wall or breaking character has been done for years, by masters like Shakespeare to Groucho Marx. Breaking the fourth wall is largely a comedic device that is based on surprise and absurdity.

Characters talk to the camera, or as in some of the early cartoons, interact with people in the movie theater. Some of the early MGM™ and Warner Brothers' cartoons always tried to create stranger and more surprising gags that would break that fourth wall. Examples are when a character runs off camera with such force that we see them leave the film and as they run by, the audience sees the sprockets of the film (see Figure 2.1).

In other cartoons, the film goes out of frame and the characters jump from one level to another like an elevator stuck between floors. This is esoteric humor because it not only breaks the rules of storytelling, but it also relies on the viewers understanding some basic principals about film, projection, and frames. If a viewer didn't get the reference and didn't understand the joke, it wasn't that important. Many of the classic cartoons and comedies that used this device had so many levels of humor going on that the viewer was bound to follow another line of humor.

FIGURE 2.1 An animated character physically "breaks the fourth wall" by stepping off the film itself.

Early cartoons like Tex Avery's work and Chuck Jones' *Duck Amuck* cartoon focused on the creation of the animation itself; the tradition continues in many episodes of *The Simpsons* and other modern animated television shows, including shows about being an animated character. Using the fourth-wall technique, early cartoons relied on the film's environment and poked fun at the theater projection medium by creating a "hair in the gate." Often with traditional projectors, the spinning metal reels can cause static that makes the film attract hair and dust as it moves through the projector. These hairs and dust stick to the film, pass through the film gate, get stuck in the field of view, and become visible on the screen. Since the film is constantly moving, the hair or dust specs dances around in the corner of the picture. Hair in the gate is an annoying visual distraction, but was inevitable with huge reels of film exposed to air and people.

In several classic cartoons, what appears to be dust or hair is actually drawn on by an animator. After the audience has been fooled into thinking that the projectionist isn't paying attention, the animated character will pull the hair out of the gate and fling it away. Similar gags flirted with the edge of the frame; for example, silhouettes of audience members getting up from their seats further down in the theater. All at once, the character on the screen notices the figure, yells, or cracks the figure on the head exclaiming, "Down in front, Mister!"

These jokes leveraged off the fact that at the time, before widespread television, most cartoons and movies were watched in theaters; when translated to television, the gags don't work well or don't work at all. The idea hasn't been forgotten, but is harder to pull off with a television and has been sparingly used. An episode of *The X-Files* featured a story about killer cockroaches and at the end of the show, the show's creators digitally added a cockroach that appeared to be crawling on the home viewers' television screen. The effect was very shocking and fooled and frightened many viewers. The insecticide company Orkin featured the identical technique. A fake commercial for shampoo or bath products run in the background while a cockroach crawls on the viewers' screen. The technique is simple: film a cockroach on a blue screen, composite that over the shampoo commercial footage, and add some reflection and some shading consistent with something attached to a glowing television screen. The image becomes very convincing. These commercials were so convincing that several viewers broke or damaged their televisions when they threw an object at what they thought was a real cockroach crawling on their set.

There are also fourth-wall gags that don't involve physical comedy; early film comedians like Groucho Marx have a long history of talking to the camera or addressing the audience directly. From Bugs Bunny and Daffy Duck talking to the camera to Woody Allen, who used the same technique extensively in the Academy Award-winning film *Annie Hall,* breaking the fourth wall is a legitimate technique.

Addressing the audience is another complex level of humor and can create a sense of the viewer being truly included in the character's thoughts. The structure of the story has to be created in a way where such a departure from the norm doesn't detract from the main emotion that is trying to be conveyed. Often, it can just be a glance at the camera, signifying that the character realizes he is in a story and makes a connection with the audience as if to say, "This is fake, and I know it, but I'm still playing along." Still, breaking the fourth wall is a drastic and unusual departure from conventional storytelling. It is usually confined to comedy that doesn't rely on the complete illusion of story and the connection with the story and the emotion is lighter. Voice-over or standard narration is considered a classic device for story, where a character tells the story outright and the visuals follow along; a standard narrative can quickly cross over to break the fourth wall simply by what the narrator says. It's not necessary for an actor to face the camera or reference the medium of the theater or the film. Characters simply stepping out of character can have the same function of deliberately breaking the illusion.

In comedy, laughs and humor are the main focus. The complete illusion of the story can go in and out and not harm the film. Because of the nature of humor, even if the audience is aware or made aware that the story is make-believe, it can still be humorous and entertaining.

In other genres breaking the fourth wall would be a disaster, akin to seeing the microphone or a reflection of the camera and film crew in a medieval epic. Even though audiences welcome the illusion of a movie, misplaced objects or events can easily create a disconnect. Other visual disconnections can be items that are unavoidable: the condensation trail of a modern airliner streaking through the sky over a Viking movie, telephone lines in a 16th-century drama, or modern vehicles in a period film set at the turn of the century. Mistakes like out-of-time pieces are often removed digitally at great expense.

Dramas, thrillers, and mysteries that rely on the suspension of disbelief and stepping out of the story or acknowledging the medium rarely work, because those types of stories rely on a complete illusion. Characters can tell a story to the camera, but rarely does a straight narrative or epic drama stop and then feature someone addressing the camera. However, done correctly and cleverly, it could of course work as an exception.

Expert filmmakers, like the team of Ismail Merchant and James Ivory, who have made a career making films based in history like *Room with a View,* are keenly aware of the power of misplaced items. Many keen cinematographers and directors will go to great lengths to ensure that the real world never is even hinted at in the unreal world. Fanatic directors of the early 1920s often had actors in period films even wearing period underwear so that they would "feel" different and that would somehow be visible on film.

With modern productions keen to hide the hand of the film, every shinny surface is a problem. In instances of reflection, with large windows or polished surfaces, the camera crew and other equipment will shoot from behind huge black curtains with only the lens poking out from behind the material to ensure that reflections on coaches, armor, and other reflective objects never pick up any modern images; people in modern clothing, camera equipment, and light stands are examples of items that could break the mood and cause a disconnect. It is another level of detail, and another level of expense, but is important for distancing the "old" story from the "new" tools.

Breaking the fourth wall has evolved with the sophistication of audiences and exists in more subtle forms; camera shakes and vibrations are a once-removed version of breaking the fourth wall. Huge shockwaves, explosions, and heavy objects hitting the ground are all examples of breaking the fourth wall by having the camera being affected by the event. In essence, a big explosion in a movie suggests that it's so powerful that it rocks the fourth wall.

Theme-park and specialty films such as motion rides extensively use the fourth wall to send objects hurtling toward the viewer. Theme parks also go one step further and synchronize them with in-theatre effects, such as wind, mist, fog, and large and small motion simulators. Big-budget action films now often feature shots in films that break the fourth wall, as pieces of debris from an explosion, a hurricane, or tornado fly at the camera and appear to smash it, sending the virtual energy into the viewer's mind.

STORY ELEMENTS AND PROPS

Telling the story without words or people is often part of a larger picture of storytelling. For example, take the cliché. A cliché that has been used again and again, but always to great effect, is the spinning newspaper that flies in with a headline. Even if it's not spinning, a newspaper headline speaks volumes with one shot. Seeing a newspaper tells the viewer several things instantly: whatever it is, it's big news if it's on the front page and everyone knows or will know. The next cliché shot is someone in the story reading the paper and seeing the story. There are also other ways to tell a story with objects and shots that aren't clichés, and even a cliché turned on its ear can be new, fun, or original.

In feature films and plays, props are basically anything that anyone handles. But props and even certain set pieces in movies and animation are important potential players in telling the story and setting a mood. The use of props and sets should be considered as important as the use of characters.

In the Disney classic *Snow White and the Seven Dwarfs,* sets and props are used perfectly to help tell the story and to give more vivid characterization and story texture. In the story, after the wicked Queen taints the apple that she'll deliver to Snow White, she exits her dungeon to go to the dwarves' cabin where Snow White hides. On the way out of her dungeon, the Queen comes upon a human skeleton reaching out of a tiny cell; its fingers are just inches from what would have been a pitcher of water. It's a tragic setting: someone died of thirst, and has been dead a long time, inches from reaching the pitcher. The Queen stops, notices, and shrieks, "Thirsty?"

The Queen then laughs and kicks the pitcher into the skeleton, scattering the bones and sending a spider running from the dried out water pitcher. In the course of the film, it is a scene that could have easily been omitted, because it doesn't add any information to the plot. Instead, the Queen has the tainted apple and could have simply left her dungeon on her way out to trick Snow White. The next shot in the film, which easily could have been cut to, showed the Queen outside the castle on her way into the forest. But the scene with the skeleton says so much about the cruel Queen who has obviously been cruel for a long time. It's a frightful idea, dying of thirst, and it's been so long that the prisoner has long turned to bones, but the Queen still has no sympathy. She ruthlessly kicks the empty pitcher for the final indignity, scattering the bones. It's a great sequence, not essential to the story, but essential to showing that the Queen is mean and ruthless and reinforces the evil nature of her heart.

On a much more straightforward level, the short film *Shards of Death*, on the CD-ROM titled **Shards.mov**, has four props that characters handle, all of them strategic. Some are quite simple, and don't even move, but are for hand use.

ON THE CD

In the film, a pair of glasses sits on a desk, obviously owned by the monster. This is a dynamic prop, because it tells more about the monster without having to spell it out. He's got poor eyesight—a normal "human trait" that says something about him. The second prop that is handled is the pencil that the green monster is using. He's looking over the blue fairy creature's résumé while tapping his pencil. Again, the humor or charm should come out of the hideous monster, absently tapping a pencil, like anyone would do.

The next prop is a box of tissue that the zombie awkwardly offers to the fairy when he realized that he's blown the interview. The tissue box is a good prop because it becomes a setup for another gag when the little character, instead of blowing his nose, tries to impress the monster by making the tissue into a flower, only making itself cuter. The job requires the fairy to be scary and the fairy just can't do it; anything he does is cute.

People and creatures use their hands. Animated characters that also use their hands become more believable, showing their complexity and ability to do two things at once.

ANIMATION IN STORYTELLING

Storytelling is about conflict. There has been so much written on telling a story, and it all applies, but animation has some unique requirements and even more unique opportunities.

Creating a story for animation is similar to any storytelling, the mechanics can be compared to music, and the tempo or the beat of the music is the pacing (not that pacing should happen to the beat of a drum). In music as well as in visual storytelling, there is a rhythm in which things happen at a rate, and that rate is decided by the mood and the motivating elements. It is completely subjective and has to be one of the most intangible ideas to develop. Other jobs of a storyteller can be fleshed out with processes. In filming you can cover it with a wide shot, close-ups, and interacts; follow the action, and then create a few unique shots to pepper in, but how they fit together and how long they stay on screen can only be discovered by trial and error. This trial-and-error process is always paret of animation depending on the stylization often requires longer or more specific shots to read poses and gestures. Directors need to be aware that even though they've become accustomed to an animated character's look, the viewers might need a split second more to fully digest what they've just seen.

Animation Story Considerations

A story that is going to be adapted to a film is decidedly different from a story that only appears on paper. Written stories can be plotless and have tragic endings, but feature films, whether animated or live action, have been shaped by the viewing audiences over decades and decades of films and animation. Short animated films, and now even video games can have a totally unique angle, but by and large, feature animation is geared toward children and families and follows the standard structure.

Writing for animation is its own unique challenge because unlike live action with actors, animation is all created from scratch; only the voice is used to inform the performance and differs from a talented actor doing his interpretation of a scene. In a very real sense, short animated films can often be more daring and explore unique storytelling angles that would be more difficult and risky in a feature film. Feature films, specifically animated films, have to be crafted carefully. The audience doesn't have any real-world references, and it can prove harder to keep an emotional connection to animated characters than to real or live action characters.

CHARACTERIZATION

Often the most interesting characters are the characters that are the most flawed. Superman is a well-known fictional character, but having incredible strength, good looks, and a heroic sense of morality isn't interesting for very long. In fact if that's all he had, he'd become uninteresting because no one can relate to such a figure because none exists. It's the conflict that makes Superman interesting: who he's fighting and what he's up against. If Superman didn't have bad guys with kryptonite, the only substance that weakens him, he'd be boring. He needs foes and he needs big scale action to work. He also is the poster boy for good versus evil, which is one of the most basic story themes.

Simpler characters that are internally flawed or conflicted can often be far more interesting. Television's Archie Bunker was chauvinistic, stubborn, and racist, but worst of all he thought he knew everything and his view was the only correct view.

The humor and the drama that came out of a character so flawed was from his dysfunctional logic. When he backed himself into intellectual corners he couldn't get out of, or when he realized that he'd gone too far and had hurt the ones he loved with his pigheadedness, Bunker became more of a mouse than a lion. People can relate to a character because others often act like that, perhaps not to the degree Archie Bunker did, but to some degree. Mr. Burns from *The Simpons* is very similar, but more exaggerated. He is greedy, evil, and sinister, but also cowardly, fragile, and often helpless.

Empathy for a Character

It's not absolutely essential that the audience always root for, love, or even like a specific character, but they do need a character intricate enough, that they care for in some form, to want to follow a character's story. If the character is evil or bad, the audience can't wait to see them get their just desserts, but making an interesting bad guy is just as complicated as making an interesting good guy. Often, truly interesting characters are a little of both. The traditionally perfect good guy is now a fairly one-dimensional concept, except when turned on its ear. Often, bad guys have a lot of good in them and vice versa.

For the hero or protagonist of a story, often it is essential that the audience like or at least relate to what the main character is doing. In order to further truly emotional connections, it does become important that the audience likes or appreciates a character if that character is going to have the traditional role of a lead in a story. Tony Soprano from television's *The Sopranos* has done some awful things, but his true feelings about right and wrong are conflicting with his continuing to be a gangster and the conflict is torturing him; besides being a killer, he's funny, clever, caring, and ultimately just wants peace. He's complex and likable by some. Tim Robbin's character in *The Shawshank Redemption* is a completely cut and dry character who is virtually impossible to not empathize with. He's wrongly convicted, sent to prison for life, abused, used, and finally escapes and gets his just desserts. There's nothing that he ever does that makes the audience question whether or not he is worthy of their empathy or feelings. Instead, everything he does reinforces his noble character.

The character Gollum from *Lord of the Rings* is driven by his flaws: his addiction to the ring and his internal fight between who he was and what he has become. He was so conflicted that he split into two separate personalities—a clear mental disorder. There is entertainment in watching that conflict, because everyone has been conflicted about something on some scale. Whether the conflict is about a mythical ring, or something mundane, the conflict is always real, and people can identify with it.

Nonhuman Characterization

Talking animals and other nonhuman characters can be anything from talking robots and talking plants to talking toilets and talking bugs. If done poorly, talking critters is a cliché, but talking and communicating verbally can make a story imperative, specifically when telling a linear standard structured story. One of the simplest ways for creatures to communicate, emote, and create humor is to speak, and a huge amount of animation has its roots in talking animals and creatures.

Even after decades of talking animals, animation companies can find new ways to meld the two relationships between humans and animals or creatures. The idea of either species exchanging traits has always fascinated for millennia; the Egyptians have the enigmatic sphinx, which has the body of a lion and the head of a man, while the Greeks have the centaur, a creature that is half horse and half man. The attraction is obvious: take the brain of the man and put it into the much more powerful body of the creature. In essence, the idea is to become that creature while still keeping the persona the same. It is a fascinating idea, and continues to fascinate and entertain audiences. A werewolf is the horror extreme of such a combination, as is the genetic disaster in the sci-fi standard *The Fly*.

Humor has a much longer lasting relationship with animals and humans trading traits and persona. Many animation studios owe their successes to animating nonhuman characters. Disney used to be the icon of that animation, but in the new millennium, Pixar is at the forefront of nonhuman animated characters becoming a massive business worldwide. Besides the surprise of a nonhuman character talking, and beyond the basic idea of being able to take all the traits of animals, there is also an inherent conflict with nonhuman characters that act human.

The human traits, the human desires, and language juxtaposed against animal or creature behavior is limitless in its possibilities. Pixar's *Toy Story* is a classic example. The characters are anthropomorphic toys; they speak like and have emotions like humans, but also have the background of being a toy and feel conflicted. Talking dogs and cats play both sides of the personality. They talk like people, but act like wild animals, verbalizing what humans have always thought or assumed their pets were thinking.

Like any animated object, creatures must be true to their nature in order to stay that creature, and be bound by the laws of their physical characteristics. Dogs have four legs that stick out in front of their bodies. Unlike a human, they cannot reach behind their backs with their front paws to scratch, so they use their back legs instead; their paws just don't bend like a humans arm.

If an animated dog were to scratch its back with its front paws, the dog would be going against his physical traits, and this might unglue the "dog" part of the character. Still, in cartoons, dogs, cats, rabbits, and ducks can act like human's, use human poses, drive cars, and work. The entire history of MGM's and Warner Brothers' cartoons is decidedly that: creatures of all kinds doing all sorts of human and animal behaviors, for comedic effect, over a span of many years in many cartoons.

As animation evolved, certain animal characters stopped being their creature and just became characters. Mickey Mouse is a mouse, but does nothing mouselike. Deputy Dog is a dog, but is more sheriff than dog; he never eats from a dog dish, nor does he bark. Bugs Bunny is a rabbit, and does eat carrots, but everything else he does has nothing to do with a rabbit.

With the short seven-minute cartoon, the main rule was humor. If a duck drove off in a car, it wasn't necessary for the duck to adjust the seat or explain how the pedals were reached. It was just accepted because in the world of cartoons, visual gags and surprise supersede plausibility.

ALTERNATE STORY FORMS AND PERSONAL TASTE

Not all forms of film, television, and animation require a "story" in the standard setting to be entertaining, but virtually all forms of entertainment have a story of some kind involved. Although it's often many levels deep, even a genre like a game show with its simplistic nature, would be uninteresting if average people weren't involved. In fact, every game show begins with the contestant telling a little about his life story, and on that basis the viewer either dislikes or roots for a fellow person.

Sports is about "us versus them" and is a story about good defeating the bad: the rival team, the stories behind the players' trials and tribulations, and the things they've said and done. Reality-type entertainment has gone to another level; the handheld cinema vérité is now a huge form of entertainment in modern culture worldwide. People are interested in other people's lives; whether better or worse off, people are entertained by the real stories of their neighbors near and far.

From the realistic and uncut live interaction of people's lives, voyeurism becomes slightly more visceral as audiences have grown to enjoy "confrontainment:" entertainment combined with confrontation. From reporters asking intensely personal questions, to people screaming insults at each other, to all-out physical altercations, the stories behind these lives drive the conflict.

Like many forms of entertainment, not everything is for everyone, but there are millions of people worldwide who find the most interesting stories, unwritten and unstaged, in their next-door neighbor's house. Film studios are very sensitive to specific genre films, for they can measure the success of a film by its audience. Films that cross all audiences and are successful, and films that combine genres often are created to bring in specific audiences. It has little to do with filmmaking, but characters are often added to bring in certain audiences.

Even movie advertisements will be edited in several versions, showing a single picture as almost different stories. The studio will cut a commercial that shows the comedy or the buddy relationship. It will also cut a trailer that features only action so that it appears to be an action film, and then it will cut a trailer that is all drama so that it appears to be a dramatic film.

Tips for Future Projects

Determine the Point of the Story

It's impossible to tell anyone how to create a good story, but certain elements are inherent in good stories. Stories have a point, and some type of truth, however obscure or buried. Stories also usually have a big change of some type, where something happens, and stories almost always have some sort of basic conflict. The longer a project is, often the more developed a story must be to keep it interesting. Animation can in short bursts be based on pure absurdity, and the stories can be parodies or loose frames to simply hang visual gags on. The simple story of a cat trying to eat a mouse or bird has fueled literally thousands of cartoons throughout the years. When animation combines with humor, and there are enough interesting characters providing enough entertainment, stories can completely depart from normality and break the fourth wall and beyond. Drama, thrillers, and mysteries aren't as forgiving because the nature of their story must be grounded in reality for there to be any drama, thrills, or mystery.

Deciding on Plots, Points of View, and Subplots

Figuring out how a story is going to play out visually or in written word is where true talent shines through. Many storytellers start with a scene or a core character in mind, or they start with a point of view that interests them. Each writer and creator has his own method of development. But perhaps the biggest influence on the method will be the motive for telling the story—what is compelling then to tell this story. This motivation will greatly influence the decisions about characters, points of view, and subplots, and will help answer the question of how the story should be told.

Break the Fourth Wall

In developing comic or comedic projects, what are other ways to create scenes like breaking the fourth wall? Comedy can go anywhere and do anything. What new way of surprising an audience can be achieved by referencing the medium itself?

Strip Down a Story to Its Basic Components

Knowing the fundamentals of what forces are driving a character and a story—good versus evil, greed or revenge, basic motivations, complicated or simple—help define how a character behaves and what it does. Conflicted characters do conflicted things. Frankenstein's monster has the naïveté of a child, but also has the brain of a psychopath, the combination of which causes moments of simple tenderness and sadness offset by acts of complete rage.

Reverse Engineer a Story

Reverse Engineering a story often comes out of some other limitations or some outside forces on the story. Reverse engineering means accessing all the elements that a project has, and doesn't have, and figuring a story from those elements. A simple example is a filmmaker who has no recording equipment but wants to make a film, he must then reverse engineer a story around the fact that he cannot record field audio. Instead he'll have to create a silent film, or a film with just music and sound effects, or a story that has no spoken words, or a story that is campy and could be over dubbed later.

ON THE CD

On the CD-ROM, the short film, Shards of Death was reversed engineered because the characters already existed. So the story was written around the two characters that were going to be used. This idea of reverse story telling goes against the ideas of the "word is golden" but a script is not poetry, a script is a blue print and words are flexible.

INTERVIEW WITH DEAN WELLINS

Dean Wellins started his animation career doing animations on an Amiga computer. He attended Cal Arts and worked as an intern at Turner Feature Animation before working at Renegade animation. Dean has worked on *The Pagemaster*, *The Iron Giant*, *Osmosis Jones*, and *Treasure Planet*. He is now currently head of story on an upcoming feature from Disney animation.

Mike Wellins: When did you get serious about doing animation?

Dean Wellins: I guess when I went to Cal Arts from 1990 through 1992. Then from Cal Arts I went into the Turner Feature Animation internship, where I was a trainee animator under Bruce Smith, who is a well-known animator. Bruce is an amazing animator, and I learned I wanted to be [in] an animator from him. I wasn't sure what I was going to do at Cal Arts: character design, I didn't know. I saw his animation and I was like, I want to do what he's doing,

→

however he's doing it. He was my big influence. And then I went to Renegade Animation and worked on a bunch of commercials under Darryl Van Citters, the director. I learned a lot about storyboarding and animating, animating fast, because they're commercials and you only have two weeks to do it. I spent a little over two years doing that. Then from there, Tony Fucile, who is the head animator at Pixar on *The Incredibles,* was working with Brad Bird at the time. He was actually going to lunch with a guy who was doing freelance for us, and I was doing layouts for all the animation that we had to do for all these games that we were doing. So this guy was picking up work to take home and work on, and the guy who was driving picked up the stuff and set it in Tony's lap in the passenger seat, and while they're driving, Tony was looking through the layouts I'd done and he said, "Who's doing these?" And so that's how they got my name, and then Brad Bird got my name and then I got hired on [*The*] *Iron Giant* as an animator.

The thing was that the head of story on *Iron Giant,* Jeff Lynch, thought I was a storyboard artist, because the only office they had available was in the story area. Jeff assumed I was a storyboard artist. So Jeff came in and went, "OK, this is your first sequence; you gotta do this!" and I was like, "OK, great! I can storyboard, really exciting!," and then I started working on this thing; it was the part where the giant finds the deer in the forest. I was really excited and I started doing all this stuff with the animals and all these things like atmospheric things like the giant looking through the trees and rays of came in and said, "Hey, what's he doing? He's an animator—he's not a storyboard artist!" And Jeff said, "Oh, I thought he was a story guy." "No no, no, no, he's not doing storyboards."

So then I just hung out for like a month with Tony Fucile who was the head animator. He would do drawings and I would kind of just explore drawings, just like busy work, drawing characters, and then finally, I guess Jeff really needed sequences done in the storyboard. Finally, Tony took those little thumbnails that I did of the giant and went to Brad and said, "I think these are really good and I think maybe you should give him a shot at it, because we need it done and he's not really doing anything important." Brad gave in, "Alright, alright, he can do that one," and that was the beginning. I did a pass on three quarters of the sequences in that movie.

M. Wellins: *Where does the animated feature* The Pagemaster *fit in?*

D. Wellins: That was the Turner internship that was *Pagemaster.* I did cleanup on that and I actually animated two scenes, just on the side as an animating assistant.

M. Wellins: *Do you think all that was valuable? Do you feel like any of that was wasted or do you think it was all valuable for your experience?*

D. Wellins: All the animator stuff was all very valuable. Going through cleanup was definitely valuable because I was putting the final line on everything so I knew what an animator had to put in. I knew what information an animator really needed to put in for me to clean it up right. So when I started animating, I knew the trials and tribulations of cleanup people and I knew I'd better do this right because I knew what cleanup people needed to make it look good, so going through the cleanup job helped when it came to animating. At Warner Brothers, I worked on *Iron Giant* and then I worked on *Osmosis Jones.* I did the Thrax character, and then from there I went to Disney and worked with Glen Keane on *Treasure Planet.*

→

M. Wellins: *What's the most rewarding part of doing animation, for you?*

D. Wellins: I think it's the initial rough out of the scene: when you lay the dialogue on it and you shoot it and you hit play and it just suddenly looks alive. It looks like the talking is actually coming out of their mouth, that they're breathing that air. That's when it's exciting; that's when you're animating. Then after that you have to get in between it all, and then you gotta do the tedious part of animation, which is frame by frame by frame. You gotta get it all in there.

M. Wellins: *So is the tedious part worth it?*

D. Wellins: Oh yeah, especially at the end. But you want the end product to look great. Animation is just inherently tedious.

M. Wellins: *A lot of beginning animators ask me about going to the level that the classic animators do. A lot of CG [computer graphics] movies aren't done that well and still are successful. Pixar has done really great CG character animation, but it costs them a fortune to pull it off. Why bother doing a good job?*

D. Wellins: CG is one of those things that your eye just so instantly believes that it's a living, breathing thing just by being rendered and by being fully 3D. So there's bad movement, [but] still a part of your brain believes it just by virtue of what it is. 2D is not like that, because it doesn't have the automatic 3D space CG does. It is harder in CG, but I do believe that the thing about being a great draftsman or being an animator is that it gives you the ability to be subtle. I don't think you can get subtlety if you don't have that accomplishment of being able to really animate and know timing. You won't have the subtlety in acting, and you won't get the kind of emotion that the story requires. Even though you maybe get it 80 or 90 percent and if it's more or less animated decently, it's not great. If you look at movies like *Finding Nemo,* if you look at the expressions of the fish, that marlin and stuff, I don't think *Shrek* comes close to that. I don't think you feel the same emotion in *Shrek*-type movies that you do in *Nemo*-type movies because you're not seeing it in their face. I feel like you really see their soul when you look at Pixar characters. [With] *Shrek,* I don't feel that same thing, even though you can't argue with their box office—that's for sure. But some of that is just novelty. I think there's an absolutely untapped world of acting, of storytelling, that animation has yet to even scratch the surface of.

M. Wellins: *What are some of your favorite influences in animation?*

D. Wellins: I'm a big Warner Brothers fan. It had great subtlety. Bugs Bunny used to in the old ones, like in the 40s, like Bob Clampett had great subtlety. Rod Scribner animation and stuff like that.

M. Wellins: *What kind of cartoons or animated movies do you look at and say, "I want to do that"?*

D. Wellins: *Peter Pan* is my favorite Disney movie. It's my favorite as far as atmosphere. It's just that escapism. To me, that's pure animated fantasy.

$\rightarrow$

M. Wellins: So now you're head of story.

D. Wellins: This is my second go with being head of story. There was this feature project they were doing in Florida—Disney Florida. They pulled the plug on it because the story just wasn't marketable.

M. Wellins: What does head of story do?

D. Wellins: I think it's up to the person who's head of story to make it whatever you want it to be. When I was first head of story, the first fear is that now everybody thinks, "Oh, he's head of story." And you look at yourself through other people's eyes and think, "Man, I have to have all the answers." If somebody asks me a question, I have to have an answer. That was my first reaction. I gotta look like I know what I'm going, or know that I have a plan and that I have strong philosophies. The big realization is that I really didn't have to have the answer; I could just rely on people, and go to other storyboard artists and go, "That part of the movie I think really lacks. What do you think we should do?" and they go, "I think we should do this and that." I actually feel that they more appreciated me that I do not have all the answers that I would say, "I don't know. Maybe we should all get together as a group and figure it out."

M. Wellins: Do think its presumptuous for directors to think they have all the answers?

D. Wellins: I think it's seriously dangerous and I know with a few we've had where we ask, "Are we going to do this or this?" and they say, "Well, I think we should do this, so we're going to do it." [T]hen we'd say, "Well, maybe we should talk about it with the other guys or something?" "No, that's it. That's what we're doing." Then you'd say, "OK . . ." Invariably, they might not know what they're doing, and they're not being honest if they don't know what they're doing. As long as you're honest, and I think everyone to a certain extent feels like they don't know what they're doing—even the greatest veterans. It's that complicated.

M. Wellins: What's the key to translating the story to animation?

D. Wellins: When you're head of story, it comes to you through a script usually, unless the story is extremely broken. But if it comes from a script, then you're translating from a script. That's the story, and then that's translated through the story department with people always trying to better what they've been handed. It's always fussing at every level, not to the point where you overanalyze it, but to the point where you just feel it's getting better, and knowing when to stop.

M. Wellins: Is there one underlying plan where you say, "OK, here's the script and now we're going to translate this into visuals"?

D. Wellins: I don't know if there's just one, but the key is to let the story become what it wants to be. Most stories that I've dealt with being a story artist at Disney, and working with *Iron Giant,* you can feel the story wanting to be something, when you start working. You feel it wants to go in a direction, and you let it go in that direction. Or if it feels like it's veering, and

→

you push it back in that direction. Let it guide you a little bit, and then when things are starting to veer away from the original idea, then you've got to steer it back to the original premise that got you excited about it in the first place. At the same time, if it's already headed in that direction, don't mess with it. Just let it go.

M. Wellins: Is there a problem when you're working on something that takes so long? Is there a danger in overthinking things?

D. Wellins: What you'll find is you'll find designs and things that have been on the wall so long that when they take them off, there's a black square where they were. It's been there so long it's just old, even though the rest of the world hasn't seen it and it might be really cool. Now everyone wonders, Is it old? and then they get worried and say, "We gotta do something!" I'm tired of looking at these same designs. I'm tired of talking about this same story. And so many babies go out with the bathwater that way. It's still funny, but we've watched it 80 times and we don't laugh at that joke anymore; you get a fresh person in there to help. It still works. You can feel that it still works.

M. Wellins: How important are storyboards and animatics?

D. Wellins: They're the framework of the house. The house can't stand unless it has the frame, and that is the frame. If it doesn't work in the story realm, animation isn't going to save it.

M. Wellins: In a given project, what percentage of your time is spent working on storyboards?

D. Wellins: For me, probably 75 percent of the time is spent working on storyboards. With storyboards, I'm just another storyboard artist and I have all the story artists look at my stuff the same way I look at theirs. I tend to look at it and say how they can better their shots and things like that. But really what they do is, I leave it to them to put themselves into it. But really, 75 percent is spent on storyboards. Another 25 percent is meetings, sitting and editing, and looking at what we've done, which is a whole other monster; editorial is another monster.

M. Wellins: But editing and animatics is a useful monster, right?

D. Wellins: Something that completely works on boards will go down to editorial and lay flat as a pancake. Most things you can tell [that] this is funny and it will be funny if we get all the timing figured out. Sometimes it was really funny on boards, but now in animatic form it's boring. It's too long . . . It just becomes something different. I always find that once it goes into editorial, I don't want the project to go backwards. I don't want it to go back into putting it back up on boards because once it's there, you just want to deal with it there.

M. Wellins: Does it happen, where it goes back to the boards?

D. Wellins: It does . . . well, it has. I try to fight like hell for that not to happen, so that once it goes down there to editing, it's down there. Pixar is really big on that. They pitch boards like everybody else, but they just throw everything down into editorial. They throw the kitchen sink down there and they just deal with it in editorial. They make the movie in editorial, just

→

like in live action. You shoot a lot of stuff, all kinds of coverage: over people's shoulders and all this stuff and the movie really comes alive in editorial. [Editorial] sorts it all out and delivers great story points and happy endings.

M. Wellins: *There's a formula with movies in general. People don't like downer endings no matter what, unless it's a really different kind of film. In all animated movies that are 75 to 85 minutes, the good guy usually wins. Is that restrictive?*

D. Wellins: Yeah, it can be, but it can be challenging to work in that format as well. There's still infinite possibilities inside that structure, and it's Walt Disney, you know.

M. Wellins: *Was* Iron Giant *the same?*

D. Wellins: Well, not really. That one was out there because it was bittersweet when [the characters] weren't together in the end. It wasn't the same as *E.T.*, but he was resurrected. The great 'out' on *Iron Giant* was that he was a robot and we set it up early in the movie that he could rebuild himself.

M. Wellins: *Most movies have three acts.*

D. Wellins: Yeah, three acts: the setup, the same climax at the end of the second act. The worst thing happens at the bottom of the second act. The third act is the final . . . it's hard. It's hard not to do the same thing over and over, but I think you can do different things even with the three-act structure. The one I'm working on right now is a really different film, but it's got three acts and it does the same thing. The three-act structure—the emotional structure that features movies animated and live action—is really tired. The people go, "Yeah, I've seen that before."

M. Wellins: *What are some absolute do's, things you want to keep in mind?*

D. Wellins: My biggest strength is visually telling the story through boards, through shots, through cutting, things like that. The kind of recalculated depth, I learned it all from Jeff Lynch and Brad Bird.

M. Wellins: *You guys double as a cinematographer because you're picking all the shots.*

D. Wellins: It's not unheard of at Disney, but the usual way it goes is that they do storyboarding that is very simplistic. They just put it up there, get the characters generally in there saying the words, the general emotions, and then the workbook phase is where they go through and really figure out shots, pans and things like that. I came from Warner Brothers with Brad Bird where he worked on *The Simpsons* where they had to figure out all that stuff before they sent it, and they would do it all on the boards. They'd figure out the shots. So I definitely got schooled that way, that you put everything into those boards—every shot. You get creative with the shots because so much of the story is told with shots. There's so much comedy you can get out of a cut. There's so much comedy you can get out of a pan: the way you pan, what you pan to, why you do it, how fast you do it. There's a laugh there that you won't get on

→

boards unless you do it, and I feel like that's an important part of storyboarding in general. Chris Sanders, the director of this upcoming project, and I are definitely on the same page as far as, let's get the filmmaking in the boards and not wait for somebody else to do it. Same way with *Iron Giant*; Brad's mantra every time we went to workbook was follow the boards. Don't be inventive, we've already figured it out. Just follow the boards.

M. Wellins: *So what are some of the do's in creating storyboards?*

D. Wellins: Flow: working the flow from shot to shot, so that the audience is never lost. It's important to the audience to know where everyone is in the scene, and have a sense of mental geography. In storyboards, you're manipulating someone's mind while they're watching, so you've always got to be mindful of that. I don't want them to be thinking, "What happened to that one character? Where is he right now?" And now I'm seeing one character and all I'm seeing is just the head. Where's the other one standing? Is he close by? Is he far away? I can't remember now. And even though you're not consciously thinking that, subconsciously, your brain starts to cloud with things like that, so I feel like storyboards are always keeping you abreast of every little nuance that your brain is constantly asking every time a frame comes up. With every new frame that comes up, it asks a bunch of questions and you have to answer them all quickly and clearly, so they can just listen to the dialogue and watch the movie and not get bogged down wondering what's going on. It's all a part of clarity. It's clarity through cutting, and not cutting too much and not using camera moves to keep you guessing. I usually don't cut unless I absolutely have to.

If I can do a whole sequence with one shot, I'll do it unless I feel like this cut has to happen because I have to give new information in a way that I can't do where I am right now. I'm setting up a scene that is over someone's shoulder looking at someone else. If the person I'm looking over the shoulder at is talking to the other person, I'll stay on that shot forever, or as long as the other person's talking. I'll find that people will cut just to cut, because it's been going on too long. But as long as that person's talking, just keep going with the scene until the next person starts talking—even then maybe you don't. Maybe you're still on that first person, because their reactions are more interesting than the other character speaking. I always push the cut as far down as I can, to where I go, "OK, I really do have to cut to a different angle now."

M. Wellins: *So what are your don'ts?*

D. Wellins: Don't lose focus, not committing to an idea. You always have to commit to an idea. Technically, keep it clear. Clarity is probably the biggest thing that I can see that goes wrong. I sometimes get too much into the drawing and I start to lose clarity of what's going on. I start to draw in the background too much and it's not necessary. The character's talking and that's all you're going to be looking at. You don't need to draw in all the nooks and crannies on everything, even though you want to, just to make the storyboard look good. I think the biggest don't is to work too slowly. Your first pass on a storyboard should be really quick and from your gut. I can rough out a storyboard sequence, rough it out really quickly in a day,

$\rightarrow$

maybe a two-minute sequence. You should be able to rough it out in one day even if your drawings are something that you're the only one that understands. As long as you can understand them, you should be able to do it. I think a big don't is to sit there and doodle a drawing for hours, trying to get it right and you haven't even gone to the next panel.

M. Wellins: *What are some philosophical don'ts?*

D. Wellins: Not to cut too much, not just cut for the sake of cutting. Try to keep the camera invisible. Try to keep people always looking inside the frame and not to the frame itself. I think it's just something you just learn as you go along.

M. Wellins: *What about pacing?*

D. Wellins: In a grand scale, it's about pacing. I think it's the dynamics of the story. It's like in a piece of music: you have the right amount of softness, the right amount of hardness, the right amount of drama and comedy.

M. Wellins: *They say timing is everything. Do you agree with that?*

D. Wellins: I don't know if it's everything, but it's definitely a huge thing. Pacing is the very dynamics of the film itself. Timing sets the tone for the movie. It's like any kind of art. When you do a painting, you have big open areas and little tiny, tight areas that are really dense, but the contrast is what makes you feel good about it. Films are the same way. The contrast of timing is what makes it pleasing to watch: making things very dense and then going into a sequence that may be very languid. That contrast is what makes you want to go on into the story.

M. Wellins: *What is your dream project?*

D. Wellins: I feel like I already did it. *Iron Giant* was really a dream project because it was egoless. I think half of working on a film is for the people, for the experience of making it in general, and that was the perfect atmosphere for making a film. Nobody bugged us. We were filmmakers and the only people that had an opinion in the room were the filmmakers. There were no executives; there was nobody in the room watching us, policing us and our ideas and saying, "You can't do that. You have to do this and that." I feel like I've already done it. A dream would be for me to do something, but I don't know if I could create a good atmosphere that we had at Warner Brothers, which was basically, they barely cared that we were doing anything. We were doing it while the boxes were being packed up. *Quest for Camelot* was not what they'd hoped and they were going, Oh well, we tried the animation thing. They're still doing something over there. We don't know what it is, but we'll just keep going. That was really the dream job. I remember walking with Brad down the hall and saying, "I feel like this is never, ever going to happen again," and he said, "Nah, it'll happen again." Then I talked to him later and he said, "You're right, it never happened again."

II

VISUAL STORYTELLING

DEVELOPING THE TRUE CRITICAL EYE

The phrase, "mastering the critical eye," is really a term for mastering the critical brain. It involves developing an acute awareness of and being able to focus on the finest details. It also means being able to assess these details in the context of the production and in the larger scope of a performance that goes beyond animation and becomes good character acting that is consistent with the character's personality and further tells the story regardless of the material. The well-trained eye not only can see and catch every minute detail, but also has a keen sense of timing and pacing that is frame accurate. The critical eye also focuses on all elements that feed into the visual and tries to maintain a consistent production style, while still focusing and directing the audience's eyes and emotions.

EXPERIMENTATION

Experimentation happens whenever a filmmaker sets out and attempts something unknown, whether it be minute details, special lighting effects, or major performance points. Only through trial and error can elements be played against each other, and so experimentation becomes a key element at arriving at good visual storytelling. Whether ideas are experimented on paper or in front of the camera, filmmakers have the good fortune of being able to view other filmmakers' experiments and learn from their results. However, nothing replaces the actual experience. Doing visual experiments or exploring visual relationships is important. Thinking of explorations as experiments is helpful, because there are no predetermined outcomes. Often things work out great and new things are discovered, while other times, things didn't go as well as expected; that is the nature of experimentation and learning from successful and unsuccessful experimentation, is key. In a very real sense, every scene is an experiment, either entirely or by individual elements. The outcome of certain events cannot be accessed until it's in motion, edited, and has sound. Therefore, the nature of experimenting, the process of judging and learning from various processes, often simultaneously is a major part of growing and improving as a filmmaker, director, animator, modeler, or any other job in the visual media lineup.

EXPERIMENTAL FILM

The spirit in experimentation is so strong that some filmmakers began to create experimental film and nothing else. Film and animation have the-ability to morph from so many forms that show their artistic feathers that they can be considered visual and fine art. There are many fine modern artists who instead of calling themselves filmmakers call themselves artists, and instead of showing in festivals they show their films, animations, and videos in galleries. These artists use video, film, and animation more as paint and canvas than a medium of storytelling and mainstream entertainment. Often experimental film explores textures, abstract imagery, and repetition. Instead of establishing a story, these films often rely on assembling visuals and deliberately avoid classic storytelling techniques. Experimental film goes back to the early days of film in general, and one of the most famous early experimental silent films is the German expressionist film from 1920, *The Cabinet of Dr. Caligari.*

Millions of feet of experimental film have been made; even such legendary artists like Salvador Dali took a stab at making peculiar experimental films in the 1960s. Perhaps because of its perceived cost and required technical background, experimental film isn't as prevalent as it should be. Experimenting and simply shooting as visual artists is an incredible way to discover relationships and techniques and form ideas. Modeling and animating take a bit more science than simply filming with a camera, but there is valid exploration in simply creating visuals in any format. Whether it's called experimenting, testing, or designing with an eventual plan to create a film or story, experimentation is the life blood of filmmaking and animation. Experimental filmmakers and animators go far beyond the standard tools of film or animation. Because experimental filmmakers aren't bound to any rules, they often use found footage, recorded footage, and stills, while animators use all sorts of found materials, cloth, leaves, and sticks. Modern animators like Jan Svankmajer and the Quay Brothers often animate raw meat, little motors, wheels, dolls' heads, and dead insects all together to create complex and disturbing visuals that are void of any explanation of what is going on. Figure 3.1 is a scene from an experimental film that is dimensional with a drawn component, but it also utilizes bits of cloth, nylons, and actual medical clamps.

Animation and film is 50-percent science, with cameras and computers, and 50-percent emotions, with visuals, angles, and acting. Stories can grow out of experimentation, and there is no fixed rule that a story can't be reverse engineered from interesting designs created in any visual realm. Because of the complex science aspect of film and animation, experimentation is critical in learning the tools, and like science, animation and filmmaking work well with good note taking. The visuals and the emotions are less tangible, but the science side must be at least understood to begin to address real storytelling and solid character animation.

With projects that have budget and time constraints, experimentation can be risky, but innovation can happen under pressure, but it's a gamble. With the relative ease of digital filmmaking and animation, filmmakers who truly want to innovate have little or no excuse not to be experimenting with animation and shooting constantly.

FIGURE 3.1   A frame from an experimental film that utilizes drawn components, bits of cloth, and real medical instruments. © 2004 Joanna Priestley. Reprinted with permission.

VIEWING AND CRITIQUING ANIMATION

Animators can mentally or even literally mask off portions of the screen to study other aspects. For example, consider a walk cycle with a character with big eyes and a big smile. Even though the animator reviewing the work is the creator of the animation, it's still easy to get distracted by faces and eyes; the human eye always goes to other eyes, but the animator needs to work on the body animation. The animator may choose to turn off the sound, since tracks can be distracting, and with a card or even with the hand, he may simply mask off the head so it can't be seen. He may also mask off other areas that need to be studied, which is a simple but effective tool. When developing a real walk cycle in computer graphics (CG), it's important to preview it from every angle, including from directly above; often, a problem, a key frame, or limb out of place will be revealed simply by looking at the shot from another angle. CG is tedious and complex, but it also allows for incredible analysis that isn't possible in a medium like cel animation. Often to compensate for the lack of dimensionality, cel animators have a maquette or sculpture on hand of the character that they can look at from any angle instead of having to visualize complex angles.

Visual clarity is important and poses need a clear read and a strong outline. In 3D or digital programs, animators can simply render a scene with an alpha channel and then view the alpha channel at speed. The idea is to render animation as an alpha so that animators can see the shadow-puppet effect of the character's outline of black on white. This technique strips away all the surfaces, colors, and textures so animators can focus on the mass, cleanness, and readability of the character poses and outlines. In applications like Moho or Macromedia Flash, animators can simply run a mask layer so that the animation is then cut out, turn the mask layer to black on white, and view it from there—another effective tool.

THE FINE ART OF PUSHING

Dynamic animation is based on extremes: extreme action, extreme color, extreme noise, and extreme movement. When developing animation, extremes reveal a great deal about a project. When exploring or establishing key elements—a look, animation styles, action, or motion—it's helpful to push every aspect to the extremes. The art of pushing means taking stylization, design, and motion and pushing them to where they're so abstracted that they no longer work. Often by pushing toward the impossible, animators and artists discover new relationships that actually benefit from truly extreme treatment. An example would be a character that is human, but is exaggerated to the point where it is barely recognizable as a human; the character has pencil-thin legs, a tiny head, and a thin ribbon for a torso. Depending on the animation, that type of stylization can often work and have real artistic value.

RAPID MOTION AND MOTION BLUR

Being able to dissect fast motion, analyze, and adjust it to maximize effect is an incredibly hard skill to develop. With the advent of video, we are now able to watch things repeatedly and quickly, and are able to go frame by frame, which makes judging fast motion much easier. However, massaging single frames is still an innate desire driven by the style, pace, and the tone or mood. Many things happen faster than a 30th of a second, and manipulating motion to create real or even super-real movement can only happen after being able to correctly dissect what is wrong with a motion. Beginning CG animation, whether it's 2D or 3D, often suffers from any sharpness in motion. Things float from place to place, nothing has weight, and objects just seem to motor from point to point. CG animation has always had the perception that the computer was doing the work, and animation was just that much easier, but that was never true. Motion is easy; making something move from one place to the next is as simple as two mouse clicks, but doing true dynamic motion that is sharp, quick, full of energy, responds to physics, and adheres to the rules is never easy. The computer does do a lot; it creates every frame, applies color and shading, and keeps shapes consistent. However, it does not, for the time being, create animation.

The human eye can recognize when energy is used incorrectly, and the animator has to know how to recognize this and fix it. For example, an exaggerated character, a baseball pitcher, does a giant windup and throws the fastest pitch ever, and visually there is a huge release of energy. If the catcher catches the ball without event, the energy is undermined; unless it was done for effect, the energy needs to smash into the catcher, knocking him into the stands if the extreme nature of the energy is to be consistent. When the ball hits the catcher, the explosion of energy is instantaneous and needs to seem as such. With such force, the catcher could move a matter of feet in one frame as he's hurdled a great distance in a very short amount of time. In the extreme pitch scenario, as the catcher catches the ball, the ball could be one gigantic motion blur that streaks for one or two frames before the catcher is ejected backwards. Again, the modern animator and editor use the flexibility of digital editing to study, over and over and frame by frame, and massage such motions and study the effects when frames are added and subtracted. This way, the feeling of energy is consistent with what has been presented and with the scene's physics, while still packing the biggest punch.

Often in creating these important bursts of energy, animators create motion blur and stretched frames. The float of poorly animated CG was the opposite problem for traditional cel and stop motion animators. The development and discovery of huge sharp action, takes where a character changes or moves dramatically from one frame to the next, is for some cel animators the truly fun frames to draw—the key frames.

Motion blur hints at an idea that is crucial to developing a critical eye, and animators, editors, and directors need to be able to read and create motions and motion blurs that convey clean, quick, and often clever movements. Like lens flares, motion blur is an artifact of filmmaking that has been such a big part of that visual media; when it's added to animation, it again hints at that filmed reality. Unlike lens flares, however, motion blur is a bit more indispensable when trying to create a sense of reality in CG, cel, or stop motion. Creating fast motion that often reads as a blur is often the key to crisp, sharp motion.

In stop motion, motion blur is a bit haphazard unless the character or object that is going to be blurred is on some type of motion control. If that's the case, then the motion blur can be repeated, and it's also possible to create a similar blur by adjusting the shutter angle. The idea of "go motion" is again exploiting the ability of stop motion to take longer exposures than a camera running at sync speed. Go motion can have a simple rig where the puppet is pushed or moved during the frame exposure, causing it to blur. Often, a stop-motion animator will give the puppet a good sturdy flick of the finger, making it vibrate, and then expose the frame. Although the technique is a bit uncontrollable, it's also a good way to unwittingly commit to a frame or series of frames that didn't work out that great. Since almost all animation goes through a post system at some point, it's often best to add motion blur in post, where it can be tested and dialed so it looks the best.

If time is a luxury, a stop-motion animator can take advantage of digital compositing and essentially create a second pass or shot simultaneously while trying the go motion. The idea is simple. The first frame of a movement is clean with no vibration. Then there is the go motion on the same frame, so essentially there are two takes of each frame: 11, 22, 33, 44, 55, 66, 77, and so forth. That way, they're both there if the go motion doesn't seem to look right. The ability for compositors and digital editing tools to be able to essentially unzip the two sequences from one source makes this possible. Theoretically it could be done analog as well and print every other frame, but it would be very laborious. To that point, stop-motion animators also can leave notes for the editor or compositor to remove frames that they decided didn't work, but only after it had been filmed. Because of digital accuracy and ease, editors and compositors can easily remove single or sequences of frames. This technique is known as a cutback, and it is a last resort for a fix.

Motion blur is again one of the iconic effects of filmmaking. Its ability to add reality to film for animation perhaps lies in the fact that the human eye sees things as blurs as well. According to the National Science Foundation, the frame rate at which the eye sends impulses to the brain is 25 pulses per second. Film runs at 24 frames, which is comparatively close in speed. That is why video and television, which runs at 29.97 frames, has a different look when it comes to motion: video versus film. There have been some major experiments with frame rates. Douglas Trumbull, a legendary special-effects wizard, pioneered Showscan, a process where films or animations are created at 60 frames per second, and then shown back at 60 frames per second, giving an incredible image of sharpness and clarity. Essentially, Showscan forces the eye to see more than it normally can. For every one pulse of the input to the brain, Showscan is stuffing two more images into the space. A baseball flying at camera, for example, would have no motion blur, where as in reality, a baseball thrown past a viewer's head would be a stretched white blur. Showscan theatres are around the world in theme parks and similar venues.

To the trained animator, motion blur is far more than just a way to punctuate movement; it is another tool that can be used to enhance animation styles, humor, and hide awkward transitions. In the classic style of Warner Brothers films, motion blur became a serious comedic effect. Even though it usually only lasts for a few frames, it is the visual signal that a tremendous amount of energy has been released and that an object has moved at a terrific speed (see Figure 3.2).

FIGURE 3.2   Motion blur frames often show a large burst of energy in a short amount of time.

The classic cartoon exit—the anticipation pose and then a motion blur for the actual exit—is commonly used in animation. The humor can come from the surprise, because the character or object almost disappeared since it has moved so fast. The big moves are the obvious ones, but motion blur also works on small moves and arm gestures, snapping from pose to pose.

A motion blur, as seen in Figure 3.3, is essential to most snappy fast action. But a motion blur doesn't mean that the image has to physically be blurry. In many classic animated cartoons, quick motion was super-exaggerated, with characters being stretched and wrapped around landscapes for a frame or two. Instead of a simple blur shape that simply shows motion, animators, who are drawers, had more fun creating ridiculous and stretched images, even when it was only visible for one or two frames.

FIGURE 3.3   A motion-blur frame that is more exaggeration than blur.

Creating these complex and often absurdly exaggerated frames crosses from an effect to good character animation. This is because the shape of the blur and the distortion, even though it's only visible for a frame or two, can still be felt; they add a sense of motion to the character whether it's fast, rubbery, or completely distorted. Motion blur and elements of speed and snap move too quickly to be able to focus on, but they are always felt and border on the subliminal.

Animation can happen slowly like slow motion or faster than the eye can really focus on. When evaluating fast motion, like blur frames, animators can begin to get a feeling for judging relationships that are constantly changing. In a 24-frame walk cycle, each frame is different and one full step takes place in one second at 24 frames per second. If there's a frame that isn't working, has missed timed or is out of sync, or is not following the same arch as the other frames, it will only be visible for 1/24th of a second. A walk cycle is used to illustrate, but it is an obvious rule of motion played at 24 frames per second. A good animator can catch such a fleeting mistake and fix these hitches and bumps. Fixing every bump and smoothing every curve can really polish the work and help move characters beyond just animation and into acting and performing. To begin to polish to that level, the animator has to first be able to recognize the problem, however small, before he can fix it. Luckily for modern animators, watching their scenes over and over and being able to finesse frames makes such smoothing possible; it also creates such outstanding character animation that is associated great animated movies and shows.

Tips for Future Projects

Studying the World Around You

Developing a critical eye has so much more to do with the eye and the brain than with what is actually being observed. It's been said over and over, but it is true, the best visual artists never stop being artists, and are always studying the world around them. Whether it's studying motion, composition, or relationships, visual artists are rarely bored when there's something to observe and learn from.

Repetition, Repetition, Repetition

When watching things in reality, many things happen faster than the sharpest eye can catch, but in animation and visual media, creators have the amazing luxury of repetition—watching a shot or scene over and over and over. In the course of a short but well animated commercial, it would be completely standard for abn animator to have viewed his scenes thousands of times.

Slow Motion and Frame by Frame

Being able to see time slowed down, allows animators to see frames that aren't necessarily viewable at full speed. Photographer Eduard Muybridge, known for his epic motion studies began his whole photographic exploration of motion because of a bet that a horse lifts all four hooves off the ground at the same time when running. Watching a horse running it's hard to say, but a still frame shows the results clearly. For animators and anyone trying to solve animation problems, slow motion shows curves and arcs of movements, and reveals pops, bumps, and movement that aren't flowing correctly.

Flopping an Image to Study Balance

Whether using a mirror or holding a sketch up to the light in reverse, reveals compositional details and visual balance. Doing the same thing digitally, known as flopping the image, can also reveal the same potential issues.

Study the Work of the Masters

This is a popular cliche, but it is a pure truth that is echoed by many of the artists included in this book. All of the best works in animation and visual media are available to be seen and studies. Use them to investigate and evaluate story concepts, styles, and techniques—the critical eye.

INTERVIEW WITH BARRY BRUCE

Barry Bruce has 30 years of experience in professional animation and production. Barry originally was an architect, but the business was unpredictable and a friend had begun making sets at the fledgling Vinton Studios. Barry signed on to help with sets, and Will Vinton got him into animating. Barry planned for his animation stint to last six months. Twenty-eight years later, Barry is still in animation as a director, master character designer, and all-around expert when it comes to making animation work well. Barry has worked on countless projects, from the California Raisins, to the M&Ms®, to the only clay animated feature, *The Adventures of Mark Twain*. Barry has garnered and earned more awards than one could count, including an Emmy as a co-writer on a *Claymation Easter Celebration*. Barry also clay animated the legendary film *The Great Cognito*.

Wellins: *One of the most impressive things I immediately noticed working with you, early on, was your critical eye. What is it that you do that enables you to have such a visual grasp of animation?*

$\rightarrow$

Bruce: I think maybe the most important thing that I discovered came as a realization when we were working on the film *Adam and Eve*. If you go into your daily review session to view animation with a whole bunch of things on your mind, a list of things you're going to check: did this work, did that work, you wind up bringing preconceptions to the first viewing of a scene, or even a second and even third viewing. You tend to not really see it, but instead see it with your preconceived ideas. So, what I tried to learn to do, over a period of time, was to view a scene and not think about anything except what my eye was doing—where I looked first, what I watched, what caught my attention—and to focus on what you were really seeing, not what you were thinking about seeing. To me, that got me 75 percent of the way. You know there are things that you've got to watch out for. If it's a story you're telling, you've got to make sure you're getting the story point across. In terms of art direction and staging, let your eye tell you what's going on, because if your eye is going to the wrong place, and if you're going to miss the action, or the focus of the scene, then that's something you've got to change.

Wellins: Would you say that holds true for lip sync?

Bruce: Yes, that's right. Especially if you over lip-sync something. For instance, an animator is trying to hit every consonant, and winds up exaggerating it, and then it winds up that you're mostly aware of this big flapping mouth. For me, lip sync should be completely transparent, so that the viewer is not even aware that it's happening.

Wellins: Why is it if you rotoscope a live action person's lip sync exactly, frame for frame, it looks great in real life, but very flappy and poppy on the animated character?

Bruce: I'm not completely sure. It has something to do with getting close to reality. It's not a very simple thing, and it's one of those things you have to learn as you go along. Somethings you follow exactly and it's OK; other times it gets flappy [and] other times, it doesn't seem like a big enough move. Over the years, I just began to get a sense of where it would go. One of the obvious things, which wasn't that obvious when I started, was having a recording of the dialogue right there with you on the set, so you could hear the emphasis, inflection and all that. The temptation is to just take out a log sheet and just hit the Os, consonants, and vowels, and think you're going to be on it, but the emphasis really drives it.

Wellins: Now that you can drop a wav file or a type of sound file into a software program and have it right at your fingertips, do you still have a need for a log sheet?

Bruce: I still log it out as a director, just because it helps me log the action. Your action is so much driven by the dialogue; if someone is going to be talking they're going to be gesturing to the rhythm of their talk, so I need it for that. But then also it's also a good way to check the animators. I find that modern animators, using a wav file in CG in their scene tend to hit it pretty well. There are still some surprising things that slip by. A lot of times you want to emphasis an M or B with an extra closed frame—those are really important to nail—and if those slip by it slurs over and it looks like you're not on it. With a wav file, you only hear the sounds and can't get a fix on when the lips close, hence a log.

$\rightarrow$

Wellins: *When you were animating the California Raisins, you used specific celebrities or someone with a distinct mouth. Did you use reference films or pictures?*

Bruce: For the most part we would do that. In those days, we shot reference film for all the voice talent so that the animator had it right there to look at frame by frame. Even then you could trick yourself because you could hit a consonant between frames, following exactly what was going on and you'd never actually have a frame where the mouth was closed. [I]t looks fine in live action, but if you animate it that way it looks sloppy so you had to know when to push the close frames, which really only comes from practice.

Wellins: *I've noticed that it's almost like a house of cards. If you miss one or two mouth shapes and it starts to draw attention to itself, then you lose track, and then it completely falls apart. It just keeps getting worse and worse.*

Bruce: I think once you draw the audience's attention to the lips then you're in trouble because they're never going to be that perfect. Sometimes maybe, but the trick is never to draw the attention down there and that goes right back to the eyes. The eyes are the key. If you're close enough, like a medium shot, or sometimes even a wider shot, we're always watching the eyes. You wonder if they watch anything else. The eyes start not working and you start losing it, and the character will stop being alive and they start looking somewhere else. It is like a house of cards. With eyes, the most important things is never let them walk off with the head, unless you want to have a character that look like he got hit on the head or is losing consciousness. Then if the head turned, the eyes would stay locked. Otherwise, your eyes are always jumping and adjusting, and then jumping and adjusting if there's no focus. If there's something you're really intent on watching, you're just on it. When you move your head your eyes stay right with it.

Wellins: *The rule I always used was unless you're drunk or something, eyes never move slowly. It is really the head that moves slowly. The eyes move from one location to the next in one or two frames. Is there a process? In CG, we'd often hit the big mouth shapes, closed mouths, and then go back and finesse the little shapes and smooth out the transitions.*

Bruce: My experience with lip sync was always with stop motion lip sync, which is straight-ahead animation, and I haven't really had a chance to do it in the computer and then go back and tweak it, because when computers came along, I was already directing and didn't do hands-on CG. I assume that would probably be a good way to do it. Take your consonants and then go in and adjust your vowel shapes.

Wellins: *That must have been laborious with the filmed reference being on film, not having video and the likes.*

Bruce: We had these little tiny editing machines out on the set. So you'd know your frame count and you'd have to keep track of your frame count, because there was no way for them to be sunk together. And even then you could trick yourself, because you can hit a consonant between frames, so if you're just following exactly what's going on you would never close the

→

mouth. And it looks fine for some reason on film in the shot, but if you were ever going to animate it that way it would look sloppy, so you'd have to know when to do that.

Wellins: *And that really only comes from practice. I can't imagine sitting there on set with a film editor. Isn't it amazing how easy it's gotten relative to how it used to be?*

Bruce: We used to have all those little surface gauges—you know we didn't have video back then. We didn't even have a video camera on it for a while. We'd just have the surface gauges out there, and if a character fell over we'd kind of just guess where it was and keep going.

Wellins: *It must have turned dailies into real nail-biters.*

Bruce: No kidding! The hardest decision was when you had been shooting for a week or maybe two weeks in, and a character tips over and you think you know where it was. But are you going to risk the week that you just went through and shoot another week or are you going to go back and use that? Oh, I hated those decisions! They were just the worst.

Wellins: *When you had your shot, and you were going to start clay animating, you had the log and you had the footage. Is there anything else that you do to prepare? Especially when you're doing a shot that's going to take a couple of weeks, is there something you'd do or a way to make sure that when you get down the road things would keep working?*

Bruce: I first listened and looked at film—over and over and over with the film. I just had it in my head. I would say it over and over and watch myself saying it over and over so you'd just basically absorb the scene. And then having the log sheet and in those days you had to really make sure you run your numbers and make sure you're clicking your editing machine and keeping it in exact sync with the camera before checking it off. These days, nobody has to worry about that now. In those days, like with *The Adventures of Mark Twain* or clay animation in general, we'd have a split jaw, and you'd remove the lower jaw and so I'd have like 10 or 20 lower jaws already in approximate lip shapes. So then I'd have all those categorized. So I had all those ready to go. And once I had all that stuff, I kind of felt I was ready to start.

Wellins: *How may frames a day could you expect, or what was the comfort zone for creating that really great lip sync like the Raisins or any of that really sculpted clay animation?*

Bruce: Like with *Mark Twain* when we were really rolling, if I had a single character to do and a medium shot I could do probably 10 seconds a day—maybe 200 to 240 frames. Add more characters or lines and then it really slowed down. I would double frame a lot for lip sync. I know a lot of people don't like to do that. There are a lot of places where you could double frame through and nobody will even notice it. You just needed to know when you need to single frame and when you need to double frame.

Wellins: *Prior to working at Vinton Studios, were you interested in animation and had you made animated films before?*

→

Bruce: Yeah, a little bit. My friend Don and I were in architecture school and we had a little Super-8 camera and on our thesis project we animated a few things, and that was the first time I'd done any of that. It wasn't character animation—it was just pieces of architecture moving. It was so much fun to do that it got me sort of interested in it.

Wellins: *Do you still like animation?*

Bruce: No [laughing]. I've been sort of tempted by the computer, but I've done enough of it. There's hardly anything I'm tempted to do.

Wellins: *Do you enjoy watching it?*

Bruce: I don't even like watching it much anymore. There are some things that are really beautiful and I love watching, but for the most part I don't watch that much. I'm more affected by live-action films that are really well made than animated films.

Wellins: *Going back to lip sync, how important are the tongue and teeth? I see a lot of beginning animators shrug it off; unless they have big oversized teeth they don't even bother. And then they can't figure out why the lips aren't working, and they now need the tongue for certain sounds.*

Bruce: No, it's absolutely true. A lot of times with the tongue, like with sounds like N, you just see the tongue starting to rise to the roof of the mouth in the frame before it happens and just seeing that little flick of color in there makes that lip sync work. The lips aren't really moving—it's that tongue. And you don't have to see a real tongue. When we were doing clay animation, I would just stick a piece of red clay back in the mouth. Just as long as I saw something in there that flickered. Your brain wants it to work, and so when you see it, it just confirms it for you.

Wellins: *It's a cliché, but it really is about feel. So much about animation is what you don't see. I'm trying to get that over and over. It kind of sounds like that Hollywood guy, "Well, it doesn't feel right to me," but it's actually a really valid comment, especially in animation.*

Bruce: No, it's true, because a lot of it is pretty subliminal stuff. Pretty transparent things and they should stay that way. You start bringing them up to the foreground and it just ruins it. There is so much information we take in that we don't know we're taking in, so animators have to know what that information is and provide it without pushing it in people's faces. And when you get that, I think it's that level of information that is what convinces people of the liveliness—that something uncannily seems alive and they can't put their finger on it. I think it's a lot of those strange, transparent, and subliminal feelings.

Wellins: *And it's the best when an animation rises to the level where it seems like it's happening and it doesn't have a hand making it happen. It's not deliberate; it's just happening. If there were a character where something accidental happened, like someone stumbles and trips and falls, it's really hard to do pull off in animation because it's accidental. Because it just happens and everything about animation is that it often feels like someone's doing it.*

$\rightarrow$

Bruce: Yeah, exactly. I think the other thing I was sort of referencing that was a big revelation to me was that most people, although I suppose there are some people who pride themselves on looking for flaws, who aren't really there to just be entertained, but most people want it to work. Your brain and your eye will contribute as much as needed. Your brain is adding as much sometimes as your eye is seeing. As long as you don't do something that flies in the face of those expectations, you can get away with leaving out a lot. It's sort of saying it's the opposite of what I was saying before, but it's also true. You don't have to give them everything. You just want to keep the flow going and not deny what the expectations of the brain are, and work your audience so that they fill in that other stuff.

Wellins: *If you rotoscope to someone's mouth on a character, frame for frame it looks like he's saying two words for every one word, even though it's spot on. For whatever reason that reality jump to "animation reality" is huge.*

Bruce: When we were doing Flash animation, just the nature of it forced us to try to condense everything and abbreviate it. It surprised me, even as much animation as I had done before, how you could just indicate the beginning of an action and the end of an action and never have to show the in-between of the action at all. Your brain just put it there, and there was no real image there at all.

Wellins: *When you're watching animation classic, Warner Brothers, Disney or whatever, there's a sense of disbelief that you automatically go into, the viewer thinks, "OK, this is cartoon." But if you start to watch something like Shrek, which is flirting with reality, the scenery looks virtually real. When he [the character Shrek] starts talking, you're now using all the tools that you would use when you watch real people, which is totally different. You know, it goes back to people reading other people's expressions. The first time someone stuck his face in your crib when you were a baby, people learned to read the human face. If somebody has a big abscess in his mouth, you can tell. You can instantly tell when something's wrong with someone's speech. So as soon as Shrek starts to look real, you start to think, "Is this guy real?" You notice, Hey, wait a minute! His muscles don't do this when you do that. But then if you see South Park, it just is how it is. No expectations. You understand that's what it looks like and you don't apply any of those rules to it.*

Bruce: You know it's really true; it's that slippery slope we get on. The more you add something that's a little bit real and then there's something that's not as real as that, you have to bring it up. [P]retty soon you're just chasing yourself and it gets more and pretty soon you have to be absolutely hyperrealistic when you're starting down that slope. CG is really a nasty one for that, because it wants to make it more real than any drawing—even more than most clay sculptures could ever be. So you're really halfway down that slope and you just tend to start sliding right down into chasing reality.

Wellins: *It's a real pain, so to that point, stylized lip sync: are there any big considerations for that? It's obviously much more forgiving?*

Bruce: Yeah, I think you just want to hit the most basic—just puppet-sync stuff. Where you basically are just opening and closing and want to get the consonants and the vowels. Not the

$\rightarrow$

shapes of them, but just the beginnings and the ends of them. And to some extent I think that's fine, if you set that as your style. If you had the realism of *Shrek* going, and you did stylized lip sync it could be terrible. It would get so much criticism. But with *South Park* and with the Muppets, look at how much the Muppets just open and close; there was a little bit of shaping but very little.

Wellins: Yeah, the Muppets almost reserved the shaping for special moments.

Bruce: So I think, depending on what style you're animating in, you can just kind of dial that degree of reality and try and match it to what your style is so you don't make it too real and you don't make it too low—just don't draw attention to it once you get it.

Wellins: People who are trying to learn more about making a film should use stylization; it is a great way because it's much more forgiving and if it's done well, then it can be really unique. The opportunities to stylize are so broad that it frees you up from all these things that go along with chasing photo real. Especially with CG, because its ability to look real attracts animators and film-makers because of that eye-fooling illusion, which I think goes back to special effects. Too many animators start out trying to do photo-real stuff, which isn't about animation, and getting photo real to look really good is really difficult. It can be discouraging, where as an animator could really get stuff done if it were stylized.

Bruce: It's sure a hard lesson to learn. I just preach that all the time and it just never seems to sink in with any CG animators.

Wellins: Why do you think that's so? Obviously there is something really attractive about the photo-real illusion. With special effects movies, animators think, "Man, that looked really real!" There is some attraction to that illusion of, "Was that real?" But I think photo real doesn't have much to do with animation, or much to do with storytelling either.

Bruce: I don't think so either. I think it's a number of things. One thing is, if you have a big team of people and particularly if you're doing commercial work, and everybody's trying to get it in their head what it is you're talking about so they can all agree before it's made what it's going to look like, one of the most common vocabulary everybody shares is reality. [J]ust that communication problem tends to slide everybody toward reality.

If you're talking about a new style, how do you put it in words? You can get somebody drawing it, but a lot of times even that isn't going to work. If it's a 2D drawing on something that's going to be 3D, the translation there is so drastic. There's a tremendous amount of pressure to go toward reality that way because it's a common point—something we all share and we have words for it. But I also think that style is . . . I mean there is an infinite number of styles, and that choice can be intimidating. It takes personal taste and confidence. So unless you are an artist who understands and knows style, unless you're used to taking specific looks and making them look a different way, it's not that easy. It's not going to come very naturally for most people. I think for CG particularly it's important to have art directors and production designers who are strong stylists, because they can fight that gravity realm of reality and push people back up out of it.

$\rightarrow$

Another thing that's interesting about style too is that most of the time I think people think about style, and if they understand style and think about style they think about it in terms of visual, like what does the person look like, what's the character design, what's the world look like. But you can actually stylize animation. You can take the way movement happens, and you can give that a style. Like have a smooth parabolic feel to a character's movement, the paths [he] follow[s] round, as one example. Even the way that movement works, that in itself is a stylization, which I don't think many people take advantage of.

Wellins: *Is it a little bit of laziness? Just not opening your mind up to go to those levels? Have you seen the character animation of the maître d' in* The Triplets of Belleville? *There is really nice stylization in that movie.*

Bruce: Yeah, exactly. I mean that's really taking advantage of animation, where you can take a character of somebody and force it into some kind of a visual representation you never see. It's perfect for the story.

Wellins: *That animation was a virtual impossibility, except in animation.*

Bruce: It's kind of where we started out when we were doing the early clay stuff, because we could. One film that never got produced was *The Million Pound Goat,* and there was a character in there who we had decided he was going to be hyper, and he either had this really long, long sad face, or this incredibly gigantic smiley face. And he jumped back and forth constantly between these two things. It was a really fun thing to watch; it added to his character so it was part of the story.It added something to the story you never saw in real life. It was the same with *Jumping Frog,* where we gave some of the guys mustaches that were so gigantic that they were larger than their heads and they just crashed around while they talked so it was nothing like reality and yet it represented lip sync in a new way. It was transparent enough that you believed it, yet it was interesting enough and it added to the peculiars of the story. That was really fun. I liked it when we could do that kind of stuff.

Wellins: *I wonder why it doesn't happen, because people enjoy watching it when they see very stylized stuff. I'm thinking of stylized characters with a mouth that is just a line, and then when it speaks, the movement drops down below the line— just a little bit. It's hilarious. Now today if they did it you know they'd have a fully realized mouth.*

Bruce: I just saw that there's a new trailer for *The Polar Express.* It's just horrible. First of all, there's some really beautiful stuff in it, and you can tell the amount of work that's gone into it. I mean, every frame has like thousands of dollars of money, but all of the faces are frozen. They're moving probably 25 percent as much as they really would. The characters are like somebody who's had their face injected with Novocain™. The most important thing in the whole film is the one thing they couldn't pull off. They wanted the reality so much and they went ahead anyway, and I just can't believe that—for all that money, just hyperreality.

What's the point of having the conductor really look like Tom Hanks, when he could be something more interesting than that? Why not just do it live action? I do not understand what

→

they're doing. I can only imagine that it's probably so hard to get it to that level that it may seem like a success. Otherwise, I don't know how it ever got by. On *The Polar Express,* it looks like they got a tiny step further than *Final Fantasy.* It wasn't quite that bad, but still was the exact same flaw and it's so significant still. It's going to take all the energy out of it. They just don't care.

Wellins: What is it with CG people? Nobody seems to notice that it always looks like there's light coming out of their mouths. Take Shrek, *for example; obviously they put all the money into Shrek himself. They have good features and good poses and all these textures around his mouth, and then you get to the humans and they open their mouth there's all this light shining around in their mouths.*

Bruce: It's like they're illuminated. Ever since the beginning when I first started working with computers, I would ask that same question and it was like nobody noticed it or something. Are the mouths going to look like that? And they'd say, "What do you mean?" "Is there a light in there?, and someone would say, "Well, no." "Well, why does it look like it's glowing inside?" I'd rather see nothing in there than see glowing teeth, and it goes all the way back to the wisdom teeth too. When we were doing stop motion, we would always line the inside of the mouth with black clay. Even a flesh tone in there was too bright. Black worked great because it made a nice, crisp graphic shape and you could read the lips better.

Wellins: Is that important to see iconic shapes, to see a nice round O open up and others?

Bruce: I think it harkens back to 2D animation. The nice thing about 2D animation is that it's such a stylization to begin where there's not that gravity well of reality. You already are stylizing a three-dimensional shape into a two-dimensional shape, so as a result it's pretty natural for people to look at how graphically pleasing it is or not pleasing. So you tend to make the mouths be simpler shapes and easily read shapes. Even when you jump up to clay, which is more stylized than CG, I found it was really hard to get stop-motion animators to look at how graphic an image was, because it is going to be a 2D image on the film. To get them to look through the camera and think about the contour of the character and the shapes—just to see if the contour of the character is selling what's supposed to be being communicated [or] whether a face or mouth is graphically where it should be—is really a hard thing to get people to think about. I think in a lot of cases it's because the animators haven't really grown that much. They've never gone through that process of translating three-dimensional space into a two-dimensional space and dealt with all the cheating and the reasons for the cheating that you do. So they just figure, "Hey, I've got a thing that changes like a human body. It's in front of the camera. It's facing the right way on the set, so why should I not click the frame right now?" So you get all these scenes with hands pointing directly at the camera and everything stacked up; you can't really read what's going on. As opposed to breaking it out so the contour, and the outlines and the basic shapes help make it read, using cheating makes things readable. And I've seen it even worse in CG.

→

Wellins: *If you were going to try to do Tex Avery-type extremes, you'd almost need another physical model, switching out models to do that stuff, and it's just unheard of in CG.*

Bruce: Ever since we've been doing CG I've been preaching replacement animation. Don't try to do it all with one character. I still don't know whether the reluctance to do it is based on some horrendous technical problem that I'm asking of them or whether it's just a preconception about CG—all I know is I still can't get them to do it. I'll demand that we do it and still when it comes to the end I'll get maybe one other replacement character—very peculiar.

Wellins: *There certainly is a culture around CG that it has to be a button pushed or a way of automating things instead of really ever doing it frame by frame.*

Bruce: I mean, there's some computer stuff that's been pretty good, but by and large the majority of it really is terrible. In many cases it's not some kind of magic thing that would change it. If you just pay attention to the basic thing people have known for 50 years about animation you could open up tremendously. I think it's because the history of the computer—and I think we're still in the midst of that—that most of the people came out of a technical background and as a result it's that same old thing where reality is sort of their base goal. They haven't done something else. They haven't drawn. They haven't sculpted. They haven't translated the world into a different view of it, and so as a result they just want to refract the world with this magic medium.

Wellins: *To that point, you're also a really amazing character designer. What do you do when you set out to design a character?*

Bruce: That's a little hard. If you wanted to put your finger on the very simplest kind of visual appeal, it's just the slope of the eyelids. If you have a character and you slope the eyelids downward from the middle out, you'll get a relatively friendly looking character, even if they bring their brows down and look angry. They don't look evil. They just look angry—like a normal person who can look angry. If you slope them the other way, you get an evil person. You get a really hard gaze. That's one of the things I kept running into with nonstop-motion animators; they would use the eyelids to give them emotion. If you do that, your characters change from being who they really are. People can actually change their eyelids a little bit when an emotion happens, with slope in the eyelids, but not very much. A lot of times, I would see people taking the eyelids if the character's angry; they'd slope the eyelids way in and slope the brows way in, and suddenly a character you're supposed to still be sympathetic with, even though they're just angry. [Now they're] like evil and you lose all sympathy because they seem to have turned into a demon as opposed to a simply angry good person. That for me was one of the easy tricks. And if you want to play against it, you can. It's a nice trick to keep in your back pocket. If you had a situation where you wanted to really surprise your audience and have somebody who seemed jovial and friendly and then become evil, well, the place to start is to slope the eyelids.

$\rightarrow$

Wellins: *If you had one thing you could shout out about lip sync or any of these topics, like one big do or one big don't, what would it be?*

Bruce: I guess the biggest rule with lip sync is don't over lip-sync. That's the biggest mistake I see. Because most people, it's pretty obvious they want to be closed on the Bs, or on the consonants, and open on the vowels. They need to be able to know when the character—if one person would slur a word and roll over it. Maybe one other thing about lip sync is that when you log lip sync, like if I were going to log the word *we,* I wouldn't put W and an E as I go down the sheet. I would start out with a U, then I'd go into an aah sound, and then I'd go into an E sound so I know when it's going through. Because those are the real sounds you're making. There is no such thing as a W sound. So if that's the way you log it out, according to the sounds you're actually making, first of all it makes you think about it when you're logging, and then it reminds you, when you're animating, what you're really doing with the vowels.

Wellins: *What's a big note on the critical eye? How can one develop that?*

Bruce: Just try to stand back, and I think a lot of times before we make something we have a picture of it in our head, and then we make that thing and many times you don't know it, but you're putting that picture in your head on that thing you made. It doesn't really look like that but you think it does, and I think the trick is to turn that picture in your head off, and somehow get yourself to where you can actually see what's really there. For me, I've never had many classes in art direction, but I found that being able to it, solved most of that for me, because I didn't have to have somebody tell me that saturated colors come up and desaturated colors drop back. I sat and looked at the shot or the film and I realized, the background's coming up in front of the character and what to do. And if you step through the scene frame by frame with that frame of mind, when you first look at it, look at the whole thing and see what the effect is, know what the effect you want is and see what the real effect is and then step through it like that. Separate each part of the frame separately and see what's happening.

More than that was just watching it, and I think another thing to do is you kind of have to be sensitive to what you're feeling when you watch something. Feelings can be really fleeting, and sometimes if you're watching something and an eye's not working right, there'll be a feeling for a really brief moment that the energy went out of the character. But you're not fast enough to see what's causing it. You need to single frame to see what's causing it, but you can feel it as it comes back. So you go, "Oh, there was something that's making me feel something so I'm going to slow it down." So I think you need to watch for those and not dismiss them. It's easy to gloss over those feelings, and it's all about feelings.

DIRECTING

Visual Storytelling and Directing

A director's primary function, despite all the complexities of the job, is profoundly simple: use all the tools and elements of a production to find the best solution for creating the visual language to tell the story in the best way. The best judge of whether this is achieved is when the film stops being a film. It becomes a memorable story that truly moves or changes people.

Directing can be an incredibly difficult task, but in the director's corner there are almost limitless tools to help create that emotional connection. Directors are masters of time and space; the director's view can move through walls. For example, it can go effortlessly inside a bank vault, and come back out again to show if the robbers are making any progress. The director's point of view can be invisible in the most intimate conversations, zip ahead 10 years into the future, or go back 10,000 years in the past. Stanley Kubrick's *2001: A Space Odyssey* starts with early man, who is more ape than man, and jumps ahead a million years to man living and working in outer space. The director can be deceptive and trick his audience, aiming their attention at false clues and deliberately confusing them. In Jonathan Demme's *The Silence of the Lambs,* Demme deliberately misleads the audience. In the film's final resolution, the FBI thinks it has discovered the house of the killer, and as the agents push the doorbell, the next shot shows the bell ringing in the basement of the killer. When the killer goes to the door, however, it's not the FBI agents— they're actually several states away. Instead it's Jodie Foster. The FBI got it wrong, and it's a complete deliberate misdirect that ends in a shocking conclusion: the main character is now unknowingly alone with the killer. The director can tip the hand of what is going to happen, and often does, showing things slightly ahead and around the corner. This way the audience is one step ahead of the characters as well, feeling as omniscient as the director's view and anticipating what is going to happen next.

Being able to see just slightly ahead is unique in the visual language because it's used a great deal to the point that the audience isn't aware of it. For example, a man comes down a hall, while a burglar with a candlestick waits for him. Without seeing the burglar, it might be confusing as to what happens when he's attacked. In another example, a car roars down a dirt road. A shot that sees beyond the present scene shows a deer crossing the road; the car quickly rounds the corner, and the driver crashes into a ditch.

The director's view can distort actions, slow them down, or speed them up. So strong is the director's view that it can actually go into the mind, see dreams, and hear the most intimate thoughts and recall the most distant memories. Without saying a word, a director can tell an audience what a character is thinking or what they're about to do, often by the character's expression alone.

Directors make it so that an audience can tell what a character is thinking; nowhere else is the act of thinking more important than in animation. Seeing an animated character think is essential in creating a living character. Whether the character frets and tosses over a decision or makes a split-second decision, thinking is the core level of life for an animated character. The eyes and eyebrows are the first direct line to seeing a character think, and a director is always aware of showing eyes and facial expression clearly if emotions are to be read.

A director can lay out a story without judgment and without feeling, simply showing the facts. He can also judge, being as condemning and as biased and slanted as the story demands.

The director's view of the story is also very much a chameleon; it can go from one scene of intimate reveal, such as a dying woman's last words, where the camera is inches from her face. A scene can also be the opposite of intimate, such as an angle behind a crowd of people and reporters in front of a locked gate trying to get a glimpse of an infamous person, with the audience, only catching images and vague visual clues. The director can also misdirect the audience and deliberately feed them false clues. He can shoot opposites for effect, panning off a violent scene and instead showing a pastoral painting, as the guttural sound is heard off camera.

True experience and a critical eye count for a great deal, but good directors across the board have a vision of how they see telling any given story. Whether a feature film, a short, a video game, or an industrial film, a truly creative director can be handed any script and devise any number of ways as to how to visually tell the story as well as take the written word to the visual level, while expanding and elaborating on the written ideas as they become physical. A director has a vision of how he sees it, but he also has a vision of how best to explain and illustrate the ideas to emotionally connect to the audience. Technically turning ideas into frames is the tricky job of changing feelings and expressions into concrete shots and scenes.

Directors may have any number of processes they use to discover the best solution to telling a story. Whether it just comes from studying the initial reading, viewing similar work, or doing sketches or notes, directors by their very nature should always arrive at an approach on how to best tell a given story. Mike Leigh, British director of *Secrets & Lies* and *Naked*, uses very loose scripts and allows his actors to improvise and live out characters and often creates whole scenes from those improvisations. Other directors and filmmakers do similar things; Robert Altman, Larry David, and Christopher Guest all work with the almost same group of actors and allow the actors to create the characters and often large plot points of the story. In the animated version of a scene, it is the director who tells the master animator to make the scene look good and nothing else. A voice director lets a voice talent ad-lib and come up with the talent's own words for an animated character.

A director might not have every single shot in mind after reading a script, but by and large, they have a feeling about how things can go. Directors truly work a juggling act when developing a production. They not only think of ways to visually stage each shot or sequence, but more importantly, they have a definite and often specific plan on how the actual character performs and acts, sometimes down to the word. Above all else, directors direct performance, whether the performance is a person, a drawing, or a digital creation.

Directors have a vision—a vision of how that performance is presented and how the production is paced—all the while figuring out how it is to be filmed or animated based on the vision. Whether or not the audience or the viewers align with the director's vision or performance, visual language and pacing ultimately determine how developed and effective the director's visual storytelling skills are.

Film and animation are a medium meant for viewers and audiences, and unlike art forms like poetry, for whom an artist may never show his work, visual media demands an audience's consideration by its very nature. A director's role is simple and complex simultaneously: tell the best story, but also be sensitive to subjective ideas, and be able to go beyond personal tastes and feelings to consider an unknown audience.

Directors wear many hats, from the very technical to the very subjective, and to be successful they must be masters of all. Directors who walk around with a viewer, figuring out strange and unusual angles, are doing an important task—still only one of many of their important jobs. Recording the performance, whether people or animation, is a huge equation on its own. However, getting the performers and actors to create their characters, both through their actions and then their lines, is even more important.

At a specific point, preferably long before actual production begins, directors have to decide on a very clear idea of how they want things to go on almost every level of the production. Good directors are always open to new and better ideas offered up by anybody and remain flexible on every level, but the final choice that is committed to film is up to the director. The director also has to be able to mentally juggle the story ideas as well. He must keep an eye on the overall picture, overall emotions, and the actual point or meaning of the story, but also must focus down to the very frame or pixel.

The director can take credit for a lot of great people's work because they've directed the process, but the director is also personally responsible for anything that doesn't work. Whether it's casting, lighting, music, sound design, the director, by his very job title, is responsible for every frame and every sound, unless he has to respond to other factors outside the production. Directors by nature enjoy all the various levels that need attention because when it works and comes together, it truly is a sum much larger than its parts. Directors should like having everything planned, because every unplanned shot is a potential loss for the story.

To the successful director, the highest level of achievement is when the audience goes beyond the production and is truly entertained by a given story, diverted from their ordinary lives and completely captured by what they are watching. In the most ideal situation, the direction becomes invisible, and is merely the perfect fitting vehicle to deliver emotions and actions. To the audience, there is no sign of a director's hand deciding this or focusing on that. When it's truly successful, the director doesn't exist, nor does any other element of the filmmaking process; only the story exists, as if the story itself created the film.

Filmmakers and directors ultimately are out to create illusions that have a strong emotional connection. Whether it's sad, funny, poignant, thrilling, or terrifying, the goal is entertainment. The pinnacle of entertainment is a such a strong emotional connection that the filmed experience touches the audience and changes the audience for a couple of hours, a few days, or for the rest of their lives. How many people still won't swim in the ocean after seeing Steven Spielberg's *Jaws?*

Creating Story Visuals

By the end of a successful animation project, no one should know a project as well as the director—not even the producer or the writer will be as intimate as the director. The producer's job is to deliver a tangible product, watch the money, and make sure all the physical elements are in place and working. The writer is responsible for writing the story and inventing the entire story, but it's the director's job to create that story; a sentence that a writer dreamed up in a few minutes could take a director months to realize.

For example, a writer writes, "New York City, a rainy New Year's eve, in the year 2086. A giant sea monster closes in on Time Square." The decisions for the director on a shot of that scale would be monumental, but an important part of the visual job; what a writer can hammer out in five seconds, a director can spend countless hours actualizing. Creating a believable scene that suspends an audience's disbelief is so much more than figuring out giant special-effects shots, although it is important and exciting. A director's role and relationship with the performers can be far more important. The writer largely concentrates on words, but the director has to go beyond the words. The director has to discover how the character thinks and how the character's thinking makes him behave, so that the character goes beyond animation or acting and acts so well that he is completely believable.

In another example, the writer writes, "The delivery boy enters the elevator. He is nervous." How does the audience know he's nervous?

Does he fidget? Does he glance around or stumble when he tries to speak? Is the delivery boy so nervous that he trembles or drips with sweat? What's he like? Is he a boy or a man? Is this delivery boy the type who can play it cool and keep calm, or have the circumstances pushed him to the point where he is about to completely lose his cool and break down? Where he's going, what he's doing, and who he is will dictate how he acts. What he's doing and who he is come from the story. Being nervous can mean so many things: the delivery boy is being forced to carry a bomb or the delivery boy is standing next to a girl he likes.

Even before the director decides how to play the character's nervousness, he has to consider technique and the mood he's trying to create. Audiences, like the medium, have evolved and become sophisticated. Is the nervous delivery boy in a lighthearted and playful comedy that has plenty of slapstick? If so, then the acting can be over-the-top to fit in with the humor and the silly jokes. Is the story a modern drama, based on real problems and on situations that are close to what the audience knows and experiences? If the latter were true, then a performance might be much more subdued, stiff, and stilted, closer mimicking what a real person would do in a similar situation.

ON THE CD

Shards of Death is a short film included on the CD-ROM under the file **Shards.mov**. The short animated film was directed with the idea that humor comes from core conflicts and other comic tools: extremes, opposites, and surprises. Although the film is animated, and there are many unique considerations for directing animation, many of the directorial ideas would be the same regardless of the medium: live action or animation.

In creating a direction that would best execute the script, the nature of the humor had to remain intact and uncomplicated. The characters are extreme by their very nature, so having them act extremely would be redundant and could complicate their specific simple attitudes toward the scene. There is inherent humor in the characters acting subtly while being visually extreme; humor can be drained or even ruined if too many elements are extreme and compete with the story. The interviewing monster furthers this idea by juxtaposing its grotesque appearance with a very sensitive nature. He is a huge monster with horrific scars and features, and yet he acts like a modern sensitive human conducting a mundane interview for a run-of-the-mill job. The very fact that being "in" a video game would seem like a job to a video-game character, and that there would be a formal and almost mundane interview process, adds another level of absurdity that is immediately evident.

There is an element of surprise and humor in this unexpected opposite behavior, with the monster being kind and sensitive and having a soft-spoken demeanor. The monster interviews the small blue fairy creature: a cute and sweet creature that is true to its appearance. If the fairy creature had performed like the monster, specifically acting opposite of the idea of a fairy, then the surprise of a personality that is opposite to how the characters appear would be overworked; it would have worked against the basic story and the overall humor.

The humor of the film is based on the conflict that at its root is a "square peg in a round hole." It is a hopeless situation; a cute character applies for a job in a violent video game, and the scarier the character tries to be, the cuter the character becomes. In directing both characters, the setup of two such extreme characters creates a natural dynamic of tension and absurdity. To have them act extreme on top of being extreme characters would complicate the idea and draw away from the core conflict. To feel empathy and awkwardness, it became important for the characters' performance to be close to real and true and sincere. The fairy creature becomes sad once realizing its poor performance on the job interview. If the creature's sadness had been extreme and over-the-top, with blubbering, screaming, and bawling, then that performance would be another extreme on top of an extreme character, making the creature seem less real. Instead, the creature cries subtly, and its body posture is defeated; this reserved performance helps the audience feel the creature's sadness, because it's closer to reality and has a sense of sincerity that helps tie the emotional connection between the character and the viewer without the character acting overtly.

The monster character's humor comes out of its demeanor as a caring personality in a terrifying body, but additional humor comes from the monster's performance that is anything but scary. The monster is awkward, and reacts minimally to the blue fairy creature's efforts to impress him. The character uses subtle humanlike hand gestures, while trying to break the news to the fairy creature that the interview is going badly. The monster tries to be encouraging and truly empathetic with the fairy creature, even though the situation is clearly hopeless—another behavior that makes the character more unique and complex.

The overall direction is very limited, drawing no attention to the shots or angles and using no wild camera movements. There is a slight camera movement that keeps the camera from becoming stagnant and slightly adjusting for on-screen movement, but there is no benefit in this story to drawing attention to the direction. The opening shot does hold the viewer back by not showing the fairy creature and creating a late reveal that is built on surprise, but other than the initial starting shot, no other overt camera techniques are used.

Shots are set up to allow performance against a mundane and dull background. The humor comes out of the performance, not out of how it was filmed.

Hundreds of thousands of films, short and long and good and bad, have been made. Many directors try and dream up new ways to tell what fundamentally are the same stories over and over. With technological advances plus an audience willing to accept new visuals, filmmakers and directors are using many tools, some new and some old, as visual story-telling devices. Some devices are ideas, while some are pieces of new hardware, from Steadicam®s to the entire 3D CG revolution.

Combined with stabilizing lens, shots can be smooth, with incredible complexity and motion all in one. Cinema verité, the filming of real life, has made a huge comeback, and forms that have a verité feel, whether or not they are "real life," is unimportant. An important part of that feeling of reality being filmed is the handheld shaky movement, the opposite of Steadicam. Modern films now use scenes on mixed-film stocks or are shot on low-budget equipment to create that amateur feel, such as the film *The Blair Witch Project.*

At the opposite end of the handheld spectrum is the wide variety of almost robotic cameras. Motion control systems create impossible moves; speed systems go beyond slow motion and fast motion to show the time lapse of days passing by, slow motion going at hundreds of thousands of frames per second capturing drops of water, or an ultra slow-motion explosion. The prevalence of hidden cameras and security cameras has become a storytelling tool due to their familiarity. Beyond the huge epic crane shot of the camera flying over the crowd, are the opposite microscopic scenes, often created in CG, of cells and internal structures; these all become simple tools trying to exemplify a story idea.

Pacing and Timing

Pacing is of paramount importance to storytelling; it's the pulse from which the production flows. From quick shots to long shots and from hyperediting to slow motivated cutting, all are used as the visual tools of adjusting pacing on a technical level. With actors and characters, performance and energy dictate a pacing all their own. Using pauses on words or silence, being soft-spoken or loud, or using quick or slow movements are all input elements that impact pacing.

Modern filmmaker David Mamet creates stories with a standard pacing, but with a fast-paced stilted banter of talk. His characters, influenced from the stage, speak a great deal more than in reality and have unusual cadences and word usage. To achieve that unusual verbal pacing, Mamet, during rehearsals, often uses a metronome to perfect the timing and pacing. He also creates a unique pacing with the stilted speech set against very real backgrounds. Sergio Leone's beginning sequence from *Once Upon a Time in the West* is a very slow and plodding sequence but because of the characters' look and behavior, the suspense builds because the characters are obviously up to no good.

Like a stage play, filmmaking and animation have another dimension that most other forms of visual art don't have: visual media, animation, and film require a specific amount of time to experience the art form. In a painting gallery one looks at a painting or a sculpture as long as he's interested, then he walks away. The person may have missed some subtle symbols or forms that the artist thought was important, but didn't give it that much inspection because his feet hurt, the museum was closing, or a number of other factors. In classic art forms, the viewer's life and day set the pacing for viewing or experiencing that art. Visual storytelling is more like music in the way that it is created, and with demanding a specified amount of time from an audience there is a huge responsibility to deliver.

Music and visual media are close relatives when it comes to the use of time and the intent of emotional connections. Music tends to lead the listener's focus and move it around with all the tools of music. Similarly, animation and film directors using their tools must lead the viewer through the visuals and moreover through the story, hopefully keeping that emotional connection strong. Music is also similar to visual media in that it uses pauses, soft parts, loud parts, frenetic parts, and soothing parts to make an emotional connection. At the same time, it keeps an interesting variety; as events take place one after the other, there is always a sense of discovery and surprise. Depending on the story, and with a few exceptions, every production should have those traits that music has: stops and starts, ups and downs, loud and soft segments. Of course, there are great examples of films and television that have few breaks and go at one extreme rate. A heavy-metal rock video will seem to do that, but even a short song at heavy-metal speed will begin to numb the listener; the video is often broken up with a slow-motion sequence, as is the music is with a specific instrument performing a solo. Breaking up the pace is necessary because using a frenetic pace for too long loses energy, and the viewer or listener becomes accustomed to it.

It's the first burst of that frenetic speed that surprises the viewer. Then by slowing the speed down, it gives the chance to build up again. This is similar to a roller-coaster ride, which functions the same way for reasons of suspense and practicality.

Like music, there's also a great deal of difference of opinion about storytelling. When emotions are involved, viewers get very particular about how they spend their time. Some people only watch action, while some people hate a laugh track and others feel left out without one. Some viewers don't like black-and-white films, while others don't like sad movies. With the massive history of films, games, stories, and shows, viewers are able to find and tailor their watching to their own specific tastes.

The Evolved Audience

Even though the story is crucial to any film or animation, audiences and fans of cinema and animation have evolved to understand and enjoy complicated visuals. Stories within stories and subplots can also serve as departures while still being in line with the overall project, especially as films and animations go longer.

Audiences will now accept hearing and seeing a specific scene and then have the visuals focus on something else, even though the scene is still being played out. Flashbacks, daydreams, and forward flashes are commonly used devices. Dreams are also used in films and animations and are often used to show symbolism. Although a dream is not required to be symbolic, symbolism is another way of creating complex ideas that work on subtle levels.

Symbolism

Symbols are visuals and concepts that represent a larger idea; they can often be subtle or vague, but still have impact on a story. Some symbols are overt, such as a crucifix, which denotes religion. Other symbols are more ethereal, such as a sky becoming dark and brooding when the criminals roll into the small town. Symbols can also serve as premonitions. For example, a small group of people go out on a small charter boat, and as the happy passengers pile on board, the shot pans off the happy passengers and sits on a long shot of a life vest. Immediately the audience knows that there is going to be trouble at sea—a life vest is a symbol of trouble. The decision to use a foreshadowing or a premonition is left up to the director. Using another example, a man tells his friend he's going to drive home; he picks up his keys off the table, which were sitting next to a half-empty bottle of wine. If he has a drunk-driving accident, then it was foreshadowing, but if he arrives safely, it suggests that he is flirting with disaster.

On a much larger scale, even seasons can be symbolic in film and animation. Spring represents birth and growth. Summer represents warmth and comfort, fall represents sleepiness and slowing down, while winter represents lifelessness. For example, a tragic romance movie starts with a young couple meeting in the park in the spring, and ends with one leaving or dying in the dead of winter.

Like symbolism, and metaphor is another complex angle of a story. Metaphoric use is where one story goes on and may hint at or represent a larger idea. Vampires are a popular subject in both live-action and animated films. Vampires can be a metaphor for evil, but also a metaphor for temptation, because they are able to grant everlasting life. Sunlight is a metaphor for goodness that triumphs over evil and turns vampires to dust. A metaphor is often part of the basis of a story. The various versions of the basic conflicts—man against man, man against himself, and man against nature—are repeatedly represented metaphorically in films. Alfred Hitchcock's *Lifeboat* is a combination of all three. In the film, survivors of a passenger ship sunk in World War II are stranded in a small lifeboat with injured people, limited rations, and countless other life-threatening elements. Because the people are stranded on the sea, the conflict of man against nature is a big problem, but there are other common conflicts used. The passengers represent the man against man conflict, and the personal fortitude to try to survive such an ordeal represents man against himself; it's a simple setup for a film, yet very powerful and compelling. Francis Ford Coppola's *Apocalypse Now* has the same roots. It uses the conflicts of man against man (the war) and man against nature (surviving in a hostile environment [the jungle]). It also shows the conflict of man against himself. Martin Sheen's character is conflicted about knowing he is being ordered to kill a rogue officer, Colonel Kurtz, played by Marlon Brando.

Filmmakers like David Lynch and Ken Russell, and animators like Jan Svankmajer and the Quay Brothers have taken symbolism to new levels. Instead of using theme in the standard formula, the symbolism becomes skewed or distorted, and what the ultimate meaning is is for the viewer to decide. The same group of filmmakers also pushes the audience to the limits with disturbing and confusing imagery and flirts with entertainment that is so strange and convoluted that it can become repellent and interesting at the same time. With their types of work, audiences are clearly divided on these films that push boundaries and standards.

In *Shards of Death*, something as average as a desk is actually a symbol of authority; it insulates the interviewer from the interviewee. Judges and lecturers often sit up higher than their audience. One reason for sitting higher is visibility, but also there is a separation and a positioning that says that a judge's tall bench is a symbol that the judge is above the fray in the courtroom. A podium to a lesser degree is a symbol, but there is also a strategically implied sense of importance over someone sitting on a folding chair. This sense of positioning was also used in *Shards of Death* when it came to composition. The monster doing the interview is the authority figure, and is always looking down at the blue fairy creature. In turn, the blue fairy is always filmed from an angle above to make the character seem smaller and more vulnerable. This film shows that symbolism can be used literally, like a life preserver, or metaphorically with a condescending camera direction.

For example, a man is in jail and talking to his lawyer, and the man is always filmed through the bars in front of him. The bars are a symbol of imprisonment, and seeing the man in that way can be important to his acting, his stress, and his predicament. However, the lawyer is not imprisoned and is just visiting, so the return angles of the lawyer don't have bars in front of them, even though traditional camera placement would be behind the man in jail and aimed back out through the bars. Animators like the Quay Brothers, in their film *Street of Crocodiles*, use imagery that carries a great amount of visual weight. The scenes are thick with grime and dirt and everything seems neglected and burned. The animations include many sharp things, strings that go off to nowhere, strange characters peering through dirty and fogged glass and windows, and disembodied dolls doing strange and abstract things. All the animations are very symbolic but what they symbolize is truly up to the viewer.

Often, symbolism works best when it isn't overt or obvious. Symbolism can be very abstract and metaphorical, and film historians and film studies endlessly lecture on the meanings of significant films and filmmakers like directors Ingmar Bergman and Federico Fillini and the meanings behind their specific uses of symbolism, both large and small. Filmmakers are sometimes unaware of the symbolism, that they may have subconsciously included in a film, and may not even recognize it for years.

Diplomat Between the Production and the Story

For the director, having a grasp on the core ideas of the story as well as the fundamentals of filming or animating makes the director the only person who can decide when to push and pull from either end of the spectrum. The director knows that certain elements or plot points are absolutely necessary, but how they are laid out is up to him. Knowing these fundamentals is key to being able to edit and modify for reasons of pacing, time, and ultimately, costs. Being able to strip the story down to the bare essentials allows for flexible production and production planning to help deal with the real-world difficulties and challenges of making films and animation.

The 30-Second Spot

Commercials are sales tools, and advertisers know that making an emotional connection, often through repetition, is a powerful way for them to glue their message and sales pitch into the brains of viewers. Some commercials are innovative, while pragmatically some commercials are forever the same. Car commercials, for all the creative effort that goes into them, are still about showing the car and showing how it drives—that isn't going to change anytime soon. Other products are smaller or aren't physical, such as services, which open them up to a much greater level of diversity of storytelling and trying to enable a connection. Commercials, whether for a car, a cellular phone, or for life insurance, all come from the same family in that they have to be concise. As a matter of storytelling, the idea of compressing ideas into a fixed format, such as a 30-second or a minute spot, is a good proving ground for shots as well as what is superfluous and what is required to tell a story, make a joke, or make a very succinct point.

Let's say there is a commercial for a microwavable breakfast meal. The main point of the commercial is that the microwave meal is quick, easy to make, and tastes good. The concept is a woman getting ready for her workday. She wakes up, puts the product in the microwave, and sets the timer. She then returns to the shower, brushes her teeth, dresses, and feeds the dog; the microwave finishes cooking just as she heads for the door. She grabs the meal, takes a bite, and is pleasantly surprised as she heads out the door.

This is a simple concept that is repeated throughout commercials all the time, and commercials are designed simply because they have a fixed amount of time. A standard 30-second commercial will usually have a product shot in it, which can be 3 to 7 seconds, leaving a mere 23 seconds or so to tell this idea: the product is easy to cook, fast, and most importantly tastes good. In the story, she wakes up, feeds the dog, and puts the product in the microwave oven. Any of these activities would easily take longer than 23 seconds, so basically the iconic symbols of what is being done are shown in quick cuts long enough on screen to be read and then goes on to the next shot.

Instead of showing the woman waking up, opening her eyes, and yawning, which could take all of the 23 seconds, the shot starts with a hand slapping the alarm on the alarm clock. Next, the dog wakes up. The shot shows the groggy woman shuffling through the house. Even though the story has only 23 seconds to take place, the images still need to spend enough time to show that she's still waking up. Instead of getting out the dog food, the audience instead sees a low angle on the bowl as dog food is poured in and the dog starts to eat. The showerhead blasts steamy water, and immediately the next shots show the woman slipping her feet into socks, drying her hair, brushing her teeth, and putting on her jacket. The product is done in the microwave and the timer sounds just as she heads out the door.

Showing that something tastes good is easy. All the viewer needs to see is that the woman takes a bite, smiles, or makes a face that shows that she's enjoying the food. She doesn't need to eat it all; the viewer only needs to see one shot of enjoyment.

This idea of compressing the visuals and focusing on the most crucial images is a great way to move a lot of information quickly. British director Guy Ritchie used that truncated effect in his feature film *Snatch* about a diamond heist gone incredibly wrong. In the film, characters fly from London and New York several times; the idea of traveling isn't crucial to the story. In fact, it's cumbersome, but necessary to cleanly explain how the characters got where they did. In the travel sequences, Ritchie used iconic shots very quickly, spending a second or two on each. Instead of showing the character standing in line at the airport and going through security and showing the airplane taxiing onto the runway, the shots were cut down to a simple burst of shots. Shots included the airplane door closing, the seatbelt being buckled, the nervous passenger taking airsick pills, the plane landing on the tarmac, the plane's front wheel rolling to a stop at the gate, and an extreme close-up of a passport being stamped at immigration, showing that the character has arrived in London.

The flash editing is a sharp and effective device that also conveniently eliminated any filming at an airport and is fun to watch. The device works well, and indeed some type of device needed to be used. Characters generally cannot show up in a scene carrying a backpack and explain something away like a transatlantic flight; it's too simple and it doesn't ring true to audiences. Audiences need to see what happened to stay connected with the story. Instead of begrudgingly creating a normal airport scene, Ritchie instead used a difficult plot point to enhance the pace of the film with hypercutting in a clever plan—a difficulty was turned into an asset.

Idea Farmer

As a director of a project, the director always has ideas and plans on how to tell the story. However, when working with a group of animators, editors, sound people, artists, and the rest of the production crew, it's always wise to get as much input as possible. Like a render farm on computers, multiple brains bring that much horsepower and diversity to the mix. Directors focus on the whole project, but often talented animators and artists have the ability to focus on aspects of the production in greater detail than perhaps the director can. Animators might have a fresh take on how a character is animated. A person responsible for the costumes, or surfaces depending on the medium, might have specific ideas that are unique, funny, or reinforce the character. The director says, "Our character is an old, decrepit hobo. Dress [or surface] him like a hobo," and then the director moves on to his next problem. But the surfacers or costumers might have ideas about details that go beyond dressing the character like a hobo. Maybe it's a simple ironic statement like a hobo wearing an obviously fancy, but ruined jacket, or an ironic T-shirt that says, "party animal." The same goes with people who build sets. Whether the sets are full-sized, CG, miniature, or drawn in cel, the set builders can add and offer details that the director hadn't thought of and aren't in the script. A theoretical scene calls for the hobo trying to get in a restaurant that won't let him in. In a wacky comedy, the set and prop people could take it further with several signs that say, "No vagrants," "Loitering will not be tolerated," "No bums," "This means you," and "Keep moving, buddy," pushing the dilemma over the top. Still it's the director who must take the very best of the ideas, in relation to the mood of the story and the budget, and decide which things are or aren't possible. The various signage may be too silly for the tone of the project, and the director may morph the idea into a legitimate sign that says, "No trespassing" or "No loitering." These decisions are about the tone. If it's a sad moment, then a bunch of goofy signs would draw away from that and the director is always sensitive to the mood and the tone in every last detail, if necessary.

Techniques

Live-action director Jonathan Demme and documentarian Errol Morris have realized the value of actual eye contact—having the actor look directly into the camera. In most films, direct eye contact is avoided, but both these directors, makers of very different films, recognize that the illusion that the viewer is not only looking directly into someone's eyes, but that someone in a way is looking out. To that point, Morris created a system where his interviewees are looking directly at a video image of him listening, so that he is on television and the interviewee is looking directly into his eyes via a beam splitting glass, while also looking directly into the camera. Having a character making that kind of direct contact is tricky, and often the trickiest part is the transition because the viewer becomes aware that the character is aware of the camera. When telling a narrative of a fictitious story, directors must be cautious about such an unusual technique. However, when used effectively, looking straight into the camera is very powerful.

Each director brings his own technique, and like all great art forms, there's a massive history of great filmmaking techniques all readily available from around the world. Sources range from the films of F.W. Murnau, to legendary classics like *Citizen Kane* and *Raging Bull*, to everything in between.

Stylization can infuse everything: sound effects, music, angles, lens, editing. With extreme stylization, from CG models to practical sets, everything must be created, but starting from scratch also allows for maximum control. Directing in its own right is largely about a style that the director is using to tell the story. A live-action example would be contemporary filmmakers. A traditional action director would do a cowboy gunfight with multiple cuts and extreme angles, showing people, often in slow motion, diving for cover behind bars as windows and bottles explode—expected mainstream normal filmmaking. Independent filmmakers like Jim Jarmusch, who's made many acclaimed live-action films including *Down by Law, Stranger than Paradise*, and *Mystery Train*, finds stylistic ways to film his productions.

In Jarmusch's western *Deadman*, Johnny Depp is a misplaced Easterner turned fugitive. There are several gun battles in the movie, but stylistically Jarmusch treats the shootouts as if the characters were only talking. There are no close-ups of guns or faces; most of the shots are wide and locked off. It's strangely ironic, a send back to the early days of film making this period piece feel older and vintage, but it also gives a new sense of reality and makes the gunfights seem extremely stoic and incidental. It works well in the context of this movie that is filmed in a very downplayed sense. The filming is as simple as the times of the Old West, the time period when the movie takes place. Leone's *Once Upon a Time in the West,* is a classic piece of visual storytelling, and still seems to stay within the bounds of the time period. Stylization of camera placement, the lens, and editing can have measurable impact to a production, but it has to work with the story and the feel.

In a modern-day action or drama movie, a composer can use any array of music styles from a rock-and-roll track to a simple single guitar. Depending on the story and the production, in some instances, the single instrument gives a grittier feel. In making a western or a period piece, a single guitar could easily be used, but it might seem out of place to use a rock or reggae band.

Characters in a medieval animation can't have modern haircuts or wear glasses, so designers of characters and productions need to keep in mind that there is an element of what the audience expects in every aspect of telling a story. If something is understood to be in a specific time and place, then everything should reinforce that. A director wouldn't pick Hawaiian music in a movie about the Antarctic, unless he was making an ironic joke. Animation and film have a massive history, and filmmakers and animators, both beginners and advanced, are fortunate that the best work in these genres winds up on the screen. It is a function of the process that good work is recorded; style, movement, and dialogue therefore easily give up their secrets to anyone who cares to look.

By studying early comedic films from Buster Keaton and Harold Lloyd, filmmakers can see, learn, and find inspiration on timings and gags from watching both old and modern masters. The same is true with the script and direction. There are cartoons in Tex Avery's heyday that Disney didn't want their animators looking at because of the potential influence of seeing such extreme poses. Avery is just one of many animators who all animators should always study. The style has been mimicked and copied over and over for years, but the originals are still the best and the takes and giant exaggerations are far more than just visual gags. The gags that Avery directed were complicated, smart, numerous, nonstop and together are some of the most outrageous animation set to film. All reasonably new DVD players and videocassette recorders can go frame by frame, and the Avery's genius is easily decoded in any of his work. Going frame by frame is incredibly useful. Not only does it show how the action works, but it also shows how those animators kept their pacing, kept the motion flowing, and didn't dwell on the mundane, dismissing certain actions to get to the next gag; it's all there, ready to be studied, as is the cinema from the very first films to the latest masters. True directors are film and animation fans at heart.

The Montage

Most modern feature comedies now always have a music montage or two as a strict formula in the editing. Obviously, the studio wants to sell records as well, but a montage is an effective tool to show a lot of activity, a great distance, or the passage of time. Unfortunately, many of those types of light comedies, romances, and family films suffer from the lack of a well-planned story, and instead concentrate on the one-liners and the action.

In addition, many movies will have a montage or a modern effect that doesn't really work, and it can be a disconnect because most viewers associate certain genres with a certain style of filming. A montage to a rock song doesn't necessarily work in a Victorian romance. The feature film *Paper Moon* is a film about a con artist and his child partner in the early 1930s. The film is filmed with long, wide shots that are often minutes long, avoiding fast and snappy cutting or unusual shots. Instead, since the film is based in the early 1900s, it is similar to Jarmusch's techniques in *Deadman;* they both are similarly directed like an old photograph with long, wide, lingering shots, and the style and technique is closely tied to the story and the mood. Montages would seem completely out of place in films like *Deadman* and *Paper Moon*. Still, there are countless ways to create a montage. Montages are a number of scenes put together; 30-second commercials and the sequence discussed earlier from the film *Snatch* are examples of short montages.

DIRECTING FOR ANIMATION

The most popular animated TV show of all time, *The Simpsons*, is keenly aware that writers and animators are different animals. Each episode is written for about 21 minutes, which is approximately the length of a half-hour show with commercials. The show is then edited down to about 18 minutes and then handed off to the animation directors and animators to enhance the visual humor.

Directors often need to have the best ideas about poses, and they need to be clear on which pose conveys which emotion the best. Animators can come up with great poses, but it's the director's responsibility to provide clever and fun poses when the animator doesn't have anything solid. It's also the director's responsibility to recognize when an animator's idea of a pose has surpassed the director's idea for the same pose.

Directing for animation is unique, and there are serious considerations that apply to directing animation that go above and beyond directing people or live action. Animation is based on abstraction of some sort, and abstraction isn't always easy for the mind to digest. In filming live action, people act and perform, but it's not up to the director to make sure that every frame is informed. Good actors carry a level of intensity by how they are performing, how they look, and how they carry themselves. The same is not true with animation. Since none of the natural personality comes across in a drawing of an inanimate character, it's up to the director to make sure every single thing an animated character does informs its personality and performance. Animation is not reality, but it's beyond reality. In order to sell that new reality, a director and animator must leave nothing to chance when it comes to an animated character.

In traditional cel animation, the key frames must be drawn well and stay on model; the in-betweens must be drawn just as well or the entire animation suffers. The same is true with performance. If only the big comical or pointed gestures are planned and the small details are glossed over, the story and the character suffer and there's less chance of making a connection. Similarly, live action filming often offers up locations, lighting, and various elements. Animation is wholly different and starts with virtually nothing. Even physical laws like gravity and inertia and how light behaves aren't a given; everything has to be created or controlled in animation.

Animation directors also direct the characters indirectly because an animator usually does the animation. In a very real sense, the animator is the actor and will often bring a level of interpretation to a character's performance.

Animation, particularly good character animation, is a pleasing illusion to watch. Depending on the level of stylization, it often requires unique directing solutions. Stylized animation with extreme characters often benefits from direction that is simplified. Animated characters that have extreme designs aren't as easily recognized by the eye as a human being would be. Human beings are incredibly tuned to watching other human beings and can read subtle expressions quickly, but the same isn't always true with animated characters. Certain subtle gestures need more time to be read, even if it's only a few more frames. Direction and editing that would work fine with filmed people can often be too quick with animated characters, because viewers require additional time, however small, to establish what they are seeing.

Often, animation studios will have large floor-to-ceiling mirrors that animators can use like a video reference to study a step or specific turn or move. This method is effective, quick, doesn't require any videotape, and is just a logical extension of the lip-sync mirror that is an absolute must for all animators doing lip sync and facial expressions. Even when animating nonhuman characters, people and actors can go a long way to improvise movements from other creatures.

Exaggeration

Exaggeration is a large part of animation, mostly for effect, but some of it comes out of the strange nature of animation's expectations. Creating lip sync that wholly works in animation is an exaggeration; most movements that are deliberate and clear in some form are on some level of exaggeration. Another example of useful exaggeration in animation is when characters or objects are small, figuratively way off in the distance, deep in the environment. For example, a tiny figure is on a mountaintop, jumping up and down and trying to get a rescue helicopter's attention. In animation, this type of exaggeration would not seem like exaggeration. In fact, having the character jump normally like a human won't read as jumping at all. Generally, as objects become smaller in distance, whether in CG, cel, or any type of animation, their movements can be gradually exaggerated proportionally to the distance they go. At some point, the exaggeration would become too distracting, but pushing the animation to discover how far the exaggeration can go and visually work the best is the animator's job.

The director's job, above all else, is to be the best actor of all and understand how every performance should act. Whether it's a physical performance by an actor, digital or real, or whether it's the performance of the lighting or the editor it is ultimately up to the director. The director is the keeper of the story, the mood, the timing, and most importantly the telling of the story and every element that contributes to it. Whether they are broad stroke tools like design, editing, and lighting, or specific choices like costumes or facial reactions are ultimately up to the director. A director who doesn't at least try to consider every aspect of the production is missing the key aspect of his job. He ultimately makes the project work or not, and combining all the elements of a project is one of his most important roles.

Tips for Future Projects

Physics Apply to Editing and Cutting

Physics dictate how actions can flow and objects can move from scene to scene, and directors control the performance and motion. Whether it's emotional weight or physical weight, directors are always conscious of the physics of storytelling.

Be Flexible and Resourceful

Rigidity of ideas can be disastrous depending on what's going on. A successful director is measured by how he deals with the good as well as the bad: the perfect shot and the disastrous shot. Directors don't have to accept the order of shots and can shuffle them around, if the story permits, in a big way or a little way, either by performance or impact. Directors have everything play to the camera and avoid spoon-feeding emotions to the audience. Directors are masters of relative problem solving and thinking on their feet. In order to accomplish this, they have to know the roots of what is going on: the roots of the story and its intent and the roots of the performance and what needs to be conveyed and what can be omitted.

Keeping It Moving

One rule of directing is to keep cutting until it hurts. Whether cutting the script or cutting in editing, the idea is that less is more. If something good had to be cut because everything else was better, then that director and project are in good shape. Directors shouldn't fall in love with a sequence or an idea, but instead should try to think about the overall timing and pacing, which is often more important. Directors also need to evaluate what they have, and how those elements can be combined to keep the pace alive and thriving. Suppose a scene in a film features dialogue; although the scene is a bit long, it is essential to the film. A second scene features action that is not essential to the film, but follows the previous scene. A good director might take those elements and combine them to have two things happen simultaneously, developing both the dialogue and exciting action visuals. He must be able to intertwine scenes and ideas to better present the project.

Rehearsing

Nothing can replace trial and error. Repeatedly rehearsing, practicing, or trying other ways and ideas whether with people, CG characters, storyboards, or pencil tests is often useful. Actors bring a great deal to a play or film. In animation, studies and tests from other animators can bring, modify, or evolve performances, jokes, gags, and even story points, but only through trial and error can they be discovered. When working with talented people on every level, directors also get the best of all worlds, knowing that several creative brains are all working on separate yet connected pieces of a puzzle.

When a director trusts the other artists' judgment, then he's truly free to concentrate on the biggest ideas of performance, emotions, and entertainment. Good directors are never passive and never leave anything unconsidered. That in itself is the true skin of a director who realizes that everything is at his control, especially in animation, and to leave something unconsidered would be like not doing a complete job. Directors often rely on talented people to consider the minutia. In perfect scenarios, there is a rapport between the director and the people he's working with, as they are extensions of the overall ideas, mood, and tone. However, the director has the biggest picture and always makes sure that everyone's work conforms to or works within the global framework.

Directors need to be like detectives, hammering away at the truth and never accepting what they get by default. They must push, pull, and drag all the elements into play to get to the ultimate truth. Likewise, film-makers and modern animators must use these same tactics to get the per-fect vehicle for a story, rehearsing and trying new things and always attempting to improve anything and everything. The real trick is to be able to recognize when the first idea was the strongest and the best. It is just as important to know when things aren't to be messed with and are as good as they're going to get. It's worth repeating over and over: although repetition is invaluable in solving certain problems, it is also a death sen-tence to humor. What was funny or surprising on the first pass will no longer be funny 30 viewings later. The truly tuned-in director has to be able to recognize and remember the initial reaction to certain things, and trust that reaction six months later during postproduction. In the end, the technical side of directing is complex, but is also driven by many hard and fast rules of science and physics. Although these rules can be worked out to some point, the subjective choices of directing are truly what separates good directors from great directors.

INTERVIEW WITH DIRECTOR CHRIS SANDERS

Chris Sanders is the creator of Disney's *Lilo & Stitch*. He has also worked on *Aladdin* and *Mulan* and is now directing an upcoming feature for Disney.

Wellins: *How did you get started?*

Sanders: I went to Cal Arts. Walt Disney was in a period of decline and they'd been through a bunch of strikes and stuff, so they were definitely not hiring. So I went to Marvel Productions, were I worked on the *Muppet Babies* show. That was my first job in animation. So I worked there and they made me do all the things that I'd previously refused to do before in school, which was you should draw everyday things—mundane things to really teach yourself these things. Then I got to Marvel Productions and I drew everyday mundane things for three years. Chair, table, vacuum cleaner—I did turnarounds of them for all the departments.

Wellins: *You were always a drawer, filmmaker kind of person?*

Sanders: Yeah, I did my little Super 8 films. Drew my little comic strips and published my in-house, in-home newspaper, which I distributed to the family. I had one of those typewriters like an old Underwood that would go, clack, clack, clack, and the ribbon would get stuck a mil-lion times. And some of the things would get really dim at the end, and we would never get a new ribbon!

Wellins: *What were some of your early influences in animation on film?*

Sanders: In art in general Carl Barks was huge for me, and still is. Early on I was able to detect which comics he had done, and I separated them out so they would never get thrown out.

→

Beatrix Potter I loved. In film, the only films I really liked a ton, as a kid, were silent films. When I saw my first silent film, like a Keystone Cops film, it was the funniest thing I'd ever seen in my life. I was thinking, "Why do they have sound these days? They should always be like this!" So I tried to get as many of those as I could, but you couldn't find them—you just had to watch them as much as you could. So Buster Keaton, Keystone Cops, things like that. And the only animation that really stuck out in my head, I never liked the Disney features as well as the little shorts they did. I loved Ichabod Crane [film: *The Adventures of Ichabod and Mr. Toad*], and I loved *The Ugly Duckling*, and I loved *Lambert the Sheepish Lion*. Some of those little shorts I think were still some of the best things they did. The one that continues to be the pinnacle for me was *A Charlie Brown Christmas*. That one, *Rudolph* [*the Red-Nosed Reindeer*], any of the more crudely built specials that had a great deal of heart to them. The actual super-good animation, it definitely impressed me, but not as much as the other things that these other things are transmitting. The emotional impact of these things as a kid, I just could not get enough of that.

Wellins: *What excites you now about doing animation?*

Sanders: That's a good question. The thing that makes me really psyched right now is the thing that's been so horrible for a lot of people to get through, which is the transition to CG. I understand the difficulties now in having to build a character, having to set up environments and it's more arduous to just begin one of these films and the whole art form changed. But what you are about to be able to achieve is so many things that live action has gotten away with for all these years that you could never touch. A slow trucking shot, all the the camera work, dolly shots: the things that a grip would be setting up on the set. That's the stuff that I would constantly reference when I talk about a scene or I think about a scene. And that's the part I don't want to skimp on for this film. For *Lilo & Stitch* we couldn't do any of that. There was no budget for something like that and it was so horrible to get something like that done. For one shot of the airplane flying down the street, which we ultimately cut from the film, we worked for a year to prepare for that shot, and at the last minute we had to pull it out of the film, which was incredibly disappointing. But the idea that now that would come with the territory is huge.

Wellins: *So it's the live action tools that are now represented in 3D that you're most excited about?*

Sanders: It's the actual virtual camera work that you can do. It's the lens changes, the camera work, the camera movement—that's the stuff I'm the most excited about. I am excited about trying to get it, but I don't think anyone's really gotten it yet. I have yet to see a CG film . . . *Ice Age*, strangely, was the one that did it for me the best, more so than any of the Pixar films, so far. That scene at the end of *Ice Age* where the little sloth goes up to that saber-toothed tiger, who has been so hateful and horrid to him the entire film, and he says, "C'mon, c'mon you can make it," and he says, "I'll carry you." That just broke me up—that was the sweetest thing I'd ever seen. That emotional thing is something I've yet to see repeated. So far all the CG has been so dazzling, but it hasn't carried a lot of emotion yet and I know it can.

Wellins: *What do you find the most tedious about animation? Is it the fact that you have to go so slowly?*

→

Sanders: The biggest danger with speed for us is the threat of change. You actually can indulge yourself in too much change. You're liable to become bored with something and change it when you maybe shouldn't have changed it. The thing that has proved tedious for me are the things you just can't get: something like a costume that would be so important, and you just can't make it any more complex more than a few little colored lines separated on a shirt. Like we had a little emblem we wanted to put on one of the character's shirt and we just couldn't afford it. Again, to have the now, something that you can achieve, is huge for me. I think it does mostly have to do with the process. It really isn't the people who you have to deal with. I've always felt like, and it's been my experience, that almost every single person just brings things to the party and there couldn't be anything better. That I think is just like a live-action film. If you have a good designer, you have a good cinematographer, [and] you have a good wardrobe person, they're just going to plus what you're doing; that was always wonderful for me. And I had to be careful to separate the input from the process. Getting input from people really is never bad if you're able to sort through it. But the way that our process is sometimes set up is, rather than helping to make a film, it seems to be counter to making a film. It seems like they're almost trying to stop you from making a film. The worst experience I had filmmaking in that realm was *Mulan*. We had a group of creative executives who constantly sent us a massive set of notes and it was always titled "The Group" and the group felt X and Y and Z about these things. What they were really asking was to make everything logical: I don't buy this. I don't quite understand why she went to war. I don't buy that the dad loves her this much. Why would he stand up against society and love her at the end? And all these things, and certain ones were OK to think about, but a lot of it was asking us to make a logical film and that's impossible. Human beings are not logical creatures, so the things they do are utterly contrary to logic. They should be helping me make a film that doesn't lose you, but they should not be trying to make me make a logical film, because all that does is make something nobody would go to see. So that was one of the biggest fights we had.

Wellins: *What was your role in* Mulan?

Sanders: I was head of story on *Mulan*. And that was an interesting situation because we fought so hard on that movie to make it the right movie that I actually got a writing credit on the film. I'd never officially written things but so much of the story crew was in the film. I think most of the film ended up being the story crew's actual material that we were granted that, which is a big deal.

Wellins: *As a writer/director, you obviously have a clear vision. You wrote it and you're now bringing it all together, which is rare, not unheard of, but it's rare. A lot of great stuff comes from a unified vision and not the vision distilled from a group of people. But since you've written and are directing it, is there any conflict when other people go, "Oh, I think I like this better . . . ?"*

Sanders: No, it's always helpful. As long as you can sort it out, it's always helpful. As long as you keep clear the film you wanted to make in the beginning, all the stuff can help, even if you completely disagree with the notes. If for some reason there's a multitude of notes on some

→

one thing, there's something going on. It may not be completely wrong, but it may be wrong. But it's a great indicator of something. I've always felt like the experience of getting notes is a really good thing, but the exact notes you wouldn't want to be slavish about. You would want to take them as a generality, like, "Oh, everybody's giving me a note on X." What is it about that? Sometimes it's really obvious, but other times you're like, "Hmmm, what's going on here?" When an audience sees something, sometimes it's so positive. I never got notes from a test screening with an audience, until I did *Lilo & Stitch*, and I got those packets of notes from test audience members. People got questions like, "What did you like about this movie? What did you hate about this movie?" Under "What did you hate about it?," I got a note where someone had said, "I don't like so and so." Well, that person they don't like happens to be a bad character, so I was thinking maybe it's good that they don't like character. So I said to myself, "Be careful about how you take this."

Wellins: *So the prescreening test audiences filled out stacks of cards?*

Sanders: Yeah, the cards, and we eventually got the book that they took away from us. We got a black book, a little pamphlet. I don't know how much it cost for them to put those together. There was a company who did it; I don't know who it was. But they were the people who took the notes from the screening and compiled it into a mass of information that the more you read it the more you didn't know what to do with it. [The notes said] "75% of Eskimos and soccer moms didn't like the color blue in your film," and then later on other notes would say that audience members like . . . the color blue very much. You'd go through this, and the information was broken down a thousand different ways and they would put different filters on the information until you were going, Ugh! I don't know what to do with this.

But the thing that was the most valuable was the experience of sitting in the theater and watching how the audience reacted, because there's no question that as a mass, they engaged or disengaged or laughed or reacted to the film. So you could just write down: Lost audience at scene 5. Audience gone. People getting up and walking around. People talking. One lady was on a cell phone through most of my film—right in front of me. I felt no compunction about it. The phone rang and she got it and started talking. Actually she was the anomaly in that particular screening.

Wellins: *What was your process for developing* Lilo & Stitch?

Sanders: You know, I wish that I could go back to that a little bit because I'd never really done that before. I had a co-director and a co-writer, Dean DeBlois, and the initial idea, the start of the whole thing, was a failed children's book I had in my head. The thing that drove most of the process was just the idea of having the villain and the hero be the same character. It's something that people don't comment on very much about that film, but the idea of redemption was huge—that no one would die in the film. The thing that started the process was we were talking about how we would kill the bad guy in *Mulan*. Should he fall to his death or should he do this or that? I had this bright idea that we would blow him up, that he'd be hit by this rocket. I was so excited about this idea that I actually kept it secret until I presented it in

$\rightarrow$

my storyboard. I thought it was really cool and it ended up verbatim in the film. He gets hit by a rocket at the fireworks stand. But it was odd to me because here I was working at Disney Studios and we were having yet another discussion about how to kill someone. If you think about it, a lot of villains die in Disney films. Well how should this one die? They always fall to their death; let's think of something different. I began to think to myself, "Does it have to be this way? Why do they always have to die?" That's where I started thinking about this little character I have and I thought, "Why couldn't the villain be the hero? Why couldn't he turn it around at the end and do something really good?"

If you watch *Lilo & Stitch* now, the way it came together it's much more about a little guy who's an orphan. He's sort of the ultimate orphan finding a place to live and belong and stuff like that. Really and truly the way it started out was a villain becoming a hero—that was the thing that drove the entire process. As for the process, we just dove straight in at the beginning. We never had a script complete. We wrote sequences and started gluing them together. We did have an outline board, but we started with an outline board, talked about that for just a few weeks or months, and dove straight into the board. We wrote a sequence and boarded it, wrote it, boarded it. We would just divvy things up. Do you like that part? OK, I like this part. So we'd each take a sequence, and we'd each write it, then board it, and see if they glue together.

Wellins: *When you're creating, do you get a lot of ideas by doodling and drawing or do your ideas come more by writing?*

Sanders: I had never written really anything and then boarded it until I got onto *Lilo & Stitch*, and before that I just sort of started drawing. I had a little piece of notebook paper and I would write it on this big, cheap yellow notepad and then board it. So I had a miniature of that process when I first started doing it in actual final draft. It was really neat; it was fun to do that. It was so easy and abstract to write it, and then when you have to board it, it becomes a lot more tedious. They fight. It becomes . . . ugh, 300 drawings. Up to that point I'd been so negative when it came to pages like, "Oh, what idiot writer wrote this?" and I would throw the pages in the trash and do what I thought I should do. Not completely impudent, but I would do that because it really didn't seem to work. But then I'd write my own pages and finally I didn't have to go through that.

As soon as I took my pages and started drawing them, I went, "Well, this doesn't work!" The same thing. The very same thing happened. I was going, "Geez, what was I thinking?" The one thing I'm really good at is trading up. I will always trade up. I say, "That's better? Good! Old goes, new is ours now." We don't have to agonize about it. If it works better, use it. A lot of writers say, "We should just go back to what I did." And you know he's going to come back with that. My biggest concern now is that as you keep driving forward, you lose those spots with nobody talking and it just becomes a lot of business and more manic. I felt really sad, because when we went into the scoring session for *Lilo & Stitch*, the poor composer. Not poor, he did a great job. I felt bad for him though because Alan Silvestri was expert at writing music and he would just duck under all the dialogue. He'd clear for the dialogue and he built his music around it. So the frustration came from great musical moments that can carry great emotion being drowned out because the film kept getting filled up with lines. I'd hear a

→

theme and it would start to build and it would duck under some dialogue, and keep ducking. The stuff I love to listen to on my little iPod® are themes that grow, build, and then vary. They start varying themselves. The composer never got to the point where he could really indulge a piece of music because he was being so considerate of the film. I received such an education on that because, for example, he came into an early scoring session, and he wanted to know about what we were doing. He really wanted to know what the emotional changes were, where these turns were happening. He had a lot of questions and we talked for a long time and had several sessions like this. He really wanted to understand what we were up to. This was my first time doing this and I didn't know you ever did that. I just never thought about that. He had a great question. He said I didn't really catch the part where Stitch changed. Where did he go from bad to good? And we had to sit and think about it and I said, "I guess it happened between those two scenes. I guess it kind of happened off screen." He said, "Why didn't you show it?," and I said, "Well, it felt so awkward to show it." Then he said, "If you put it on screen, I'll do it for you." I said, "Oh, I never thought about that," and he did it. There's a moment where the music makes this profound little shift, and Stitch has a new idea in his head and he did it for me.

I've got to remember that the score can carry more story than you would ever suspect while you're busy working everything. You're trying to solve it all, and this guy's going to come in and carry stuff so much more eloquently than you can, and we've got to remember to clear big areas for that. We were talking about doing a sequence that is largely just score and/or a song, and make everybody shut up for a while, and let that happen. I'd like to find at least another place or two like that.

Wellins: *Music is language as well as words—it's feelings.*

Sanders: Yep. When we started doing *Lilo & Stitch,* we never talked about the budget. The budget was sort of a thing you didn't talk about, but they would tell us we didn't have much of a budget. So we said, "Whatever this budget is," and we didn't know how much it is, "I would like you to saw off enough of the budget to buy the best score humanly possible and we'll make the movie with what's left over," and they did do that. It was pretty neat.

Wellins: *What do you think is the most important role for you as a director above everything else? Obviously you're wearing two hats as writer and director, but put all that away. What is the single most important thing that you do?*

Sanders: Just keep the flavor of the movie the one that I wanted in the very beginning, but aside from that, allow everybody else to make the film, really. I will be one of the people that joins in with them. I really want a storyboard as much as possible, but that will be it. I want to allow as much creativity as possible that will build that shapes a film.

Wellins: *What are some of the important do's? What would be a hit list of things that you do on a project?*

$\rightarrow$

Sanders: I would say in the process as it is now, make sure the thing stays interesting to people who are working on it. A lot of times I want to cast people to certain sequences, and then sometimes my urge is to not cast them on something they want to do. I did a lot of sequences that were very dialogue-heavy and very character-filled, and one time I asked him [name withheld] to do a sequence that was an action sequence. He said, "I don't do action sequences," and I said, "Well, can you try it?" It was a great sequence.

Wellins: *So you're kind of pushing people a little bit?*

Sanders: A little bit. A little bit of putting people in their comfort zone and then once in a while pushing them a little bit out of their comfort zone—and knowing when to do that. Not that I'm very good at it, but just to keep alive that I should be doing that. And trying to balance everything. Trying to remember that a score is going to come in and then trying to be conscious of them that you don't lose those air spaces and things like that.

Wellins: *What are some things that you absolutely don't want to do?*

Sanders: I think it would be almost the same answer. Don't limit creativity. Don't close the door on something. People appreciate clarity, but that doesn't mean [saying] no to something.

Wellins: *If you could give one or two tips to aspiring directors or filmmakers, what would it be?*

Sanders: To do something that you are familiar with and makes you happy. Don't try to make a giant space epic if that's not what you really want to do. If you want to make a film about your next-door neighbor and his troubles with his car in the driveway, then do that and you're going to have a better project. You're going to feel happier. It's going to come out easier. It's a mistake I've made several times. Like, "Ooh, I'm going to do this project, but I want to be like this other thing that I like." I'll take a children's book I admire and go, "Ooh, look. It's all done in oil paintings." I want mine to look like oil paintings, but I don't oil paint. So I'm going to waste like a thousand years trying to get an oil painting going, and I should do it the way I feel comfortable doing it.

Wellins: *Writers always say write what you know.*

Sanders: It is true. Look into yourself. What experience, as mundane as it might be, is unique to you? I wouldn't do well writing a western, so I wouldn't necessarily want to jump into that right away.

Wellins: *Writing and directing, being a filmmaker—that's a pretty good gig. Is this one of your dream jobs, or what would be a dream project for you?*

Sanders: I would love to do a book. The people I admire most are people who draw and do comics and do stuff in print. If I could ever do something like that, it would be a giant thing for me. The other thing would be I would love to do a documentary of something. I have a couple ideas for something I'd like to do, but to have time to be able to do that would be great.

→

Wellins: *Do you have any interest in directing live action?*

Sanders: You know, a lot of the things I write down are live action films, and yeah, I definitely want to do that. I'm not one of those who can't wait to get away from animation. This stuff is great and the neat thing about it, especially now more than ever, now that CG has come in [it] has somehow stepped closer to what live action is getting as far as people connecting to the film—immersion that you experience being in the film. So we're way more into that territory than we ever were. I'm so glad I was born when I was and I didn't miss this. I'm so happy! That line [between live action and CG] is so blurred, if even existent now. And we're all sort of trying to achieve the other thing. We're always trying to achieve these moments of emotional clarity and interaction that feel real between bizarre characters. For me, that's my taste. I love Bugs Bunny cartoons, but I've never been comfortable doing slapstick and gags. Whenever we had a gag session, I think I contributed nearly nothing to any gag session we were ever at. But if you talked about a scene where somebody was having trouble with something and it's a more internal thing, I feel much more comfortable contributing stuff to that kind of discussion. That's the kind of style of filmmaking that I do. As bizarre as the characters may be, and as bizarre as the situation may be, I want them to react inside it as though it's real.

Wellins: *It's really important for the audience to be able connect. If it's so abstract that you don't have anything to connect to, then you lose them I would think.*

Sanders: There's also levels of convention as far as an animated thing. Like [*Who Framed*] *Roger Rabbit*—those were characters that came from [a] Warner Brothers kind of a world and they got squished flat and popped back into shape, and I liked *Bambi* better where they were trying not to get shot. If they got onto ice they'd slide, but when they hit the ice they stayed themselves. That's what I like. Again, as crudely as it's animated, *A Charlie Brown Christmas* is real. I like that. I don't know why.

Wellins: *You're just getting going on this project, but what's next? Do you think that far ahead? What would you like to do next?*

Sanders: I do have a little idea of what I'm going to do next. If I could, ideally I'd have a very short-format little movie I'm going to make. I'd love to make a short right after this. If not, [I will] jump onto somebody else's project and help them out. I think I'd like to do a short.

ART DIRECTION

Art direction is another vast level of interpretation required in the production design. The goal is to create visual appeal that will enhance and help the story. When the script for *The Wizard of Oz* called for the Emerald City, the art director decided what it look like and how it fit into the scene and the film as a whole. The director may speak in broad strokes or can be specific about some scenes and feelings, but the art director fills in these spaces, and offers up a number of options from which the director can choose. Art directors need to have every sketch and know every details of the story. If the film calls for underwater scenes, what does that mean? Can you see the bottom? Is it cartoonish and iconic with starfish and treasure chests, or is it more realistic like a kelp forest? Is the water the color of real underwater, which has its own huge array of colors, or can it even go beyond reality and use all colors? The underwater theme can be abstracted to the point where it becomes a backdrop like the undersea feel in the television show *SpongeBob SquarePants*. The show is iconic and cartoony, but is still clearly underwater.

Art directors are artists who take the hardest look at the overall visuals. These visuals can include an overall color treatment of the film, such as a story told in the Old West where the film is tinted in sepia tones, to the detailed specifics of set and character design, costumes props, color schemes, lighting schemes, styles and textures, and everything else in the visual spectrum.

Animation is capable of taking art direction to impossible levels, and the animation art director has complete control over every visual element. He not only focuses on the general story and ideas, but also focuses on specifics and ranges. Art direction can enhance or even completely create a mood. Science-fiction movies from their earliest incarnations always painted science fiction as sterile, clean, and polished; these movies were influenced by the National Aeronautics and Space Administration (NASA), the rigors of science, the television era, and B-movies, where stark and simple was a stylistic choice driven by budget.

Art direction and visuals changed dramatically, however, when the sci-fi classic *Alien* was released in 1979. All at once space and science fiction were gritty, dirty, greasy, and worn out, featuring broken objects and flickering lighting. *Alien* is more of a horror film than a science-fiction film, but the creators of the film forced horror-film art direction onto a science-fiction film with astounding success.

Art directors can help focus abstract ideas and often create or identify a style of visual treatment that helps tie the story pieces together, or depending on the story, set the pieces apart. Art direction is anchored more in the theatrical than in storytelling because storytelling usually resides in the characters. But while directors can plan every word or every step a character makes, the art director plans everything else that is visible in that scene. Art direction also creates visual depth and can hint at different levels of story. *Alien* has a brilliant designer that goes beyond simple set creation; the art designer told the viewer more about the world and hinted at a history that went far beyond what was seen.

In *The Wizard of Oz*, the art direction takes a dramatic change when reality itself changes as Dorothy and Toto go from Kansas to the land of Oz. The jump from black and white to color is the obvious artistic change, because Oz is a fantasy world and Kansas is not. The tornado that destroys the Kansas farmhouse is very realistic, while the Emerald City in Oz looks nothing like a city, but instead is a beautiful stylization of a city. Reality has changed, but the reality and the fantasy bend and twist to accommodate the story. In contrast to the Emerald City, the Wicked Witch of the West's castle is a foreboding castle that is closer to reality than stylized. The reason for these changes in style is to affect the mood; a stylized castle would not be as scary as a large stone medieval castle, and a real tornado is much more threatening than a fake one. The land of Oz uses extensive colorful background paintings to set the mood of a happy, fantasy world. Such is the complex nature of art direction. *The Wizard of Oz* is an obvious use of art direction and shows how important the link between beauty and art is. But art direction has different tasks for different stories, many of which have nothing to do with beauty. Art direction can also be deliberately dull and flat or distorted and warped, creating moods and feelings that are anything but pleasing. Terry Gilliam's *Brazil* is an art director's dream. Although there are scenes of beauty in places, most of the film is dismal, with sickly looking humans, who are pale and sweaty and often shown under flat buzzing and irritating lighting. Gilliam started out as an artist and an animator, so his attention to visual detail goes beyond the average live-action director's.

Figure 5.1 is another example of stylized art direction. This scene from *The Lester Show*, shows Lester, the main character, leaving his home. The entire scene is designed like a stage play. Instead of filling out the scene with endless textures and objects to try to make the scene look real, it focuses on iconic objects and locations: a dismal sky, smokestacks of a factory that puff into the sky, a shopping cart, a trash can, a tire, and a car up on a cinder block. All these objects are iconic of ruin and grime. The background images are also like a background painting of a stage play, and the houses and buildings are simple, painted, and graphical.

In Figure 5.2, the design technique is the same. The focus of the scene is textured and rich, and the background elements, which are corners of buildings and such, are extremely abstract with visible paintbrush lines and sketch lines. Together, the 3D set against the 2D artwork helps to create the story's very surreal world. From an emotional standpoint, there is visual complexity, and a sense of grime and feeling of the underbelly of society. This plays against Lester, who, in his mind, lives in a fantasy land where everything is just fine. The art direction for the film is the focal point that makes the film less about a strange character and instead hints at a metaphor for something not as funny and perhaps more tragic.

FIGURE 5.1 A scene from *The Lester Show*, with its specific stylized and textured art direction. © 2004 Allan Steele. Reprinted with permission.

FIGURE 5.2 Another scene combining 2D and 3D from *The Lester Show* (see Color Plate 1). © 2004 Allan Steele. Reprinted with permission.

VISUAL CONSISTENCY

Art directors try to use the visuals to help tell the story the actors and characters are telling, but the art director also pays strict attention to the mechanical details of consistency throughout the visual presentation. Even in *The Lester Show*, the consistency is 3D against a 2D world. In creating worlds and characters, it's often important that characters come from the same vein so that they all feel connected.

Figure 5.3 shows character studies and designs for an animation with stylized dinosaurs. All the dinosaurs are distinctly different, but share the same world when it comes to relationships, line weights, and details. In animation anything can be done, so it's possible to have designs that come from all sorts of different worlds. Ultimately the scenes that are rendered or animated will "glue" the styles together. However, mixing of styles is a delicate maneuver, specifically when the driving force is a story.

FIGURE 5.3   There is a wide variety of characters, but they are all in the same graphical vein.

CREATING THE ENVIRONMENT

The lighting, texture, and set are rich in Figure 5.4a, with rich deep colors and textures that tell the story of a well-worn and antique desk on which the insect performs. The lighting also hints at stage-play lighting, with each character being featured with its own glow that visually pops the characters out of the backdrop and focuses the viewer's attention. Instead of lighting the desktop like a standard desk, the art direction mixes settings, creating a dynamic and rich environment that goes beyond how a desktop would normally be lit.

The great surrealist painter Salvador Dalí did backgrounds in 1946 for a short Disney film titled *Destino,* a six-minute surreal exploration. *Destino* was abandoned, but was finally finished after more than 50 years in limbo. The fact that Dalí did background paintings says a great deal about something as banal sounding as a "background." Production design, sets, landscapes, buildings, and entire worlds that have been created for movies have been some of the most innovative art in the last 100 years. From Georges Méliès films, to the classic worlds of animators like Ray Harryhausen, environmental design is as important of an element as any other aspect of making animation and creating scenes.

Set pieces are often just as important as props; just like the story, sets and set pieces and environments are all part of the feeling. There's no question of the importance of design because it's always noticeable when it's bad; one can tell when a set looks cheap, whether real or animated.

ON THE CD

The *Shards of Death* (on the companion CD-ROM) set plays the story as straight as the filming, music, and performance. It's about extreme characters in a rather banal and awkward situation. Awkwardness comes from pauses, silence, and long beats, not strange set designs. *Grime Shoed*

ON THE CD

Diaries (on the companion CD-ROM) goes much further with set design, pushing the visual ideas of a huge, faceless, and unsympathetic city.

Live action also has an advantage when it comes to scale. In live action, everything is instantly recognizable in real-world settings. Even exotic sets are grounded in reality because people and everyday objects are of a common size. But, animation has to be clear about scale, because there is often no instant size recognition. Animation, however, is also capable of creating incredibly dramatic uses of scale from the very significant to the very small. A large segment of modern special effects are large vista shots and epic scenes, and CG has now changed flat matte paintings into 3D environments that are limitless in scope. With every environment, whether a natural vista or a fantastical landscape, it's important to remind the audience of the scale, and tiny figures moving over the landscape or toward the vista are an instant comparison for the viewer. Classical landscape painters like Albert Bierstadt and Fredrich Church painted huge panoramas and striking vistas of giant mountain

FIGURE 5.4a   The world of *Insect Poetry* is an antique desktop, which has a
stage-play feel (see Color Plate 2). © 2001 Marilyn Zornado. Reprinted with permission.

ranges and dramatic skies, but those artists also almost always added a
few deer, cattle, settlers, or Native Americans in their paintings simply to
reinforce the scale. Common objects like people, animals, cars, vehicles,
and houses all have an instantly recognizable scale in the viewer's mind,
and a tiny figure against a large backdrop instantly defines the scale (see
Figure 5.4b).

FIGURE 5.4b   A conceptual drawing showing massive scale, but without the human
figure in the foreground the perceived size is relative.

COLOR

Color is another tool that animation can push further than live action. Bright pure colors that animation can use are extreme and rarely exist in the normal visual world. In the real world, other factors influence color, such as lighting, atmosphere, dirt, and shadows, but animation starts at the opposite end with vivid and pure colors.

Basic color theory states that warm colors (e.g., red and yellow) come forward, while cool colors (e.g., shades of blue) recess visually. This happens partly out of recognition and partly out of physics. When it comes to color in animation, stylization is not bound by reality. Animation is a very forgiving media in certain areas, and because stylized animation has very few preconceptions in the audience's view, color can be used creatively and to effect. *The Lester Show* (see Figures 5.1 and 5.2, color version on the CD-ROM) and Color Plate 1 for Figure 5.2 is a film set in a seedy, grimy world. The color palette has plenty of weak and pale colors, but also has areas of almost psychedelic bursts of color that help with the peculiar mood of the film. Color can be consistent, or it can change with mood and emotion subtly or overtly like in *The Wizard of Oz*.

Limited color palettes are also a tool of animation because unlike live action, every color can be controlled. Limited palettes can create moods and feelings and can have graphical connections that have the feel of comic books and graphic design.

Animation can use the spectrum of colors, no colors, or one color on a black and white backdrop. Color is like music when it comes to mood, and art directors try color schemes and look for a color combination that visually works well but also says something about the character, story, or scene.

The color palette in Figure 5.5 (color plate 3) spins the color theory that warm colors come forward and cool colors recede. There is a cool lake at the foreground, but a warm tree and a dirt bank screen right, which are the foremost objects composed in frame, tie the two areas together. The colors, although vibrant, fade as they move toward the back, and the sunlight source highlights the facets of the distant stone mountains. Figure 5.5 is also a forced perspective set and is in reality no more than six feet deep.

Figure 5.6 is a stop-motion set of a forbidding castle. The rocks have tremendous texture and power. The castle is slightly lighter in color, but is as gray and unfriendly as the rocks that surround it. The castle sits perched in this mountain of rock as a very formidable structure. Color is

FIGURE 5.5   A rich yet specific color palette (see Color Plate 3). © 2004 Paul Harrod. Reprinted with permission.

FIGURE 5.6   A miniature stop-motion set with a limited and cold palette. © 2004 Paul Harrod. Reprinted with permission.

ON THE CD

tied to mood; a gray rock against a black sky is menacing and works well with a scary castle.

On the other end of the spectrum are bright and vivid colors. Figure 5.7 is a scene from the short film *107.6 Degrees* on the CD-ROM (**1076_degrees.mov**). The top image is a conceptual drawing of the characters, and the bottom images are the final rendered image. The final color palette was far more brilliant, if not fluorescent, in the final CG rendering. The look works with the idea of the story; its main motivation is heat and the extremely bright sun. The colors work with the lighting, but are also a fun departure on the strange characters. Figure 5.7 (see also Color Plate 4) is also doing double duty as a key pose drawing, and the final actual pose, which with the elongation of the characters, reads much clearer than the initial drawing. Figure 5.8 shows a tree design and then the CG execution. The short takes place in a baking desert, but it's a stylized desert of a stylized world with good use of colors.

FIGURE 5.7   A conceptual drawing and the final rendered scene (see Color Plate 4).
© 2004 Amila and Patrik Puhala. Reprinted with permission.

FORCED PERSPECTIVE

The scenes in Figure 5.5 and Figure 5.6 were both created for stop motion. Both figures utilize forced perspective, which is when objects are deliberately designed to create a fake diminishing of size as things go off in distance. It is done in stop motion for economy because sets are limited in

FIGURE 5.8 A drawing translated to the model of the burning desert world where the story takes place. © 2004 Amila and Patrik Puhala. Reprinted with permission.

size, but its design impact goes far beyond economy and creates a truly unique and designed world that has depth and space. The castle in Figure 5.6 also is built with forced perspective, which is so seamless that it looks perfectly natural. This model shows how effective a subtle forced perspective can be not only on the illusion of size, but also on pushing the visual design cues. CG modelers often default to the almost blueprint-type design that comes naturally when using a CG modeling program, such as straight perfect lines and perfect right angles. However, making an extra effort to distort and change that sterile, normal perspective is often a great mood creator and helps bury the sterile CG feel (see Figure 5.9).

Figure 5.10 is an extreme forced perspective with everything warping to the idea of a fish-eyed view of the world. The shot is unique, and creating other shots off the precise perspective that the shot is mimicking can create truly unusual shots with strange distortions. Force perspective isn't out to fool the eye in Figure 5.11. It hints at the perspective in the room, but it's off slightly by design, creating a warped fun and unusual feel. Instead of a normal and perhaps dull classroom set, distortion and forced perspective have fun with the surroundings that naturally translate to the animated final. This figure is also another image that deals with interesting lighting. Force perspective often means seeing the ceiling, and lighting has to be addressed.

FIGURE 5.9   A forced perspective shot incorporating complex elements like the freighter built with depth to give it more perceived size. © 2004 Paul Harrod. Reprinted with permission.

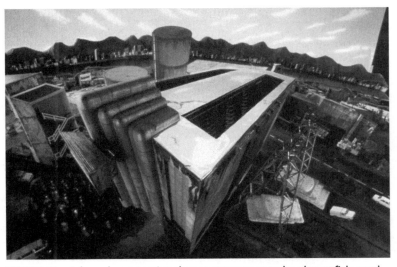

FIGURE 5.10   A forced perspective shot so extreme as to be almost fish-eyed. © 2004 Paul Harrod. Reprinted with permission.

Animation, because of its extensive use of graphical drawings and illustrations in all sorts of media, blurs the lines between not only artist and animator, but character designer, art director, cinematographer, and production design as well. This is because they all can come from the same pencil or from different sources, and often they must all be considered simultaneously in animation. Forced perspective can be worked into an animation and overall design as in Figure 5.12, where extremely stylized and iconic characters have forced perspective or a wide-angle lens worked into the artwork as a very stylistic choice.

FIGURE 5.11   A smaller stop-motion indoor set with forced perspective that is more style-driven than an illusion of depth. © 2004 Paul Harrod. Reprinted with permission.

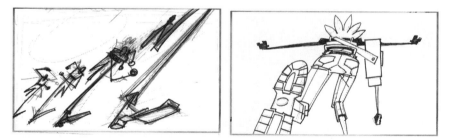

FIGURE 5.12   An illustration of extremely graphical characters with force perspective or fish-eyed view built into the artwork. © 2004 Guy Burwell. Reprinted with permission.

LIGHTING AS VISUAL TEXTURES

Lighting for an art director can mean anything from a brush stroke to a physical 1000-watt or CG light. In animation, art directors work closely with the first line of production: the director, the cinematographer, the director of photography, and the producer. Lighting is a big consideration that affects everything from mood to cost. Texture can be literal, but it also applies to all the skins and surfaces applied to every object. Whether drawn as a design, or painted on a stop-motion puppet or the skin of a CG character, texture is again an aspect of visuals that live action usually gets from the natural surroundings, so the texture is simply enhanced. In animation, texture is another tool in the artist's toolbox to create visual depth, atmosphere, mood, and style.

Figure 5.13 is a scene of a Flash animation. It is very stylized and graphical, and the tropical texture and the bright colors are lighting choices that are tied closely to design. Figure 5.14 is the opposite of a graphical design, but incorporates extensive use of real textures on every surface, except the character, which separates the character from the scene for visual clarity against wild and diverse textures and patterns.

FIGURE 5.13   A scene that is purely graphical isn't lit, although it still has a sense of bright, full light. In Flash, cel, and 2D, lighting is more flexible than any other form of animation (see color plate 5). © 2004 Laura DiTrapani. Reprinted with permission.

TEXTURE MAPS AND SURFACES

Whether a stop-motion, cel, or CG project, texture is the treatment surfaces get. In live action, most objects come with their own texture, and the art department often enhances textures. In animation, texture, like lighting and design, can go to extremes that would never work in live action. Figure 5.14 shows a visually textured scene in a very artistic and painterly style.

FIGURE 5.14   A highly stylized stop-motion scene rich in texture, except for the character, making the character a clean read and an easy focus (see Color Plate 6). © 2004 Joanna Priestley. Reprinted with permission.

CG animation probably creates the most challenges when creating good texture maps and surfaces. In cel, Flash, and stop motion, the work of creating textures is very straightforward, as in painted or sculpted surfaces, and is readily apparent when working or not. Paint can be applied thick or thin in stop motion with sponge brushes and varnishes, and paints can create any surface. Cel is simpler because it's flat and can use photo textures or even full photographs; it can even use old artwork, like Terry Gilliam's stop-motion/cel animation done for *Monty Python's Flying Circus*. Actual textures of cloth, wood, and stone can obviously be used in stop motion, but earth textures can even be scanned and added to cel or Flash animation, giving a very tactile feel. Live action comes with real-world textures, but CG starts with everything being very smooth and flat, and a great effort has to be made to give textures that have a tactile feel. CG textures further complicate the issue because they often wrap around surfaces and follow geometry that warp and distort the uniformity of the texture, which the human eye is very sensitive to. Stretched, pinched, and distorted textures smack of poorly developed CG.

CG-dimensional animation also creates all the depth and textures either in geometry or in bump maps and displacement maps. There are infinite possibilities between all the texture properties than can be tweaked and adjusted in CG. Character performance also makes a big impact on surfaces and how they react. Characters that have big moves and stretches can distort and stretch surfaces unnaturally, and geometry or models must be tweaked to compensate for this. CG, in its complex 3D mimicking of reality, creates great imagery. However, it takes exponential time to get the surfaces and textures looking right.

With cel, shiny objects would be a complete illusion and the reflections would be painted into the artwork. In reality and in stop motion, shiny objects will reflect light following the rules of physics. CG knows the rules of physics, but applying the rules of reality (e.g., diffusion, secularity, gloss, reflection, and refraction) doesn't always behave the way they do in the real world. Running turnarounds on objects that reflect light or imagery from around the object must test to see how the visuals react with the surface, texture, bump, and other maps. When using reflections, CG technical directors often take cues from photography and incorporate large white or colored shapes just off camera, so that the object has elements to catch reflections from, especially when dealing with truly reflective surfaces like chrome or polished metals.

ON THE CD

On the CD-ROM, a surface test on a chrome character called **Sunny. mov** was created to see how the reflection surfaces react on a shiny character in relation to its performance and visual appeal as it moves. The green monster in *Shards of Death* also had complicated surface maps to create the leatherlike textures. The monster is a Frankenstein assembly, so that parts of the skin have different textures to give the idea that the character was sewn together from separate parts. Creating different skins required manipulation on many levels of the skins; gloss, specularity, diffusion, and bump all had to be manipulated to create the different types of skin looks and textures.

Creating texture maps when closing in on photo-real characters can go far beyond the level of *Shards of Death*. CG creatures like Gollum from *The Lord of the Rings* and the dinosaurs from *Jurassic Park* are laborious combinations of geometry that mimic muscles and are then covered with skins and textures. At that level of realism, the art direction encompasses mimicking reality and moves character animation into the realm of special effects while doing both simultaneously: fooling the eye while creating compelling performances.

FIGURE 5.15   The unwrapped UV texture maps of the green monster from *Shards of Death*. The ultraviolet (UV) textures in *Shards of Death* were painted by Sheila Bailey in a combination of Adobe® Photoshop® and Deep Paint 3D®. The monster was skinned by technical director Stephen Bailey.

Whether creating photo-real characters that combine many maps and textures or CG characters that are more stylized, testing is still important so that you establish a look that isn't instantly recognizable as computer generated.

ON THE CD

On the CD-ROM is there a series of texture tests on the green monster character. **ShTest1.mov** is an early animation with no textures at all and simple shading. In CG production, while animation evolves, texture designers continue to develop surfaces. For animators, it's often easier to animate without surfaces so that reading animation poses is simplified. Animators must also consider the textures and check how the textures look in conjunction with the performance to ensure that readability isn't lost once textures are applied. **ShTest2.mov** is an early texture test that

ON THE CD

was less monsterlike and more zombielike, with more decay and more humanlike skin. The sutures and wounds were all created with bump maps instead of geometry to keep the feel that the characters were from the game world.

The early tests for the monster's surface were a departure from the original designs and a bit of exploration to go more realistic. **ShTest3. mov** is another version of the same scene with the first tests of textures on the walls, props, and signs. The texture maps in the tests were a departure from the original designs, and ultimately the green monster was an easier and cleaner comedic read being less human; the texture designs returned to the original drawings.

Tips for Future Projects

Don't Get Hung Up on Preconceived Ideas—Be Flexible

If time is allowed, art directors should explore a full spectrum of ideas and new visual relationships. Doing what is expected and routine is acceptable, but exploring new avenues often yields new and more engaging ideas.

How Are the Story and the Art Direction Connected?

The art direction creates the world, but also reinforces the story, and the level of detail, and the placement and stylization. How does the art direction help create mood and emotions? Does the art direction change or evolve with the story or does it stay the same throughout? How can color, or lack of color, add another level of emotional connection to the story?

How Are the Character Design, Animation Design, and Art Direction and Art Direction Tied to the Scene?

Art directors are all about adjectives: spooky, fun, hyper, empty, claustrophobic, creepy, gritty, grimy, slick, sterile, busy, calming, and so on. Art directors are about applying those adjectives and feelings to a scene, taking it from a standard scene to a scene that resembles a piece of art rather than a snapshot photograph (see Figure 5.16).

FIGURE 5.16 A scene from *Sesame Street* that features a focus on the letter X. All the elements on the scene help focus the eye with color, position, and backdrop. A child climbing on the X helps establish the size (see Color Plate 7). © 2004 Laura DiTrapani. Reprinted with permission.

Create a Production Plan from the Animatic

Like everyone else, art directors have a budget, and art direction can become a huge budgetary factor when it encompasses costumes, sets, vehicles, and props. Art directors have to reign in their fanciful side and deal with real-world issues like budgets and time. At ths point, stylization means deciding on key elements to use to create the mood or tone, instead of creating entire worlds. Icon elements can be used to do this and prevent directors from having to create every single concept. An example would be to use a headstone to suggest a whole cemetery. This type of icon use works well, if done correctly. (Animatics are covered in detail in Chapter 9, "Animatics.")

Experiment on Paper

Whether creating collages from scrap, doing hundreds of drawings, or creating foam core or cardboard mockups or models of sets, art directors can truly make huge gains by experimenting first.

INTERVIEW WITH PAUL HARROD

Paul Harrod is an art director and director who has a long and varied carrier in animation and film. Harrod has worked on the original *Pee-wee's Playhouse* and the movie *Mars Attacks!* He also directed five episodes of Eddie Murphy's animated show *The PJs*, as well as countless commercial productions.

Wellins: *How did you get started?*

Harrod: I've probably been interested in working in film since I was about 10 years old. When I was about 12 years old, I decided to do a *Planet of the Apes* makeup and pretty much learned what I could about makeup. That was kind of my entrée into the business. After I finished at Cal Arts, I really became associated with a lot of animators, because it was such a great animation school that Disney founded. [I associated with] lots of talented animators like people like Joanna Priestley and others. I did do a brief period working in the makeup business and sculpted an alien for the worst *Star Trek* movie—the one that [William] Shatner directed.

One thing I discovered when I was in art school was that I was a little more interested in environments as opposed to character design, so I started moving into art direction and set design. I had done a lot of experiments. When I was in college, I became really fascinated with force perspective set building: the idea that you could conceive of a frame and simulate a level of depth within a very small area. Part of my thesis project at Cal Arts was working on a film that involved compositing live-action characters in front of forced perspective sets that I had built, and I got pretty good at it. But what really started fascinating me was what would happen when you

→

started looking at a force perspective set from the wrong angle, from the side or whatever, and whatever bizarre distortions that you would get, which I realized was in large part where people like Tex Avery and Chuck Jones were drawing a lot of their inspiration in set designs. Also it seemed to tie in with German Expressionist film set designs, like *Cabinet of Dr. Caligari,* and others.

Wellins: *Could you define forced perspective?*

Harrod: A forced perspective set is one where basically a vanishing point and perspective lines are actually established on the set. It's designed to be looked at usually from one angle. You're compressing space so that the scale in the very foreground may be 1/6 scale and the scale in the distant background may be 1/500 scale. In fact, some of the sets that I was building when I was in college would be a very detailed city street where in the foreground I was working with model cars that were 1/24 scale, but in the very back in the distance there was a waterfront area, a pier like in Seattle or San Francisco, where I was working with things as small as 1/2400 scale, like ships. It would just get really detailed, even in the background, and in some cases these sets would be built on a pivot so that I could have a stationary camera and simulate camera moves by actually moving the set. There I would have a whole city scene with all the background with a set that was only about six feet long by about four feet deep.

Initially I started out trying to be as realistic as I possibly could be given certain limitations, but as time went on as I started working with other filmmakers I decided to use the same perspective techniques to create a cartoon expressionism, where you had a lot of conflicting perspectives working against each other. When you look at cartoons like *Little Rural Riding Hood* and that Tex Avery one with the country wolf and the city wolf, you have images of the city and you have buildings that get wider at the top, and you have really bizarre, nonsensical perspectives. In that case, it just works really well to create a sense of the confusion about the city. It feels very busy because he's got all these conflicting perspectives. So that became something that tied in pretty well to what was going on at the time in the stop motion I was doing. In the mid-eighties, when things like *Pee-wee's Playhouse* were being produced, suddenly the idea of translating those design ideas into three-dimensional sets was starting to take root, and I just happen to be fortunate enough to be on that particular wave.

Wellins: *Describe your job as art director.*

Harrod: Well, the first day I usually do a lot of banging my head against the wall. I'm very subject to a kind of blank-page syndrome. When I'm coming into a job where no work has been done on it, there's usually a very anxious period where it's like, well, nobody's really told me exactly what they want, and there are about 50 different directions I could go in. A lot of anxiety is generated over which direction it will be. Then oftentimes, I spend a lot of time just looking through books until something hits me. I have a lot of art and architecture books that I look through.

Wellins: *Is there any book or artist that you always go to first?*

Harrod: There are a couple of really great books on film design that I have a tendency to glance at just to spark my imagination. One is called *Designing Dreams: Modern Architecture in the*

$\rightarrow$

Movies by Donald Albrecht, which is mostly about art direction in film before the forties, so it focuses on what was going on in Europe in the teens, twenties, thirties, and the sort of Hollywood art deco fascination. Those things get my mind racing. Another book called *Film Architecture: Set Designs from Metropolis to Blade Runner* by Dietrich Neumann is also quite good and deals with some similar ideas. As far as what artists inspire me, that's tough because it so often depends on the project itself. Recently for instance, I happened across some Grant Wood landscapes and I was helping out with a bid for a commercial, and I started really integrating the Grant Wood, almost naive style into trying to conceive of how to make some three-dimensional sets that have this quality. It's a very interesting approach to perspective for one thing. It's almost like looking at a map at times with three-dimensional elements placed on it.

Wellins: *Once you decide on a route or an angle, then what do you do?*

Harrod: Because I'm not really much of a draftsman, what I like to do is a quick drawing, which is followed by a foam-core model. But lately, what I've been doing is grab a camera, photograph the foam-core model, and in Photoshop start adding in a lot of details. A foam-core mockup would be a matter of essentially building a scale model of my proposed set. Pretty much scabbing something very quickly together in Photoshop or out of foam core, oftentimes just drawing onto the surface to get the main landmarks of the architecture established. Then put together a small tabletop scene that can be hammered out in an hour or two. The point is to do it very quickly and to photograph it from a few different angles to find the ideal angle approach or the ideal composition and then from there start to fill in all the details. Then once we're all happy with the basic illustrative set design I'll go in and start to do schematics. I do less and less carpentry nowadays, and more time is spent on focusing on being able to hand the carpenter very specific dimensions. They have to be pretty exacting, especially when you're doing a forced perspective model because most carpenters or even model makers are not used to working in forced perspective—they're used to doing scale models. You take a film like, say *Blade Runner*, which has amazing model construction, but it's all done to a particular scale and often the model makers can count on doing a certain amount of kit-bashing. In fact, I think a lot of the models in *Blade Runner* were done in N scale so that they could find things like gantries and speed rail and windows and ductwork and everything within a particular scale that's available to them and assemble it from there.

With forced perspective, because you're not dealing with any one scale, everything has to be made. Oftentimes, you'll build a fire escape or something on the side of a building and every part of it has to be diminishing in scale, so that it gets smaller towards the back, and this can be really confounding to a classically trained model maker or carpenter. It's wrong; it doesn't look right. I've run into real frustration from a lot of people—why do you want to make it so hard? But the fact is in the end it looks great and it photographs beautifully. One of the main reasons we use force perspective in stop-motion animation is that we're constrained by the space that we have. Most animation I work on is not big features where you can build your city in fill scale in a 5,000 square foot space. You really have to economize on your space and so forced perspective becomes the answer. Also, beyond just the practical problem of economizing on space, there's a look. There's something that comes out of it, where you look at it and say, "Yeah, this doesn't feel

→

like something I could've built with my erector set as a kid." It doesn't feel like a toy. It ends up creating its own space, almost in the same way that a Hudson River School painting does. People of that school, when they did a painting of Yosemite Valley or some such place, they've taken all the elements within a 180-degree panorama and compressed them into a smaller area. They've taken the foreground and background relations and compressed them a little bit. Everything that was going on within their field of vision when they originally looked at the place, they've condensed into this place and the result is this kind of magical place. It feels on one hand miniaturized and the same time quite epic. You were asking me about some of my influences; one place I go to a lot is actually a cheap little book I have on the Hudson River School, particularly when I'm dealing with landscape. That's it for creating fantasy landscapes. In fact, if you look at the really dramatic matte paintings in films, a really good example is in [*Star Trek:*] *The Wrath of Kahn*. There's this scene where they're in this underground cave on the Genesis planet and there's a classic matte painting where the Star Trek crew are in the foreground and there's this waterfall and it's pure [Albert] Bierstadt. That approach is a really important part of the film language.

The idea of cutting away everything that's not essential and bringing together all the most essential elements. Basically, you're condensing space but there's always something to look at. When I was a teenager I was such a nut about this kind of stuff. I would go see really bad films just to see the matte shots over and over again. This was in the seventies when we didn't have home videos, so those damn studios made so much money off of me if they would throw in a matte painting because I'd go three times to see it. Or a good miniature shot or something like that, and most of these were pretty awful movies. I must have seen *The Hindenburg* five times because it had so many beautiful matte paintings that had such great compositions. Albert Whitlock was the king of that; he wrote the book. He did all the matte paintings for *North by Northwest*, which was one of the first examples of a film that was trying to treat light as the eye sees it as opposed to how the camera sees it.

Wellins: As an art director you get a script and you're working with the director. How do you decide on texture and color, and what are the main influences when working with somebody to decide all those key elements?

Harrod: Of course it's going to depend on the director, because some of the directors you work with have very strong opinions on all these things. A few directors I work with, the first day on the job, I come in and they've got a stack of books or a stack of things that they've pulled off the Internet and they say, "I'm really loving this. Is there any way we can do this three dimensionally?" Lately I've turned a lot of people who I work with onto painter Mark Ryden, because I think he's one of the most interesting contemporary painters right now, and it's coming right back at me. They say, "I love this painting by Mark Ryden. How can we achieve that look in a three-dimensional world?" It's very challenging because they're focusing on all these painterly elements, and I think achieving that real painterly look is going to be much easier in the CG world than in the stop-motion world because you're not fighting physics in the same way. Then there are the directors who just shrug their shoulders and say, "I don't really know where to go with this."

→

Wellins: *Between the two kinds of directors, what do you bring to it that they haven't expected?*

Harrod: More than anything else, it's experience. What is a dangerous road to follow and what is a practical road to follow? Over eight or nine years, I've been involved in easily over a dozen projects where the client, usually in advertising, wants a Rankin and Bass style. They say they want it to feel like *Rudolph the Red-Nosed Reindeer.* My experience tells me that they don't really want it to look that way. I say to them as diplomatically as possible, "What you want is to get the same feeling that you had when you were six years old and you saw that for the first time, but you're not going to get that feeling by replicating that style. We have to actually sophisticate that style a little bit and give it a little more depth." And sure enough I've been fairly spot-on in most of those cases. If somebody does a test where it really does feel like Rankin and Bass, they say, "Oh gee, it looks a lot funkier than we thought it was going to be. But that style is actually a funky style, you know?" A couple of things that I'm oftentimes very wary of in designing stop-motion animation is when people want to get very realistic, and my philosophy especially now with the verisimilitude of computer animation is why? Why try to pursue realism in stop motion and animation? It should be its own language. There have been two camps of stop motion from the very start. You had Willis O'Brien and his protégé Ray Harryhausen on one side, attempting to create as realistic a representation of life as possible, largely because there was no other option back then except for a man in a creature suit. You can look at *Destroy All Monsters* and see how that works. Then on the other side you have people like Ladislas Starevitch, the Russian animator, who was working more with a stylization and exploring stop motion as its own kind of visual language that was disconnected from our reality and more related to cartoons.

Wellins: *Isn't that the difference between animation and special effects?*

Harrod: Maybe it's not necessarily the fundamental difference between animation and special effects, but between cartoons and special effects. *Spider-Man* and all those things are heavily animated and they've got vast teams of animators. When you see the end credits they're like looking at the Manhattan phonebook. They're working away on creating very lifelike movement, but for the most part these are trained animators and some of the same people actually cross over between doing a *Star Wars*-type movie and a *Finding Nemo*-type movie. You'll find people using similar skills to very different ends. Not too long ago I looked at *Robocop* again. *Robocop and Pee-wee's Big Adventure* were the two films that came out in the mid-eighties that signaled a rebirth of stop motion. *Robocop* had quite a bit and *Pee Wee's Big Adventure* had a bit. There were things that really stood out, and in *Robocop* we were seeing something explored in stop motion that we hadn't really seen in a long time. But I looked at it again and even though I've seen so many of these technological transitions, I realized stop motion can't hold a candle to CG in terms of representing reality. It's not as good a tool for that. So I was really happy to see that in the late eighties and the early nineties, there were a lot of short films coming out with stop motion that were really representing stylistically where you could go with it. Films like *The Sandman*, the work of Aardman Studios, films like *Balance.* Most of it was going on in Europe, not so much here in the U.S. But there were the films that were really defining the language of stop motion and less successful were those films that were trying to simulate reality.

$\rightarrow$

Wellins: How does the story influence the art director?

Harrod: The funny thing is working in animation, I haven't been involved in too many projects that are serious dramatic representations. For the most part it's been fairly lighthearted. And what's interesting about that is when you decide to "go dark" or "go gothic" or something like that it's generally meant as a sort of parody. I love the opportunity to actually parody serious cinema because so often serious cinema is using a lot of design and lighting conventions that are really kind of hackneyed, and animation is a great place to point out how hackneyed they really are. We got to do that a lot on *The PJs*. We pushed the drama until it became completely absurd, and in the design sense when you did something, a scene in the sewer that in a serious film would have been trying to elicit a sense of creepiness and dread, in an animated production you're really pointing out how artificial those emotions really are in a film. With regard to story, more often than not it really depends on where the story is coming from. In *The PJs*, when I was designing that, we had the first couple of scripts and I looked at it and I felt that this really wanted to be a somewhat realistic representation of the ghetto. It did not want to be a heavily cartoonified, softened, or friendly ghetto. It needed to have all the dangers and the broken-plate glass and the trash and the rust and all of those textures, but at the same time it didn't really want to be *Alphabet City*. You didn't want to be too aware of the spent condoms and the hypodermic needles on the ground and that sort of thing all the time. That was going to just really turn people away. There was one short film that had been made, *A Junkie's Christmas*, the William Burroughs's poem that had taken place in the ghetto and it was really dark and creepy and very effective for what it wanted to get across, but not funny.

To me, environment needs to be another character. For instance, one thing that I always present to my students when I'm teaching art direction is design a set with no characters in it that tells a story. You can have objects. Say you've got a room. Maybe the room has a wheelchair in the corner and slowly as you start to add things to this room, they're just objects, they're just bits of decor. Even a stain on the ceiling tells a story. I think the most frustrating jobs for me are the ones where I'm essentially asked to treat the sets purely as backgrounds, that they're going to be some kind of out of focus blur that suggests maybe some kind of a space behind the characters. And that's the kind of confounding thing where I say, "No, I want the set to be a character and to provide as much to the story as the actors." Not that the audience, the viewer, is ever going to be aware of that. It all works subliminally for them. Certainly, you can go way too far where the set is giving way too much information and that's certainly something you want to avoid—where your characters are competing with the environment. Many first-time filmmakers have made that mistake, of building an elaborate environment for their action to take place in and then proceed to film the scene, and two things can happen. One is the set is somehow competing with the character and the viewer ends up not being able to make any sense of it because too much is going on. Or the character blends in a little too much [and] doesn't actually stand out. I've seen a lot of first-time films where the character ends up kind of dissolving into the set. Oftentimes you're actually not able to differentiate between the two. You're going to have a very hard time following a story.

→

Wellins: *A lot of things happen in CG that would not be allowed in any other kind of animation. If they open a scene and it happens to have default light and they say, "Oh, the ambient light is set so here we go," whereas a cell animator has to compose everything in the shot.*

Harrod: The thing that frustrates me the most with CG is that they can place the camera anywhere, so they do. Even in pretty well-made films like [*The*] *Lord of the Rings* they say, "We can fly the camera along here and swing it around and go down this chute and go between the legs of that guy and..." Just because you can do that doesn't mean you should, and I look at that sort of thing and to me it's pointing to the CG-ness of it. What impresses me is when computer animation is used to replicate that which you could potentially film with a camera. A good example is the film *The Perfect Storm,* where there are several shots of this boat set on a CG ocean, but the position of the camera is locked maybe about 10 feet away from the deck of the boat in a shot that you would never be able to get out on the sea. I thought it was a huge mistake in that film to constantly do the shots that you could never ever get if you had the most elaborate rig out on the ocean. What you want to do in that kind of realistic special effects is to try to get the idea across that if you suggest that there's a camera crew battling to get this really difficult shot in these high seas, then I'm going to believe the action in front of the camera too, but I didn't believe any of it because it was all so artificial. It's something that comes out of CG culture. One of the seminal pieces of environmental CG work, going back to *The Wrath of Kahn,* when the device, known as the Genesis effect, took over this entire planet. It was where you had a camera that was orbiting around this planet and then in concentric circles it was getting closer to the surface of it. Everyone was just so wowed by it, we all were, and it became integrated into the culture of CG, but the fact is it tends to distance you from what you're looking at.

Wellins: *On the other hand, there are the shots that are so shaky and so crazy I can't tell what's going on. In some scenes, locked off works best, where you can see the whole thing happening. It's great.*

Harrod: That's an editorial decision, and I would like to see editors brought back into the process of filmmaking. Not that they're not there, but the modern trend is to go for as much quick cutting as possible. People are just terrified of lingering on a shot for a while. You have to go to indie cinema to see a shot that's 30 seconds long. I really welcome it, and actually the more the merrier. In Gus Van Sant's film *Gerry,* there's this shot that's 10 minutes long of one thing and there were people who were getting up and fleeing the theater, because it was so terrifying to their sense of what cinema is supposed to be, and I was sorry when the shot was over.

Wellins: *I'm a long-shot guy. Long shots pull you in and say, "You look. You figure out what's going on. I'm not going to give you a close-up. You have to use your brain."*

Harrod: There's a really interesting experimental filmmaker named James Benning. In the sixties, Andy Warhol did *Empire,* which is a single shot of the Empire State Building for 24 hours, and nothing happens except lights go on and off and a plane flies in the background—that's going a little far. I don't know anyone who actually sat through the whole thing. But sort of born from that were a lot of experimental filmmakers and James Benning was one I particularly liked. It's

→

amazing: after looking at a single one of his shots for maybe five minutes you start to see details. And again it's the whole idea of a story. The little details here and there are actually starting to tell you something of a story, and I would love to see people's minds being exercised in that way. It's like the child just ripping through all their presents on Christmas morning as opposed to sort of unwrapping it, savoring the experience. I'm not saying it should all be that way, but I would love to see it explored a little bit more in mainstream entertainment. The movie *The Rock* and that horrible chase scene with the Humvee [is] one of the most appallingly stupid chase scenes I've ever seen. I think the greatest chase scene of all time is still the one in *Bullitt*. In *The Rock* what happens in several shots instead happens in one shot in *Bullitt*. The camera will follow a car going down the street, speeding down the hill, go around a corner, and then the camera will pan back and see the car pursuing it—it's better. I feel like it's really happening.

If you take the same thing and tell the story in 50 different shots over the same period of time, I don't know where I am. I don't know where anyone is in relation to anyone else and that's a key thing. To me the most important thing in visual storytelling is to know where you are and where the characters are in relationship to each other. So often the martial-arts films, action films, and especially the superhero films—they're one of the worst offenders. Half the time I don't know where I am or where the characters are in relationship to each other. I was very impressed by what [Quentin] Tarantino did in *Kill Bill: Volume 1,* because in the massive climactic battle scene at the end of the film, I was amazed that even though there was a lot of quick cutting, I knew exactly where I was in relationship to the characters. When one action started I saw it carried out, and it wasn't just trying to confuse me into thinking I was seeing action.

Wellins: *Any more CG considerations?*

Harrod: I've designed a little bit for CG. It becomes a little tougher to ensure a specific effect in CG, because there tends to be a lot more people involved and so many specialists. It's really different from stop motion where we say, "OK, we want there to be this layered atmosphere on this particular set, so we'll create these places where we'll stretch the muslin and create the illusion of diffuse lighting sources." My biggest frustration working in CG is whereas on the stop-motion set it's usually me, the director, and the DP [director of photography] sort of figuring out how to achieve all this stuff, in CG there can be a lot more people involved and oftentimes the danger is that we fall back on a lot of defaults. More and more I think that the most important thing in developing CG as a language in animation is to bring a lot of non-CG people into the mix. Classically trained painters and sculptors, people who are going to demand a lot of the medium, who are not going to settle for the idea that the machine just won't do that. These are the people who are going to say, "Why not? Let's figure out how we can make machine do this," as opposed to somebody who simply is satisfied with the limitations of the software. And I do think that the best work in CG is coming from that. John Lasseter is a classically trained animator. He learned from the pioneer Disney animators about composition and certainly how all those things relate to story. Subsequently his work becomes very watchable because the technology is so transparent, and the work that does not hold up very well is that which is shackled or hobbled by technology.

CINEMATOGRAPHY

C inematography encompasses all the people and technical aspects of shooting a film from technical camera and lighting decisions to selecting lenses, angles, and distances. In live-action filmmaking the director of photography is generally responsible for these technical aspects, and he bases his decisions on cues from the cinematographer and director. The cinematographer is responsible for helping to tell the story by selecting the right angles, symbols, tgextures, movement, and visuals. The cinematographer films the scripts and creates ways to show descriptions that the audience would never read, such as "it was a dark and gloomy night." There are an infinite number of ways to show a dark and stormy night and set the tone for that scene, but it's up to the cinematographer to determine the best way to bring the idea to the screen.

In digital animation, the cinematographer and the director of photography's job are often split between the storyboard artist and the technical director. The storyboard artist has the responsibilities of the cinematographer and the technical director takes over the tasks of the director of photography. This varies from production to production, however, and in small productions, the technical director does everyting but the animation. For larger productions, the technical director might actually become a technical supervisor, because lighting, surfacing, rendering, texturing are often broken off into separate departments or people.

Regardless of whether the production is live-action or animation, the desire to discover new ideas and techniques continues and by studying the vast history of cinematography, filmmakers can find new tools for telling their stories. One excellent resource is Shadows and Light documentary that illustrates the great history of work and fundamental ideas of the true pioneers of cinematography.

PHOTOGRAPHY

For thousands of years, artists spent their lives studying and perfecting compositions. Greeks and early civilizations sought perfection in compositions of symmetry and balance that were massive in scale and planned out to be mathematically accurate. Eventually artists slowly began to create new compositions, but it was photograph that was truly revolutionary: its snapshot effect changed artistic composition forever.

The portable camera with reasonably fast shutters was taken out of the structured, posed studio to grab time and freeze motion indiscriminately. There was still proper and geometrical composition, but with the prevalence of the camera everyone was able to take pictures—even people who knew nothing of artistic composition. The indiscriminate way cameras with a simple click recorded everything they saw in what was considered art. Previously, art was something an artist created, but now anyone could take a picture that recorded a beautiful expression or scene and others could view it as art. Not only did photography change art, but in an equally important respect it changed the way everyday people viewed imagery as art.

Being able to capture and freeze a moment in time had an enormous effect on the viewing public's perception of pleasing visual imagery. Newspapers, books, and magazines now featured dramatic news images, average people, fantastic images of other lands, great beauty, and great tragedy. The subject matter alone made photography a legitimate and powerful art form and form of expression. Professor Ira Latour, art historian, photographer, and student of Ansel Adams, explains that the photograph's ability to freeze any random moment in time began to influence other art forms and quickly took hold. For example, photographs most likely influenced the French painter Degas to paint images of people walking out of the frame.

In Figure 6.1, a photograph taken in Italy in 1953 of a family on their way to a funeral illustrates the departure from classical painting composition when subjects had to pose and hold still. There is energy and motion in this complex composition: feet are blurred as they move through a step and body postures illustrate forward motion on not casually walking, but moving rather quickly. All of these elements are pleasing to the eye. The elements that combine to create the image draw the eye through the picture and a "happenstance" shot uses empty space to perhaps eerily hint at

FIGURE 6.1   A photograph illustrates a captured moment and frozen motion. © Ira Latour. Reprinted with permission.

a missing family member in the photograph. The composition beyond the family has another level of complexity with a man on the street. The man, who also seems to be in motion and is aware of the photo being taken, sends some of the voyeuristic qualities out of the photograph and back to the viewer, almost as if the viewer is also being watched. Photos of this complexity that aren't staged are difficult to capture. It's only by the sheer number of photos they take that master photographers can capture such powerful compositions. There is nothing wrong with staging a scene like the family going to the funeral. In fact, that is the world of a director, cinematographer, and a director of photography: to create dynamic and often complex compositions that have the illusion of happenstance or the reality of a captured moment.

Photography is the big brother of cinematography, and in stop motion there's very little difference between the two. Stop motion is the process of taking stills one frame at a time and flipping the pictures together. Digital filmmaking and CG are one step removed from the traditional analog process, but many aspects are similar or identical. CG cameras still use lenses, exposures, and f-stops with their virtual cameras. It's no coincidence that CG cameras in software function almost identically to cameras that are 100 years old. The convention of f-stops, exposure times, and shutter angles are all based on years of serious scientific study, and they are the proven system and controling worldwide standards for lenses and exposure settings. The f-stop, which is a photography standard for all lenses, was created so that photographs could consistently calibrate the amount of light that passes through a lens with a specific-sized diaphragm or aperture and lens size. Similarly, lens sizes and shapes are also identically treated in a virtual camera, so that there is a consistency of rules to provide users familiar with photography with a benchmark of control. Animation and filmmaking, whether analog or CG, all rely on physics and the rules established and discovered by photography, almost without exception. Naturally, CG has the ability to bend and stretch the rules of light and lenses, but its foundations are photographic. A true cinematographer is on a basic level the consummate photographer, by virtue of using a system to gather light and record it in a specific way with a compelling composition.

Black and White

Early photography used many processes, and for most of its early life photography was only able to capture black and white. Films and prints were often tinted or hand painted with dyes to mimic color, but it wasn't until much later that reliable color film became available. Still black and white is alive and well and exists in many forms. Black-and-white photography is more economical for newspapers and printed material with many pictures that do not want the added cost of printing full color on every page. However, whether the decision to use black and white is determined by money or aesthetics, a black-and-white image has its own sense of reality.

Very few mainstream modern films are ever made in black and white. General viewing audiences tend to not watch black and white, as evidenced by the trend to colorize classic black-and-white films. However, black and white has its own feel whether in film or still, and perhaps it's because once real-world lighting gets dim or dark, the cones in the human eye that perceive color stop working. The color cones aren't as sensitive to light as the rods, which pick up light and dark, so in dim lighting humans actually see in levels of reduced color nearing black and white. Because of this black and white is uniquely in that it allows the viewer to concentrate on form and composition and light and shade, and not be distracted by color. Perhaps it's that connection to night that makes black and white excede a mood of somberness. But like music, it's not for everyone, or most people as far as film and animation go. Still black and white is frequently used for effect in a flashback, a dream sequence, or a scene that stylistically wants to set itself apart from normal color.

For live filmmakers, the video revolutions started when a video camera could be added to the eyepiece of a movie camera and record the take. Most professional motion-picture cameras have eyepieces that include a video tap that can record what the camera sees. Before video, only the cameraman got to see the exact take, because only one person at a time could actually look through the analog optical viewer. Using the video tap, once the video signal was recorded and saved, it could be simultaneously broadcast to everyone and now everyone on the crew could see what the camera sees. Everyone from the director to the special-effects people to even special-effects puppeteers controlling animatronics effects could now watch what the camera was filming; the video tap was a true tool in making film. Early on, a tiny unobtrusive video camera that fit onto the eyepiece of a movie camera had to be sensitive enough to expose on all the settings of any lens, so for a long time it had to do this in black and white.

Through the use of video, directors could remove the color from a scene and study the composition like a black-and-white photograph. Color video taps quickly came along, but directors now use black and white, simply on a switch, to often judge composition.

Negative Space

Negative space is not a new idea. To use empty spaces in compositions to balance out solid objects and shapes visually has attracted artists for a long time. It is a bold approach and sets its own tone when used in film and animation. CinemaScope™ and wide angles lend themselves to huge amounts of negative space, all to great effect. Unlike a painting, where nothing is painted, the space can truly be dead—a blank canvas. The viewer gets the idea that the image stops when the paint stops, but photography and film always record something. Stark empty walls begin to have weight, empty skies have weight, and even the blackness of night has a weight, so that the filmed or animated image doesn't ever have dead space like a half-painted canvas. The filmmaker needs to realize the visual weight and balance of negative space.

This is what makes a great cinematographer: someone who can use abstract relationships of objects and characters to compose pleasing, exciting, and unique visual relationships. Judging such composition isn't completely subjective and neither is every composition, although feelings, experience, and talent ultimately rule. However, the story, the scene, the flow, and the shot before and after the current shot all influence the cinematographer. The cinematographer also has to answer—and potentially leave the final decision on every detail—to the director.

Figure 6.2 is a photograph take by Ira Latour in 1955. He says that, "the negative space behind the woman has weight and can balance with the figure. It's not a composition that the classic painter Rafael would have painted, but it is a photographic type of composition and has just as much validity, in my view, as if you put the figure smack dab in the middle of the frame."

FIGURE 6.2   A photograph illustrates a dramatic use of negative space. © Ira Latour.
Reprinted with permission.

Audiences have become more sophisticated and more accepting of unusual compositions like this photo. The idea of negative space has evolved and has become such a universal idea that it's something framed dead-on tends to be viewed as flat and undynamic, unless being used for effect. Aesthetics often prevails over practicality. Showing what needs to be shown is the first order of business, but aesthetics is the next ruling factor when it comes to framing shots. There is, of course, a compositional balance and weight, because objects have real-world weight. For example, take a shot of an elephant; anyone watching knows it's an extremely heavy visual just by what it is. There is also a visual weight that is defined by color and its relationship to other colors; the busyness of surfaces or designs all have visual weight as well. For instance, dense patterns, complicated thick textures used visually against a white or light background can have the same "visual" weight as a shot of an elephant, allegorically speaking. Whether a cinematographer frames for weight and balance or frames a shot deliberately off balance, visual weight and balance are always factors on every shot.

The "rule of thirds," illustrated in Figure 6.3, is the idea that the viewing area is split up in thirds, both horizontally and vertically; it's more visually pleasing and easier to sort out for the viewer's eye if he works with the idea of being conscious of what the lines of thirds are. Rule of thirds is a valid starting point, but many factors contribute to the composition of a shot, so adhering to the ryule of thirds all the time can be too limiting.

FIGURE 6.3   The rule of thirds. The frame is cut three ways, both horizontally and vertically, with the intersections being the focus of attention.

DEPTH

The human brain actually seems to want to see depth. Even where there is no depth, it welcomes and creates illusions. Seeing shapes and images in clouds is an experience that almost anyone can identify with. Our brain's imagination and its recognition centers are always searching to make some sort of association with recognizable shapes, distances, and depths. Imagination is so strong that even when given a blank screen, blackness, or emptiness, it starts sending out images. In the dark, people see things—shapes in the branches or faces in the wallpaper—because they're excited or frightened. Other times, people with perfect vision don't see things right in front of their faces, because they have a mental image already in their head, blocking what they see. It's this recognition and acceptance of illusion that makes film and animation possible as well as illusions like weight, balance, depth, and distance.

Look at Figure 6.4. Even though there are no clues to where the character is in space, the brain generally wants to imagine it in some sort of space, because we exist in 3D space. Also, the simple fact that the character is standing implies that it has to be standing on something. So strong is the imagination that in order for a character appear like it's in a void, it almost needs to be in a floating pose, which still defines some space.

FIGURE 6.4   A 2D-drawn character in limbo.

The imagination is creating all the illusions of relationships, but in creating compositions, a director can help the illusion or confuse the illusion. This could create a confusing moment for the viewer and cause an emotional disconnect. In animation, it's important to break the lines; this also applies to live action, but is more crucial in animation because spatial cues do not automatically exist as they do in 3D (see Figures 6.5 and 6.6). In Chapter 14, "Character Animation," you'll learn that it's important to create clean outlines and poses. The same is true with objects, sets, and

FIGURE 6.5   An example of how a simple shadow under the character will tell spatially where the character is, and that there is a ground plane of some sort.

FIGURE 6.6   By adding a horizon line, the shot immediately tells the viewer that there is substantial space.

locations; if too many elements become stacked so that they are all lined up behind each other, it can become confusing spatially. Stacking happens frequently when things pass behind each other in motion. But if a composition creates too much stacking that doesn't change, it's visually confusing and potentially creates too much weight in one area.

So keep in mind that it's important for the character to cross the horizon line, especially if there's any chance of spatial confusion. This isn't just a cel issue either; this is very applicable to flash and even to simplified CG. When dealing with simplistic stylized scenes, it's imperative that the audience never gets confused spatially. If the character breaks these lines, then it becomes a clarifier and reinforces spatially where the character is.

Because of people's familiarity with things they've seen all their lives, in live-action productions it's a given that common sizes of people and objects and other recognizable relationships will be clear. However, in animation (CG, cel, or stop-motion), and with various forms of stylization, it isn't always clear. If a set is so minimal, the horizon might start to read as a simple line over the character's head, as in Figure 6.7. Sometimes shooting square or perpendicular to the camera, may have a stylistic necessity, meaning the animation is stylistically presented in a straight angle. However, a more dynamic angle might be an angle from one side or the other, so that the character moves at an angle. Stylistically, there are certain stories where a flat or 2D character is desired so that the character is flat on a flat surface. If that is the stylistic choice, then it has its own set of rules as well.

FIGURE 6.7   Is this line a horizon, or a line above the character's head? Breaking the horizon is crucial in animation, especially in stylized animation.

But be careful because a shadow showing that the character is flat, or other signs of "flatness", can read as extremely shallow depth. A "stiff," locked, or flat presentation can also be very effective, but it shouldn't be a stylistic or a default choice to not have the camera move simply because it's easier not to move it. More important, because of CG cameras, wild camera moves are far too prevalent and should be kept in line with the tone of a scene.

Aiming the camera and deciding on the shot, whether it's an extreme close-up or a long or wide shot, is extremely important. Above picking interesting angles with textured compositions, the choice of shot when a character is acting is crucial. From our experiences living with other people, we all have an innate sense of how close to get to another person, and all sorts of factors can be involved.

When recording a character's or actor's performance, using the proper distance from the character is important. First there are practical considerations. If the character is doing something or manipulating something and that movement is a key element, then the shot must be framed to show it. Comedies that rely on physical movement, such as full body expressions, need to have a wide angle of view. In fact, framing is so tied to perception and the proper distance that an audience can sense when there's too much activity out of frame. Having too much movement tells the audience they're missing something, expecting a cut or a pull to show what's going on off screen.

Consider a very simple shot: an old man tells a story but uses lots of big hand gestures. Close-ups are important on key moments of emotional connection, but the fact that he uses his hands so wildly requires cutting back wide to capture what is going on. Even though the audience realizes he just makes grand gestures, they still need to see the gestures. They need to see how the shadows are moving across his face, how his head moves, and how his shirt collar stretches around. The options are to either widen the shot or try to in this case stop the man from moving his hands so much as he speaks, if that's the appropriate tone.

For the audience, it's instinctual. If something is going on, the audience wants to see it. It could be a huge explosion or a twitch of the lip, but if it's significant, it needs to be seen. Whether it's framed tightly filling the entire view, or is subtly, mixed in with other elements, it is intended for the audience to discover or notice.

Let's say a couple has a huge verbal argument and comes to an impasse where they are no longer talking. They walk passed a fixed camera and go down a long busy street, and in the far distance, they eventually hold hands. There is no close-up of the hands or the exchange of eyes, but only a subtle gesture is shown. If the storytelling were done correctly, the audience would be focused on their backs as they walk away and find a pleasant and charming surprise in this subtle gesture. Because it's not broadcast on a grand scale, it leaves work for the viewers and draws them into the story even further. If the story is set up correctly, the audience will be invested in these characters, hoping that they reconcile and watching for any sign.

The prescribed idea of using and covering things in specific shots, such as wide shots, medium shots, and long shots, is a solid system for production. Covering scenes and shots a number of ways is a useful tool, and being able to stop and go and redo is key to dialing timings and performance. However, that is not so in animation; there is no such thing as getting coverage in animation, so animation requires much more planning. In CG, it is possible to reposition cameras and render scenes from different angles, but often so much is played or cheated toward the camera that multiple shots on a certain set need to be planned well in advance.

Evolving the idea of standards further is to use the performance, focus of the story, and the emotional connection of the characters to drive the positioning of the camera (see Figure 6.8). Certain pragmatic parameters will always apply, whether a story imperative or a physical element. Beyond that, the story and performance should be the true guide for shot and composition. Similarly, the director and editor have to be aware of the shots that go before and after a given shot; this is where a director and a cinematographer can develop a style or a structured way of adding another level of feeling to a film or animation.

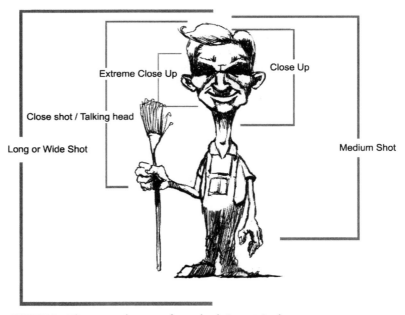

FIGURE 6.8 The general range of standard cinematic shots.

Sequences of shots can build energy or slow energy, and framing is an element that can reinforce that energy for each separate shot, while working in conjunction with similar shots. Extreme close-ups on a large screen are intimate and very intense by nature. The vast majority of extreme close-ups are about strong feelings, whether the close-up is a whisper, a tear in the corner of the eye, or simply the expression of a character contemplating something.

In cel animation, drawings are the language everyone speaks. In other forms of animation, drawings, doodles, and sketches are important for establishing great composition but aren't used to their full potential. The idea of three dimensions—the space all humans live in, move through, and exist in—can't be truly recorded in standard film and video. In fact, filming or rendering out from the CG three-dimensional world or the filmed live-action dimensional world ultimately converts everything to two dimensions.

This is because the depth that the animator can see in a 3D program, a stop-motion set, or full-sized set can't truly be recorded by standard film or television or video, with the exception of stereoscopic recording. Because of this illusion, directors have to always find and reinforce familiar scenes of depth, such as a wide vista. In this case, they may have to move things through the depth or move the camera. Digital animators, by virtue of the dimensionality of the software, are able to preview work from multiple angles. And animators, modelers, lighters, surfacers, and digital cinematographers have the luxury of running their scenes from angles other than the camera and using that information to see relationships in depth and space.

Any sense of depth that a viewer sees in standard film or television is as big of an illusion as the medium itself, but there are infinite clues that filmmakers and animators alike can use to recreate a sense of depth that will ring right to the viewer's eye. For example, consider that things in the distance moving away and upward get smaller. If the horizon is somewhere in the middle of the frame, then things below the horizon line will move down as they move forward and grow in size, and things taller than the horizon line will move up as they approach the camera. Depth of field will also reinforce the illusion of depth. This problem of no actual depth in standard film or television can also be used to the film-maker's or animator's benefit.

The simplest of these cheats is the shot where someone holds a small person in his hand. In reality, the small person is much farther back than he appears. The composing of the shot and the person with his hand out both seal the illusion that the small person is standing in the other person's hand. The hand is also tilted in a way that the contact point between the feet and the hand are naturally obscured. This effect isn't applicable to cel because everything is in 2D to begin with, but it does apply to live action and CG. In *Shards of Death*, (included on the CD-ROM

ON THE CD

under the file **Shards.mov**), and with all CG and stop-motion projects, it's important for the director to keep that flexibility in mind. For example, the desk was modeled in *Shards of Death* long before animation began, with all the items on it, including a blotter, glasses, pencils, pencil jar, phone, intercom, lamp, and stapler—all normal props. Similarly, there are set pieces like the file cabinets, potted plant, chairs, and other props that were also created dimensionally.

Like a live-action film, it would almost be derelict for the director to not consider where each item sits. Once the camera is up and being looked through or once the animation layout begins, then real composition can begin. In *Shards of Death*, once the green monster character started to act and move its arms and interact with the other character, moving the props from shot to shot to find visually dynamic positions for each became routine. Also, positions are chosen so that the props would be consistent throughout the film, not getting in the way or intersecting with the monster's gestures. If the props were to move slightly from shot to shot to accommodate the movement and avoid intersection as well as work with composition, then the movement is acceptable because it won't be noticeable.

In stop motion, like live action, item placement is crucial. However, other elements can become unwieldy or not worthwhile, adjusting for subtle composition finessing. In a live-action film or even in stop motion, it might be too expensive to completely move a window and its frame a few inches or feet so that the corner of the window is visible in a shot. Instead, it might be easier to move the desk, character, and file cabinets. If set up right, in CG everything is adjustable and items normally fixed in reality like a door frame, wall, window, or a whole room can be moved or nudged. In that respect, it's always important not to get preconceived ideas about rules in a world that actually shares very few rules with the real world.

When working on projects like commercials, it is common to have many quick and disparate shots. When compositing CG characters with live action, it is absolutely standard and often necessary to size the characters for almost each separate shot, in relation to other real people and filmed elements. Characters and their relation to other CG characters, as well as their relation to the camera angle, all influence how big or small a character should be. In fact, when CG is combined with live-action plates, it is rare that a character can stay the same size in several shots, simply because of the perception of where it is in space in relation to the environment around it.

So many factors can be brought into play. For example, if a background is bright, it tends to come forward, and darker, cooler colors tend to recede, causing characters or elements to look or feel bigger or smaller. This can work for or against the director or animator, but he must be aware of these relationships to control them to their advantage. Many early special effects exploited this inability to truly be able to judge size and distance in standard television or film. Filmmakers figured out that they could build miniature models, and if placed right, they could look full-sized. The problem was that if the camera moved, it instantly betrayed the illusion, but filmmakers also quickly figured out that the rules of perspective didn't discriminate on size; if a camera panned and the pan revolved around the nodal point of the lens, then the perspective stayed intact. The nodal point of the lens is the exact center of the lens. If the camera panned around this point via a special tripod or mount, it was possible for a pan to be done with a miniature and a full-sized background visually stuck together. This made it possible for special-effects modelers to create huge set extensions that were actually tiny models hanging close to the camera.

This has now all but been replaced by digital production, but still illustrates the power of manipulating depth, size, and position. Stop-motion animators have always made great use of forced perspective sets—sets that are built with perspective in them. The idea is that a deeper looking set is created without having to build a huge set. This is also used extensively in stage plays, because the audience primarily watches from one fixed angle, and a set can be distorted to create more perceived depth. Not only can forced perspective sets create the sense of depth of items disappearing off into the distance, but in a more subtle sense these sets create a dynamic feel. In the world of stop motion and miniatures, it helps to reinforce that the sets aren't small, but instead human-sized or any size.

Forced perspective can be built into computer models, or it can be created by rendering in layers: rendering a background with a wide lens, and then rendering characters or foreground elements with a standard lens. Forced perspective was covered in detail in Chapter 5, "Art Direction."

Using 2D Stylistically

Often the aim of animation is to go beyond the drawings or models so that artwork comes to life, but there is also a rich tradition of embracing the elements of drawing and art. Animation, and specifically drawn animation, such as cel and programs like Moho and Macromedia Flash, can be a stylized in a way that draws attention to being drawn or modeled. Its charm and appeal arise out of the unmoving and unwavering eye, as if the animator's pad had come to life, or it reads as a throwback to a simplified type of animation or a moving comic book. It's nothing about reality, but instead it is artwork that has come to life, and creates yet another form of story.

The sequence in Figure 6.9 could have plenty of cuts to feature all sorts of angles, but there is inherent value in letting animation be animation, letting the performance be the focus, and having the cinematography do little more than record the scene. As simple as the scene is, it still uses the horizon as a true horizon and utilizes the edges of the frame as well. The charm of the storyboard exists in the simplicity of the character: the

FIGURE 6.9 A storyboard for a short animation. It is s a straightforward, locked-off shot, and reads perfectly clear as a comic strip. © 2004 Colin Batty. Reprinted with permission.

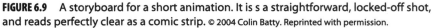

setup, the action, and the resolve. Deciding when to move and where to go is a stylistic choice. Some truly interesting ideas aren't feature length, and animation works at any length.

Figure 6.10 is shot at a standard angle. It's an acceptable shot, but the idea is to increase the pathos for this lonely child. All the audience knows is that the child is sad; she could be a spoiled child or could be crying because she got in trouble. Stylistically there is very little information. That revealing of information may be important to how the story unfolds, but it must be a conscious effort. Figure 6.11 is in thirds, a standard convention that is well tested. Thirds is a faithful dynamic but doesn't automatically mean that the shot is automatically dynamic simply because the rule of thirds has been applied. A more dynamic angle would help sell the mood of the scene. Figure 6.12 might be a better choice of angles to help sell the vulnerability of the child.

FIGURE 6.10   A lonely child stands alone on a street, but if shown too close up, the audience has no knowledge of how desperate the child is.

FIGURE 6.11   A composition that is basically in thirds, which is generally a acceptable frame, but not very dramatic.

FIGURE 6.12 A bird's-eye view that makes the child seem more alone and lost. With motion and a moving camera, all of the shots can be accomplished in a single moving shot that starts high and then moves down to an extreme close-up.

If the girl is directly in the middle, it can be flat; the focus is a bit too close on her. If the shot is wider, and there is negative space, it starts to suggest the bleakness of the scene—there are no adults around. Her clothes are now apparent and they show that she isn't all right. Still the shot is fairly standard. Perhaps a better angle is an up-angle view, making the walls more foreboding. The result would be dynamic perspective that is up and down instead of side to side. The frame is symbolic; she's smaller and the camera is up, looking down. The angle diminishes the girl, which makes her seem that much more vulnerable. It's a stylistic choice if the audience is supposed to feel sorry for the girl immediately or not. By showing her predicament, there is instant sympathy, which may be essential to the story.

Unlike photography, film and animation composition is often in flux. This is compounded when the camera is moving or elements, people, vehicles, or objects also move, creating complex compositions and infinite possibilities. There are many possible ways to shoot or animate something, and many of them are mundane and average. As with all the other elements, the story should dictate the framework of the composition and factor in the characters, action, mood, and rules of physics; determining whether they're real-world physics or animation physics will help decide the composition.

The Lester Show is a short film by filmmaker Allan Steele. The film was created in Maya®, Photoshop, and Corel Painter®. Steele is creating a truly unique world, and as a painter he incorporates his painterly style to every scene. The story is bizarre: Lester lives in a broken down car, the world around him is grimy and dirty, and yet he is delighted with life and is in a fantasy world where everything seems great. The composition is always unusual because the story is so strange. The camera is often dutched and frequently finds extreme angles, but the shots still have a solidness to them so that the animation is readable as shown in Figure 6.13.

FIGURE 6.13   A shot from a strange film (*The Lester Show*) that warrants strange compositions (see Color Plate 8). © 2004 Allan Steele. Reprinted with permission.

ON THE CD

In *Grime Shoed Diaries,* the short film on the CD-ROM (**Grime.mov**), the opening scene starts several stories up in a massive city. Immediately, the shot drops down through the city, a train passes, and the shot then pushes into a diner and dissolves inside. This cinematic choice establishes a large city and then introduces the main character.

Because film and animations are tied to classic photography and classical art, there are countless books on composition, the golden ratio, staging, and composing. All this information is valuable, even to just survey visually. Animation is as always unique for several reasons in that an animation camera, at least in cel and CG, is unlimited to where the camera can be placed and where it can go. The flexibility of an animation camera shouldn't be misused simply because it can find strange locations and movement, however, the movement should be forever tied to the storytelling, pacing, and tone.

FOREGROUND AND BACKGROUND ELEMENTS

A person runs desperately through the woods, while the camera runs or dollies alongside the person. The brain expects to see trees and bushes zipping by between the camera and the runner; if trees aren't there it seems like the person is running down a cleared path. An extreme example would be a scene in a World War II submarine as in the German film *DasBoot*. A submarine movie is a curious genre because the set is a given, but the actors have to sell the idea that they are in an underwater vessel. Usually there's no window to see out of, so the actors always look to the surface as they listen for the enemy depth charges. They could easily look down, and hear the same thing, but they're selling the idea that an enemy ship is above and they are in a steel drum under crushing depths of water. Similarly, selling the claustrophobic idea of the submarine should also be in the director's and cinematographer's mind, because the danger and the fear of being underwater is a great source of intensity and suspense. Because a submarine is basically a tube packed with pipes and valves, low ceilings, and thick bulkheads, the dominant feeling of claustrophobia needs to be constantly shown.

ON THE CD

The QuickTime movie on the CD-ROM (**Sub_interior.mov**) is a cel-animated animation on a digital multiplane shot, using foreground and background elements that move to create depth. In the shot, images and sequences are mapped onto polygons and physically separated in depth in a 3D space; this happens to be set up in LightWave 3D®. The same could have been created completely in 3D with all 3D models, but this is stylized with drawn animation elements, making use of the 3D program (see Figure 6.14).

FIGURE 6.14   A frame from 2D/3D animation of a claustrophobic interior of a submarine, punctuated by pipes and machinery crowding into the frame.

Foreground information helps create the mood, so that the viewer is watching or peeking in on the scene. It's a powerful tool, however, and if the camera angle becomes erratic or handheld, then it becomes familiar horror-movie territory. Handheld shots from behind trees and cars and up in the rafters have a powerful effect. The audience gets the feeling that they are now seeing a character's point of view, a handheld view. This view, which is almost peeking from behind something or under something, is almost locked into the collective expectations of the viewers. It's simply the evolution of the viewers that has dictated that a handheld shot behind foreground objects (or if the camera is "sneaking" around) always feels like the character's point of view. If it's not the character's point of view, then it's a shot out of place, making handheld a complex element in composition and staging that can have two very different feelings and be virtually the same sort of shot.

Playing toward the camera in cel animation is a given—the scenes are staged with the camera in mind. When designing or actively drawing what is going to be seen by the camera, a skilled animator, director, or layout artist would consider the angles of all the characters and important objects or items in the scene. Because it started on paper, usually some amount of thought has been put into the composition. Items are bent, twisted, and cheated toward the virtual camera, which not only creates the best composition for the shot, but also makes exact placements of items, set pieces, and characters. Once a camera becomes involved, whether an analog camera or a camera in software, things are overlooked that wouldn't get past traditional animators' designs. Often because of their physical properties and their perceived position in reality, objects wind up in a specific place, regardless of how they appear in the camera. In *Shards of Death*, the desk lamp sits on the corner of the desk, where it would be in the real world. When the shots feature the green monster, it became useful to float the lamp off the desk and cheat it toward the camera so that it worked better in the composition of the shot. Although the lamp is floating off the desk, it isn't visible in the shot. The cheat idea is that a digital director, like a skilled drawn animator or layout artist, can manipulate any and all objects to enhance the shot that is being recorded by the camera.

PHYSICAL STAGING

Stage plays play to both an audience and a theater. In stage plays, the most personal secrets are spoken so loud that they're heard at the back of the room. Whispering is impossible without microphones, and everything is done with large gestures so that everyone gets the same visual message. If someone has a long speech or sings a solo, he often moves downstage toward the audience, while secondary characters find a graceful way to move into positions and hold them.

Staging in plays still has relevant rules to staging characters, places, and props, because the camera is the eye of the audience and needs to be controlled at that level. Whether with light, composition, or the simple act of having the focused character stand very close to the camera, the idea is to focus the audience's attention on the important action in the scene, which is often an actor, real or digital. Staging can be done in thirds, with compositions that mimic classic painting masters, while other directors rely more on the mundane or abstract compositions to create unique feelings. Focus of attention can be aimed in countless ways. If a close-up is one way to have an actor emote a line, then a person walking 100 yards away with a telephoto lens can have as much or more impact as a close-up, depending on the story.

In the short film *107.6 Degrees* (on the CD-ROM, filename **1076_ degrees.mov** and Figure 6.15), the entire motivation for the film was staying out of the searing sun. The one and only tree in the film became an extremely important object and almost became a character itself in this scenario. In a sense, the tree plays the straight man or the pile of gold miners would fight over. Shade is the main thing that the tree offers to the scene. It needs to be framed to show that it has a large overhanging branch that provides the shade that starts the ruckus among the characters.

Directors are always looking for an abstract and yet interesting composition to define a tone when shooting a shot, but basic ideas always work: dark areas tend to disappear and the eye always goes to light areas, focusing on people and their faces. Figure 6.16 also has a sense of vignette. It is a scene where the edges are rounded in to focus the eye on the characters.

FIGURE 6.15   The tree creates the shade and motivates all the other characters to seek it. In a scene like this, the tree goes beyond being a prop and is central to story. It almost plays a character as the straight man and needs to be framed that way. © 2004 Amila and Patrik Puhala. Reprinted with permission.

FIGURE 6.16   The background character is speaking, but the foreground character is thinking about what to do next, so the audience is focused on how he's thinking about solving the problem. Even though the background character is speaking, speaking can be secondary to another action. © 2004 Gesine Krätzner. Reprinted with permission.

Rat Trap, a short animated tale from Gesine Krätzner, features two unusual and well-meaning characters who have a problem with a large friendly rat. As shown in Figure 6.17, after capturing the rat, the characters take the rat through a dense and strange jungle that defines the world where the story takes place. The composition serves the mechanical purpose of getting the characters from one point to the next. It also goes much further in creating depth, space, and atmosphere, all with dynamic and usual color and a vivid use of light and shade.

FIGURE 6.17   *Rat Trap* makes use of multiple levels of composition, with the angle looking through the trees and mist. This creates a rich and dense atmosphere (see Color Plate 9). © 2004 Gesine Krätzner. Reprinted with permission.

The world in which Rat *Trap* takes place is strange and although there are similar items, everything is its own world, with very few straight edges or sharp curves and a unique palette of color. As illustrated in Figure 6.18, by design it's familiar enough for a viewer to not have to figure out it's a house and recognize a familiar scene, but it's also different enough to tell the viewer that this is not the real world; it is a fanciful world. Even with the areas of bright color, the viewer's eyes are lead to the floor, the composition is a low angle favoring the rat, and the floor is relatively clear and well lit so that the eye is drawn down. With a combination of simple yet unusual sets and simplified colors, a very strange and unique design is still instantly recognizable and readable, but moreover is also visually pleasing and enjoyable to watch. CG 3D software knows all the rules of perspective perfectly, and that precise repeating of real-world perspective allows for all the big-money special-effects shots and set extensions that are seamless. However, it's also a very telling visual, and animators working in CG often fight the rigid real-world perspective with objects, sets, and worlds that go against the rigid and visual rules of physics and perspective.

FIGURE 6.18   The design is unique but still familiar, and composition still focuses on the action. © 2004 Gesine Krätzner. Reprinted with permission.

Depth of Field

Some of the first and most beautiful examples of forced depth of field are in the classic Disney films. Using a multiplane camera two stories tall, the Disney animators took advantage of the properties of the lens to create animations that had backgrounds and foreground elements that were in soft focus.

The advantage of animation is that depth of field can be easier to pull off than with a practical camera or filters. But depth of field is a solid tool that can also be used very subtlety and still be very powerful. In animation, depth of field is often an extra production step, but it's usually well worth it when it's tied to composition. For example, take a scientist in a laboratory. There are myriad interesting things in a laboratory; the feeling of a lab is lots of clutter, and there are strange objects that crowd the scene. Specific elements, whether in focus or not, can help to create a visual atmosphere. More clues draw the viewer in and suggest a scene beyond what the viewer is seeing.

Light and Dark

Light, darkness, and everything in between are where visuals exist, and filmmakers and animators, depending on the story, need to use the whole spectrum of light. In staging, a person can walk out of the shadows to be revealed and to feature what they're saying. Similarly, someone can be seen, perhaps silhouetted in the shadows, and remain there, obviously trying to keep their identity concealed. For more dramatic effect, a person can be half lit in darkness or shadow or have a swatch of light that defines his eyes or mouth, while the rest of his face stays in relative shadow.

Moving in and out of light is an important tool in the cinematographer's toolbox. Metaphorically, light can represent many things. In vampire movies, light represents goodness that destroys vampires. Light can also be a symbol of knowledge. On the other hand, darkness represents impending doom, friction, evil, or confusion.

Using light to go beyond lighting to express ideas, metaphors, and symbolism is yet another level that filmmakers can weave into a story. In Figure 6.19, the character devises a solution. The composition is enhanced by light as if the idea were illuminated, radiating from behind the character like a halo of a new great idea, just as the character speaks the lines. Outside, beyond the scene, is the strange flora of this world, thick with atmosphere. The distance goes out of focus and volumetric lighting adds to the sense of depth and texture. The world of *Rat Trap* is fanciful and every decision reflects that idea.

FIGURE 6.19   Another shot from *Rat Trap* where the character has a solution and the light around his head is allegorical for discovering a fix to his problem (see Color Plate 10). © 2004 Gesine Krätzner. Reprinted with permission.

CINEMATIC PROPS

Important props that help tell a story need to be seen and recognized. Objects that are not directly part of the story are dealt with as quickly and simply as possible. For example, a romantic scene takes place on a train, where a couple sips champagne; the champagne is taken from the chiller and glasses are filled, but showing the champagne label would be distracting and take away from the scene's romantic feeling. Similarly, showing close-ups of the champagne in the ice bucket and how much champagne is left are not necessary, unless they're integral to the plot. The same goes for visual staging. Unless going for an abstract composition, the focus of performance is usually about the character and the face. Whether or not a director considers it, people are always watching other people.

Staging and using sets and props and texture to reinforce that idea results in appealing images like the ones in Figure 6.18. If an element becomes more than an enhancer and is integral, then it almost becomes its own character. Having a moving camera, whether in 3D or in reality, adds to the ability to create complex and interesting staging and blocking scenarios. However, like drawn animation, sloppy inbetween frames make a lackluster animation, and unplanned moves can be clumsy, confusing, and dull. Filmmakers and especially animators have the ability to compose visual staging that is frame perfect, and need to compose their shots in 3D so that the movement is enforcing and enhancing the story by including visual texture, such as filming behind flasks and beakers in the laboratory or a having a shot crowded with pipes and tubes in a submarine. A harrowing scene of a person hanging off a cliff isn't harrowing if the audience cannot see how far the fall is.

In a play when one person speaks, the others hold still, and stage actors help direct the audience's attention to whomever is furthering the story at that point. The same is true in animation. If one character is speaking, the other's movement is minimal, unless distraction is the aim of the shot. However, when it comes to movement that is telling or furthering the story, clarity is usually the key. Confusion can be the goal, such as in Peter Bogdanovich's screwball comedy *What's Up, Doc?*, a loose remake of *Bringing Up Baby*. In *What's Up, Doc?*, four identical travel bags, one with top secret government documents, one with normal clothes, one with priceless jewelry, and one with geological specimens, all wind up at the center of a madcap slapstick comedy, and the deliberate confusion is at the core. By and large, however, confusion is rarely desired, and movements and staging should be planned for clarity and conciseness.

Another useful trait of all cameras, whether real or CG, is not only what the cameras see, but also what they don't see and what can be hidden out of frame. What is done in *Shards of Death* with repositioning the desk lamp so it fits the composition holds true to live action. A simple example would be a real-world setup of filming a scene in the woods. The director and the director of photography (DP) decide on a perfect angle: a mountain is visible in the distance and a stream is the midground. The scene could still use more color, so the set decorator alters Mother Nature and brings in potted trees that are placed in the foreground.

The "cheat" toward the camera is a cheat because from any other angle, it doesn't look right, but the camera only sees what it sees. Often when filming a film, a director will tell two actors who are talking to each other to get closer so they fit in the frame. In reality, they could be uncomfortably close, closer than two people who aren't romantically involved would get, but to the camera it doesn't read that way. In fact, it often looks fine. Two actors face off and one happens to be so short, so the director has the short actor stand on a box—another cheat. Turning a character or an actor's body more toward camera and turning his head away might feel awkward, but can read as dynamic in the camera, depending on the shot.

Cinematographers also compose shots so that objects on a wall that are behind an actor's face aren't well lit or are simple and not distracting, unless done for effect. Cinematographers also have to be sensitive to how actors and characters turn, enter, and exit to either link up with similar scenes or to avoid too much time on a character without seeing the character's face. In *The Lord of the Rings*, director Peter Jackson always had the characters Frodo and Sam going from left to right, so that it always felt like the land of Mordor was to the right of the viewer and home was always to the left.

SHOTS AND LENSES

It is a strange dichotomy that the more sophisticated audiences become, the less sophisticated the technology can become. Examples include handheld shots, or shots filmed with available light or low-resolution equipment. A recent example would be *The Blair Witch Project* or *28 Days Later,* which was shot on a Mini DV. Still, certain rules apply. When telling a visual story where people do subtle things, in order to clearly show events, the camera must hold still long enough to see them.

Most directors mix up a variety of shots, while still obeying the rules, such as staying on the eye line or getting master shots and close-ups. This is what is expected and it also feels right, but the director is always pulled to the creative side, wondering if a more unusual shot will create more of an effect. It's a fine line, but when creativity starts to be noticed, then it may have gone too far.

Master director Alfred Hitchcock in *Dial M for Murder* plays a guessing game with keys that open an apartment. The keys are often hidden in hands, under a carpet, under a saucer, or on a table—important clues that tell the story of how the main character is attempting murder. To see the keys, to keep up with which one is which and who put which key where, the shots have to be extremely close, especially when someone is trying to conceal the key. In shots where someone is going to hide a key or move about the apartment, the shots are long and wide. If the audience ever becomes confused, then there are huge problems with the story being a mystery. Of course Hitchcock tells it masterfully and the audience takes away a feeling of being one step ahead of the would-be criminal, without even noticing the visual direction. As the story is created, the images seem so logical that the audience knows no difference; everything plays out exactly: surprise, suspense, all of it built, but never having that feeling.

Handheld rapid-fire cutting could not tell the story, show the subtle clues, and build tension and suspense any better than Hitchcock laid out. Less is more and when it comes to clarity. Locked-off shots obviously have a solidifying effect and work well with subtle human movements, and comedy is often subtle. Locked-off shots have a calming effect and hearken back to a stage play: they're grounding. Locked-off shots are often used to focus on something going on. Since there is no movement, the background can be dismissed and the action focused on, or elements and compositions can sort of saturate the viewer's sense of visual composition as the action progresses.

The late Stanley Kubrick was the master of smooth incredibly long shots, whether locked off or moving on a dolly or Steadicam. Kubrick's film *Full Metal Jacket* is a clear example of his technique as well as how it ties to the reality he is trying to create. In the film, the camera often runs for several minutes without editing. In incredibly long shots, where a modern action movie might encompass hundreds of short shots, Kubrick to great effect chooses one single shot. There is arguably a reality that goes with Kubrick's dolly shoots following Marines through boot camp and into the Vietnam War; the shots that don't cut are like the unflinching eye, and the perspective has no omnipresence, so that the viewers feel like they are the infantrymen as the shot moves through a blown-apart city in Vietnam.

In one long Steadicam shot that pushes forward, the actors' actions work in perfect synchronization with the movement of the shot. A soldier rushes up to a pile of cover and takes an offensive position. The camera continues forward at a continuous rate and the next solider runs ahead, finds cover, and stops as both soldiers systematically leapfrog forward, aware of enemy fire at any moment. The movement feels real, and to the viewer, the feeling of running alongside the Marines is palpable. Cutting away to their boots, feet, or faces might work, but the effect that Kubrick creates definitely works just as it is. Creating these shots, without having the luxury to cut to other shots, means massive preparation and rehearsal and often involves shooting and reshooting the shots until the visual timing is perfect.

Kubrick reverts to the all-important rules of cinematography when a normal dialogue scene takes place. He was truly a master of incorporating the traditional rules of film while creating his own rules where they would perfectly fit. The director also avoids using a wide-angle lens and instead keeps all his shots within a simple range. In *Full Metal Jacket*, there are very few texture shots or shots of visual imagery that aren't part of the story. There are no telephoto shots as helicopters fly in front of a setting sun, and there's no glorifying or trying to show images of beauty that don't include the soldiers that the story is following.

Filmmaker Terry Gilliam is an avid fan of the extremely wide-angle lens that distorts images and bends and warps lines for the feel that it gives. With a wide lens, the warping gives a disjointed and often claustrophobic effect when pushed into a tight scene or an actor's face. It's a feeling and a style, and it's the type of underlying feeling Gilliam likes to use. Not so for Kubrick. In *Full Metal Jacket*, the shots stay very close to the range of what the human eye sees normally to continually enhance the feeling that the audience is standing right next to the drill instructor as he berates the recruits. From a wide fish-eyed lens to a dramatic telephoto zoom into a shimmering sunrise, it's all stylistic. Instead of simply grabbing the lens and shots and arbitrarily fitting them together, a valuable lesson is learned from all accomplished filmmakers who use the lens as a tool for the story, mood, and tone.

Wide lenses weren't considered that viable for a standard narrative film because a wide lens, depending on its width, creates considerable distortion on the horizon or any straight lines. The distortion increases as the line gets closer and closer to the edge of the viewable area of the lens. Now wide lenses, even extremely wide lenses, are used regularly, regardless of the distortion. In live-action, stop-motion, and CG films, sets are often built to camera for obvious reasons. However, if a wider lens is used in any of these media, the sets become much smaller in frame and edges become visible. In stop motion this is most critical, because generally there is no real-world sky; instead, there is a studio ceiling with light rigs and other general building fittings. If a wide lens is considered, then the distortion it creates must be evaluated before committing to its use.

In stop motion, a wide lens on a small character can create an access problem for the stop-motion animator. If the lens is too close to the subject, it's possible to create a situation where the animator can't comfortably use his hands or tools to make character adjustments without bumping the camera. Access for stop-motion animators is a serious issue, because they are required to reach in and adjust things hundreds, if not thousands, of times. Using a wide lens extremely close on a stop-motion character can require the use of a motion-control system that can index the shot. Indexing allows the frame to be photographed or recorded. Then the animator triggers a sequence that will move the camera out of the animator's way, so he can comfortably make the necessary motion changes to the character. Once the animator is finished with the moves, the camera is then indexed and returns to the exact next spot to photograph the character. Indexing requires a lot of patience and a motion control that is extremely accurate to be able to return again and again to the same point in the sequence and have it be exactly in the right position. More time is used up in this process, extending the time it takes to animate the shot. Large motion-control rigs often vibrate and jiggle when they move, and the motion-control operator often has to program in a few seconds of settle time as well, giving the motion-control rig time to let the vibrations dissipate before the frame is exposed or recorded. Settling only takes a few seconds, but like indexing, a few seconds on a 500-frame shot will add up and add a considerable amount of time to complete the shot.

A zoom lens, however, doesn't have nearly any of the power of a push or moving camera. When a lens zooms in, no new information is gained; it is only magnified. With a short push in, foreground and background elements move in and out of the frame, a push or a pull also creates obvious depth between elements that a zoom cannot do. The strangest combination of lens is the track-and-zoom shot. The camera is pushed in, but the zoom lens pulls out, creating an expanding background even though the character in focus stays relatively in the same place. The same effect can be achieved by doing the shot in reverse: pulling the camera out, but zooming the lens in simultaneously. It's an interesting technique, but has become somewhat of a cliché to emphasize an extreme reaction of a character. The technique is similar to the wide-angle lens close-up, but even more so because the background is actually warping and stretching in a hallucinatory effect. The track and zoom shot is severely limited.

The Lester Show is a strange, dreamlike film, and the extremely wide angles help that feeling of distortion. They also take away the sterile feeling of the perfect perspective that CG naturally creates (see Figure 6.20).

Figure 6.21 is a scene from *The Lester Show* where Lester has a conversation with George Washington on a coin. The scene is more painterly than any other in the film, and the distortion and the composition are truly warped beyond any lens, taking the film to a new level of unusual visual composition and incorporating the visual bend both in artwork and lens setting. Still the composition is clean and relatively balanced with only a few iconic images left to define the strange scene.

FIGURE 6.20   A still from *The Lester Show*. The camera lens is extremely wide, distorting all the lines and bending the horizon (see Color Plate 11). © 2004 Allan Steele. Reprinted with permission.

FIGURE 6.21   An almost psychedelic scene from *The Lester Show* (see Color Plate 12).
© 2004 Allan Steele. Reprinted with permission.

CAMERA MOVEMENT

Moving a camera is unique to film and animation because the illusion of movement can make a viewer feel as if he is moving through space. An extreme example of that movement is a motion simulator, where a filmed sequence of a roller coaster makes stationary viewers feel sick. In a sense, moving the camera always has that type of effect to some degree. Moving the camera draws the viewer into the scene, even if it's only to peek around a corner or plunge over a cliff. It's a powerful tool whether slow or fast, large or small. Because film and animation are normally recorded as two dimensional and ultimately wind up on a flat screen (the television, computer, or movie screen), the movement of the camera also helps to illustrate depth. A simple shot consisting of a camera aimed forward on the front of a car going over a steel bridge is visually dynamic because everything is moving. The camera is inside a huge cage, and the perspective is changing on everything on the screen. The depth is dynamic and is always interesting, which is why so many car commercials feature a car going over a steel bridge or through a tunnel.

In its most subtle form, camera movement involves emphasis. If the story asks a question of a character such as, "Did you know about the stolen money?" the story asks too and the camera moves in; the viewer and the director press the actor by being physically closer, studying the character's face to see if he'll be truthful. Going physically closer can have the feel of a prosecutor on a witness stand: "Well, did you know about the stolen money?" By moving in to an extreme close-up, the character is visually trapped and every a blink is subject to suspicion.

Very subtle camera movement, not simply turning on a tripod but instead dollying or moving through space even just slightly, has a strong visual effect because of perspective; things appear to slide at different rates depending on their relative depth. This diverging movement makes it easy to visually pull the characters out of the background and possible to punctuate the focal point of the shot, whether it's a location, a character, or a person's face.

The viewer always looks to the human face, or the face of any creature, because it always says something about the mind. The human face is made up of six facets, and even in a simple scene of a person talking, moving around the face helps solidify the facets and reinforce depth and dimension by making the facets of the face more readable and interesting.

Camera movement also reveals new information, but can also be used stylistically to focus ideals. In *Grime Shoed Diaries'* opening shot, the concept is to go from macro to micro. The scene starts large on the faceless city to inform the audience of the backdrop, and then the shots take the audience on a mental-focusing trip and the camera finally focuses on one man alone in a diner. It's a classic moving establishing shot, verging on parody, but it's not set in stone that it had to go that way. However, there is an emotional master shot to say where both stories, the city and the man, are taking place. The film could have begun on a close-up of the detective and then pulled wide to reveal the city, but then to follow the man's story, the shot would figuratively have to go back down again, so it became a standard choice. The film could have started with the main character and then discovered the city and his predicament as he left the diner. The film could have also started with the character accidentally shooting himself as it plays out at the end and work backward; either of these scenarios is stylistic and both are capable of their own angle of truth.

Camera as a Character

The camera can be all-knowing and look ahead of the action. It can give the audience large or small clues, or, conversely, it can be totally uniformed. For example, say there is a scene in a movie where a man finds out that a friend has passed away. The shot is in the hospital and there are infinite ways to photograph it. The camera can be omniscient, and be over the shoulder of the doctor, recording the man's face, or it can be outside in the hall, where the viewer can't hear the words, but instead gets the message from the doctor's and the man's actions add expressions. Which approach, close up or third person, is more powerful? There is no easy answer and with cutting and shot coverage both could be used. But would it be better to stick with one for more impact, because going from omniscient to third person observer might have a jarring effect.

A character coming toward the screen is usually more interesting than a character just crossing from one side to the next. Namely because we can see the character's face and front. He is moving but also growing in size—it's dynamic on every level. In live-action filming, CG, or stop motion, it's easier than in cel, where it's a more difficult drawing, and often the drawings can't be repeated. A repeated sequence of drawings will only work up to a point, because when the character starts to move across the screen, unlike its real or CG counterparts, the perspective doesn't change unless the way it is drawn changes. Stylistically, however, a sequence of drawings can be used, and they simply repeat as they go off screen, giving a flat look because the eye immediately notices that the perspective isn't changing. This isn't necessarily a bad thing; it can be a style.

If the style of the animation is limited or very stylized, something on the order of *South Park* for example, then it's more a point of how the animation moves than mimicking reality. It's also much easier to cycle 12 drawings than it is to create a whole scene with the perspective slightly changing. There is also an in-between solution: using a sequence up to a point and then changing to a perspective sequence toward the end of the shot. This can also work, but again needs to be incorporated stylistically with the project and the programs and techniques being used.

Camera Shake

The camera shake is a relatively new idea that probably has its roots in documentary handheld filmmaking. It's possible that war footage was some of the first real recording of shockwaves from a force. In war, the force is an explosion: the idea that the explosion or force has jostled the camera. Earthquake sequences are the most obvious use of a camera shake, but it can exist when any force is felt or comes in proximity of the camera. In a submarine movie or a science-fiction movie, camera shakes are essential when explosions or huge forces of energy are released. A depth charge in a submarine movie, for example, helps accomplish a difficult task when there's no real connection between visuals because the audience can't ever see the submarine and the sailors inside at the same time. Instead the audience sees the submarine being attacked with depth charges, the scene cuts inside, and then the audience sees the effect of the depth charges on the crew. The action and the reaction are separate unlike a regular battle, so camera shake helps to complete the force that the depth charges are inflicting.

There's also a bit of breaking the fourth wall that goes on with the camera shake, because it gives away the idea of the camera as impervious or completely omniscient. However, the trade-off is well worth it. Since audiences are used to seeing filmed things, like war documentaries with real camera shakes, it's becoming acceptable and in fact almost necessary. The camera shake is now a key special effect, and is used in video games and animation alike. Animation is always fighting to keep its illusions consistent, and depending on the story, the camera shake is just another "real" effect that when animated makes the animated scene more real. Like animation, the camera shake can also be stylized instead of organic; it can be very mechanical and only move on the y-axis, up and down. This is a stylized approach, something the cartoon *The Flintstones* would do when a big rock fell over.

The camera shake is a close relative of dutching angles, which is breaking normal level shooting and tilting the ground plane and the horizon; in the final frame a "dutched" camera creates a disjointed feeling. Both the camera shake and dutching the camera are sometimes overused in action sequences and become so shaky that they can't even be viewed. More subtle uses include showing dinosaur footsteps approaching, which start as a vibration and get bigger, so use these options wisely.

Tips for Future Projects

Master the Rules

Like so many aspects of film and animation, a brief chapter is incapable of encapsulating all the subtleties and special circumstances that go along with the discipline of cinematography. Cinematography falls into one of those major categories that is so tied to art and photography that its depth cannot be covered in 100 books, let alone a chapter. But unlike lighting, which can be so subjective, there are some steadfast rules about how shots are created, how they are framed, how the line of sight is dealt with, and many other elements. Audiences are keenly aware when the rules of cinematography aren't working, but when they are working in conjunction with the storytelling it's invisible.

There are many complicated scenarios when shooting, a table full of people: some people are standing, some are sitting, and some are getting up and moving around, moving the line of sight. The complexity mounts when trying to best frame each shot, and it can only be mastered by studying techniques through trial and error. There are many excellent books on cinematography written by seasoned cinematographers, and books on photography are often equally as useful. Still, a pile of books cannot hold a candle to the actual process—cinematographers never stop shooting. By that same token, cinematographers never stop watching either. Whether watching master filmmakers or the world around them, cinematographers are always mentally shooting. In live action and animation, some shots merely require recording an event, while other shots can be composed for impact and power on dash overtly or subliminally.

Establish a Tone or Style

When possible, try to create a tone that works with the story and the mood, whether through a lens, long shots, short shots, or handheld shots. Is the camera omniscient, or is it more like a distant observer? Does the tone change with the story? What, if any, are the subtle feelings that can be enhanced with color choices, darkness, raw light, or diffused light? How can light, and almost more important, darkness, be used to enhance feelings?

Compose Each Shot

There are no throwaway shots. Virtually every single shot can help set the tone and flow by angle, movement, and composition. Shots that would be dull to the director or the writer, such as a character simply getting into his car and taking off, should be the cinematographer's playground. His job is to create a composition out of the mundane that says something about the character, the tone, or the story. He can also create an interesting visual relationship among the character, the car, and the character's surroundings that has balance and visual weight. Every frame counts and every frame costs something.

The age-old image of a director wandering around with a viewer, or using his fingers to create masks, is a laughable trait and almost the international symbol for the job of director. It is, however, often the most powerful tool in creating feelings that connect to an audience. Directors use many ways to devise shots. They can do elaborate storyboards and can then wander around with a viewer to discover compositions. For the director it's all about the composition—a visual composition that is both interesting and clearly reinforcing the story or mood. Directors can take cues from traditional artists by stepping back from visuals and looking at overall balance

Some artists, including this author, set their eyes out of focus to judge densities, general weights, and abstract compositions. Reversing images is also a powerful tool. To the artist, hand mirrors are effective for judging symmetry, while an electronic artist can flop images digitally. Still photographers often use a Polaroid™ back on their still cameras loaded with black-and-white film; even when shooting color, they instead use black and white to judge compositions, densities, and values without the distraction of color. Whether one is a cinematographer, animator, lighting, or technical director, each person must find a specific mental tool that is set beyond just subjectivity to judge compositions. Subjectivity has the absolute final veto power, but knowing rules and techniques is valuable when subjectivity isn't so clear.

PREPRODUCTION

PREPLANNING AND PREPRODUCTION

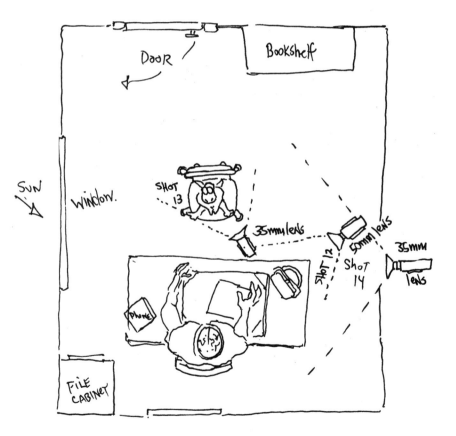

There are only a few instances when a production does not need to follow the preproduction process in some form. One instance would be if an individual were just creating a small short film, or a simple stand-alone. There is also experimental animation, which is a constructive form of animation and filmmaking that starts with just playing and experimenting. It is a valuable tool for generating ideas, momentum, and enthusiasm. Experimental animation and film can be a very pure artistic expression of the medium, but as soon as it becomes a project, film, game, or story, it needs a production plan. The plan can just be a simple plan jotted down on one sheet of paper or it can be weeks of production laid out into a spreadsheet. Having a production plan safeguards against wasting time and helps insure that all the expended energy, effort, and budget are spent the right way. The plan also makes sure that the idea of making your art into a cohesive final production uses all the most powerful workings of animation, film, design, pacing, and resources: everything involved to reinforce whatever it was that made you want to make the film in the first place.

STARTING A PROJECT

One of the greatest animated films is *Powers of Ten* created by Charles and Ray Eames, although there's very little animation in the amazing film by the husband and wife design team. What is so extraordinary about this film is how the filmmakers used art and simple animation to simply explain some of the biggest ideas humans have ever happened upon. In this short film of a man sleeping on a picnic table, the Eameses create an extraordinary journey that starts with a field of view that is 1 meter squared and every 10 seconds the size is doubled. Quickly the shot moves up and the man recedes. As the shot grows and grows, it's obvious that the sleeping man is in a park near Lake Michigan; the shot continues to double until the entire Lake Michigan is seen, then North America, and then Earth. The film continues to double and zooms out to the very edge of the universe, and then it quickly backtracks and goes into a cell on the man's hand and down to the limits of the subatomic level. In less than 10 minutes every major concept of science is shown. It's an extraordinary film that is essentially about size and space. It combines all the fundamental ideas of astronomy, biology, and physics in a clear and amazing presentation.

The film was created with a series of camera moves and dissolves, and it only feels dated today because of the strange music. *Powers of Ten* was remade into an IMAX® film that takes advantage of excellent CG graphics and compositing that didn't exist back then for the Eameses. The remake is an excellent film, but all the credit goes to the Eameses for making the original film and its story. Without the use of animation equipment, techniques, and effects the film would have been nearly impossible, but as an animated film it stands as a shining example of the power of what are essentially flat images in a flipbook. Never before have such huge concepts been so easily understood, but more than that, it runs through dozens of concepts and ideas that are all huge in their scope but easily understood because of the perfect visuals. It is the perfect combination of art and animation to tell a story of galactic proportions that has never been so easily and cleanly explained before.

Of course, not all films have to be to that caliber, but *Powers of Ten* illustrates a point about how the medium melds with the idea, and how a film like this works so well to visually explain complex ideas so clearly. Walt Disney's *Donald in Mathmagic Land,* a film millions of kids see in grade school, is a brilliant telling of some of the fundamentals of music, math, and geometry, all of which are notoriously dry subjects.

In the film, Donald Duck leads the viewer through a beautiful world that shows the fundamentals of math, physics, and proportions with great clarity. Any other form of explanation would be hard pressed to improve on how this small Disney film lays out the ideas. Not only does the film explain the concepts clearer than ever before, but it makes math funny and entertaining, and present dozens and dozens of complex ideas in a very short amount of time. The key to the film is that animation is what explains the concepts so clearly; it clearly shows why using moving illustrations to convey ideas is such a powerful tool.

One of the absolute necessities of making a film like the *Powers of Ten* or *Donald in Mathmagic Land* is that the filmmakers had to understand their subject completely before beginning to design ways to visually explain the ideas. All films and animations are done this way. Whether explaining something as concrete as algebra something as abstract as a broken heart, the filmmaker needs to understand the subject, the concept, and the story before he can lay it out for someone else. It is important to know what story, motivations, and feelings you are going to convey. You also need to know who your characters are and what they will be doing. Even if the writer and the director don't know all the answers to every specific detail, the director and the production and design team need to know the basic key concepts and point of the story.

In making a movie to explain math, the concepts are concrete, but in telling a story about human emotion, it isn't as straightforward. An excellent technique is to deconstruct the story down to its basic components. Chapter 2, "The Story," illustrates how the basics of a story are discovered or created.

There are always exceptions to that rule, of course. For instance, filmmakers like David Lynch and Ken Russell create and present ideas that they don't necessarily understand. Russell's *Gothic* and Lynch's *Eraserhead* and *Blue Velvet* are films that were created from a purely experimental and visual level, without admittedly knowing what the scenes were about. Although both filmmakers experimented visually, they did so at a mechanical level, because they know that their departures have to be grounded in some reality, or they will lose that sense of a "movie."

Animation lives in a world of extremes, and it responds well to extreme ideas. So why take a story to the animated level? Is the story impossible or too elaborate to create practically? Does it feature nonhuman characters or fantastic locations? Not all animated things have to bounce off the walls and morph into other things, but animation's ability to do things live action can't is a serious consideration. Can the medium of animation help tell a given story, or is some complexity of the story actually going to make the animation harder? Is that extra work worth it? Would the project simply be better and the story told better if it were filmed as live action? There are many reasons to go with animation, but questioning those reasons isn't necessarily that important; what is important is to find the best animation style to fit with a story or concept. Simply wanting to make an animated film is motivation enough to make one, however, when working from this point, it's important to be able to reverse engineer the idea so that the animated film was worth making when it's completed.

With today's desktop animation and editing systems, small, or even solo, animators and filmmakers can take on big-story concepts and create films and animations that have a big-budget look with virtually no budget. In order to get that big-budget look, however, those solo animators have to spend much more time or have a truly fantastic story. It's never been easier to create animation, but *good* animation is still as difficult as it has always been.

With the *Shards of Death* animation (the author's own short), the reason behind the animated project is complicated. Stylistically, animation fits well with two characters: a monster and a cute fairylike creature. Their stories say they are both from CG animated video games, so the use of 3D CG was logical. Since we were a group of 3D animators and creators, the film served to feature the team's talents in storytelling, characterization, performance, design, and execution.

Shards of Death would have probably worked fine in cel, stop motion, or any other animation program, but the characters are from video games and needed to be created with the tools that are used to create the video games. Suppose the animation team had been a cel animation team and the goal was to create a film that would show the talents of a cel company. In that case, the story could have been adjusted so that the interview was for a "job" that was closer to cel, perhaps in another cartoon or animated show.

The personal goal of the group was to feature the team's talents, but also to create an entertaining film. Creating a visual match for a given story goes beyond lighting and camera direction, but in animation the story can be matched with a specific technique. All animation techniques have their strong suit, whatever animation technique is used, but that stylistic point should match the story and the mood.

PLANNING CHARACTER CREATION

Before beginning to model, a design phase should be run through. This ensures that before anything is modeled, there is a plan for the type of characters, what they will be doing, and how they will be modeled and rigged. Beyond the design phase, the project needs to be dissected to discover how far models and sets need to go. If a CG or stop-motion film has a character seated in a chair for the entire film, then it might not be necessary to rig the feet. If a character's feet are always hidden under a table, then feet don't even need to be built or modeled.

In stop motion, this type of planning is common. If a background character is just sitting and doing nothing, an armature can be built that only addresses the head and arms. If a character has a very small part, cheaper materials can be used, such as a lead-wire armature as opposed to a full ball and socket-manufactured one.

Decisions should not limit production because it would be a disaster to get down the road and wish a character were rigged differently. Filmmakers need to look objectively at what they're going to do, which goes back to having a cohesive and detailed plan before any modeling or building is even begun.

In *Shards of Death,* the green monster was actually a character for a video game that never developed, so he was modeled and rigged in the traditional T-pose that most CG characters are. When it came time to do the film, the green monster was simply imported and animators started animating.

Shards of Death focused on character animation and the film was deliberately locked to this idea by having the characters sit across from each other and act fact to face, which is ideal for good character performance. As animators started to animate, it became apparent that the monster's character rig was set up for a general purpose movement, such as walking, jumping, and general monster-type, video-game movement, so it needed to be adjusted.

ON THE CD

The file **Monstertest.mov** on the CD-ROM is a very early blocking test for the monster in an early version of the game set. In the test, the monster is walking, leaping, and being very physical. He doesn't focus on subtle movements like sitting at a desk and feeling awkward. The model set is far more evolved than necessary to start motion tests, but anything that can be incorporated can be helpful. The overall plan should be to test elements as often as possible, so that the modelers and animators get a true measure of progress and can have the flexibility to finesse and change all models, surfaces, camera moves, and animation simultaneously.

The character rig from the game setting wasn't working well for the monster because the character mostly kept its hands well in front with its elbows often on the desk. After a few frustrating days of animation, the rig was reworked. The animators paid the price and were then able to use an existing character and get on with making the film. Ideally, the monster would have been thoroughly tested with a full range of motion relative to what it would be doing, but time and budget didn't allow for such tests and often don't.

Planning Before Modeling

Ideally, in all productions it's important that the modeler, texture artist, and anyone who is dealing with the character see all the animatics and all the storyboards, so they know what angles they can expect. This way, no one does work that is not going to be seen, and no one is surprised when his character is called on for a close-up. Obviously on feature films this is all part of the testing phase. However, on smaller projects, it's also important for animators to explore and test the limits of the characters, test interconnection with other items and props, and resolve parenting issues with those items and objects.

For models, there are many reasons why it's also important not to overmodel. For all studios, large and small, rendering is spending money, but for small productions it often means tying up every processor and slowing down other work. If a character is never going to have a close-up, then its polygon or point count should reflect that. Again, no one wants to compromise, but there are numerous ways to speed up the process and cut corners. These are not corners that hold the project together, but rather are smart corners that no one would ever see.

For thousands of years, stage plays have used metaphor and symbols to dress a stage with epic ideas. Suppose there is a play or musical that has a scene in downtown New York City. How does the stage department sell this concept to the audience? They do it with metaphor, iconography, and symbols, to create a New York street with the noise of cabs, flashing lights, throngs of people, neon signs, and buildings rising up and out of view. Because these are solid ideas and concepts, the animator and filmmaker are able to choose the very best iconography. Equally as important, they don't have to bother with the images and ideas that aren't iconic, or are counter to the story and too expensive or complex to produce.

In animation, this idea is enhanced tenfold because the possibilities are limitless. In a very real sense, animation can be the response that the artist has to ideas bigger than reality, similar to the way iconic sets were the response to creating a metaphor of reality on the stage. For example, in a stage play a room can be rendered with a simple door frame and a window. No walls are required, because theater audiences understand the suggestion of the door frame and window.

Animation can go further, however, by picking and choosing its iconic set pieces. And in animation, the door frames don't hang on wires, so they can open to anything the animator can dream up. Often with live-action film, reality and physics drive a lot of the world that the story lives in. In a basic sense, things that break reality require extra effort. In the *Lord of the Rings* trilogy, for example, the prop department didn't have the luxury of being able to buy anything off the shelf. There were no door knobs, cups, chairs, tables; everything had to be created because of the stylistic design choices. Animation always involves creating everything from scratch, so using extreme design or stylistic choices should always be considered.

But when making choices, remember that the vast majority of stories audiences see happen to real people in settings that the viewer can relate to. Whether it's the seasons, room, places, etc., there's a level of familiarity to which everyone can relate. When developing *Shards of Death*, we considered having the setting in a more familiar environment for a monster, such as a cave or a dungeon because the interview was for a job in a very violent video game. Ultimately it was decided that the interview taking place in a dungeon would be too "on the nose" and too expected. In a sense, a dungeon setting wouldn't let the audience draw their own conclusion or figure out what was happening. An overt background would have been doubling the joke, and it would also have taken too many liberties on a well-known process: the job interview. Everyone knows a job interview is usually dull and usually takes place in an office, sitting face to face in front of a desk.

But because job interviews are viewed as boring and mundane, they play well against something as extreme as a monster interviewing a little fairy for a job in a violent video game. If the interview were in a dungeon, it would perhaps be too removed from the interview, and the main conflict in the scene. In a mundane office, the two unusual characters stand out on their own and don't compete with the backdrop. They approach the story on equal footing. Neither character is in its own world; both characters are sharing the mundane world of a simple office.

The office also addresses the issue of visual pacing, and playing opposites against each other to create unusual imagery. An office with monsters is potentially funnier and more unique than monsters in a dungeon, where viewers would expect to see them. The office also works well with the drudgery of the job that the monster reflects. The familiarity of the set tells the audience that the monster is a lot like people, so the audience can assume that the monster must get paid, have an office and a home, have to pay bills, and lead a weird yet ordinary life.

It's this simple choice of a set that can tell so much about a character without having to spell it out. If the scene were in a dungeon, the film might not have a place of reference, because in a dungeon, it might be more confusing. The audience might wonder—does he live there? does he get paid? etc. The humor that should come from the monster lies in opposites: a horrible creature, works in an office. This is the type of visual planning and decision making that tells a good story.

Animators and filmmakers can be handed a script or story, but it's up to the filmmaker and director to take the visuals to a level beyond what is written and try to create more interesting dynamics. Creating these types of visual layouts usually happens as drawings and notes, long before design or storyboarding starts.

Taking Full Advantage of Technology

Animated filmmakers are always conscious of the story, but should also explore the technical options and recognize processes that can speed up or streamline production without affecting the final product. If a scene is taking hours and hours to render and the frame is locked off, then it might make sense to do a composite. For example, in *Shards of Death*, two characters sit and talk. The background is rendered with depth of field and radiosity and each frame takes a long time to render. There are also several scenes from the same angle. Depending on the scene and limited camera movement it can be faster to render a single frame and then render the character separately with an alpha channel then have a compositor put the two together.

But when using short cuts, planning becomes crucial because shortcuts often limit other options. Also, creating some short cuts actually only passes the buck from one department to the next. Short cuts don't always speed things up, but instead simply shift the work to someone else. And many fixes are glossed over and left to be fixed in postproduction, which is notoriously expensive. This is why coordination and a complete understanding of processes and the time needed to do specific jobs and tasks are essential in managing a production. Simply expecting problems to all be fixed in postproduction is the least desirable path to take, especially for the postproduction crew.

Why Use Animation?

Because animation technology is so available and has so much impact, it is used everywhere, at every level. Advertising and television commercials occasionally make spots that have no business being animated, but instead should have been created using live action, animatronics, or something else. Unfortunately for some, animation is a just another visual technique that is inherently fun with bright visuals that they thought could somehow fix a flawed or weak story. Animation, which provides the power to create powerful and fun images, can do just that: make a dismal idea passable. But using animation to solve story problems is a sorry state of affairs, and in the end, animation as a cover really has little to do with good storytelling. Animation works best with good stories, however abstract, bizarre, or straightforward. Although animation can work as a sort of eye candy, that use is really a miscast of the whole idea and a wasted opportunity.

Animation often works best when the story can't be done any other way, such as in *Powers of Ten,* but the lofty ideas of this film have nothing to do with the quality of the story being matched with a technique. The *Beavis and Butthead* cartoon series is also a story that really works best in aimation. Two people sitting in a restaurant talking about the stock market would be fine to animate, but to what end? It's difficult to get the emotion on an animated character's face that an actor could do without even thinking about it. It can work, but should it?

As mentioned earlier, wanting to make an animated film just because it's animated is a completely valid approach. That drive, that love of animation, and that illusion of things coming to life have driven some of the world's best animators to create the fantastic work they do. If the intent is to make an animated film, dissect the story, premise, or idea with a keen eye to determine what animation brings to it and how animation can extend the ideas. If it's on the line, meaning it's a good story but is still a bit pedestrian, work on what it is that will make it an animated film, not just a film that has been animated.

VERY FEW HAPPY ACCIDENTS

The overall goal of preproduction and preplanning is to try to minimize, compartmentalize, and set up a framework so that as a storyteller and a filmmaker and animator you can try to minimize the technical difficulties, completely avoid disasters, and focus on the really hard stuff. It is your job to go beyond just animation and create the illusion that the characters are real acting individuals, capable of being players in the given story. In live action there is often a sense of spontaneity; actors can pull off a fantastic performance, or the sun can suddenly break through and create a dramatic sky. Animation has no such luck. Things that go wrong usually look wrong. Stylistically, animation can be incredibly forgiving as a medium. However, storytelling and transferring the heart of a story to a physical medium is far more complicated, because too many things can go wrong and ruin a good story.

If a story is sound, when things go wrong and don't look right it's essentially always because the design, production, and execution wasn't adequately planned out, practiced, finessed, or sometimes completely overhauled. If the story isn't working, then it's another major element that should be fixed before going down the long animation road.

FRAME COUNTS AND NAMING CONVENTIONS

Frame counts and naming conventions are both important for clarity and organization of a production. If a filmmaker or animator is working on his own on a small minimal shot project, frame counts and conventions aren't crucial. However, as soon as another person is added into the mix, it becomes vastly more complex, whether the new person is directing, surfacing, animating, lighting, or even doing the music. A running on-screen frame count becomes indispensable once two or more people are involved who will be dealing with common scenes. When working with animators, whether it's computer blocking of a character, pencil tests, or pop throughs, frame counts on the screen create a place for specific comments, from any department, that are clear to everyone. An animator needs to have a prop appear on a specific frame, and having running frame counts on every scene makes talking about specific movements and cues precise and frame accurate. Frame counts are also immensely important to the editorial department and help to keep the editorial cut conformed and in check.

As with frame counts, naing conventions aren't important when working alone. But as soon as another person is added who needs to access the same footage, files, and other elements of production, a consistent naming convention is imperative. This becomes even more important with multiple projects that all reside in the same hard drive, server, or even a storage cabinet or film vault.

Whatever the predominant name of the project is, it should be the first description in a name. While in production, *Shards of Death* didn't have a final title, but everyone working on it referred to it as "The Interview," which described what happens and was a working title from the script.

In a naming convention, the project needs the flexibility to incorporate any element that must be created so that all files, including film, spreadsheets, and shot cards, are uniform. This way, anyone working on the project can easily find the files, elements, and tapes. More important, the convention idea safeguards against work being accidentally redone, saved over, or erased. There aren't any rules on how to set up a convention. For example, letters can be used instead of numbers, but it can become clumsy if you get into hundreds of versions and wind up having to use double or triple letters. A combination of letters and numbers can work well. The production designer, producer, and technical directors need to account for all the specific variables for the specific problem and then create a naming convention according to that.

Eliminating confusion and avoiding expensive mistakes is the goal of naming convention in folders, scenes, and directories. For animators, the safest way to save all work is to use versions. Animators using professional software usually cannot rely on undos for any real performance, because animation, with all its plug-ins, connections, and scripts to other files, is hit or miss with undo. It is not unheard of for CG animators to save hundreds of versions of scenes, knowing that they can go back and load any specific or major change.

Certain software can automate the naming convention, so that every time an animator saves his file, digitized scene, or drawings it automatically saves the proper version. This is extremely useful, especially when the project gets into a pressure situation or goes into crunch time. At this point, work often becomes more frantic, and animators start to buck the convention because they're going fast and of course mishaps near delivery day can multiply to disastrous levels. In order to prevent problems like this, set up a convention, print it out, and tape it to the monitors of the animators and crew if necessary. In a production setting, organization is absolutely essential so use the automated functionalities of the software to help. For example, LightWave 3D, the software we used on *Shards of Death*, defaults to LightWave folder setups. Separate folders are created for scenes, objects, images, and surfaces. These folders were divided by a specific scene that was designated from the animatics when it was broken down after a tentative "lock" on the animatic.

Handles

Handles are a few frames that are added on the ends of scenes for editing flexibility, which allows sliding the animation around within those frames. Handles are useful for finessing, editing, and action hookups and should follow the established naming convention. The number of frames for a handle is up to the production. Using five frames is fairly standard, but it can be more or less. Fewer frames give less flexibility, and more frames mean more animation.

Handles are also useful for animators to start a big motion, and know that they can build up energy so that the handle frames give the animator room to have scenes already in motion when the shot actually cuts in. If a scene cuts in on frame 6, the animator can use frames 1 through 5 to get the character into motion. This way, when the shot cuts in, the character can be moving already, giving the animator a few frames to adjust the movement. When using handles, animators always need to know which frame is the first frame that will appear on screen, and work backwards accordingly.

LOCKING A PROJECT

Television spots are unique in that they have an absolute "lock," which means that they must be exactly the size they're sold as. A 15-second spot is 15 seconds to the frame, as is a 30-second or a 60-second spot. Timing is nonnegotiable. But having a tentative lock on a short film is acceptable because it can be as long or as short as ultimately needed. The term is also used to "lock" everyone's approvals. A lock can be a point in a project where the client or producer decides and says, "I agree to make no more changes to the cut of the project." Animation can be tweaked. Lighting or anything visual is still open to adjustment, but adjustment in timing cannot change from this specified point. Animation locks to the vocal track, and if the project slides around, it can affect every shot thereafter.

A lock is valuable in that it allows animators to know they can discard ends and shots that were in flux; it is also extremely important to the audio, whether it's music, additional dialogue recording (ADR), or sound fx. With a lock animators and sound mixers now know that they're working on absolutes and can begin to finalize production. However, a lock is really a frame of mind. Many times, clients decide on an 11th-hour change that breaks the lock and sends editors, animators, and sound people scrambling, usually at an increased expense.

TESTING

Like any form of testing and proving, when cost and time is an issue, there can be a point of diminished returns. With infinite available versions and infinitely adjustable elements, it's often harder to keep focus on the original intent and the original design. With near effortless flexible editing and adjustments, it's easy to overthink a project just as easy as it is to not plan enough. Time is a dangerous enemy of humor, and it's important to rely on the initial energy that made it worth making in the first place; the funniest joke or the cleverest gag can start to seem tired when it's been watched over and over.

A "fishing trip" refers to a process where the director is unhappy with various elements, but has little or no plan and can't see a clear path for any or all of the elements. This can occur for many reasons, but it's possible for problems to arise that no plan can cover. The worst problem is a fundamental problem with the whole concept or a major technical problem that caused lost footage or imagery. Other less disastrous problems could be with a scene or performance or an edit that isn't working or isn't as strong as it should be for whatever reason; the director, editor, and all interested parties try to resolve these problems and often at great expense.

In the end, because of the creative aspect of animation and film production, many important and pivotal choices are ultimately subjective. When dealing with such complex emotions like humor, interest, taste, and perception, there is a great unknown quantity that cannot be accounted. This is proven time and time again when a huge movie has all the right elements—good cast, good story, good direction, good everything—and still the sum isn't that good. The opposite is true as well; a

COLOR PLATE 1 Scene from *The Lester Show* combining 2D and 3D. ©2004 Allan Steele Reprinted with permission

COLOR PLATE 2 The world of *Insect Poetry* is an antique desktop, which has a stage-play feel. ©2001 Marilyn Zornado. Reprinted with permission

COLOR PLATE 3 A rich yet specific color palette.
©2004 Paul Harrod. Reprinted with permission.

COLOR PLATE 4 A conceptual drawing and the final rendered scene. ©2004 Amila and Patrik Puhala. Reprinted with permission.

COLOR PLATE 5 A scene that is purely graphical isn't lit, although it still has a sense of bright, full light. ©2004 Laura DiTrapani. Reprinted with permission.

COLOR PLATE 6 A highly stylized stop-motion scene rich in texture, except for the character, making the character a clean read and an easy focus. ©2004 Joanna Priestley. Reprinted with permission.

COLOR PLATE 7 A scene from *Sesame Street* that features a focus on the letter X. ©2004 Laura DiTrapani. Reprinted with permission.

COLOR PLATE 8 A shot from *The Lester Show* showing strange compositions. ©2004 Allan Steele. Reprinted with permission.

COLOR PLATE 9 *Rat Trap* makes use of multiple levels of composition, with the angle looking through the trees and mist. ©2004 Gesine Krätzner. Reprinted with permission.

COLOR PLATE 10 Another shot from Rat Trap where the character has a solution and the light around his head is allegorical for discovering a fix to his problem. ©2004 Gesine Krätzner. Reprinted with permission.

COLOR PLATE 11 A still from *The Lester Show*. The camera lens is extremely wide, distorting all the lines and bending the horizon. ©2004 Allan Steele. Reprinted with permission.

COLOR PLATE 12 An almost psychedelic scene from *The Lester Show.* ©2004 Allan Steele. Reprinted with permission

COLOR PLATE 13 A scene from a Flash animation that shows the layout board that incorporates extended elements for panning or creating the illusion of depth by moving them at varied speeds. ©2004 Tracy Prescott MacGregor. Reprinted with permission.

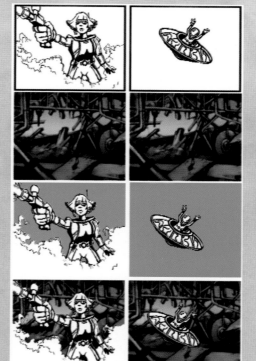

COLOR PLATE 14 An illustration of the foreground elements, the back-ground, and the element on a green-screen layer, and then the final combined elements ready for movement.

COLOR PLATE 15   The weevil conceptual drawing alongside the final animation puppet.
©2001 Marilyn Zornado. Reprinted with permission

COLOR PLATE 16   A Flash animation with high detail and well-created design that ultimately looks closer to cel than to what is usually thought of as Flash animation. ©2004 Tracy Prescott MacGregor. Reprinted with permission

COLOR PLATE 17   The final result of the technique of using Photoshop to create the rosy cheeks on the Eskimo character.
©2004 Tracy Prescott MacGregor. Reprinted with permission.

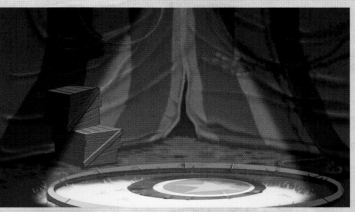

COLOR PLATE 18 A backdrop of a circus animation, with lighting effects created in Photoshop.

COLOR PLATE 19 A scene from a purely graphical animated film. Lighting is inherent in the graphic design, instead of being lit with individual lights. ©2004 Laura DiTrapani. Reprinted with permission.

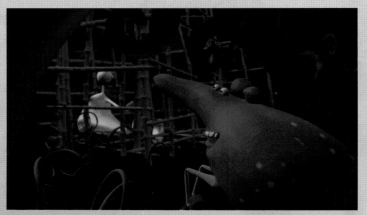

COLOR PLATE 20 Dramatic blue lighting fills the scene with an ethereal and pleasing version of nighttime. ©2004 Gesine Krätzner. Reprinted with permission

COLOR PLATE 21 A still from a cel- and computer-animated combination that uses geometry and fog to create a stylized underwater effect.

COLOR PLATE 22 A graphic design with a limited palette and a removed or rotoscoped outline of a person. The composition is geometrical and graphical. © 2004 Toni Smith. Reprinted with permission.

COLOR PLATE 23 A very straight-on square composition for a *Sesame Street* episode, with a simple "school-play" depth. ©2004 Laura DiTrapani. Reprinted with permission.

poorly acted movie with a bad script, bad production, and bad direction turns out to be a good movie, although it's rare.

With the complexity of storytelling, emotion, visuals, and all the equally complex other details that go into a full-blown animation production, it is possible that major problems do wind up needing fixing at the very end. However, planning can divert most problems so that there isn't a huge scramble or crunch at the end that involves a lot of compromise or less than desired results. A creative complex story that isn't figured out well in advance can succeed, but if people are getting paid and there's a fixed amount of time and a fixed amount of budget, fishing trips are bad news in production and can be even worse in postproduction. The reasons are obvious. As a production moves through time, it gets increasingly expensive at every step. Scripts, artwork, and storyboards are the land of fishing trips and wild exploration. Testing time, when available, can be cents spent and dollars saved. In short production cycles with limited budgets, clients want to see every dollar on the screen, and testing often falls by the wayside. However, when a new character is created, it's important that the character, the cameras, the computers, the postproduction, and anything that is unusual and new be tested when possible. There are always contingencies and design issues that can't be discovered until all the equipment is in place and the characters have gone through all the paces. An example would be a character that is built or modeled, rigged either in stop motion or CG, and not adequately tested. Once shooting or animation begins, it's discovered that because of the design style, the character's arms are too short to hold objects above its own head, which is an important scene in the film.

It's not uncommon for an animated character to have an oversized head. Drawings may have been made and approved, even of the character holding an object. Even though it was sculpted in the T-position, modeled, and rigged, but not with the prop in mind, for whatever reason the two never came together. Now a problem must be dealt with involving either a resculpt or a stretching the arms—an extra expense large or small.

Storyboards are where all the basics are sorted out, and then smaller fishing trips are allowed during the animatic phase. After this phase it's ideal to have as many concrete plans as possible as well as contingency plans. You can't plan too much if someone else is paying for the production. Planning doesn't preempt improvisation; just plan for it, allow time for it, budget it, and have it be part of the plan.

No amount of planning can ever catch every last thing. Occasionally uncontrollable forces wreak havoc. Editing and final postproduction sessions become logistical nightmares, trying to fix problems with existing footage or discovering missing footage. It's an unfortunate place to be, but it often happens when doing film and animation as a business; there seems to be never enough time or money.

INTERNET/INTRANET

With large and small productions it's possible to set up intranet and Internet virtual editorial rooms that can be accessed by the building or the world. Whether as a Web site or a file transfer protocol (FTP) site, it's possible to create a site that features the working cut, and elements as QuickTime files that animators and other production people can access. The edit cut can be updated daily or hourly, and animators can see their scenes cut in at whatever level they're working. They can also have access to the digital storyboards, notes, animatic versions, and anything else required of the production. In small production companies, there was tremendous expense in sending works in progress on videotape, not to mention the loss of time while tapes to be reviewed were in transit. Internet or intranet sites speed up the production and allow for almost immediate feedback the world over.

ASPECT RATIOS

Aspect ratios used to be the result of the equipment used and was standardized by the equipment, but working in animation or digitally now allows aspect ratios to be tailored to any project. Today's 35mm film cameras mostly shoot either in Academy 16 × 9 or in anamorphic CinemaScope, whereas 16mm and television are close to a square presentation. The result when using an aspect ratio other than television and then going to a television format is the "letterbox," where black bands are above the field of view. Digital imagery can render at any image ratio whether doing a final film out or not.

In modern cinema, the collective tastes of viewers have come to accept the idea of a cropped screen on television. Many television shows deliberately shoot out of the television aspect ratio to make the show seem more movielike, with a movie aspect ratio. In animation, it has become nearly a simple matter of choice and another dynamic that might be considered for a story. CinemaScope or 16 × 9 forces a completely different type of composition than a television screen does, and knowing what the final outcome of the film might be can impact the decision. Images now can be rendered in any aspect from nontraditional to anamorphic and then recorded. Aspect ratios dictate how wide shots will be and how wide sets are, so aspect can influence animation.

REVERSE ENGINEERING THE STORY

Animators and creators of media are out to do one simple task: tell the story in the best way possible. Writing for animation is simpler than pulling off the animation and the story, and the writing must be as flexible as every other aspect of the production.

There is no conflict of integrity with creating a story backwards. Creative problems and puzzles are to be solved, and the fact that words are flexible should be used as a creative tool as well. Originally, *Shards of Death* had a more elaborate sketch involving multiple sets, and several more characters, but was scratched because it wasn't practically doable. The idea was simple and two characters were already rigged and set. A set was built and tested.

Set_test.mov on the CD-ROM is a very early test of the basic objects: desk, doors, and an outer office. With a simple set like an office, it was easy to build it out completely, which gave flexibility when shots were being selected. Other sets can be too complicated to build out completely just for camera placement flexibility, and therefore a shooting plan must be more decisive.

The general idea of the interview was sound and simple, so between practicality and the longevity of the joke, extra characters were eliminated and effort was concentrated on a simple idea. Dragging out the simple idea over too long of time with other characters might have stretched the idea too thin, and then the idea would lose its momentum or worse. From the very beginning, animators know that complicated animations are always reverse engineered to some degree. Reverse engineering can go beyond the animation process, and certain outside factors can contribute to having to structure the story around other aspects. Examples include those projects that must follow a specific style or point of view: a film that has time constraints like a commercial, a film that is educational and must explain certain elements, tests and pitches, trailers, and industrial or specialized films.

Building a film with a purpose is important. It must be engineered so that it fits a whole host of opportunities that don't compromise the film or the story. Writers who write for animation are different from writers who write a story or a novel. Writers for animation know the process is a true give-and-take production. In live action there seems to be the tendency that the script is golden and can't be changed and the animation or the film has to find a way, however difficult or impossible, to conform to the words. There are probably legions of writers who fume at the idea that filmmakers can take their words and change them, but if they are fuming then they shouldn't be writing for animation. Unlike models, sets, and motion curves, words are the easiest to change.

Creating a film or animation to showcase work, and perhaps generate more business and help develop further animated projects, is an important tool of the animation business. Herein lies the true challenge, the filmmaker's challenge: to use what he's got to get stuff done and create some sort of connection.

THE GRAVEYARD OF UNFINISHED FILMS

It is a unique and unfortunate quality of the medium, but there is a massive graveyard of unfinished films in basements, closets, and garages around the world. Probably the single biggest reason for so many dead projects was the filmmaker being overly ambitious. Depending on what was committed to the film, it can be devastating to filmmakers both financially and creatively. There's no clear answer, but it's unfortunate because there have been many films and works in progress that could have been really interesting, engaging, and at the very least fun to watch. In most art forms, repetition is how one improves: painters paint, writers write, and dancers dance. The same is true with animation and filmmaking. Yet filmmakers often get the idea that a film project's quality is directly related to the size and the scope of production. For traditional artists, it's easy to make a sketch; it can be done in seconds. With film and animation it isn't possible to create a film in seconds. However, a short film, even as short as a 30-second spot, if done right it can have its own form of impact.

It is possible to experiment, and with the ease of digital desktop editing and filming, the mechanical labor has been trimmed away. A filmmaker with a basic amount of gear, can continually create animated films. This isn't to say that films of huge scope and complexity aren't worth it, but to experiment, learn to develop styles and techniques, and tell different kinds of stories in unique and compelling ways require experience that can only benefit from repetition. If it takes years for each project, it can severely limit the number of different projects an animator can do in his working career.

With all the highbrow notions of a classical story and making a film properly, it's important not to get too lofty about film and animation creation. Most of the ideas about the importance or the making of big statements come from the fact that because film and animation at a large scale are so expensive on so many levels, the end result must be fantastic. It's also important not to get bogged down with the medium, and film has a tendency to do that. Because it is so powerful, complicated, and expensive, it's hard to not aim high and try to create a landmark film like *Powers of Ten*. To that cause, lots of other films are entertaining in many other ways, whether based on the scale of the universe or the simplest visual gags. Doing animation can be managed on nearly any budget, and wanting to make good animation is reason enough to get started. If a filmmaker wants to just mess around and make sequences solely for his own amusement, that is reason enough to delve into film. One of the filmmaker's goals should be to make whatever effort made in film or animation a positive experience by avoiding traps.

It is easy to get swept into the technological frenzy of the latest and greatest equipment. Every filmmaker would love to work in the highest format possible, but there has to be a reality check. Making films shouldn't be about spending money—it should be about telling a story. Not that long ago, to be considered a serious filmmaker meant having to work in actual film; video just wasn't there.

Professional video equipment has been around a long time, but in the early days it was bulky and as expensive as film equipment, and it didn't have the same quality. Times have now changed for both equipment and viewers. In recent years, many independent films have been shot on Mini-DV camcorders. The films *Timecode, Dancer in the Dark,* and *28 Days Later* were all shot on Mini DV, posted electronically, and finally printed to film for theatrical distribution. Various companies now have "film-look systems" to add a film feel to video and recompile the video from 29.97 frames to 24 film frames; many affordable cameras now run at 24 frames per second to mimic the film feel as well as go across directly to a film output.

All of this is a clear response by filmmakers enticed by the portability and the inexpensive nature of Mini DV. Professional film cameras are bulky, heavy and expensive, require tons of setup, and can only hold 10 minutes of film without a special magazine. Even with film look, matte boxes, and professional lighting, Mini DV is nowhere near close to the image quality of film, but to the filmmakers who use Mini DV, it's a compromise well worth it. Mini DV doesn't look like VHS or Digibeta. It has its own look—a look that viewers are getting more and more used to. The big part of the acceptance of digital formats is that the audience doesn't view them as low resolution anymore. From reality shows like *Cops* to home-video shows, QuickTime files, and Internet movies, the audience isn't that put off by low resolution, and collectively watch it as a legitimate format. On the high end, high definition has moved vigorously into the professional shooting realm as well, and with professional lens and running at 24 fps, it can easily be printed to film. The most obvious use of this is seen in the latest *Star Wars* films, which were all digitally recorded and not filmed on traditional motion-picture film.

However, high definition is still expensive. Filmmakers can rent a high-definition camera, but then it's necessary to secure a high-definition editing system. If a filmmaker or animator is going to invest in making a film or an animation, he must decide what is going to serve the project better.

How is effort and money best spent? If a filmmaker can afford all the latest and the greatest, then they're fortunate. But for a film on a budget, what is going to work better? For a hypothetical project, a $10,000 budget has been set aside. This is just an exercise to look at cost from a creative point of view. Rates are approximate.

Option One
Rent a high-definition system
$450 a day, production can shoot for 10 days
High-definition editing, $500 per day
Production can edit for 10 days
$50 dollars can by one high-definition tape

Option Two
Buy a 24p DV camera, with filters, batteries, tripod
$3,500 (production owns the camera and shoots as much as they want)
$5,000 (production buys the latest desktop editing system and computer with gigs of FireWire™ hard drive space and loaded with RAM, plus a program like Speed Razor™, Final Cut, Premiere, or Toaster Edit)
Production can also buy hours and hours of tape, FireWire cards, and film-look software.

The comparison between the two options really asks the question is high definition so important, and for specific applications and even specific stories it is. In the filming scenario, using DV video as opposed to film could potentially mean sacrificed visual quality for a lot more creativity. Also, in the first option, the production doesn't need to learn how to edit, and instead uses an in-house editor. The second option requires a fair amount of computer savvy on the production side, and the quality is still far less than the first option.

When it comes to quality, animation doesn't need to suffer at all because a camera can be replaced by a scanner or rendering software. There are certainly projects that would warrant spending the money and going ahead with the high-end production. With most animation, proper planning and digital production doesn't mean having to sacrifice visual quality to the level of film versus video, if at all.

WORKING WITH AFFORDABLE RESOLUTION

In most cases, animators and filmmakers want to work with the highest resolution and latest equipment on every project, but that's just not reality. It would be great to have a Steadicam, a massive render farm, or a whole host of other items, but an animator or filmmaking team has to gauge what they've got and what they can do in a reasonable amount of time. Films have their own curious ability to turn into unmanageable monsters, and that starts from the concept on down.

Evaluating a project at the beginning may seem to take away some of the creative spark and some of the spontaneity, but evaluating what is realistic and affordable and comparing that to what is being attempted is important and often overlooked. Starting a project is more than just experimenting and having fun. It means evaluating what the production has, what skills it has, and how the film going to be finished. Films aren't like a painting that can be half finished and still be a painting. Films are just footage until they are finished. Animators need to work through the pipeline of what they have and what they're going to need and determine how that balances out with what the story asks for. Huge studios with millions of dollars can afford to make expensive changes indefinitely, but for everyone else that's not a reasonable way to tell a story. Film and animation involves to a large extent compromise, if you are ever going to finish.

There also is another aspect of this cost versus creativity—chasing the latest computer technology. This is one of the most counterproductive problems for filmmakers and animators. Obviously, animators and filmmakers don't want a computer that can't handle whatever they're doing. Computers need to work well. In addition, the software, whatever it is, needs to work exactly as designed; digital filmmakers want to avoid anything that has bugs and frequently crashes. Software packages are constantly upgraded and often they add new and useful features. Truly talented artists, animators, and filmmakers are constantly approaching the artistic endeavor from every angle. For many, animation and film is more than work and more than art, it is ingrained in their lives. As true artists, most are reserved when it comes to upgrades and new equipment. Artists like to make art; they don't like to put in drives and download drivers.

Software and hardware have morphed into desktop-based powerful systems that are respected equals to their expensive professional counterparts. In fact, desktop power and ease has brought huge professional companies scrambling to create packages for desktop systems and a much broader customer base. With this revolution, things have become obsolete at a staggering rate, but it's important not to overshoot a system's obsolescence. If a filmmaker has a good working system with software he knows and understands, then he should use the system for as long as he can before upgrading. If the filmmaker is limited in some important way, then it's always important to keep up with the tools needed to do the job, but it has to be evaluated on the real-world costs versus creativity.

Artists need to make art, and not all upgrades are revolutionary; sometimes they're more about selling upgrades. Anyone who has ever made films the analog way, with film cameras and upright editors and "A" and "B" rolls of actual film, and analog systems, can easily appreciate how easy it has become to make good film and animation. Never before have so many traditional technical problems been stripped away so that the filmmaker can concentrate on telling the story. Yet often the first reaction is to make the process too difficult by adding too many expensive tools. Unlike most art forms, film and animation are unique in that cost is always a factor. Writers can write on recycled paper with a pencil and painters can paint on cardboard if necessary, but films always have a significant cost. As one of the newest art forms it relies on many technologies like sound, photography, and more.

When creating a project, all these ideas need to be considered. This way, filmmakers and animators can avoid burying another project in the graveyard of unfinished films.

Tips for Future Projects

Break Down Stories to Basic Elements

Knowing the basic motivations of characters and the point of the story, while being aware of the tone, the mood, and the emotional connection at its most basic level, allows one to make every critical decision, from creative ideas to budget concerns. Knowing the fundamentals makes it possible for the director or creator to be able to compromise or trim certain elements, lines, characters, or whatever is required, while still keeping the core emotions intact. For example, if the film is a comedy, plot points might be removed or diminished to focus on gags and laughs.

Take Good Notes

Animation has a lot of scientific aspects, and science works better with notes. When testing anything relative to film and animation, detailed notes are often indispensable. Often, with tests of motion, lighting, textures, camera moves, and other complex elements, more than one aspect can be tested simultaneously. A character test of motion can also feature special shades, lighting setups, costumes, or surface details all going on simultaneously, but keeping track of all the variables isn't as simple as hitting the render button. Organization and notes maximize testing, and keeping track of elements both digital and physical are important so that work isn't redone.

Breaking down scenes to create what is required is the key. This breakdown can include characters, props, sets, lighting setups, but large concepts like lighting also dictate how the other elements are to be seen. Knowing early on that a scene is a night scene might mean not having to create as much detail on set pieces and objects. Conversely, if it's known that a close-up of a character is needed, adding extensive detail to the face is then required and planned for.

Break Down Scenes and Shots

With the exception of solo projects, projects that have an unlimited budget, or projects that are all "in the box" (one animator who does everything from start to finish on his own system and is just fooling around), breaking down scenes and shots isn't necessary. Still, even for a solo animator, shot planning can be crucial, even if simply to avoid redoing stuff, keeping up momentum and production. Using storyboards or the animatic, a shot plan can be created that is specific to each set and its limits. Shot plans can be created as a list, but it's often helpful to create a shot plan that is a drawing. Often from above a scene that shows every camera setup and where characters, props, and elements are, a shot plan also helps establish staging, preblocking, and helps avoid confusion with line-of-sight and line-crossing issues (see Figures 7.1 and 7.2).

Whether extensive notes or specific shot cards, when more than one person is working on an animation project, shot planning is always beneficial. With each additional person who works on a job, notes, plans, and

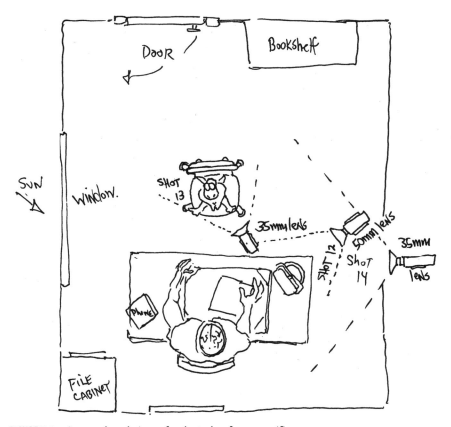

FIGURE 7.1   An overhead view of a shot plan for a specific scene.

FIGURE 7.2   A scene from a Flash animation that shows the layout board that incorporates extended elements for panning or creating the illusion of depth by moving them at varied speeds (see Color Plate 13). © 2004 Tracy Prescott MacGregor. Reprinted with permission.

shot cards become more and more important. In Chapter 15, Figure 15.1 is an example of a shot sheet from the film *Shards of Death*. Shot sheets often need to be tailor-made depending on the project. Knowing what the camera is required to do in a specific shot is important in animation, regardless of technique. In creating cel animation, which is going to incorporate a pan, layout artists know they have to create a background that is often many times bigger than the frame so that the camera has imagery to move through. If those layers are broken out separately, then moving layers faster as they get closer to the camera can create the feeling of depth. The same is true for Macromedia Flash and Moho as well as dimensional animation, 3D CG, or stop motion. Sets need to be created that can handle any specific shot.

Create a Production Plan

On personal projects with no budget, a plan can be little more than a storyboard. On bigger productions with a budget, timeline, and numerous people, a plan that breaks down each day with specific shots and tasks is extremely useful. Budgets can be an excellent way to reverse engineer how long a job can take. They can show the amount of money and the amount of costs from fixed costs like equipment and services and wages and rates for anyone involved. Often in jobs that are for hire, the client or the company footing the bill will require a very specific breakdown of what the costs will be. Animation has the flexibility of having levels of polish. A full-blown dimensional CG character animation in the *Shrek* or Pixar category is expensive, while a Flash production can be relatively cheap compared to full-blown 3D animation. With respect to a budget or a fixed amount of time, the style of animation can be dictated out of practicality and feasibility.

The following is a broken-down budget that was made from looking at the storyboard of a given commercial production. The budget is for a 30-second commercial; all rates are estimates. It is effective for whoever pays the bill, but also an effective tool to calculate how long things will take to animate, build, render, and it also shows what paid people will need to be involved. Table 7.1 is a budget for creating an animatic for a typical stop-motion commercial production. Creating a budget for a CG project is nearly identical. Although there is no live-action filming, there is render time. Whether built practically or virtually, sets must be built and either painted or surfaced, which takes artists time to do.

TABLE 7.1   Sample Budget

ANIMATICS	QTY.	WEEKS	RATE	TOTAL
Director	1	Fee		5,250
Art Director	1	1	1,800	1,800
Producer	1	1	1,700	1,700
Storyboard Artist	2	1.5	1,500	2,250
Editor	1	1.25	1,800	2,250
			Labor Total	13,250
			Total inc. allocations	2,400
			Grand Total	**$15,650**
Demo Sound/Music		Per animatic		**1,500**

In creating animation for a commercial production, animatics are absolutely essential. A job that is on time and on budget cannot be done without an animatic, unless it's profoundly simple like a single shot or something similar.

Table 7.2 shows a schedule for a production that incorporates everything required to complete the animated spot. There are sound and talent payment issues not included, but that often falls to the advertising agency commissioning the spot. Some weeks are relative, and although a storyboard artist is put in for a week, it is possible that the actual work will be done on an hourly basis, where a storyboard artist is hired to come in and fix panels during animation.

TABLE 7.2   Schedule for Production

CHARACTER CREATION				
LABOR				
Direction				
Director	Fee			**15,600**
	Quantity	Man Weeks	Weekly	Total
Production Management				
Producer	1	6	1,700	10,200
Production Assistant/Runner	1	6	500	3,000
				13,200
Art Dept.				
Art Director	1	4	1,800	7,200
Storyboard Artist	1	1	1,500	1,500
				8,700
Characters Fabrication and Creation				
Character Designer	1	2.5	1,700	4,250
Sculptor	1	2	1,600	3,200
Moldmaker	1	2	1,500	3,000
Armaturist	1	3	1,400	4,200
				14,650
Sets Fabrication and Creation				
Set Designer	1	2	1,700	3,400
Set Builder	1	2	1,500	3,000
Wrangler	1	2	1,400	2,800
Painter	1	3	1,200	3,600
Model Builder	1	2	1,200	2,400
				15,200
Production and Animation				
Director of Photography	1	3	1,800	5,400
Gaffer	1	2	1,400	2,800
Grip	1	1	1,300	1,300
Animator	1	3	1,500	4,500
Animator	1	3	1,500	4,500
				18,500
Post Production and Finishing				
CG Artist/Post Flame Artist	1	3	1,500	4,500
Editor	1	3	1,800	5,400
				9,900
Labor Total				**$ 95,750**
Labor Markup, Benefits/Equip. Alloc.				**$24,045**
Postproduction	Hrs	Rate		Total
Film Transfer to Digital Media for Plates	4	550		2200
Final Color Correction/Tape to Tape	5	340		1700
Avid Film Composer Online Edit Session	4	275		1100
Post Total				**$5,000**
Nonlabor				
Shipping, Postage, Media				1000
Animation Tables, Magnets, Video Lunchbox Rental				
	8	200	1600	
Animator supplies, Art Dept & Character Supplies		2900		
Off-site Shooting Location		2925		
Nonlabor Total				**8425**
Grand Total				**$ 133,220**

Table 7.3 is a 12-week production schedule for an average 30-second spot. Animation can be rushed when the budget shrinks and man weeks can be removed to shrink the budget and schedule. However, less time and less money allows for less iterations of design and testing; with less, generally the quality is less as well. A detailed plan with or without a budget can help manage all the elements and avoid surprises and still have room for unexpected contingencies. Table 7.4 shows a budget for a purely CG dimensional spot, with a shorter schedule and a much smaller production in general. The format is slightly different. There is no standard; it's only important that the budget be coherent and cover all the essential elements. The following template can be used for live action, CG, or stop motion; categories that aren't applicable simply remain empty. Even a project that is done strictly by volunteers and has no money involved can use a template such as the following as a checklist of jobs and the people who perform them.

TABLE 7.3   Schedule Summary

Week 1	**Week 7**
Project award	Complete character modeling,
Rough animatics	Complete set/secondary character
Character/set design	modeling
Begin voice casting	Begin prelight of sets/pop-through
	and character turnaround tests
Week 2	
Continue voice casting	**Week 8**
Continue character/set design	Begin animation
Week 3	**Week 9**
Voice record	Continue animation
Continue animatics	Begin music/sound
Lock character design	
Continue set design	**Week 10**
	Complete principal animation
Week 4	Begin reshoots
Begin character modeling	Continue music/sound
Lock set and secondary character	
designs	**Week 11**
	Complete reshoots
Week 5	Complete music/sound
Continue character modeling	
Begin set build/secondary character	**Week 12**
build	Final film transfer and or color correct
	Post and effects
Week 6	Mix
Continue character build	Delivery
Continue set/secondary	
Character modeling	

TABLE 7.4 Template for Budget

A: DIRECTOR/CREATIVE FEES FOR PRODUCTION	QUANTITY	UNITS	RATE		ESTIMATE
#1 Director/Animator (3 weeks total)					5,600.00
				TOTAL " A"	**5,600.00**
LABOR (PRODUCTION) ESTIMATE					
#2 Line Producer	1.5	1750	402.5	1600	2,400.00
#3 Prod. Coord./ Scheduler	—	650	149.5	0.00	
#4 PA/Runner	—	500	115		0.00
#5 **ANIMATION (PRODUCTION)**					
#6 Senior CG Animator	—	1750	402.5	—	0.00
#7 CG Animator	—	1600	368	—	0.00
#8 SM Animator #1	—	—	—	—	0.00
#9 SM Animator #2	—	—	—	—	0.00
#10 Cel Animator #1	—	—	—	—	0.00
#11 Cel Animator #2	—	—	—	—	0.00
#12 **FX (PRODUCTION)**					
#13 CG Supervisor	—	2000	460	—	0.00
#14 Tech Director/Modeler	1	1500	345	1500	1,500.00
#15 Tech Director/Texture	1	1350	310.5	1600	1,600.00
#16 Tech Director/Lighting	1	1700	391	1600	1,600.00
#17 Tech Director/Rendering	—	1600	368	—	0.00
#18 Programmer—Shaders/Particles	—	1800	414	—	0.00
#19					
#20 **ART DEPT (PRODUCTION)**					
#21 Art Director	—	2000	460	—	0.00
#22 Storyboard Artist	—	—	—	—	0.00
#23 **CHARACTERS (PRODUCTION)**					
#24 Character Designer	—	—	—	—	0.00
#25 Sculptor	—	—	—	—	0.00
#26 Moldmaker	—	—	—	—	0.00
#27 Armaturist	—	—	—	—	0.00
#28 **PROPS / LABOR (PRODUCTION)**	—	—	—	—	—
#29 Prop Fabricator	—	—	—	—	0.00
#30 Wrangler (props)	—	—	—	—	0.00
#31 **SETS/LABOR (PRODUCTION)**	—	—	—	—	—
#32 Set Designer	—	—	—	—	0.00
#33 Set Builder	—	—	—	—	0.00
#34 Wrangler(sets)	—	—	—	—	0.00
#35 Painter	—	—	—	—	0.00
#36 Modelbuilder	—	—	—	—	0.00
#37 **POST(PRODUCTION)**	—		—	—	—
#38 Editor	—	2000	460	—	0.00
#39 Asst. Editor/Dailies	1	1000	230	1230	1,230.00
#40 Compositor	0.5	1200	276	1500	750.00
				TOTAL " B"	**9,080.00**

→

C: STUDIO / HARDWARE ALLOCATONS

(PRODUCTION)	QUANTITY	UNITS	RATE	ESTIMATE
#41 Facility Fee Allocation	1.50		wks @ 750.00	1,125.00
#42 CG Workstation Allocations	2.00		2 weeks @ 200.00	800.00
#43 Editorial Workstation Allocation				0.00
#44 Compositing Workstation Allocation				0.00
#45 Rendering Node				0.00
			TOTAL " C"	**1,925.00**

D: MISCELLANEOUS COSTS (PRODUCTION)

	QUANTITY	UNITS	RATE	ESTIMATE
#46 Petty Cash			flat	0.00
#47 Air Shipping/Special Couriers			250.00 flat	250.00
#48 Phones/Fax			50.00 flat	50.00
#49 Special Insurance Certificates			flat	0.00
#50 PA , Camera Car, Scout Mileage			0.00 flat	0.00
#51 Crew Working Meals			50.00 flat	50.00
#52 Office Supplies			50.00 flat	50.00
			TOTAL " D"	**400.00**

E: EDITORIAL COMPLETION

(PRODUCTION)	QUANTITY	UNITS	RATE	ESTIMATE
VIDEOTAPE FINISHING				**0.00**
#53 Titles/GFX				0.00
#54 Film to Tape Transfer: Timed				0.00
#55 Off-Line Editing: No Editor				0.00
#56 Off-Line Editing: With Editor				0.00
#57 Inferno Online/Final Color	0	Hours	750.00	0.00
#58 Flame Compositing		Hours		0.00
#59 Tape Stock: Digital Beta Master	2	@	65.00	130.00
#60 Dubs: Miscellaneous Client 3/4	3	@	25.00	75.00
#61 Dubs: Miscellaneous Client DVD	0	@	30.00	0.00
#62 BetaSP Video Tape: Work Tape	2	@	40.00	80.00
#63 Station Dubs				0.00
#64 Audio Layback				0.00
#65 **AUDIO FINISHING**				0.00
#66 Original Music		Flat		0.00
#67 Record/Edit Narration				0.00
#68 Sound Design		Flat		0.00
#69 Final Mix	0	Hours	170.00	0.00
#70 DAT Tape	0			0.00
#71 Archive	0	Flat	85.00	0.00
			TOTAL " E"	**285.00**

→

F: ESTIMATED TIMELINE FOR PRODUCTION

Week 1: Design & Build Set and Props

Tues, July 8—Project award, receive reference material

Fri, July 11—Send image of character and environment for feedback

Week 2: Animation

Tues, July 15—Revise and approve environment and additional props

Wed, July 16—Begin animation

Fri, July 18—Send animation work in progress for feedback

Week 3: Post Production

Tues, July 22—Continue animation

STORYBOARDING

Since film and animation are anchored in the visual, a logical first step is developing storyboards. Storyboards are a series of comprehensive drawings, rough or refined, that create a template for how a production will ultimately play out visually. They are also the stand-in panels for the visuals yet to be filmed or animated once the boards move to the animatic phase.

Storyboards are often based on a completed script, but starting with a script isn't essential, especially for animators who focus on the visual. For them, the storyboard is the perfect place to draw the story. Nonverbal stories obviously lend themselves to storyboarding without a script, but even a script with dialogue can begin in the storyboard phase.

There are forms of experimental filmmaking that do not require boards, animatics, or anything else and they are perfectly valid, important forms of art and entertainment. However, in telling a story or creating a visual project that has specific characters, acts, and other technical aspects, storyboards are essential. Just as a contractor wouldn't start to build a house without blueprints, a filmmaker shouldn't start making a film without storyboards or a script; this is even more of the case for an animator.

PRESENTATION BOARDS VERSUS PRODUCTION BOARDS

There are many types of boards that serve various purposes. Two major categories of boards are presentation boards and working production boards (see Figure 8.1). Production boards are also known as shooting boards in live-action production.

Presentation boards are described well by their name. Presentation boards are a set of boards designed to share with others the basic concept of a visual production beyond the written word. These boards can be more polished and often rendered in color. They are designed to sell the concept or project and the story to a specific group, client, company, or to use as testing for focus groups, among many other uses.

With presentation boards, design is important, so they are usually created by someone with a graphic-design sense or drawing skills. Generally, presentation boards are more visually evolved compared to production boards, because they are meant to be viewed and understood by people who might not be savvy to the production process. By creating defined and well-executed images and using color and design, presentation boards bridge the gap for nonindustry people who could have trouble grasping roughly drawn or complicated technical boards that are more aimed at informing a crew gearing up for a given production.

Presentation boards can show a general sense of timing. In animation, they can hint at preliminary character and production design, which can be crucial to creating a project. They usually do not contain the important minutiae that go into working production storyboards. Early on

FIGURE 8.1   An illustration of the clear difference between working production boards and presentation boards.

in a project, presentation boards are a smart, no-fault way to present all the ideas at once in a simple but effective form that can be easily changed and modified. They serve to solidify proof of concept, and they represent the initial beginning of an actual production—the first switch over from writing to visual production.

Presentation boards can also serve as a call to action for anyone who will contribute to the project, by allowing various departments to start assessing their role and workload. Animators can roughly see how many characters and scenes they'll have, live-action crews can roughly start to evaluate how many filming setups they'll have, special effects people can get a feel of their involvement, and on down the line including everything from sound design to day-to-day planning of workloads.

Presentation boards rarely contain specifics like frame counts and direction notes. This is because none of that has been established concretely and it has little to do with getting the visual story. They can be just eye candy that specifically features all the visually interesting scenes or elements while glossing over other ideas that haven't been fleshed out.

Often, these are large in size, designed specifically for visual presentations so that people across a room can see them. In this case, they often read as picture boards or graphic novels, and they wind up being redrawn or recreated to become production boards. In presentation boards, a scene might be illustrated by one panel, but when it winds up going to production boards it might become several dozen or even a hundred panels, depending on the length of the scene and its complexity. Presentation boards should make an overt attempt to tell the story clearly in pictures. Elements like color, lighting, and composition are important to creating an environment where the story lives, and anything to clarify the story will help the project on many levels.

Working production storyboards are decidedly different from presentation boards. The fundamental difference is that presentation boards are a sales tool, while working production or shooting boards are a detailed map of the entire visual production that show how the story will be told visually.

In conjunction with the script and a working animatic, production or shooting boards by their very nature are always changing. They can be drawn very well, they can be stick figures, or they can be extremely rough sketches, just as long as everyone who uses or needs them understands the direction. As a production goes along, the quality of production storyboards drawings often gets rougher and rougher, as shots are changed, inserted, moved, and tweaked. The storyboard artist, no longer worried about the quality of visuals, but now concentrates on finding and creating new working shots.

Using Storyboards as a Working Tool

Storyboarding and cinematography go hand in hand. Storyboarding is essentially the planning of the cinematic angles and is extremely important in helping tell the story. Pay attention to the standard rules of cinematography so that the foundation of a flow can begin. Establish locations with wide establishing shots, use close-ups to see faces, move the camera when appropriate, and hold the camera still when necessary. Consider interesting compositions featuring props or characters. Changing scenes should always be motivated, just as cuts are during editing.

Pay attention to the line of sight and give characters room to perform. Choosing the angles for filming or animating as well as planning the motion of all moving elements are some important decisions. Alfred Hitchcock regarded boarding as the actual creating of the movie, and once completed he thought the actual filming was quite dull and mechanical.

Shooting or working boards, if not drawn by the director, are closely watched by the director working in conjunction with the storyboard artists. Unless the director is making his own work, he often receives input about the storyboards from the writer, client, producer, art director, cinematographer, and anyone else whose input could change the visual layout of the translation from script to visuals.

Some directors will hand a storyboard artist quick thumbnail drawings, basically asking for not much more than a cleaned-up redraw. A director will often have concrete ideas about how certain sequences are laid out and roughly sketch those scenes. The director may not have clear and immediate ideas about all the other scenes and will look to the storyboard artist to interpret the script for those sequences; the director delineates key images he has visualized and lets a storyboard artist fill in the gaps. When working with a good storyboard artist, the director can often give the artist as much or as little input as he wants, and can get another take on the visual production.

Good storyboard artists often have a much broader or different art experience than a director and can perhaps create angles and setups that the director hadn't considered. Ultimately, however, the director decides and picks the best of all the ideas that are presented. He then sells his view to the writers or clients, while trying to work within the producer's parameters of time and budget.

When there are several people working on a production, it's rare that there is an immediate consensus on the storytelling's proper direction. The writer might feel that a director's take on a scene isn't right, or the director has made too many changes to the initial idea. The producer may have comments regarding budget restraints, special-effect limitations, or countless other issues. In working with creative individuals, a difference of opinion is almost always guaranteed as visual entertainment, and storytelling relies on personal taste and subjectivity.

Working through challenges like writing considerations, art direction input, styles, angles, and budgetary issues is one of the important functions of the storyboarding phase; this is precisely where plans of this nature get sorted out. Visual and technical types of details and other certain considerations never clearly come across in a script alone. Style, set design, props, lighting, blocking placement, and staging are rarely considered on the written page, but are supremely important.

All of the elements that fall into the visual world can and should be addressed in the storyboarding phase, which can work in conjunction with changing and modifying the script to reflect the leap from written words to visuals. A simple line in a script can create a nearly infinite number of visual treatments. The line, "Two characters have a silly comedic fight," could be created in countless ways and could last a few seconds or several minutes.

It's easy to change words and easy to change drawings. This solves many problems upfront and sets the upcoming project to function efficiently, because knowing what is coming up and true preplanning are invaluable in film and animation.

Scenes can be erased, cut, and edited, all with a stroke of a pen. It also allows the director to focus on the flow, or the "harmonious structure" that F.W. Murnau recognized. Mechanical details are tested and technical issues like hookups in the action that flows from one scene to the next are hammered out, only to remain flexible later on. A visual flow isn't just cutting on the action, but it's cutting on the action in the right place so that the scenes naturally hook up with each other. Although the exact timing of the hookups won't come until the animatic phase, the director can seriously start to plan angles for each and every shot and still know that a final commitment to a specific shot or angle treatment is still several steps away. Working production boards usually have all the information about each specific shot, including the dialogue track or line.

Using rough boards and a stopwatch, you can make a surprisingly accurate timing of the whole project. Because of the cost of animation, boards and animatics have always been integral to the animation making process. This process wasn't always used in live action, although feature film is becoming so expensive that it almost warrants doing some form of boards. Plenty of live-action productions are still filmed without boards, and instead have scene and shot breakdown lists. There are standard ways to film standard scenes; however, making even the simplest storyboards or animatics for any animated or live production can create an obvious level of organization and comfort, unless the production is profoundly simple or purely experimental. When working in the storyboarding and animatic process it is immensely liberating to be organized.

Even on small solo projects, when creating a piece that has more than a couple of shots, each new panel of shooting or production boards compounds the possibilities exponentially. Going through the storyboarding process in great detail serves several purposes. It forces the director to figure out all the scenes, not just the pivotal or exciting ones. It also makes the director focus on the film as a whole, so no scene is treated as mundane or as just a connector between two interesting scenes. From an editing point of view, storyboarding presses the director to examine how all the shots work in conjunction with each other. It also makes the director create a fit between the dialogue and the picture, either by extending shots, spacing lines out, editing lines completely, or going back to the writer for different lines.

Storyboarding brings all the theories and principles of composition, screen direction, and cinematography to bear, so that many paramount decisions are beginning to be made and tested. The working storyboard is unlike the presentation boards as it is meant to be a very close representation of the final angles, where objects, characters, and landscapes are in space and have a sense of lighting. The aspect of the storyboard panel in a real sense is the first defining of the two-dimensional space where the visuals will exist. If a story is going to be created in a specific aspect, then the board frames need to reflect it. The National Television System Committee (NTSC) television aspect ratio is 4:3 or 1.33:1. The Academy flat aspect ratio is also the high definition (HD) ratio of 16×9 or 1:85.1. It is the dominant ratio for theatrical films and has been in use since the mid-1950s. To make the theatrical presentation more dynamic, CinemaScope or anamorphic was developed and its aspect ratio is 2.35:1; it is also known as Panavision and has the widest standard aspect ratio of all. Illustrations of each ratio are shown in Figures 8.2 through 8.4.

**NTSC Television
Academy Standard**

4x3   1.33:1

FIGURE 8.2   The NTSC television standard aspect ratio.

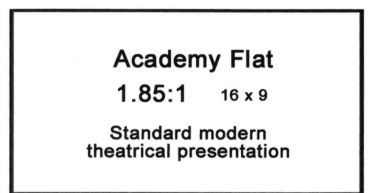

**Academy Flat
1.85:1   16 x 9**

**Standard modern
theatrical presentation**

FIGURE 8.3   The Academy flat aspect ratio or the standard film presentation.

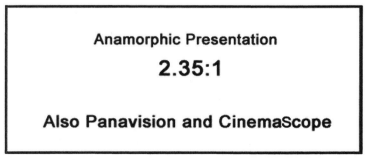

**Anamorphic Presentation
2.35:1**

Also Panavision and CinemaScope

FIGURE 8.4   The CinemaScope or Panavision widescreen aspect ratio.

Video-game cut sequences often use an academy flat aspect ratio similar to 1.85:1 that plays cut sequences in the letterbox-type scenario, but its exact aspect can vary from game to game. The Internet and projects destined for Internet or computer play don't need to be tied to any specific shape or aspect ratio. They can be completely experimental, specifically when using programs like Flash where an aspect ratio like a column could be created (see Figure 8.5). Storyboard aspect ratios need to be accurate to the actual used aspect ratio. If storyboarding is done with an arbitrary aspect ratio, and the actual production is going to be in CinemaScope, the composition can't really be thought out, because CinemaScope is a very distinct rectangle and needs to be treated as such to truly start to consider composition. In animation, and often in live action, storyboarding truly is the act of composing the shot and wearing the hats of the director, cinematographer, and the director of photography, so the proper corresponding aspect ratio must be considered.

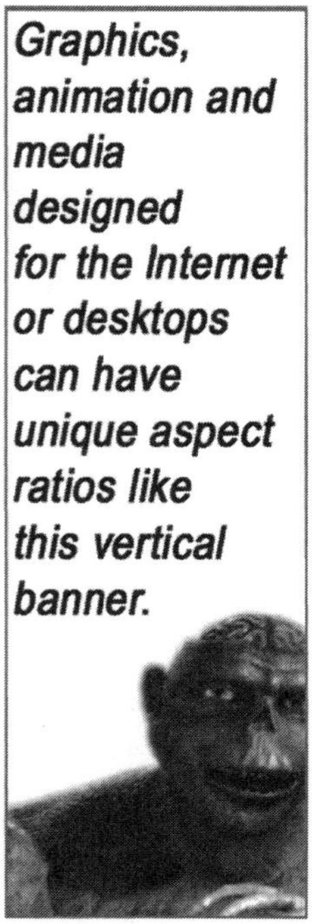

FIGURE 8.5 An illustration of the extreme aspect ratio that media and animation can have on the Internet or on the computer.

PREPPING FOR ANIMATICS

In creating complex moves or storyboards where parts are moving or some type of motion is ultimately going to be added, it's important to run through the animatic software to know how to prep elements. Making a rough matte on an element of storyboard is not a complex job. However, if many have to be made, it's wise to define how the elements are treated quickly and efficiently. In certain software the easiest way to create floating elements is to paint in the areas that are not needed with a consistent chroma key color.

Once an element is on a green screen, it can be easily manipulated in an animatic that features motion that is required for developing timing or for background separation. The level of polish on the artwork in Figure 8.6 is for presentation animatics and boards. Images on a chroma keyed

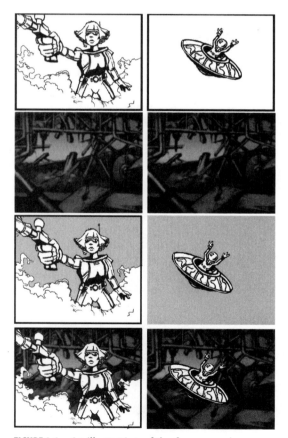

FIGURE 8.6   An illustration of the foreground elements, the background, and the element on a green-screen layer, and then the final combined elements ready for movement (see Color Plate 14).

color background are easily keyed out and also tell the editor exactly what is and isn't an element by its obvious color. Other software works quicker with an alpha channel. Depending on the software, the alpha channel can be embedded in a 32-bit targa file or saved separately. Other software doesn't recognize 32-bit targa files and instead requires a 24-bit image file and an alpha channel to be saved separately. If many drawings are being boarded and prepped to create some sense of movement, it's important to set up a system of creating and saving files so the many files do not have to be converted or reexported.

STORYBOARDS AND PHOTOSHOP

When drawing or creating storyboards, Photoshop or similar digital manipulation software can be extremely effective in creating additional panels with a minimum amount of work. Creating true working storyboards often means creating dozens and dozens of individual drawings, but being Photoshop savvy can help eliminate redrawing and can easily create clear timings for movement. In Figure 8.7, the storyboard panels started from one single drawing. The character drawing is the same and is duplicated. To create gestures, the hands are erased and then redrawn directly in Photoshop, or as a simple element, and then inserted in the storyboard panel. This creates panels that can be incredibly precise and that clearly show movement without having to draw the character over and over.

FIGURE 8.7   Panels have been altered in Photoshop to create new panels without having to redraw each one from scratch.

ON THE CD

If eye moves or expression changes are essential to timing, they too can be quickly altered in Photoshop or similar programs. The *Shards of Death* storyboards, all of which are contained on the CD-ROM saved as Figure **8_21.jpg**, illustrate this technique, as do the animatic versions that are also on the CD-ROM. The creatures' expression change is essential to the scene, and one initial drawing is modified several times to create those changes; the panels don't have to be redrawn from scratch. In the upcoming animatic phase, these types of changes appear very smooth to the eye. This is because the original panel isn't altered and the background doesn't move at all, which can help to create a clearer read.

If the panels are redrawn from scratch, then background elements move from panel to panel, creating visual bumps. These shifts aren't detrimental to the project. However, being able to utilize Photoshop can not only speed up the process, but can also improve the dynamic level of the boards, which is faster than redrawing panels from scratch. Taking that process to another level, storyboard artists short on time can draw templates and then create parts that are then brought together in Photoshop to create panels.

Like the animatic, storyboards are one step in a process designed to eliminate or minimize problems while allowing the filmmaker to concentrate on telling the best story possible. Storyboards shouldn't be the first time drawings or images come into existence on an animated production. They should begin once characters have been established in some form.

THE LANGUAGE OF STORYBOARDS

There are all kinds of systems and descriptions for labeling and indicating movement on storyboards, and these techniques can change from studio to studio and from artist to artist. There are no ironclad rules. Suffice it to say that the indicators and descriptions should clearly and concisely describe what it is the storyboards are meant to represent when it comes to turning the boards into animatics and ultimately animation.

In classic film storyboards, symbols were often used that reflected directions that were derived from analog film cutting, but those symbols were somewhat archaic. Normal language and simple words are clearer and don't require a working knowledge of outdated film techniques.

A panel that has a smaller box, inside often indicated by a dotted line, with arrows aiming in or out, describes a push in or pull out. An arrow with the description of whether the move is a push, pull, or zoom is labeled inside the arrows. If a dolly or pan move begins and ends with two distinctly different images, an arrow with the respective label can stretch across two or more panels if necessary. Panels do not exclusively have to run in a column down a page. If dialogue or other direction fills the page, then the pan or dolly indicating arrow can be broken with a clean broken or "torn" edge. This indicates that the move continues on the panel above or below the panel in question. Figures 8.8 through 8.10 show these concepts.

Boards often have to deal with movement in dimensional space, because depth is an important part of staging and composition. If a character or camera move starts close to the camera, rounds a tree, and disappears over the horizon, then the character, camera, or object is moving in depth and the boarding needs to reflect that. Creating arrows and indicators that show depth does this. Tapered arrows go a long way toward conveying 3D movement in a single drawing. Curved or tapered arrows, as shown in Figure 8.11, can indicate action or character moves or erratic camera moves. If there is confusion as to whether or not an indicating arrow is for a character or for the camera, a simple label written in the arrow can delineate what it is that is moving.

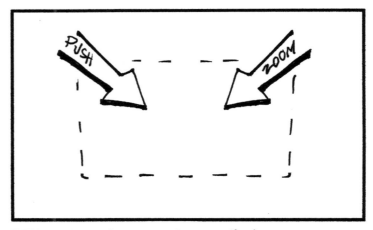

FIGURE 8.8   A move in, or a zoom into a specific element.

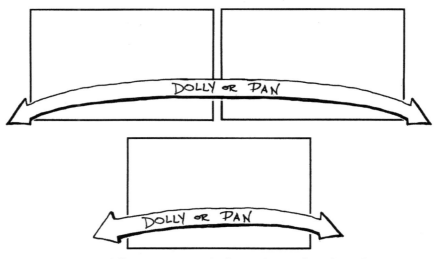

FIGURE 8.9   A pan or dolly move across a single panel or two board panels.

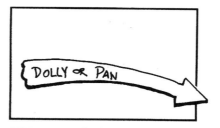

FIGURE 8.10   A broken arrow can show a move on boards that are drawn in a column or a move that continues on the next page of the storyboards.

FIGURE 8.11   Curved arrows indicate turns either by characters, objects, or the camera and are labeled to clarify.

Similar to the pan or dolly move crossing multiple panels, a tilt or crane up or down can move across several panels if different information is required in each. If a pan down or up or a crane down or up also moves in or out simultaneously, a tapered arrow can indicate this compound move. Camera shake or vibration can be simply indicated by putting action lines around a panel. A camera that is dutched or set off level can be easily represented in storyboards by simply drawing the panels with a nonhorizontal line. If a whip pan or a camera moves from one place to another very quickly, then a panel is created with a double-ended arrow with a notation that reads "whip or zip pan" added inside the arrow. This concept is illustrated in Figure 8.15. In traditional film, a diagonal line indicated wipes and dissolves across the board, but now the transitions are usually just labeled between the panels. Black frames or FTB (fade to

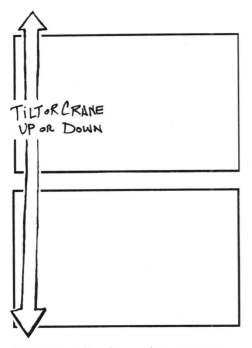

FIGURE 8.12 Tilt and crane shots can move across multiple panels.

FIGURE 8.13 An illustration of camera shake when drawing a storyboard panel.

black) indicates fades to black. In drawing storyboards, often a complex angle is hard or too time consuming to draw even for a skilled animator, and it's acceptable to use scrap, photocopies, or traces of images with specific angles. Elements that will be added later can be indicated by simple text in the panels. These concepts are shown in Figures 8.12 through 8.19.

Frames from existing films or videos can be used—anything that will clearly convey the idea to anyone who has to bring elements to the shot that is being created. Just as a costume designer can grab swatches of fabric, storyboard artists are free to use angles and images as composition references. Of course, using other artists' footage and artwork beyond inspiration is potentially copyright infringement (see Figure 8.20).

ON THE CD

Among the films on the companion CD-ROM are the two films *Shards of Death* (**Shards.mov**) and *Grime Shoed Diaries* (**Grime.mov**). Both these projects began with dozens and dozens of designs, a few animation tests, and one working scene or two and then went into an extensive storyboarding session once a script was in place and the designs were done. *Shards of Death* (see Figure 8.21) was very straightforward as a talking film

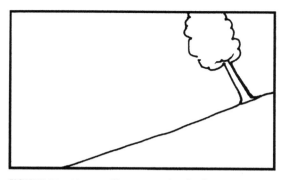

FIGURE 8.14   How to illustrate a dutched camera angle.

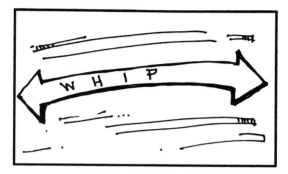

FIGURE 8.15   The standard panel to illustrate a whip pan or quick movement.

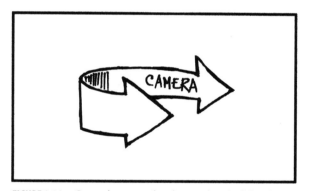

FIGURE 8.16   Curved arrows that have a level of depth to them indicate character turns or camera turns. A label is added inside the arrow to delineate between the two.

with mostly subtle movements and dialogue. *Grime Shoed Diaries* was far more complex in its scope, with camera movements, and visual layering.

Boards for the *Grime Shoed Diaries*, as shown in Figure 8.22, were made up of extensive pencil sketches. Drawings were done far more elaborately than needed, especially for a film that was a solo project and had no input from others. Working in detail on the boards enabled a level of focus that allowed the development of many ideas and visual gags and allowed for the creation of another layer of subtle humor. Boarding was truly the point where all the cinematic choices, camera placement, and moves were established. Unlike *Shards of Death* that played out on one singe set, *Grime Shoed Diaries* had many backgrounds as the character moved from scene to scene. In an attempt to create the feeling of a huge

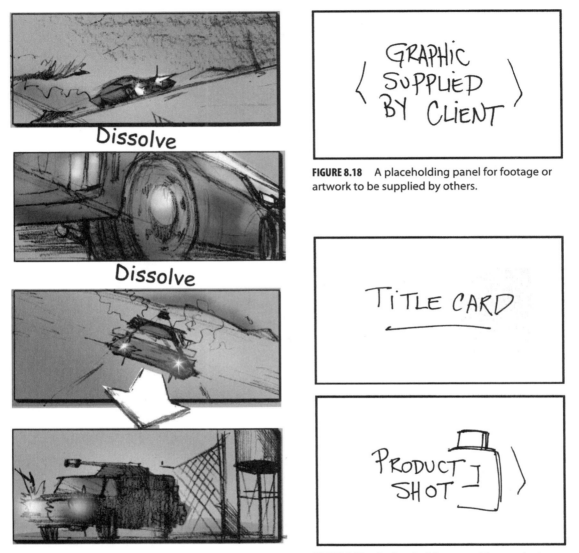

Dissolve

Dissolve

FIGURE 8.17 Dissolves are simply labeled between panels.

GRAPHIC SUPPLIED BY CLIENT

FIGURE 8.18 A placeholding panel for footage or artwork to be supplied by others.

TITLE CARD

PRODUCT SHOT

FIGURE 8.19 A placeholding panel for product shots and titles.

faceless city, it was necessary to create many shots of the detective small in frame or not in frame, with just visual texture shots of the city. Angles from high in the air give the sense of huge vertical spaces. Buildings always stretch out of frame and seemingly into infinity.

FIGURE 8.20   A vacation photo is used to create a storyboard image.

The style of the animation is still flat, like a comic book, and combines flat layers with extensive camera moves that reveal more information. The camera is integral in the film because it delivers many joke punch lines with specific reveals. The opposite is true of *Shards of Death;* punch lines came from the characters and not the camera. With voice-over narration, the camera reveals visual jokes that run contrary to the dialogue. Close-ups are used in contrast to the huge wide shots and allow the camera to focus on the facial expressions. With animation, it's possible to create shots that are impossible or nearly impossible, such as being able to go underground to see inside a coffin (see Figure 8.23). *Grime Shoed Diaries* features a quick scene where the shot zooms into the microscopic bacteria on an eyelid. Animation is made of extremes and when used correctly, inventive shots can have tremendous impact. Ultimately, boarding and cinematography are nearly one and the same thing. *Grime Shoed Diaries* is complicated visually with many moving layers, while *Shards of Death* is a comedy that is based on performance, so the camera placement plays it very straight.

In *Shards of Death*, humor developed from using ideas of opposites and awkwardness—at its root, the comedy is anchored on the well-used "fish-out-of-water" setup. Awkwardness comes out of pauses, silence, and discomfort. These elements come out of performance, and this idea informed the boarding so that the shooting is very conservative and minimal and the shots should be very unobtrusive and normal.

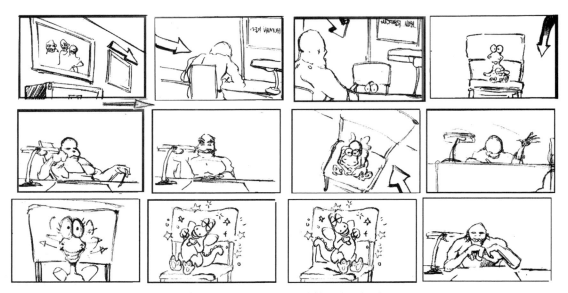

FIGURE 8.21   A series of storyboards from the short animated film *Shards of Death*.

Specific emotions call for specific treatment. *Grime Shoed Diaries* attempts to be epic in scope and parodies a gritty detective story, with many shots that attempt to create a gritty, dirty world in which the character barely gets by. The film is also a parody of a suspense film and is laid out that way, with long shots with characters moving in the shadows and lurking around in the foreground and background elements.

The story starts on a large scale, showing an entire city, and then focuses down to a single person: the detective in his office, where he works and lives. The majority of the film takes place in the city, so it was essential for the city to have the detail of the genre it parodies. The opposite is true of *Shards of Death* where if anything were going to come out of the two characters' interaction, then the camera needed to be there capturing it, silently and cleanly. With the exception of the first panning reveal of the fairy character, the camera's use of effect is minimal. It works better than wild shots, which could possibly detract from the performance. Every shot was considered and shots of the fairy character were photographed from above the creature and angled down to reinforce the character's size both in real size as well as in significance. The green monster, on the other hand, always had a desk in front of it, to keep the character feeling very standoffish, serving as a fixture of authority. The fact that he is a hideous monster at a bland desk is another absurd level of humor. The tables are turned because in a sense, the fairy is actually the straight man in the humor world, because he's acting consistent with his

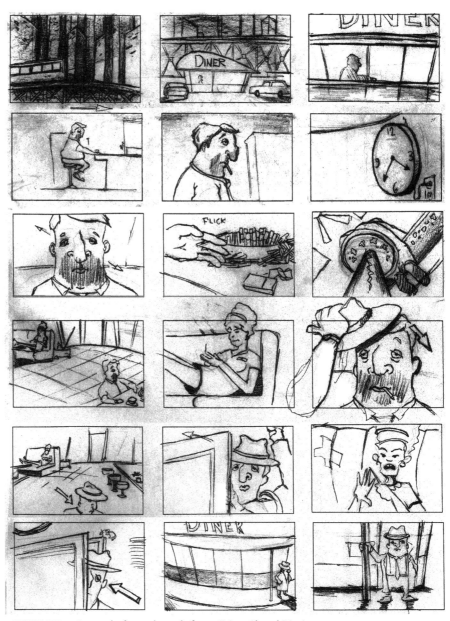

FIGURE 8.22   A panel of storyboards from *Grime Shoed Diaries*.

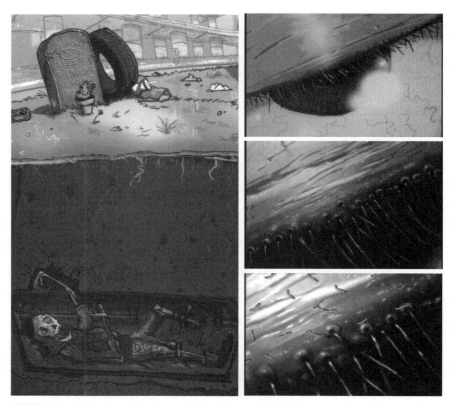

FIGURE 8.23   Animation cameras can go to impossible locations, even underground and microscopic.

nature. The monster, however, is more of the comic character because he's acting contrary to how a horrible creature or monster usually behaves, all of which was sorted out in storyboarding.

From a mechanical point of view, *Grime Shoed Diaries* had more potential editing problems, which had to be addressed in the boards. The film is almost purely a voice-over, making the visual sync-up very critical to visual gags and to animation frame lengths. The detective tells his story, and it's important for certain elements to sync-up with the running dialogue track, either by extending or shortening visuals or adding or cutting lines. Creating too few frames or too many frames is extremely wasteful, and the boarding and animatic should guard against that in addition to all their other functions.

In many instances, a set of storyboards is established, but the boarding process itself often goes on well into the production if necessary, making revisions and changes to deal with unforeseen circumstances. Much of the information on the reboarding comes from a true give-and-take process with the animatic; in modern animation production, boarding and animatic production are one process.

Tips for Future Projects

Follow the Rules of Cinematography to Establish a Flow

In live action, a cinematographer doesn't like to have all his shots handed to him in the form of storyboards. He often wants to consider the location and the lighting, and offer his own artistic input. In animation, figuring out the shots literally decides a multitude of factors of cost and time. For the storyboard artist in animation, all the issues are addressed simultaneously, but the actual rules of cinematography—cutting on action, line of sight, and staging—cannot be overlooked and need to be adhered to. Directors and animators have the flexibility of bending the traditional rules of visual storytelling. However, it's often a good idea to make the story work visually with the tried and tested standard that is cinematography before trying to establish a new look or style.

When in Doubt, Let the Story Decide

When boarding a film or animation or other project, the story weighs in on every decision. A simple process is to go from the large concepts to the small. What are the basic fundamental ideas going on? Using that notion, distill the story to its basics, distill the scenes down to their basics, and distill the characters down to their basics or motivations.

Once the main ideas and the emotions in the film or animation have been established, it becomes easier to make crucial decisions about everything from costumes and animation poses to lighting and camera positions. Is your story or the part of the story you're boarding frenetic and chaotic? Perhaps using a handheld camera would help tell that story. Is your story somber and dramatic? If so, smooth dolly moves and tracking shots can create a link with the viewer, who will feel as if he is a silent observer in the scene. If there is physical comedy, are the shots wide enough so that slapstick can play out? If the story is suspenseful, are there close-ups to show the fear or anxiousness of the characters? Boards, cinematography, and everything else should go through the "how-to-help-tell-the-story" machine.

Consider Props and Other Objects in Helping Tell the Story

A desert is a desert, but if an alien skeleton sits baking in the middle of it, it instantly becomes another planet or barren world. The playwright Leo Tolstoy said to the effect that if you show a gun in a play you'd better use it. This is true when describing the power of certain props that an audience has a level of expectation of. Props are excellent storytelling tools.

Consider Locations

Considering locations is important. Is the location normal or exotic? Does the location play a significant role in the story, such as someone being lost in a foreign city? Can a unique world be created? If so, then use it to your advantage; someone lost in a foreign city would be dwarfed against gothic cathedrals, buzzing foreign cars, or strange alleys. Perhaps angles from high up could be used as the lost person crosses old city squares. If the project is more like *Shards of Death*, then the backdrop is really mundane and bland and there is no reason to feature it. How can backdrops or sets be utilized to enhance the story and focus performance?

What Are the Boards For?

There is a huge difference between presentation boards and working boards. Presentation boards need to be well-done, colored, and well-drafted. Working production or shooting storyboards are a tool used to create a performance from a very technical point of view.

Move Quickly

The single most important idea when creating boards is to not get bogged down in any one element, drawing detail, or sound design. Block in the shot first and work from large to small. A danger occurs when too much time is spent with an element or segment; then it seems like a waste to change solely because it took too long to get to that point. Do the quickest thumbnails, be ready to do hundreds, and be ready to throw out a lot of ideas. The panels that survive can be cleaned up to show others. Be flexible; it can be helpful to physically cut out panels and have the flexibility of restaging scenes simply by reordering panels.

Focus on Clarity

At least at first, try to explain the story as simply as possible. Boarding is at many levels cinematography and photography picking and composing shots. All the rules of depth of cinematography and photography apply, from lens to composition. Boarding cannot leave important staging and positioning of characters to animatics. It must be figured out: the mechanics of where characters will be and where the camera will move to.

Boards Aren't the Place to Create Characters

Boards are often the starting point of a project, but characters need a design phase, and it should be separate from boarding.

Don't Get Hung Up on Pre-Conceived Ideas—Be Flexible

If a filmmaker has a clear idea that works and couldn't work any better, then there is no reason to work things over. However, in most cases scenes aren't so cut and dry, and experimentation often yields improved results.

Prep for Animatics

Don't draw too light so that scanning is difficult; use storyboard paper that is conducive to scanning. Try to do a run-through of what the editing software is expecting as far as size, how the files are saved and their format, aspect ratio, and any other editorial or art issues.

Photoshop and Boards Work Well Together

Using Photoshop to duplicate and manipulate panels is very effective and is an indispensable tool in the modern animation process.

In the Worst-Case Scenario, Go Back to the Writer

Because of the writing culture it's not always possible to go back to the story and have it changed. In animation, however, the process should have that flexibility. If something just doesn't work on the boards, then maybe it needs a fundamental rewrite.

ANIMATICS

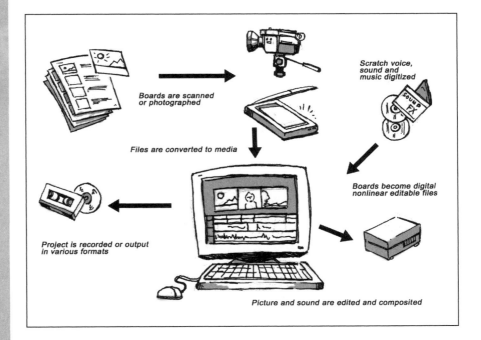

The animatic, also known as a story reel, show reel, or sometimes Leica reel, is the first pass at establishing the single most unique trait that a film or visual story has: a fixed amount of time. Animatics can accurately establish how much time the project will require and how long each scene, shot, or effect will ultimately be. More important, the animatic is the bench on which all the subjective elements are tested, such as mood, timing, pacing, and staging.

Directors have the job of figuring out spatially where things are and where they'll move, but when creating animatics, many of those directorial choices need to be made. A good director always make it clear in the viewer's mind where characters are geographically, which comes from the tried and true rules of cinematography and composition. Depending on the project, these choices and decisions should be largely reflected in the boards that move right into the animatic.

PRESENTATION AND TESTING ANIMATICS

The visual quality of production animatics can be as sketchy and as rough as the roughest boards, provided that anyone who needs to know what's going on, does. A presentation animatic is a completely different device, and might involve a lot more work and refinement than a standard animatic, including color and polished elements. Similarly, it is often unnecessary to incorporate every minute detail that a production animatic would require. Before starting an animatic and even the storyboards, it's often wise to preevaluate what the ultimate purpose of the animatic is and who is going to see it and use it.

Presentation or testing animatics, like presentation storyboards, can also go a long way to selling a project, or getting clients or other prospective parties on board. Presentation animatics can also be illustrated beautifully and fully, like comic books or a graphic novel, and can have rich colorful moving elements that suggest the final motion of the scene. Simple animation is also usually included in animatics. If certain imagery is crucial to the production and to understanding the specific elements, lip art or photographs can be utilized in animatics as well as boards. Moves, pans, reveals, and even the feeling of a handheld camera can also be incorporated into an animatic, depending on the level of finish that is required.

In commercial production, animatics are shown to test groups, so they are often extremely polished and can cost in the tens of thousands of dollars or more. For an independent filmmaker, this would be an exorbitant amount, but it's a drop in the bucket for a commercial production that will spend a quarter of a million dollars or more on a single film shoot and millions of dollars on a campaign. For this reason and others, there is a significant difference between presentation/testing animatics and working production animatics. Working animatics need only to work out the timings and mechanics of the production to provide a flexible guide to what is to happen, so adding color, movement, and animation would be overkill.

ANIMATICS BEYOND PRODUCTION

Because of the cost of animation both in actual dollars and hours, animatics are also useful in planning and reacting to a variety of budgetary issues. With animatics, it's often possible to evaluate cost issues and rework scenes based on budgetary constraints, which is a real issue on virtually every production. Examples would include being able to recycle backgrounds, eliminating unnecessary characters, avoiding expensive effects by eliminating shots that aren't inherent to the story, and many other cost-cutting measures that only become visible when the first version of the production is viewed.

Tied with modern recording systems, animatics add another level of usefulness because they can be laid off to video, burned to a DVD, or made into a QuickTime or AVI clip for later viewing. This in and of itself isn't that remarkable, but being able to revisit an animatic, an edit, or similar version is truly invaluable. Having the flexibility of revisiting a project after a few days or even weeks can have amazing clarifying powers.

Time is a brutally honest critic. Being able to reapproach a project with fresh eyes and being able to forget about all the separate pieces often helps you create new ideas and solutions that can reveal weak ideas, but most important it helps solidify elements and scenes that work well.

Both action sequences and comedic sequences that have very specific timings always benefit from a revisit when editing, but in reality everything benefits from a fresh look. Being able to view an animatic or a work in progress in other environments, such as at home in comfortable surroundings, as opposed to an edit suite or a production office, can give you new perspective and ideas. Animatics that are made portable can be viewed by anyone anywhere and are powerful and unique tools. Unlike storyboards, animatics don't have to be read; they are watched like the eventual final product.

WORKING PRODUCTION ANIMATICS

Christopher Murrie, a professional commercial editor, describes the power of the animatic process:

As an editor, the animatics are the most exciting part of my job. Because left alone I'm able to wear all the hats—I'm the director and am deciding the first pass on almost everything. I'm also the sound and music department. I can even reframe and recompose shots with Photoshop or just using the built-in tools in Avid, so I'm the cinematographer [and] director of photography as well. The animatic is really where the film is made. Once that is established, my role becomes far less creative and more operative, so the animatic is really the place where I get true creative input. Ultimately it's up to the director to decide how everything goes, but if I come up with a good sequence or a new take on how to tell the story, then it usually it stays in, and I'm making so many decisions on so many levels that I'm almost always able to add something major to any project.

Animatics are created by photographing or scanning the storyboards and other elements and then editing them to time with a dialogue, scratch track, or other temporary sounds and music. Once an animatic is roughly cut together, which is the loose joining of all the shots in some order from start to finish, then the planning of a film or animation production can truly begin. Once storyboards are complete on some level, the animatic is the next logical and crucial step in creating a working and dynamic film, animation, game, or even simple sequences. On a small, one-person project, animatics are not absolutely necessary. Even the shortest projects, the ones with a just a few scenes, can still benefit from this process. It adheres a fixed timeline to the visuals, and the creator is able to study the story and how it is translating visually relative to time. On a larger project, the animatic process becomes absolutely essential and the reasons are numerous from practicality to creativity. This process is illustrated in Figure 9.1.

When an animatic is created and the scenes and sequences are fixed in their proper positions and time has been applied, the animatic instantly becomes the template for editing, timing, pacing, and ultimately creating a dynamic project of a target length. Animatics are the first, but not final, proving grounds for how long each shot or element remains on screen. Prior to the animatic, the evaluation of screen time for each shot is erratic, and time planning is difficult if not impossible.

Shots or sequences that were estimated at four seconds on the storyboard might actually be readable in one and a half seconds. An example would be a quick reaction shot. Conversely, a shot that was timed out at four seconds in storyboards might require three times that amount to allow for a line, a beat, or a measured pause.

A filmmaker can look at boards over and over and even mentally or literally put a stopwatch to each, but until they're together, it's virtually impossible to accurately judge how the sequence of a shot's ultimate length will feel. Once an animatic is roughly assembled, the drawings,

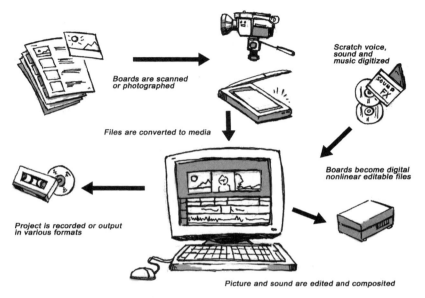

Boards are scanned or photographed

Scratch voice, sound and music digitized

Files are converted to media

Boards become digital nonlinear editable files

Project is recorded or output in various formats

Picture and sound are edited and composited

FIGURE 9.1   An encapsulation of the animatic process.

combined with time, now begin to tell a story and hint at a general pacing of that ever-evolving story. Music videos are often cut to the beat of the music track, which is now somewhat of a cliché, but cutting to the beat is an excellent analogy for cutting to the beat of the story and developing overall pacing. Pacing is crucial to keeping the story moving and keeping the audience interested.

Even though working animatics can be very roughly drawn or even just thumbnail sketched, the process works extremely well. It is remarkably accurate when trying to zero in on timing, pacing, speeds, and pauses, as well as every other aspect of a production.

Working animatics also allow the director to start to simultaneously evaluate all the combined elements, including timings, flow of action, and editing, so that it all fits seamlessly together and ultimately seems like one continuous piece and not a series of different scenes. Not all projects are meant to flow together, and projects can exist where the scenes or sequences are deliberately separate, but even with that filmic style, an animatic can solidify that approach as well.

Most narrative storytelling benefits from the seamless connection of one shot to the next, which is often referred to as a hookup. The principle behind a hookup is that every shot hooks up correctly with the previous shot and the following shot.

Like so many other elements in storytelling, scene changes, pacing, and timing are felt, but visually all elements should be virtually transparent. If during a film or animation the audience is aware of the pacing, scene changes, and cuts, then there is the potential for a "disconnect," which is the opposite of a hookup.

A *disconnect* is when technical issues draw attention to themselves or draw attention to the medium itself and begin to interfere with the viewers' suspended disbelief. Instead of going by invisibly, a cut or scene change sticks out and the audience notices the device outside the world of the story. The audience might not know what exactly they saw or felt, but something briefly kicked their attention out of the flow of the story and instead hinted at the making of the film or animation. A single disconnect isn't a complete disaster. They happen all the time in even the most polished and big-budget productions. The reasons are numerous: filming discrepancies, editorial changes, acts of nature, and so forth.

Disconnects can happen on various levels and to various degrees, and a viewer may or may not sense or feel the disconnection, depending on one's own sense of perception. If a disconnect happens, it's easy to continue on with the emotional connection provided that the following shots hook up correctly. Often a viewer can easily rejoin the story, and some hookups are more transparent than others. Disconnects should be avoided at all costs, and too many disconnects can become a veritable house of cards that can ultimately disconnect the viewer completely. The supreme technical goal of directing and editing is to find the right hookup for every single shot, short or long, and eliminate any chance of disconnect on every level. Creating a true flow of story with all the complex levels of visuals, effects, performance, and emotion is the filmmaker's greatest challenge. F.W. Murnau's harmonious structure is indeed a huge, complex puzzle, but unlocking the puzzle and getting the pieces to fit together should always be the goal.

Creating an emotional and structured flow is the first and crucial step to establishing true timings and real emotional storytelling. To represent those elements, the simplest drawings and sketches in animatic form work to inform this timing and pacing.

Invariably in the animatic phase, elements that worked in the storyboards no longer work in the animatic and require finessing. For example, scene changes are too abrupt, a given visual isn't as readable as it seemed on the storyboards, some sequences are too long, others are too short, or a string of shots or sequence is confusing. Dealing with these problems and challenges are precisely what animatic creation and adjustment is about; entire scenes can be reworked, changed, and removed, and whole new scenes added because pacing and timings are so crucial to telling the story correctly. Obviously, it is much easier and cleaner to change a few rough sketches and quick drawings and drop them into the edit than to refilm or reanimate a sequence when a scene isn't working. Emotion is the single most important driving force that informs pacing, timing, composition, direction, and performance. All of these crucial elements can be reflected in a truly dynamic animatic.

Animatics and storyboards are never truly finished until they are replaced by a final shot, and quite literally, a good animatic is always in flux. Solving technical problems is only one of many uses of a truly dynamic animatic. The animatic is also the proper place to try different versions and different cuts. With storyboards, you can have numerous versions, alternate cuts, and alternate endings: "the bad guys get away" versus "the bad guys get caught." The process of showing how the bad guys get away or get caught, and the way that the shots are laid out and sequences are timed, can only really be done with fixed timings. In certain instances, scenes can be cut together in various ways that will still arrive at the same conclusion; often sequences don't clearly read as better or worse, just different. Certain versions can use the same footage, but the individual shots are rearranged in an attempt to refine pacing, staging, and flow. Testing these sequences against others to decide on final sequencing is another valuable aspect of creating an animatic. If an animatic is valuable from a global overview perspective, it's equally as valuable at a very specific and even frame-by-frame level. Animatics can be very precise if created correctly, and even in animatic form it is possible to create and evaluate cuts and changes as specific as one or two frames. Frame-by-frame adjustment is often considered final editing business, but truly dynamic animatics have the same capabilities. Even in animatic form, a well-trained eye can tell when certain shots or hookups are a frame or two long or a frame or two short, as in the case of matching action from scene to scene.

Performance and emotion ride above all else, and a more complex example of a scene that could be massaged through an animatic would be a scene where the goal is to up the emotion by drawing out time. Let's say a person tells another person devastating or very troubling news. The person telling the bad news may have trouble getting the words out, and there could be long pauses between words. Long pauses have their time and place, and what would be disastrous during a scene of comedic banter would work perfectly in drama and drive up the tension. Elements that could be used to enhance this heavy scene could include using inserted reactions of the person hearing the stuttered line and showing the person's growing concerns over the tone; both these elements might be effective in building a brief sense of suspense on how the person receiving the news is going to ultimately react. The suspense or tension could continue to build as the person with the bad news, after several long beats, is able to whisper the pivotal line. Depending on the story, whether the audience knows what's coming or not can create another level of intrigue.

The character hearing the line may be so shocked that he says nothing for a long beat, or the person could explode in anger and not let the first person finish the last words. To allow emotions and dramatic tension to build based on the story, the right amount of time has to be provided to let them play out and develop. In this scenario, a timing beat can be adjusted to accommodate how the feeling or emotion is translating over time. Discovering that exact right amount of time simply means testing the sequence over and over with various pauses and beats at the crucial points.

In live action it's often possible to grab extra shots to edit with when making different edited versions. Examples include using an extra cutaway of an expression, creating more mood shots, or using extended sequences that don't necessarily pertain to the plot but might possibly add depth and story texture. Arbitrarily grabbing extra shots, however, is a bit haphazard. If an animatic is done well before shooting, not just in animation, the animatic can inform what extra shots need to be filmed, if time is available.

Similar to creating working storyboards, a common reaction to doing a near-frame accurate animatic prior to production is that it kills or spoils any spontaneity when filming or animating, but the opposite is actually true. Just like clear storyboarding, knowing all the essential scenes and shots that must be created before starting allows the filmmaker or animator to free up thinking about how shots and scenes will work or cut with the next, or if a certain scene was covered adequately. Since the essentials are covered to tell the story correctly, the animator or filmmaker is free to create new or inspired shots that can improve the story, while knowing that the essential elements have been completed.

Creativity comes in many forms, and visual artists need to be able to respond to on-the-spot influences: a dramatic sun set, a unique location or situation, or a unique performance or person. Planning doesn't quash spontaneity; it fosters it. It's a bit of a twisted phrase, but good animatics and boards plan for spontaneity.

If the filmmaker or animator creates or is inspired to shoot a new inspired shot that he feels might work better, then those shots or sequences can be created. If the instinct was correct, then the final production has been improved that much more. If the newly animated or filmed sequence didn't have the impact originally intended, then the director or filmmaker can comfortably revert back to the original, solid, and well thought-out sequence. Once final editing and compositing begins, it's acceptable to have many choices, but it can be disastrous to not have the required amount of visuals to tell the given story completely and correctly.

With animation, the stakes are potentially higher; the extra cost and time demands of animation can make animatics that much more crucial. When storyboards are converted to an animatic, there are always sections or sequences that worked nearly perfectly the way they were boarded. On the other end of the spectrum, there are always sections, scenes, and shots that land anywhere from needing fine-tuning to not being able to work at all. This type of story development and improvement is the highest function of the animatic: to tell the given story in the best way possible.

Animatics can also clearly reflect the sound track of the film or production. Animatics also work with roughed-in sound effects, often essential to truly evaluating motion and action in animation. Animatics also make extensive use of scratch tracks, which are the first pass at dialogue and are on-the-spot recordings of the voices, but not necessarily the final recording or location sound.

Animatics can also reflect the current state of digital editing relative to production and can easily be assembled and even have partial animation or simple motion. For example, a scene requires a bird to fly through a scene in a certain amount of time. A simple drawing of the bird or any other element can be moved however roughly to simulate the movement that can be more revealing than cutting through still frames.

Several storyboarding software packages now bypass hand drawing altogether, and automatically convert boards into working animatics on a timeline. To that point, boards and an animatic do not necessarily have to be hand drawn, but can instead be created in any visual program, whether it's 2D, 3D, or anything in between.

The idea of boarding and animatics is not to create a miniature version of the production. Trying to create boards and animatics in a 3D program often starts to defeat the purpose of the quick feedback nature of animatics, because using 3D programs can become too laborious and waste too much time. Creating 3D boards and animatics can go against the idea of flexibility and exploration that is done so easily with quick thumbnail sketches. Boards and animatics are about flexibility and extremely quick changes, so anything that makes changes and flexibility difficult or unnecessarily slow should be avoided.

Story reels or animatics used to be created on film by cutting shots together much in the same way as the final film, but digital editing systems have made animatic creation easier and more flexible than ever before. Animatics can still be created on film, or edited linearly on videotape, using drawings photographed or recorded and cut together, but film and linear tape editing isn't nearly as easily changed as its digital counterparts are. The key is nonlinear editing and even the most basic digital editing systems, provided they have locked sync capabilities, are capable of cutting together solid animatics. Programs like Avid, Speed Razor, Final Cut, Premiere, After Effects, and many more can easily handle animatics and their visual elements, sound tracks, and countless multiple versions. Additionally, programs like Flash and Lost Marble's Moho, and even Microsoft® PowerPoint can all easily handle the creation of an animatic to usable levels.

Creating an animatic in the same editing software that is going to be used to edit the final project is extremely useful and convenient, because a "drag and drop" replacement system can be used once production begins. The idea behind drag and drop in regard to animatics and editing is that finished shots are dropped right over and replace their animatic counterparts on the same working time line. By dropping finished shots into the animatic time line, as shown in Figure 9.2, it becomes possible to compare them while in production to see if all the preplanned hookups are still valid and working. Further, each time a scene is added to the ever-evolving animatic, it gives yet another chance to make adjustments to other shots that haven't been shot or animated yet. Most professional editing software now allows multiple layers of picture and sound and allows for keeping the original animatic intact, as well as alternate versions to be compared against as the production progresses. Having as many lines of defense and chances to reevaluate cuts and timing and flow only serves to solidify a true flow and cohesive story structure.

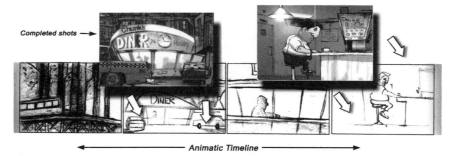

FIGURE 9.2   An illustration of how finished shots are dropped over existing shots on the time line.

Only with time running, uninterrupted, can the filmmaker truly evaluate how all the elements—visuals, dialogue, audio, and effects—fit together. From a technical aspect it also starts to inform the animators, directors, and producers how long each shot will eventually be and what elements will be involved in those shots. In live-action filming, rolling an extra 10 seconds after each shot is as easy as not turning off the camera. However, in animation, 10 seconds can be 240 additional frames that are drawn or rendered, and those frames all cost something either in real dollars or in effort.

Frame Counts

Animatics by their very nature are locked to time. As a result, they can generate real frame counts, which are crucial to animation not only for length, but also for performance. Arriving at near true frame counts allows the directors to really begin to fine tune timings in animations; it also allows animators to see the timing of the scene before and after the scene they're working on, so that actions and motions can flow from shot to shot. When more than one animator is working on a project, it becomes important for the animators to be keenly aware of what is coming after them and before them, so that the character's attitude, position, both in space and physically, are correct from scene to scene.

Transitions and Dissolves

Basic transitions and even complicated transitions can and should be incorporated into animatics. If the transition is time dependent, meaning it requires its own amount of time beyond the two scenes it's joining together, then it must be incorporated if a true measuring of accurate time and pacing is to be reached. Aside from cuts from scene to scene, animatics make extensive use of simple transitions: dissolves, wipes, or fades. Dissolves, however, are uniquely used in animatics beyond the normal use of going from one scene to the next and expressing a specified amount of time elapsed. Dissolves in animatics can also be used to show important changes or mimic camera moves in the same scene. In *Grime Shoed Diaries* there are three storyboard panels that illustrate elements that are seen as a large pan moves across the detective's office. In Figure 9.3, the three panels are dissolved between each panel in the animatic to better illustrate the idea of a pan, while still showing important information in the room.

Even when there isn't a physical cut, using a dissolve to indicate that the scene has changed adds to the level of accuracy and timing that the animatic will reflect. Many software programs have the capability of creating virtual pans where the software actually moves over the surface of an image and reveals new information. However, creating and updating virtual pans can be cumbersome. Dissolves also allow the creation of smoother transactions between subtle movements that are crucial to evaluating the story and pacing, even though they are one continuous shot.

30 frame dissolve   30 frame dissolve

FIGURE 9.3 A camera pan is illustrated in story panels by dissolves between each panel.

From the *Grime Shoed Diaries* boards, the intro sequence is again one long continuous moving shot. Cuts between those images might be misleading in evaluating the time for the shot, so dissolves between the separate panels instead of cuts more accurately reflect the pacing and ultimately the length of the final shot. The actual effect of the dissolve versus cuts is included on the CD-ROM titled **Grime.mov** and is shown in Figures 9.4 and 9.5.

ON THE CD

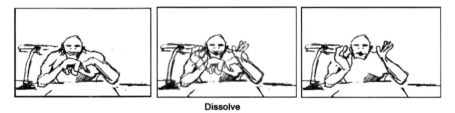

Dissolve

FIGURE 9.4 From the *Shards of Death* boards, dissolves creates a smoother transition between panels meant to be one continuous shot.

FIGURE 9.5 Dissolves between scenes as the animatic mimics the large crane shot that starts the film.

Effects in Animatics

With animatics, the more details that are added to the animatic, the more useful it will become for solving many more problems once animation production has begun. When creating animatics in Premiere, After Effects, Final Cut, or any modern editing software, other techniques can be used to create additional, visual techniques that need to be incorporated in an animatic, if they are clear elements of storytelling. For example, you can create virtual camera moves as mentioned earlier. Specific and subtle effects need to be created in some form for a complete and informed evaluation of the total time. A subtle camera device is using rack focusing or the depth of field to reveal elements. Depth of field or rack focus can be simply simulated when using a program like Photoshop. If a rack focus is needed in the animatic, it is easily created. Using the blur features in the filters controls of Photoshop, or similar programs, select all the elements in the panel that are in the background and would be out of focus on the shot. Blur those elements and save the image. Revert back to the original image and do the opposite: set the foreground images out of focus while leaving the background in focus. Save the altered image and then incorporate the two images side by side into the animatic and use a dissolve between the two to create a working representation of the rack-focus technique (see Figures 9.6 and 9.7).

FIGURE 9.6   A clean unaffected, drawn panel for creating a rack-focus effect.

ON THE CD

This technique is included on the CD-ROM titled **Rackfocus.mov**. The overall idea is simple. Use any of the traditional tools or those in your software package, and apply them to the stills. If a shot exists that requires a push-in feature in a certain element in the drawing, using any

Foreground elements blurred   Background elements blurred

FIGURE 9.7   The elements of creating a subtle rack focus in an animatic.

number of techniques and tools can do this. Whether it's created traditionally with pencil and paper with multiple panels, in Photoshop, or virtually in the editing software makes no difference, as long as the effect is readable and accurate in its timing.

When deciding how to approach and create complex shots that have moves or other dynamic features, speed and clarity are the key. Often drawing by hand is the quickest, but in other cases, using software is the most effective, fastest approach.

Programs like Premiere, After Effects, and Final Cut all have a variety of effects and transitions, many of which don't have much practical use in narrative storytelling and are instead geared toward other forms of visuals. Shaped wipes, dazzling transitions, and 3D-spinning effects occasionally find their way into storytelling. However, by and large those effects are more akin to making other visual media such as sporting events, talk shows, and other visuals that aren't so much aimed at traditional storytelling.

Being able to push in on a drawing is a powerful tool and can easily mimic a zoom or a push that would then be representative of an upcoming shot in animation or live action. The same zoom or push-in effect can be achieved by making separate drawings or Photoshop docs, and then inserting those drawings into the edit time line as a sequence and either just allowing a simple cut between each, or by dissolving between each image, similar to the earlier example from *Shards of Death*.

Depending on the software, it's often easier to use some of the built-in effects in the program to achieve the same result, if a new image isn't required. Certain storyboarding software incorporates many features and can automatically generate an animatic from the existing boards by simply adding specified time to each shot.

If the panels need to change to indicate new visual information, and an overall push in or pan is required, then a combination of techniques can be created by applying two effects at once. If the move and combination of drawings truly require a complicated combination of sequences, it is possible to apply effects to a clip, render the clip with the effects as an AVI or QuickTime, and then reimport the clip into the edit time line and apply more effects if necessary. These types of techniques are valuable when creating presentation or testing animatics that are going to be reviewed by people outside the production process.

However, from a creative standpoint, it's important to remember that an animatic is a guide for production; adding too many effects can begin to have diminished returns. Usually there is a simplified way to get the idea of whatever effect is being created with simple moves. Ultimately, a working or production animatic is a stand-in for the final animation, timings, positions, hookups, and all the other elements involved in a production. As mentioned earlier, it isn't about visual quality, and adding color and other details only slows the animatic process.

Scratch Audio

Working animatics are always changing; all the elements that live in the animatic are up for scrutiny, review, and debate. Every element should be played against other ideas, refined, and ultimately decided on. With music and sound tracks, completely different types of music and sound design can be tried: a full symphony, a simple harmonica, the natural sound in the scene, or absolute dead silence. Lines can be tried, read, reread, rewritten, and rerecorded. In commercials, this is often the case, with new lines and voice-overs being changed and reworked up until the final posting of the commercial.

Dynamic working animatics are always evolving and being updated until the final edit session, as all the drawn panels from the storyboards are replaced one by one with the final images or sequences. The animatic is never retired; it's just completely undated and made over and can continue to be referenced even after final animation or filming is done. This is especially the case if there is a discrepancy between the animatic and the final animation.

Animatics and Commercial Advertising

Animatics work for any project, long or short, but no where does an animatic prove its value more than a project with a fixed amount of time. Television commercials are a well known form of media with a very fixed amount of time. In creating a 30-second television commercial, an animatic is absolutely essential, regardless of whether it's animated or live action. In a commercial, the time is fixed and nonnegotiable, down to the very last frame. Telling a story in that very short time span requires concise and specific shots, and allows little room for anything else. Because each shot has an allotted, fixed amount of time, it becomes imperative that whatever the action is, it happens in that allotted window of time. Obviously if a shot or scene runs too long, even by a second or two, then it would have to be a cut. If there weren't enough of a difference in action, then it would become a jump cut. This would start a chain reaction that would set all other shots out of their allotted time frames, while trying to accommodate the shot that ran too long. In commercial work, every second and every frame is extremely valuable.

An advertising agency or the client who originally commissioned the commercial usually drives commercial work. In a commercial production, preproduction is essential and a vast amount of work goes on long before shooting or animation begins. Prior to filming or animating, boards and animatics have been reworked and adjusted many times. Often there is a chain of approvals from the advertising agency to the client. There can also be many layers in between who must approve the boards and concepts, and then sign off on that approval. It is, however, still acceptable to improvise and shoot or create variations, or to be inspired by the location or the performance. At the very least, it's essential to film or animate what it is the client had originally approved. For these reasons and more, animatics are complex maps that work on a multiple of levels. They are also a powerful organizational tool, unique to the medium that relies on a specified amount of time for its final delivery.

ON THE CD

The animatics for *Shards of Death* are available as QuickTime movies on the CD-ROM. The QuickTime movies are **ShAnim1.mov** and **ShAnim2.mov**. The cuts are varied and a scratch track is also in place on the first version. In creating the film, this animatic was the map, and it clearly illustrates many of the techniques used to take storyboards to the animatic level. The versions on the CD-ROM are one of many early versions and they end completely differently from the final film. The earlier versions on the CD-ROM were a bit longer, and in the final analysis it was decided to drop the extended ending. To pull off the film as it was originally boarded, with just a few more seconds of screen time, required a lot more animation, another entirely new character, and a much more extensive set model.

After much debate and weighing of the costs, both financial and in time, it was decided that the joke had already played itself out and a surprise ending would be just as entertaining. The animatics also have several early renders of animations dropped in the time line. The animatic changed daily so the included animatics were daily snapshots from the first few days of animation, which is evident by the level of render and the rough nature of the animation. These early shots in the animatic were purely blocking and animated by animation director Sean Burns.

Extensive use was made of Photoshop when creating this animatic. This fact is apparent because elements, such as the monster's hands will move, but the rest of the scene is stable, unlike the shifting effect when a whole new drawing is inserted. Using Photoshop in this capacity is doubly valuable because it's faster and easier to change just the hands than having to make another individual drawing and it is a cleaner presentation overall.

The use of dissolve techniques is also readily apparent at the moment when the little fairy creature realizes that he has probably failed the interview. His expression changes in about four drawings. Instead of cutting, these four drawings are dissolved through so that there is no confusion on how much time has elapsed, making for a smoother presentation. Having smooth and working transitions helps to truly evaluate the project. The animatic was also used for frame counts and had a scratch track and some sound effects, however simple, cut into place because specific sounds are necessary for animation timings and pauses.

Creating an Animatic

As mentioned, storyboards do not need to be complete for animatic production to begin. In fact, once the animatics do begin, storyboarding continues to change as the animatic process reveals gaps and shots that are required that weren't apparent on the storyboards. In working in a production facility, the editorial department is often a major hub of activity. If more than one project is underway, editors are regularly overbooked, and the editor's time is valuable and can be very limited. It is usually a requirement that the storyboards illustrate the entire project in some form.

In a working environment where editorial time isn't a factor, like a solo desktop project, an animatic can be created simultaneously with the storyboards. If an edit system is available unencumbered by time or cost restraints, physical boards can even be eliminated. Instead of drawing and scanning, digital drawings go straight from a digital drawing system like Photoshop, and are saved as panels and cut directly into the animatic; this approach is rare. Creating drawn boards with pencil on paper, however, can have a solidifying effect and can sort out problems prior to editing.

Either by using a scanner or a camera, the storyboard panels are brought into the computer and the edit system. Certain software packages have certain requirements, and quick tests should be run to check the throughput process of the system. Before starting the scanning and editing system, establish what format the drawings or digital images should be saved as. Most software accepts JPEG files, but some do not. If there is a conflict, then files must be converted, which is a wasted step.

The standard NTSC video resolution for the majority of edit systems is the Digibeta /D1 size, 720 pixels wide by 486 pixels high at 72 dpi. Most modern scanners scan at a much higher rate as a default, which can cause the image to be scaled up or rejected by some editing programs. In working with certain programs that work at DV resolution, the standard is 720 by 480. Some lower end systems work at 640 pixels by 480 pixels. It's important to establish the parameters for the final editing so that the panels aren't distorted or stretched or squashed. If a project has a unique aspect ratio (e.g., 16 × 9) or is mimicking anamorphic presentations, then the animatic aspect ratio and the panels should reflect that. The reasoning behind testing the process is to eliminate any conflicts between software and to avoid having to rescan or reimage. In a production setting, when working with an editor it's important to confirm all perimeters with the editor before any digital work begins (see Figure 9.8).

FIGURE 9.8   An illustration of how aspect must be considered in accurate boarding and framing.

Like other moves, push ins and pull outs can be drawn and dissolved between, so software can create digital pulls and pushes and moves. Often when using software like Avid, Speed Razor, or Premiere, when a push in or pan is created in the system, it can often break up when zoomed in on, because the image is tied to 72 dpi (see Figure 9.9).

When generating working animatics this is acceptable, because visual quality is unimportant. Timing and pacing are the goals of an animatic, and as long as the image is still recognizable it will work. If the ultimate goal is to create presentation or testing animatics, then extra effort can be made to create more polished pushes and pulls by using programs like After Effects, Combustion, and Digital Fusion, among others. If shots or panels are going to be used to mimic a push in, pan, tilt, or other move, then it's possible to scan it larger to create the move and not have the

FIGURE 9.9   Digitally zooming in on 72-dpi video frames causes breakup that is workable but less appealing.

image break up once the digital push in or move is complete. If incorporating other footage, animations, or video, again test the process to make sure that the software packages don't conflict with each other and the file formats don't conflict with the software, whether the files are AVIs or QuickTimes, or how they are ultimately compressed. QuickTime and other compression tools can create clips at any frame rate, while using various forms of compression, like Cinepak, Sorenson, or MPEG, and so forth. Depending on the editing software, different frame rates and compression formats can cause conflicts. Consistent frame rates are also essential in creating consistent motion and lip sync.

With newer updates, software is becoming less discriminating with formats, but certain formats like TIFF and PICT are somewhat outdated or suited for print design and might not be recognized by editing software. Similarly, formats for sound and compression need to be tested or at least approved by the editor, whether they're wav files, AIFF, or other formats that are specific to that edit system.

If an animatic is being created on a software package that isn't the same as the final editing software, then certain considerations need to be addressed to avoid reworking elements. This is a standard scenario, because online systems that can edit broadcast or high-definition resolutions are often cost prohibitive, so that two systems are ultimately used. If an animatic is being created offline on a consumer program like Premiere, but then will have a final edit on an Avid or other higher-end system, then it's important to try to establish a set of parameters for both systems so that files will transfer from one system to the next. Often, online editors will require all of the elements that were used to arrive at the final edit as well as a tape or equivalent of the latest animatics, sound files, and any other elements.

EDL is an acronym for edit decision list, and is a list of all the edits, transitions, and their times down to the frame. Certain software packages generate EDLs, but each software can have and saves its own format. Higher-end edit systems can export EDLs that might be compatible with other applications if an edit project is being transferred to another system. As with generating any files for software packages, it's advisable to establish early on the compatibility of the EDLs. This means establishing whether or not the EDLs can be exported or imported to other systems and making provisions and planning accordingly if the edit list doesn't translate from one system to another. At a basic level, an EDL can be exported as a simple text file that basically has the time code from the original source materials, such as a videotape that has a running time code. However, when converting a project from one to the next, a text file EDL often isn't very useful in the case of animatics. Often, the editor of the new system must simply use his eye to recreate the cut, which is not an optimal procedure but is often the case.

When making the jump from storyboards to animatics, animatics often require many more panels or images than the original boards to truly evaluate timing and pacing. With animatics and specifically dialogue it's necessary to create as many panels as required to convey the pacing and timing. Even in scenes where characters are simply talking, it's often necessary to create panels that reflect normal conversation, gestures, and poses. In a very basic sense, a still image would work on a superficial level while a character is saying a line. It is important to create panels for every gesture that will then be reflected in final animation or production. This will establish true timing and pacing and ensure that poses and gestures have enough time to be readable.

Economy is still important and an animatic shouldn't be an all-consuming enterprise. Like the storyboards, images can be recycled, modified, and tweaked to create new poses and images. Recycling or slightly modifying images is especially useful in dialogue scenes when cutting back and forth between what would ultimately be similar and the same camera setups. This is clearly how many of the images of the two characters in *Shards of Death* were created. Unfortunately, recycling panels can be limited and specific. If a camera position changes, even slightly, then a new panel is required, whether or not it's created from scratch or is a kludge from others.

Like storyboards, animatics benefit from using Photoshop or similar software to create distinct poses and reactions by slightly changing existing panels and drawings. Dialogue scenes are naturally less labor intensive. Action scenes, whether it be full-blown action like a large fight or battle or simpler action like a character moving around and doing many different tasks, often require many more panels to clearly illustrate the action. Simple gestures like head turns and pose shifts should be clearly laid out in the animatics. Even the smallest movement, such as a blink or slight expression change, if integral to the story and pacing, should be reflected in the animatic.

Most of the cues to how the animatic should go should come from the storyboards, but the flow goes back and forth, sending images from the animatic back to the storyboards. The animatic is primarily created to establish timing and storyboards where shots and angles and overall composition are sketched out. The animatic is another pass to solidify the angles and cuts on the boards and finesse or fix compositions or send them back for complete redesign when they don't work as boarded.

Blank panels are also important to show when an action has moved out of frame, but by necessity the shot has to sit for a beat to create a felt ending to the action. An example would be someone leaping off camera. A blank frame illustrates the beat from the exiting the scene and before the scene changes to the next camera angle. Classic cartoons of the 1950s and 1960s often featured extremely hyperaction. Characters often dart out of the camera's view in as few as four or five frames, and a blank frame appears after the character is gone, clearly illustrating that the event has happened (see Figure 9.10).

FIGURE 9.10   An illustration of the use of a blank frame to allow the scene to settle after a very quick action.

Dean Wellins, who is head of story development on one of Disney's upcoming animated features, treats every panel generally as two seconds of screen time. For action it can go much faster, so that a minute and a half of action on the screen could easily have 200 animatic panels to clearly illustrate every aspect of the action and how that will translate to the next step: animation production. (Read Wellins' complete interview in Chapter 2, "The Story.")

The lessons to be learned from that level of detail is to not leave anything to chance, and to that point it's almost impossible to create too many panels. It's also important to remember that getting bogged down on finessed and polished drawings can use up huge amounts of time, especially when the drawings might potentially wind up being changed any number of times. Above all, animatics, even at a highly evolved level, are still about proving and testing sequences and the project as a whole. Adjusting, tweaking, or potentially completely overhauling entire ideas, sequences, or story elements is what animatics are all about; flexibility and speed when it comes to testing is how a cohesive and emotional storytelling is visually created. If done correctly, an animatic is a comprehensive map that guides the rest of the production, potentially down to the last frame, whether it's CG, stop motion, Flash, or even live action.

Tips for Future Projects

Don't Get Hung up on Preconceived Ideas—Be Flexible

It's common to make several completely different versions if necessary, either in whole or in part.

Move Quickly

Don't get bogged down in any one element, drawing detail, or sound design. Block in the shots first and work from large to small. A danger occurs when you spend so much time with an element of a segment that it seems like a waste to change solely because it took too long to get to that point.

Create a Production Plan from the Animatic

From a production standpoint, the animatic also dictates clearly what will be required. A good producer dissects the animatic down to the last detail.

Make Pacing and Timing Work in the Animatic

Animatics are very important. If pacing and timing aren't clear in the animatic, it's not going to get any clearer during shooting or animation, without a lot of repetition and waste.

Don't Hesitate to Go Back and Get More Panels to Define Scenes

Boarding can go on long into production and should be used as an ongoing tool if necessary. It's easier to sort out problems on paper and in the animatic than in postproduction.

SOUND, MUSIC, AND VOICE

		JOHN		LUCY	DOOR			
	1			Closes	DOOR			
John—	2			Door				
"How Are You?"	3							
	4							
	5							
	6							
	7							
	8			↓				
	9	H — How			S			
Door Slam →	10	H			L			
	11	O			A			
	12	O			M			
	13	O			M			
	14	W			M			
	15	W			M			
	16	W			M			
	17	W						
	18	W						
	19			◉◉				
	20			◉◉				
	21	R — Are			Lucy:			
	22	R			I'm fine			
	23	R			I guess.			
	24	R						
	25	R		Moves	STARTS			
	26	R		eyes	ON 65			
	27							
	28	↓						
	29	▷						
	30							
	31							
	32	U You?						
	33	U						
	34	U						
	35	O						
	36	O						
	37	O						
	38	O						
	39							
	40	↡						

Sound effects, dialogue, and music have been an integral part of animation since sound was first combined with moving pictures. During the silent era of movies, live music, anything from a band to an organ or a piano, accompanied the film and played a track that reflected the mood of the scene: a solo violin played for a sad scene, while a frantic piano played for an action scene. Music was the natural partner for motion pictures for two major reasons. The first reason was that the motion picture was silent on its own, but because audiences were already enjoying vaudeville-type performances that featured a small orchestra or other musical accompaniment, music was a natural extension for movies. Second, music worked incredibly well with visuals because all people are affected by music, while still being able to focus on visuals.

Music plays some part in every human culture, and like film, music requires a specified amount of time to happen. Glued together, music and pictures created a perfect amalgam. The combination of the two created much more emotional power than a film could wield in silence alone.

Animation, being the hybrid that it is, is even more dependent on sound than live-action film is. When viewing a live-action movie or television, audiences expect a certain level of "real-world sound." This is sound that the viewer would accept being in that scene normally. For example, in the outdoors we hear wind, traffic, birds, and other natural ambient sounds. When indoors, we hear buzzing lights, clocks ticking, air conditioners humming, furnaces kicking on, and other sounds that we associate with reality. Unless being used for effect, audiences would probably pick up on missing sounds that should normally accompany a real-world situation or visual. For example, if someone shuts the door, there should be a slamming sound. Because of a lifetime of hearing specific sounds in real life, audiences, are aware of natural sound and will notice when it's missing. In animation, all sound is missing because audiences know it isn't reality; they don't have any preconceived notions about what the sounds should be.

As media have evolved, audiences have spent so much time immersed in visual entertainment that modern movie and television audiences have created a new sense of sound for entertainment "reality." They have come to expect certain types of sounds and music in certain situations, regardless of their reality in life.

For example, large city shots always have a police-car siren wailing, and low-rent apartment buildings usually have a baby crying. So infused are these expectations into the imagination of audiences that certain sounds, which are often iconic and don't actually exist, are expected. In films that feature fighting, whooshing sounds are added to big swings and kicks to add effect, and when someone gets hit, it's a much loader smack than it would be in reality. Characters often read things aloud, or talk to themselves to further a plot. In science-fiction movies, sound is always added to outer-space scenes, with rumbling spaceships and dynamic explosions, when in reality sound cannot travel in the vacuum of space. However, sound expectations evolve and change and the audience's imagination is always in sync with the latest films. Some modern sci-fi films will feature bits of silent space to sell the vacuum and the desolation. In early films, audiences would have considered a silent outer-space scene a technical error, but sophisticated sci-fi fans will recognize the reality of silence.

Sound moves incredibly slowly compared to light, but humans are so used to sound's slow speed that they mentally compensate for it. If a film featured a baseball game and the shot was filmed from high in the stands, when the batter struck the ball, the sound would happen the instant the bat struck the ball; in reality a noticeable delay would be the effect. This means that from a great distance, a viewer would see the bat hit the ball and then hear the sound much later than the actual event. Film and animation are not set in reality. If the sound were delayed as it is in the real world, on film it would appear that the crack of the bat and ball meeting would be out of sync, if it came later than the visual. Sound is a type of glue that ties the visuals together with the reality it's created or trying to associate with.

Animation again shows its ability to behave in more than one fashion. Unlike filmed live-action, animation in the mind's eye isn't bound to real sound at all. Animation can be full with 64 soundtracks, all mixed with every shoe squeak and door slam, or it can have none. Because audiences don't associate animation with reality, sounds and sound design can be tailored and manipulated to enhance the mood and to reinforce the story to a level that is impossible with the expectations of live action.

In one respect, animation is more laborious because all sound must be created and animation doesn't come with a soundtrack. However, the blank slate of animation truly is another tool for the animator, and sound mixer to use to their advantage. With animation, sounds, and an overall sound design, sound can be controlled and manipulated to focus the viewer's attention to certain actions on the screen, specific movement, mood, and emotion.

SOUND EFFECTS VERSUS SOUND DESIGN

When creating a project, it's important to evaluate how sounds should be positioned in respect to the story. As production design works to establish an overall visual look, feel, or mood. Likewise, sound design should create its own feel and mood, but with audio. Instead of simply servicing the sounds and expected sound effects in the mix, sound design tries to go further to use sound to reinforce whatever is being presented. From real-world sounds to elaborate sounds for every body movement, such as a zany cartoon that features a bizarre sound for everything a character does, the sound is always just half of the experience. Whether nearly silent or filled with sound, a good sound design finds a spectrum of noise, and sound to provide consistency in the soundtrack.

In live-action films, when filming out in public, certain sounds can be confusing or begin to pile on top of one another and create a din or a general noise. With animation, this can be duplicated if the scene requires it, but it can also go the other way where superfluous sounds are eliminated to instead focus on key sounds and effects.

Sound mixing is the act of adjusting the timings, physical positions, and volumes of all the sounds. In animation, it can go so much further by eliminating sounds or using unusual sounds that if eliminated in live action wouldn't work.

ON THE CD

In *Grime Shoed Diaries*, **Grime.mov** on the CD-ROM, the first half of the film features the main character walking through a huge city. Many sounds were added on top of a din or general city sound effects to create a grittier feel. The sounds of dogs barking, the iconic sounds of police sirens wailing in the distance, and the sound of a bottle breaking all suggest the story behind scenes going on off camera. The included short films *Grime Shoed Diaries* and *Shards of Death* both intend to mimic the real world, so a full rich "real world" sound track helps sell the reality that the films imply. In *Shards of Death*, as many noises as possible were added that were real. The squeaking vinyl chair, the monster's pencil tapping the desk, and even the soft ambient noises of an outer office were added to round out the sound track, because the reality of the film is what most viewers know in the real world.

ON THE CD

The opposite effect is a very stylized sound design. **DAE3.mov** on the CD-ROM is a short comedic animation experiment. It was designed and animated to be strange. Instead of room noise or city sounds, a strange buzzing was added as a din.

Sound has the ability to use specific sounds that are not pleasing but instead are almost to the point of irritation and yet work with a visual accompaniment. In *DAE#3*, there is no music, but there is a music cue of a short bongo drumroll that acts as an action punch and audio introduction. The animation is extreme and the sound effects are simple and deliberate so that it can hold up against such unusual visuals. Many sounds could have been layered in, but the staccato and simplistic pacing of the animation as the character freezes between poses lend themselves to simple sounds. Having sound drop out allows the viewer to again hear the strange buzzing tone and sets the visuals on edge. Effectively used, an irritating sound or effect is the opposite of cute.

In *DAE#3*, the sounds themselves are far beyond real-world sounds positioned to reinforce the animation's extreme key poses. Things that are squishy have only a very squishy sound, skin when stretched sounds like a balloon, and things crunch when pushed together; these are all sounds that tell of a creature with liquid and bones inside that is designed to be visceral.

This short film takes place in and hints at a three-dimensional world. When things fall off screen and bounce out of frame they audibly continue on, because there is still an element of real-world physics tied to the extreme animation, and that physics tends to reinforce the visual rules that have been established. Because the character sits behind a simple plane, it implies a real space. If items that fell out of frame didn't make a sound, it might create a confusing idea that the object had just kept falling, that there was no floor. In relation to the story, once the object is out of frame, the ideal situation is that it is also out of the viewer's mind; a simple sound of the object hitting ends its movement and it can then be mentally dismissed by the viewer. Sound design, both on and off the screen, whether stylized or realistic, must pay keen attention to the perceptions of space, substance and movement, and distance.

MUSIC

Music carries its own emotional ties that can have incredible impact on people and be far more personal than visuals alone. In creating a mood for a story, the combinations are endless. Different types of music create different types of feelings by simply combining a specific type of music or instrument. At the top of the scale is the full-blown symphony, which is capable of powerful emotions at every level. For example, the music of a full choir has a built-in regalness and can make a scene feel profound and awesome; a male choir can seem very foreboding and even have a militaristic feel, both of which are very serious and were used to effect in the nuclear-submarine drama *Crimson Tide*. Choirs can also be comical and can be used when someone sees an object of their desire, such as when a kid sees a giant toy robot he wants in a store window and a choir sings the "Hallelujah" chorus. Popular music is often used in comedies and chases, and music videos have had a huge effect on the musical track in films. In storytelling, however, less is often more.

A film or animation may have a sad scene, and a natural reaction is to reinforce the scene with symphonic music, such as with long notes on strings like violins and other flowing instruments. Using the standard sweeping symphony can work, but audiences have been hearing that type of sound design since movies began having sound. In modern films, this can be overkill. If it's too overpowering, the sound can become emotionally redundant and sappy, or it can have an opposite effect on a viewer. Suppose the viewer gets the feeling that the filmmaker is trying to squeeze an emotion out of a scene instead of letting it develop or evolve, whether in sound effects, music, or visuals. He may then sense that the filmmaker is trying to sell an idea, resulting in a large disconnect.

Early on, when films and visual entertainment were newer, certain types of music and sounds always went along with certain visuals. Sad scenes had sad music, dramatic scenes had intense dramatic music, and action scenes had up-tempo music; most of it was simple and one-dimensional. With modern audiences, musical tastes have evolved and changed and the combination is now far more sophisticated. Now a single instrument can punctuate a sad scene. For example, a piano can play single chords or notes with huge pauses between each measure. Musical pauses tend to hold an audience's ear, because music is made up of time and many notes, and single notes with long measured pauses can create a sense of anticipation for the audience. With evolved and sophisticated audiences, it's now acceptable to play opposites against each other with greater effect. For example, a horrific or violent scene backed with light or upbeat music is ironic. A harrowing and high-speed car chase set against a classical or operatic piece of music has the same effect, but can also give a sense of poetic visuals to what would be generally a fairly unpoetic scene.

In animation, music and sounds can have even more effect depending on the stylization of the animation. Similarly, certain music put against certain types of animation doesn't work at all. Naturally, there are instances where music reinforces the story, but there are also as many instances where the right choice is to use no music at all. In a sad scene, scaling back the music, either in volume or in the number of instruments, to the amount of music in a given time, can change the mood and feeling dramatically; in the right scene, silence can be sadder or more poignant than any music. Discovering the balance of sound and music is paying close attention to a complex set of variables.

The scenario of a little homeless girl all alone on the street in a big city is an example of normal sound-design challenge. Too much music would definitely mar the scene and could even make it seem trite or contrived. It might be more poignant to hear the faceless din of the city: loud noises, loud cars, yelling and screaming, and police sirens. It's a story question that must be decided.

For all the complexities, the best way to decide on the best combination of elements and the perfect amount of sound, music, or silence is testing. Testing sounds against each other as well as the visuals is the key to discovering the right mixture. The sound designer must repeatedly try things, as much as is needed or allowed. Good sound mixers cut in pieces of music against a scene, cut in sound effects, try different mixes at different volumes, and, of course, always test scenes with no music.

At this point, a fully evolving animatic becomes the most valuable player. Long before even a frame of film is shot or a frame is animated, a good working project should have a musical and sound design concept, and an overall plan for the feeling or mood it is supposed to create. The director and sound editor should be able to gauge what each sound or music component is bringing to the story, emotion, and pacing. Figuring out the relationships of sound and music within the story will mostly like affect and influence the shooting, performance, and animation.

BREAKING THE FOURTH WALL IN MUSIC

Breaking the fourth wall in music and sound is an effective tool and is unique to the visual medium. A simple form of breaking that fourth wall in music would be when something funny or unfortunate happens on screen, and then the music reflects the action with a musical "laugh" or "giggle." The idea is that the music punctuates a scene, but goes further to reference what is going on during the scene.

In specific places in film and animation, sour notes, which are usually always avoided in music, can be used without being considered wrong. The watchword for animation is feeling, and music and sound easily elicit feelings. In thrillers or suspense, sour notes, random musical notes, or music played off key or out of tempo heighten the tension. Music that has no melody or actually has a broken melody can work because playing that music incorrectly can elicit a certain feeling. Bending notes, which start and then bend down or up, can also create a strange and awkward feeling that can enforce the suspense or intensity. Music can also cross over into sound effects. The random plucking of a harp is often used to indicate the presence of insects or spiders or hordes of rodents by creating a mental link to the concept of thousands of small legs and the pattering of feet. Music or sounds even played backwards can create legitimate audio effects and environments.

David Lynch took industrial sounds and random noise to a truly disturbing level in his early film, and now cult classic, *Eraserhead*. Lynch created a feel like no other, with a continual track of strange industrial sounds and noises that are often unrelated to the strange visuals.

SOUND LAYERING

The layering of sound is the adding of other sounds to beef up or thicken sounds to often create a sound bed. A tiger's roar can be the sound effect of a tiger's roar, but a roaring train and a horn can be layered in to give the tiger's roar an unworldly sound. Layering can be created for a single complex sound effect or can be the layering of other sound effects and adjustments, on an overall scene. Take, for example, a filmed pastoral scene of a lake. The natural sound recorded at the location has some sounds, such as the water lapping at the bank, a few birds chirping, and other ambient sound, but additional sounds can easily be layered in: more birds, insects, a gentle breeze. If the location is exotic, the cries of wild animals might be heard. Sound effects can also blur the line between themselves and music. Quiet wind chimes can be added in to give an ethereal feel, and of course full-blown music would then create an entire level of its own.

In animation, when a voice is recorded in a professional studio, it's usually recorded in a soundproof booth that absorbs all room noise and gives no other noise of any kind, except the voice. Having the voice against dead silence is a useful neutral place to begin, but sound engineers often add room noise back in, such as the slight reverberation or echo of a voice talking or speaking in a given room size made of given materials. If a character is in a specifically sized room, it should sound like a room, and not like a soundproof booth. If a person is in a large space, like a museum, there's always some type of echo in large spaces that can be layered in as well.

Echoes

Sound bounces off of any solid surface whether it's audible or not. Audiologists and designers have labored for years to design theaters that address sounds' reflect ability to create pleasant and perfect acoustics and eliminate echo completely. Theaters designed correctly can use sound reflection to amplify the sound so that microphones and other amplification equipment aren't required even in very large halls. Echoes, however, have a special role in visual media sound tracks, and have become an icon in the viewers' minds.

Echoes ride the line of being a sound effect, and there are many scenarios where an echo becomes connected to a visual. For example, a heavy echo is always used to show someone's point of view who has just awakened from being unconscious or drugged. Dream sequences also have iconic echoes and sound distortions to sell the idea that the audience is watching a dream. Echoes are often added to internal dialogue when someone is thinking; they seem to reinforce that the thoughts are actual thoughts and perhaps symbolically are bouncing around in the skull. Echoes can also mean isolation in the middle of nowhere or a vast distance. Echoes are often used to enhance the idea of giant spaces.

Other forms of distorting sounds with delays or changing the pitch and tone of sounds also create that feeling of distorted reality. Long echoes and heavy reverb often also accompany shots of time manipulation, slow motion, or a time lapse, and can be used simply to punctuate one simple shot. For example, a gun battle ends, and the slain gun fighter falls to the ground. As his gun hits the pavement, the sounds echo and punctuate the fact that he's done for.

Sound and Music Flexibility

During production, animatics can change daily, and much of that has to do with sound adjustments. With reasonably modern editing tools like Avid, Speed Razor, Final Cut, Final Cut Pro, Premiere, Toaster Edit, etc., most audio tracks can be muted or activated and remain running simultaneously with all the others. Before digital, this idea was laborious. Now the smallest production has the power for effortless side-by-side comparison of different flavors, mixes, and any other sound elements, including all the visuals as well. Depending on the software, sound versions and audio clips can remain stored in a track and can continually be recompared against future editorial changes and final or rendered shots. For the most part, the only limit is having a computer capable enough and fast enough to be able to process a specific amount of tracks, or having sufficient drive space to store all the versions. However, compared to the storage of broadcast video, or even higher resolutions, like Hi-Def or film resolution, small audio files are nearly an afterthought when it comes to storage.

Animatics are as important to sound and music as they are to picture and production. Sound and music are always viewed as elements that are added when the project is complete, but with animation the sound has always come first. Any desktop editing system that allows for multiple tracks of sound and picture, with independent volume control on each locked in perfect synchronization with each other, represents the basic tools for working out films, large or small. In larger productions, however, the amount of time allowed for testing can range from months to days, and on short projects with fixed budgets editing is spending money. That fact helped reshape the idea of online and offline, where offline, if done right, is done for good, bypassing an expensive online session.

Under Music

Music with lyrics often has to be mixed down to the point of almost inaudibility, if the music is running under dialogue. Music or instruments that are in the range of the human voice will compete with the human voice and often must be mixed very low, depending on the track. Other sounds, such as a bass or deep sounds of specific instruments, can be fairly loud and the voice is still clearly audible. The idea of allowing audio space, or space for dialogue or lines doesn't stop at sound effects and music. Music design itself can be composed so that the music falls back without stopping when people speak. Designing music to fit perfectly with dialogue is another level of complexity that requires just as much flexibility, if dialogue and sounds are still being edited, moved, and modified through the postprocess.

VOICE RECORDING

When creating animation that has lip sync, it is standard practice to animate to the sound and voice. In the animatic phase, it is a true process of give and take because animation hasn't been created yet. Unlike live action, voice can be edited, spliced, and adjusted to accommodate pacing without having to refilm. Often in animation, the final dialogue is a true amalgam of all the voice takes of a voice actor. In many instances, even specific words can and are often lifted from specific takes and combined to get the proper emphasis and timing on every single word. Often a voice actor will read numerous takes at various speeds and various emphases, and all of them can be tried against the animatic before deciding on a final version.

SCRATCH AUDIO

A scratch track is a rough audio track, often read by someone who isn't the actual voice talent for any number of reasons: the talent is unavailable, the talent hasn't been decided on, or a whole host of other situations. A scratch track is an important and powerful tool in measuring and adjusting pacing, timing, and emotion. Scratch sound effects can be as important to animation as a scratch dialogue track. Often, certain animation movements virtually require a sound effect to be able to read the visuals clearly. For example, an object bouncing down a flight of stairs might require that temporary sounds be dropped in to get a feel for how the animation will finally work.

In more stylized and extreme animation as in *DAE#3*, sounds become even more important in selling what would be impossible actions in reality. A more extreme example is an animated character's ability to stretch its arm 10 feet from its body. To visually read if the animation is truly working or not, a stretching sound effect is almost mandatory to read the move. Often, sounds that would be almost inaudible in live action are amplified and featured to help clarify the animation. For example, let's say an animated character unscrews a small bottle of perfume. A noise that wouldn't normally be audible in live action is now featured to sell what might be visually hard to discern, especially if the shot is a wide shot and doesn't feature a close-up. In another example, a character in a wide shot unlocks a door, a relatively quiet motion that wouldn't be audible from standard live-action scene. But inserting an over-the-top sound effect immediately tells the audience what the character is doing, avoiding any momentary confusion and a possible emotional disconnect.

DIGITAL AND ANALOG LOGGING

Most modern animation software now comes with tools that allow a wav or similar audio file to be played simultaneously while creating an animation. This is a massive revolution; it was not very long ago that animators stuck to the old system of creating a log sheet for the sound track.

The simple form of this was putting a dialogue track onto a piece of mag film, which is magnetic tape that is sprocketed like movie film and plays at 24 fps so that it is in complete synchronization with the picture. A track reader, logger, or the animator would then slowly drag the tape over a sound head and mark the phonics of the sounds on the log.

Figure 10.1 shows a sound and dialogue log sheet. The frame rate is at 24 frames per second, so the sheet is split into thirds of a second. The frames run down the left of log sheet. The line for John is, "How are you?" and it is logged out in the first column. The words are sounded out phonetically. Lucy, a second character, starts to speak at frame 65, which is off the page, but the log is still valuable in logging her eye movement at frame 19. A sound effect, a door slam, also happens as Lucy shuts the door, and the slam happens on frame 10.

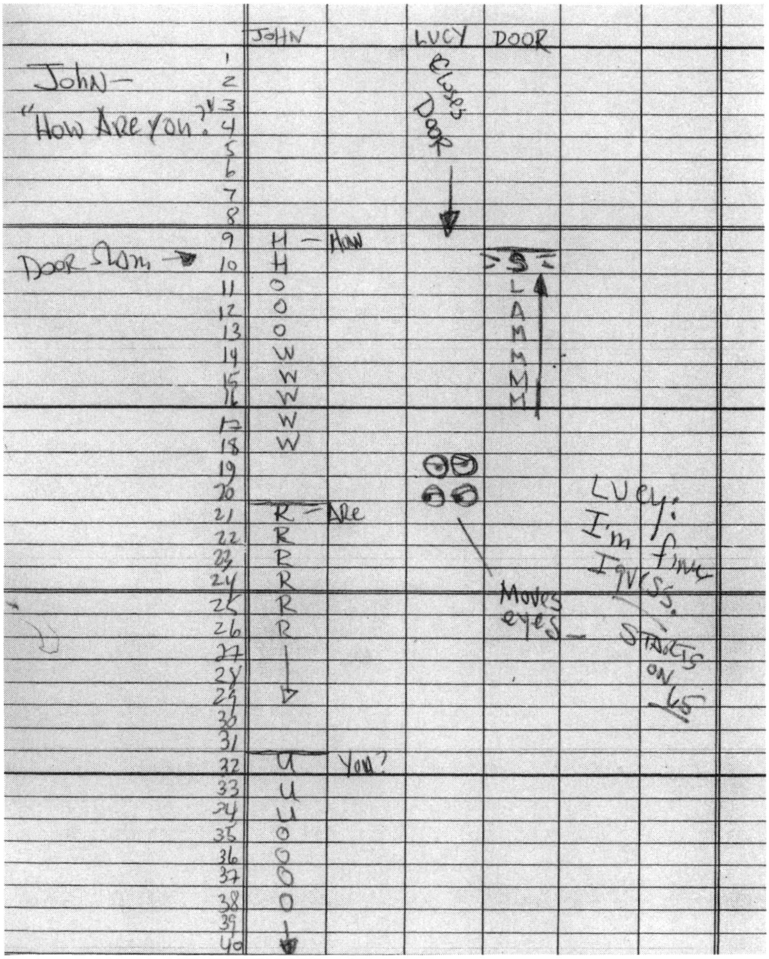

FIGURE 10.1 A log sheet for logging sounds, dialogue, and effects.

Most modern animation software such as Maya, 3ds max®, Light-Wave3D, Flash, and most professional programs can now run previews or hardware renders at television or film rate. This allows for the inclusion of a sound file that can be used and logged directly out of the animation software. Most accepted CG-animation programs also allow the "scrubbing" of the track, being able to move back and forth and pinpoint key shapes and phonetics.

There are also several sound programs for logging audio automatically such as Magpie Pro, which is a program created for doing lip sync in animation semiautomatically. Animating to the dialogue is the standard, and the voice has driven animation performance in many characters.

TEMPORARY SOUNDS AND RIGHTS

Needle-drop music, or off-the-shelf music, where a purchased CD or track is used in a production, has become a huge problematic point. There's nothing to stop anyone from buying a CD and dropping some famous music into his animation or film, and it's standard to use store-bought music during editing as a placeholder to try tempos, beats, and styles of music against the animation or film being created. However, as soon as the project is presented that music cannot, without proper written permission, be used in any form, for any reason. Music has always been, but even more so now, considered a valuable commodity that is often protected by copyright.

Not too long ago, special venues like film festivals would look the other way at "borrowed" or needle-drop music, but that is no longer always true; film festivals are big business and they often charge admission, even for student films. Once money is being made, it immediately becomes an issue because someone is making money off of music that he does not own or have the rights to use. The Internet has fueled this fire, because it is so easy for someone to make a QuickTime file, grab his favorite track, and send it out around the world. Music companies, labels, and distributors are out to stop anyone who makes money off of their music without permission.

The rights are so strict that it is safe to assume that *anything* that is recorded, even an old 78-rpm vinyl record from a yard sale, has a copyright owner who would object. Film festivals and broadcasters would be culpable if they broadcast or exhibited a film that was infringing on a copyright, so they are now very diligent about borrowed music. Trigger Street, the ongoing online film festival, disqualifies films with unlicensed music, and members must agree to legally binding statements that all music has been cleared. As to getting permission for music, it is extremely difficult without an agent who can contact the copyright owner. There are a few Web sites that offer to handle all the rights, and there are cost reductions for film-festival use only, but the cost is still extremely expensive and the process is tedious and often fruitless. Getting reproduction rights, depending on the score, can reach astronomical prices. For example, prime-time nationwide commercials that use popular rock songs can spend three quarters of a million dollars for a well-known rock song that plays a minute or less. It is so difficult to get the rights to popular hit music that it often takes contacting the musician, composer, or band itself to obtain permission.

There's also a misconception that because classical and other music are in the public domain, they can be used from a CD you purchase. Even though the music is in the public domain and was written centuries ago, the recordings aren't, and those recordings are owned by someone. Also, just because a song is old doesn't mean it's in the public domain. Often the owner is diligent and has kept up with rights and registration.

In some instances, getting a recognizable song is integral to the story. An obvious example would be a Christmas animation. Many well-known Christmas songs do fall in the public domain, but that does not mean that a specific recording does. A filmmaker using a Christmas tune still needs someone to make the music because, as mentioned, recordings aren't in the public domain. There are numerous Web sites that list songs in the public domain, some of which have mp3 files of public domain music as well. But be careful. Like all Web sites, simply looking polished doesn't mean the person necessarily did his homework in regard to copyright issues and their lists may not be correct. The quality of the music on these public-domain sites fluctuates widely, and many sites have music that sounds as if it were performed on very low-quality instruments.

All things considered, using others' music is a mixed bag at best. The good news is that the computer explosion has also created a huge army of talented musicians the world over. These people now have state-of-the-art desktop equipment and can sync up with a QuickTime or audio video interleaved (AVI) file and can deliver synced frame-accurate, perfect digital quality music as a wav file or any other file required for final editing.

It is now possible to find and hire musicians who will play classical music in the public domain. Then the filmmaker either records it himself or the musician gives him the rights to his recording, making it possible to avoid the entire agent-permission process and the license process and cost. If the filmmaker negotiates with the musician for money or any other form of payment, he can own the copyrights. Some festivals and almost all broadcast companies, large and small, now require proof of ownership or a release from the composer. AtomFilms, the online Internet movie Web site, requires releases for all music, actors, and even voice talent.

Clearly the safest and easiest way to get a usable track is to have a musician or group create original compositions. Filmmakers don't always have to pay musicians because some musicians will do it for free to get exposure, or possibly trade for filmmaking services. Whatever the arrangement, it is important to have a written agreement in which the person who created the music states he is the creator, originator, and composer. The document must also state that the creator is either giving the filmmaker permission to use the material or giving the filmmaker all the rights to the material. And finally, it should outline what is being agreed to in terms of compensation, whether it be a monetary payment or simply a credit line that appears in the film.

The deal the filmmaker strikes with the music talent is up to the involved parties, and doesn't have to be complicated to be a binding workable contract. Involving too many people in the process can open up whole new issues about fees, residuals, and contracts, which can require a lawyer and if complicated enough, require a specialized entertainment lawyer. So keep the agreements simple and uncomplicated. The idea is to protect the filmmaker and the artist, so that it is possible to use, release, sell, and distribute a project in any venue, free and clear of liabilities.

THE FINAL AUDIO MIX

In television and commercial audio, professional sound mixers mix the sounds and tracks, while listening to the project on huge state-of-the-art sound systems. But to get the most accurate sound, the best soundmen turn off their massive sound system in the studio and route the signal to a normal television set. The reason for doing this is that the vast majority of people listening to a television show or commercial are listening to it through the speakers that come with a television.

While more and more people are creating home theaters, but the vast majority of televisions still rely on their original speakers. By listening through the television, the sound engineer is able to gauge what the audience would really be hearing. Deep booming bass in the studio wouldn't pick up at all on normal television speakers, and many sound effects, voices, and music queues would have similar qualities. Testing all contingencies is an important tool when it comes to mixing sound.

Whenever possible, the best advice is to spin off tapes, DVDs, and CDs and listen to them in a variety of settings. Television sets, like computer monitors, vary greatly and so do computer speakers and television speakers. So it's at least worth listening to see if any sound problems arise in other devices.

Tips for Future Projects

Plan Out a Sound Design

Plan out a mood and a tone. How can sound help the story? Can sound become dynamic? Can sound build?

Use Simple Ideas

Scenes or animation often work well with simple sounds and music.

Audition All Sorts of Music and Sounds

Don't just rely on a first try. Try a range of music to no music at all. Try the opposite of what is expected.

Silence or Quiet Pauses

These are often welcomed after large bursts of sound.

Layer Sound

Combine music and sound effects to create an audio texture and bed of noise. Don't hesitate to pull sound out if it becomes unwanted noise.

Go Against the Standard

Earlier it was noted how in movies, the act of someone getting punched in the face always makes a terrific, if not absurdly loud, sound. Innovate directors always in search of creating new realities are aware of such movie clichés. David Fincher, director of *Fight Club*, used far more realistic sounds; he did away with the huge Hollywood crunch, which was unexpected, and made the blows seems that more painful.

Experiment

As always, experiment as much as possible.

CHARACTER DESIGN AND PRODUCTION DESIGN

The story and the character are forever intertwined and cannot exist without each other. Creating a character in visuals is different from writing a description in a short story, where the way characters are described can bias the viewer's idea of how the characters are simply by description. Writers have it harder in some respects when creating characters, but in some respects they also have an easier time than filmmakers. Writers can pick and choose which traits they want to develop and dismiss traits that aren't essential. For example, a writer can write the following:

> Gary was a dismal man, with messy unkempt hair hanging over a thick dense forehead—just like the brain inside. His lips were dry and his mouth shaped in a permanent frown, as if he was always ready to complain. He watched the world with cold beady eyes that darted around nervously.

The writer doesn't wait for the reader to decide what kind of person Gary is. He tells the reader with words like "messy," "dense," and "mouth shaped as if he were always ready to complain." By drawing conclusions and presenting them as actual personality traits, the writer draws a firm image and a foregone conclusion. The character designer can't tell the audience that a CG Gary is a dismal man. Instead, the designer must *show* all the traits, and switch the bias to the viewer. For the character designer, the adjectives are replaced by the way the character acts, what it wears, how it looks, and how it carries itself.

The writer is also free to not write about unimportant traits, like wrists, or shoes, or belt loops, because it's not necessary. Readers understand that when a character is described, it exists at level that is consistent with the story and the world. But to the character designer nothing is taken for granted. Everything has to be drawn, sculpted, and modeled from countless angles; wrists, knees, belt loops, and buttons, even if part of the "costume," must be considered.

Having to create all the details can be somewhat of a chore. It would seem rare to have something as trivial as a wrist play an important part in the story, but don't forget about the cartoon character Popeye. His wrists were truly strange, but they were also an important part of his appearance. A designer finds as many spots as he can to add to the character's nature. Not only does this include the eyes, shape of the mouth, or the costume, whether practical or digital, but the whole way the character stands, how it presents itself, and how it moves; all of these traits are closely tied together.

Audiences love good characters, and talented comedians have portrayed countless characters that audiences have enjoyed for millennia.

Good comedic actors can switch characters with no props or costume changes, and audiences accept it completely because the character is so compelling and fun. Character actors and comedians like Lily Tomlin, Martin Short, Jonathan Winters, Tracy Ullman, Benny Hill, and the *Monty Python* men create characters that are so compelling and funny that audiences love the characterizations and want to see the same character again and again in different circumstances. Audiences know full well that Lily Tomlin is a grown woman when she plays the little girl Edith Ann, and audiences know full well that the *Monty Python* troupe or *The Kids in the Hall* actors are playing characters. Not only do audiences suspend their disbelief, they almost double their entertainment enjoyment because they're watching a known actor they enjoy play a character they enjoy. Such is the power of the character; to not consider the power of characterization in animation is nothing less than negligent.

STYLIZATION

One of the most fascinating areas of possibility that comes out of animation is stylization—the idea of making an artistic interpretation of people, places, and things. Stylization is yet another tool to apply to telling the story. It is a freeing way to move away from reality, and provides the ability to strip away extraneous material so you can focus on aspects of the performance, comedy, horror, and action.

Every image in this book is stylized. The knee-jerk reaction to a word like "stylization" is to think about designing characters with big heads, little bodies, and large round eyes, or giving them the "oh so tired" look of sunglasses and tennis shoes. Those are forms of stylization. But stylization is creating a deliberate treatment or a "twist" on every process that directly adds to the feel, mood, or the humor of the final film. Stylization is by its very nature juxtaposed, either covertly or overtly to reality as most people know it. Color is an obvious stylistic tool: an untreated filmed sky is bright blue, but with filters, either digital or in front of the camera, the sky can be made brown or black, thereby creating drastic and dramatic moods, but color is only one avenue that can be stylized. Here is where animation can truly reign supreme, being able to go far beyond color, to create characters that are in spirit human but are closer to abstract art.

Virtually every process with animation is ripe for a style makeover. For example, a smooth sky can have waves of texture, or walls that are smooth can be raked with bumpy lines. Joanna Priestley's work featured in Chapter 13, "Animation," is wrought with interesting changing styles of imagery, but on a more powerful level the style works well because it deliberately and virtually sets our daily reality on its ear, which is fun. Stylization can be a way or a consistency of how things move, how they are shaped, and how similar or different they are. Stylization and the idea of an overtreatment on anything and everything is daunting without question because of its infinite possibilities. With all the animation in production, it's unfortunate that so much is expended mimicking reality, when in fact there are infinitely more interesting possibilities as reality becomes abstracted through stylization.

In a broad sense, stylization can also be what comic actors and comedians do when they become characters; they exaggerate funny traits and habits through their performance and voices. Live actors are confined to costumes and makeup to become characters, and stylization can only go so far before practical issues come into play. In practical visual terms, beyond the feeling of stylization, animation, however, is free to create stylizations that would be impossible in live action. Stylization comes from style and implies a way that something is created with a specific emphasis on any traits from line weight and textures to stylized features, exaggerated proportions, and movement. The artwork of Guy Burwell and Colin Batty in this book provides sharp examples of very different styles (Figures 11.1 and 11.2). Both create people and characters of all kinds, so their subject matter is largely the same, but the way they abstract the world they see show their unmistakable styles. All the artists in this book fall into that same category, and all the styles are as unique as the artists.

Stylization has little to do with big eyes and strange features; stylization is potentially a whole new world. It is up to the designer to create a world that works on many levels and is driven by the story and the mood and what the characters have to do. On a large organized production, design should happen before anything visual is done, and it can begin before, during, or after the script phase. The reason the design should come early is because so many processes hinge on it. A shotgun approach is when any number of design styles and rendering are applied and tested (see Figures 11.1 and 11.2).

Stylization is much more than just dodging the reality bullet; it's another huge opportunity to establish or reinforce the character's traits and create a new animated world or environment. A strange character might have a strange lip-sync system, while another quiet character might have an absurdly small mouth. Animated characters can also talk out of the side of their mouths, out of two mouths, behind huge teeth or tusks, or anything that can be imagined.

FIGURE 11.1   A stylized form of characterization so graphical that it is virtually impossible to do in live action. © 2004 Guy Burwell. Reprinted with permission.

FIGURE 11.2   A shotgun approach design study on dog characters in various styles.
© 2004 Colin Batty. Reprinted with permission.

DESIGN

Design and stylization should happen at the same time. There can be design without stylization, where things are designed to look 100% real, but design must begin to establish a stylization. When designing a character, some design process always occurs. It doesn't matter if it is a detailed planned-out process that is worked out to the minute detail with many people's input; or if it is a character sculpted on set, while the camera waits. Both are forms of a design process in which a creature or character is created.

The Academy Award-winning short film *Balance* featured elongated characters exaggerated far beyond human proportions. The film is a metaphor about the importance of cooperation and the dangers of curiosity and greed. Elongated characters stand on a flat plane that tilts as they move, hence the film's title. The fact that they are grotesquely elongated only serves to increase the precariousness of the characters balancing on a tilting plane. From a functionality standpoint, it makes the animation of the physical act of balancing and trying not to fall over more visually readable, because the characters are so thin to begin with.

If the characters in *Balance* were short and stocky, it would be harder to see that when the character raised its arms, it was trying to balance itself. Using tall, thin, exaggerated characters makes the subtly of balance much cleaner and clearer. That sort of relationship with stylization and function is rare, but is a potential goal the designer should aim for: to not only stylize for the sake of stylization, but to create a new relationship with the story, mood, humor, or functionality. The characters in *Balance* are an example where design and stylization are one in the same. They are not only tied together, but are also both tied to the story.

Some of the earliest designs are just drawings and inspired sketches that are both elaborate and simple. In animation, the design process and the boarding process are often combined. However, investing time in a design phase only makes all the other processes less abstract and answers many questions about production and telling a good story. Figure 11.3 shows a stylized caricature of a real person. The painting in this figure is an exaggeration of the man's features, but still looks exactly like a man. This painting makes a great characterization because the key shapes—the shape of the lips, the droop of the eyes, and the curve of the nose—are exaggerated, but are still the correct shape to recognize the person. Characterization is essentially taking the recognizable features or traits of a person or creature and exaggerating them in various degrees.

Figure 11.4 is a caricature of an old man whose features are bony and sharp. The back is hunched and the jaw shoots straight out. The skin is heavily lined and weathered, the ear is large and fleshy, and the jowls and skin are worn and leathery. In reality, gravity drives much of the changes of aging; gravity thins out features, tugs on jowls, and bends posture. The shape of the man's head in this figure implies that he's so old that his face has almost slipped down, pointing his head and compressing his features. All the exaggerations and abstractions are based on visual truths, which is often essential to caricatures and exaggerations. Instead of an exaggeration of a person, it's an exaggeration of an iconic type of person. In this case, it is a very old person.

FIGURE 11.3   A well-known type of exaggeration and abstraction. ©2004 Colin Batty. Reprinted with permission.

FIGURE 11.4   An exaggeration and characterization of a different kind. Instead of exaggerating the sizes and proportions of a known person's features, the exaggerations are more iconic of an old man. © 2004 Colin Batty. Reprinted with permission.

Figure 11.5 is a CG model next to an inspirational painting of the character. The stylization has huge exaggerated eyes, but a more realistic animal's mouth, which is a somewhat practical design because it needs to be able to chew as part of its performance. In the film *107.6 Degrees*, which is included on the CD-ROM as **1076_degrees.mov**, this camel character is somewhat dopey and isn't bothered by the heat; instead he just

ON THE CD

FIGURE 11.5   The painting and resulting 3D model of an exaggerated camel-like creature from *107.6 Degrees.* © 2004 Amila and Patrik Puhala. Reprinted with permission.

munches on the last bits of tree that were bringing any shade at all. The giant eye characterization, although nothing like a real camel, works to create a simple-minded camel-like character.

THE FACE AND THE EYES

Creating interesting and new characters is one of the key roles of a designer. Designers must also be mindful of what the character is required to do, how it will move, and how it will act. Nothing says more about acting than the face and the eyes. Gary Larson, creator of *The Far Side* cartoon strip, created characters that often had no eyes at all; instead, the eyes were rendered by a straight line or hidden behind glasses. When the eyes aren't visible, viewers have little clues as to what the character thinks because the eyes usually show what is on a character's mind. In

The Far Side, however, the blank looks of the people worked perfectly with the odd humor of one of the funniest and enduring comic strips of all time.

Stylization must move cautiously when it comes to facial features because certain features and expressions mean certain things. Stylization that confuses specific known looks, such as happy, sad, angry, or scared, creates a huge disconnect. Stylization can go too far, if the characters are unable to act because basic features like eye shapes, eyebrows, mouth shapes aren't readily readable, or the character is so stylized it has no eyes or eyebrows. The alien creature designed by Swiss artist H.R. Giger, from the *Alien* movies, can credit much of its scary look to the fact that it has no eyes at all, which is an uncomfortable visual to people who spend their entire lives looking at eyes for clues. Without eyes, there is no sign of what the brain is thinking. There's no empathy, which is fine for an aggressive killing machine like the alien, but would present serious problems if the alien had to act or show subtle expressions.

For a subtle expression in eyes that are recognizable, brows and eyelids both above and below the eye are often absolutely crucial. Disney characters often have large eyes, which are easier to pose and to read when a character has to perform with the full spectrum of emotions that are required in a feature film. This is not to say that eyes and faces must be fully developed. In fact, simple lines and simple shapes can often create angry brows or sad eyes, but there is a minimal amount of information or lines that are required to create the emotional expressions.

Figure 11.6 is an exaggeration of striking colors and unique designs, but the human's eyes and face must be relatively realistic to emote. A sort of geometry underscores the overall design, with many straight lines where normally they would be curved. The style is of high detail, and dramatic lighting helps to focus the scene. Even with the level of exaggeration and geometry the characters are wholly recognizable and have somewhat normal proportions. Stylization can pick and choose elements that it decides to manipulate and distort and leave others untouched. If images become too stylized, specifically for animation, it often becomes hard for the eye to follow. Early animated characters were designed on primitive shapes, such as circles and bell shapes, pear shapes, and cylinders, partly out of ease in redrawing; a consistency over a character could be maintained, but also mostly out of appeal. Creatures were based on basic simple shapes. Simple shapes with clean outlines are easy to recognize and easy to follow as they perform. If a stylization can go so far that very little is recognizable to reality, it's often hard to read the performance. A partial solution is to give characters all strange designs and proportions, but to always keep the face in a range that isn't so stylized that it can't easily and cleanly emote or act.

ON THE CD

FIGURE 11.6 An example of a complex stylization in design that is realistic in some respects, but complete fantasy in others, yet still works well together (see color version on companion CD-ROM). © 2004 Colin Batty. Reprinted with permission.

In Figure 11.7, the character on the left is clearly a dinosaur, with only a few simple shapes to create the creature. The relationship to a real dinosaur couldn't be further away, but is still present enough to recognize what the creature is. The barbs are iconic of a dinosaur or dragon, and the tiny small arms are mocking of the tiny front arms of a true tyrannosaurus. The face and eyes are purely animated and characterlike; it's a combination of dinosaur and character and can talk or roar just as easily. The two angry characters on the right are pulling scowls with their tongues out, and with a very limited amount of lines they can still convey their grimace.

FIGURE 11.7   Two different stylizations that are almost purely graphical design, but the faces and expressions are still readable as expressions with limited information. Left image © 2004 Colin Batty. Right image © 2004 Guy Burwell. Reprinted with permission.

Far too much animation fails to explore unique forms of stylization. The vast majority of stories told involve people or creatures similar to real people, so a great amount of animation features humans. Often, stylization moves toward reality, but even reality can be stylized in infinite forms and not be too far removed from a human. Depending on the story, certain types of stylizations can conflict or make it difficult for a character to act or perform. In other instances, a symbolic person will work better.

Visual Clarity in Design

Because of the relationship between animated characters and the graphic arts and art in general, the elements that govern the visual styles of artwork and design can also apply to animation. As mentioned, many animated characters are based on basic shapes such as ovals, pear shapes, spheres, and orbs, which makes reproducing the character easier, as in traditional cel animation. If a cel animator understands the basic simple shapes underlying a character such as Bugs Bunny, then it becomes easier to draw consistent poses with the character. The constancy not only goes from pose to pose, but in the case of a large animated production from animator to animator. In CG and stop motion that rule no longer applies because the characters are often made from a mold or digitally duplicated from scene to scene. However, using basic shapes has a more fundamental visual role in animated characters because basic shapes are easy to recognize, and there is a visual sense of balance that all living things have that comes from balancing on limbs to overcome gravity (see Figure 11.8).

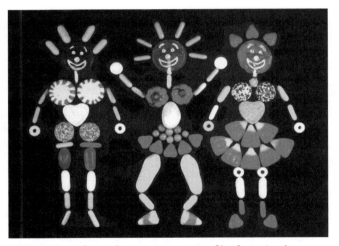

FIGURE 11.8   A frame from a stop-motion film featuring human figures that are created completely out of actual candy. © 2004 Joanna Priestley. Reprinted with permission.

When animated characters move around, it's quite different for the viewer than watching live action. In pose-to-pose animation, simple and defined shapes and clear volumes help make recognition of movement and poses easier to read. Disney has created a style of pleasing imagery, which involves making characters with simple shapes and big eyes and pleasing relationships. Disney characters have been meticulously modified and evolved over the years to entertain Disney's main audience: kids and families. For adults, Disney characters smack of cuteness, and cuteness is associated with a great percentage of animation. However, animation geared for older and adult audiences has exploded in the last few decades, creating all sorts of new stories and characters that are visually removed from their Disney and Warner Brothers' ancestors.

Art and design still have a great deal of weight when it comes to visual animation. Like the gravity that all creatures have to deal with, nature has created rules for how creatures on land and sea can grow and move. Whether a viewer is cognizant of these rules or not, he can recognize when those rules have been broken. If a stylistic approach hasn't been established, it can create characters that don't have much visual excitement or appeal.

To create pleasing and working characters, designers need to establish the rules of how the character is created. These rules often come out of rounds and rounds of drawings that are more design than animation at this point. For example, spheres and other curving balloon shapes define the overall shapes of the two characters in Figure 11.9. Although the characters have plenty of detail, the detail is clean and precise. The drawings themselves give space and room around the details to make them readable and pleasing.

FIGURE 11.9   Two stylized cel or Flash characters made up of basic shapes at their cores. © 2004 Guy Burwell. Reprinted with permission.

In Figure 11.10 the character is extremely stylized, but graphically works well and is a funny image. The character would be fine in cel or Flash, but would be a difficult task to pull off in stop motion. In 3D CG, a character could be created as extreme as Figure 11.9 or Figure 11.10, but graphically viewers will accept far more stylization than they will dimensionally. In 3D some characters' proportions that look funny or unusual in 2D just don't work once dimensionalized.

FIGURE 11.10   A simple character made of two teardrop shapes end on end. ©2004 Guy Burwell. Reprinted with permission.

Every instance of stylization and going from 2D to 3D is different, and tests are the only way to judge how far models or designs can be pushed or exaggerated. Because 3D animation is so rigid in its rules of perspective and volume, it creates a world much closer to reality than traditional animation. This is a large part of the appeal and power of 3D animation—its rules of rendering are very similar to reality. The 3D tools of the sense of space and volume of shapes are hard to avoid. As a result, certain stylizations go too far, and become unreadable in dimensional animation whereas they'd be perfectly acceptable in 2D. 3D CG brings a lot to animation, but it's also a bit of give and take when stylization tries to buck the convention of the 3D world that is inherent in a dimensional CG software world.

Certain stylizations are purely graphical and don't really even have a dimensional counterpart, yet they can work in stylized animation very well. Figure 11.11 has two characters that are created in a "flat" graphic world with no depth. This stylization is reminiscent of comic strips and a natural for animation, but perhaps not transferable to dimensional. Even though these characters could be created dimensionally in a CG program or as flat cutout art for stop motion, the ultimate feel, regardless of how they're created, is obviously designed as a flat presentation.

FIGURE 11.11   Very graphical characters that are designed to be flat, the opposite of dimensional. © 2004 Guy Burwell. Reprinted with permission.

Figure 11.12 is a graphical monkey with more clues of dimensionality. Its proportions aren't too far from a real monkey, even though it is still a very drawn look. A dimensional version could be created more readily than in Figure 11.11 because there is dimension in the character. Translating the line weights and the simplified features would be a challenge, since they don't have any clues to volume or depth.

FIGURE 11.12   Another form of stylization that is closer to reality in proportions, but is still very graphical. © 2004 Guy Burwell. Reprinted with permission.

The drawing in Figure 11.13 would make a clean dimensional counterpart; the volumes are uniform and the drawing is close to human proportions, but also is still exaggerated with a rounding of shapes and is based on basic shapes of tubes and spheres. The drawing is also adorned with graphical elements that can work in 2D or can be incorporated into 3D as a surface maps.

FIGURE 11.13   A highly detailed drawing of a graphical slightly exaggerated character and dog. © 2004 Guy Burwell. Reprinted with permission.

Figure 11.14 is extremely stylized. There are no elbows and knees, and the legs and arms and digits are exaggerated and graphical. Design always needs to be aware of the spectrum of performance required by a character as well as the tone. A character as stylized as the one in Figure 11.14 is ripe for comedy, dance, or action. However, a character that is going to act and perform might wind up fighting such exaggerations to come up with poses that will sell whatever the character is trying to say. Animation is such that if designed right, it can be both, but a design plan and the rules of the world have to be worked out.

FIGURE 11.14   A graphical human figure far removed from real proportions. © 2004 Guy Burwell. Reprinted with permission.

There is no limit to stylization, and it's up to the designers to push limits of exaggeration and stylization that is motivated not only be a new and appealing look, but also motivated by the story, what the character will be required to do, and the world that they come from.

DESIGN PHASE

Establishing a design phase is to create a project and a scope that is doable in the given amount of time and budget and has a specific coherent look that works with the story. The visual design process informs the production process, because the production process has to figure out how to turn the visual ideas into visual media. Every decision made from the number of characters and sets to character size and set size all impact a production profoundly, and designs on every level from character to an overall production design create another chance to prepare the project for upcoming challenges. Designers also compare how characters will visually fit in their world, as well as how they will interact with that world.

Expression Studies

Figure 11.15 is a few images from a traditional expression study. An expression study is a series of drawings that show all the angles and, specifically, the various visual expressions a character is going to be required to perform. Expression studies show how the character changes from different moods and feelings, and also show how the character stays the same. Without question, when creating a visual character, nothing works better than pencil on paper—the starting point for almost every character. Studies of expressions, styles, stylization, exaggeration, and visual explorations on paper or through inspired art are a key tool in creating visually satisfying, interesting characters that not only look good but also mesh well with the environment they are in, and have the ability to act and emote. Character and expression studies are more than effective tools; they are often where real visual characters emerge. Characters that are going to perform complex facial emotions always benefit from emotional and expression studies to see how the characters look when behaving differently.

Relationships and sizes, such as a head size, will dictate how large expressions can go. In the case of the little fish in Figure 11.15, it is limited to expressions that will fit comfortably on the face and work in that area, unless the design style is such that expressions can explode and grow in size like in a Tex Avery fashion. If the story called for a fish that made huge expressions or exaggerations, then the model might benefit from having a bigger head overall. For animators, expression studies are invaluable for being able to plan animations and work on a series of key expressions so that looks are consistent from scene to scene.

From a technical and even budgetary standpoint, expression studies tell the technical team what is potentially expected from a rigged model, morph targets, or blend shapes, whether it be CG or stop motion. In projects where characters are required to go through dozens and dozens of expressions, more time and money is used on the extra rigging, modeling, and animating. Does the character have teeth? When it speaks will it say sounds that require a tongue (e.g., the "th" sound)? The more a character has to do, the more technical and time considerations come into play.

FIGURE 11.15   Expression studies of a small fish character, essential for character modelers and animators.

The ongoing "reality-versus-stylized" technique battle also weighs in on the design phase. A stylized design, from movement down to lip sync, will animate faster than a lip sync that is trying to be realistic. Expression studies, model sheets, and motion studies can begin to address these complex concerns.

Model Sheets

Model sheets are integral to cel animation as the first source of how a character is created. In CG and stop motion, the character comes in with all its proportions; the CG software figures out the angles and the virtual camera is put in place. The companion to model sheets, which are immensely more valuable to CG and stop motion, is motion studies or pose studies of common or extreme poses.

A series of tests creating some of the key performance extremes (e.g., jumping, stretching, crawling, other exaggerated poses) can all break a rig. Breaking a rig in computer animation is where the CG characters push a character so far that the mesh or skin doesn't respond correctly to the pose. In the case of a broken rig, the mesh or rig then goes back to the modeler to make the pose work. Similar to this is a rig or armature that doesn't allow certain poses or doesn't have a proper skeletal system either in CG or stop motion. Riggers both in CG and stop motion need to know specific movements, such as when a character is going to go up on its toes or shrug its shoulders. The same is true for a facial animation; expression and motion studies are important in facial animation, so that animators have enough control to convey the emotions and expressions the script or story requires.

Most of the examples of characters in this chapter would be considered model sheets. Model sheets can be very specific and have almost isometric drawings of the characters from every angle, useful for passing off 2D to other artists whether drawing or sculpting. Often, model sheets are more organic and incorporate many poses and many angles. Model-sheet format is dictated by the production and the artists who use them.

ANTIPLEASING

As audiences become more sophisticated, and as elaborate and photo-real creations become commonplace, some artists revert back to simple and even crude designs; these designs aren't pleasing to look at and are intended to be unpleasant looking. For comedic effect, John Kricfalusi, creator of *The Ren & Stimpy Show,* took design elements from the 1950s and applied an extreme Tex Avery-type style that had deliberately gross and disgusting details. *Beavis and Butthead* was also created in an antipleasing style with confusing lines and an erratic sense of design, which was key to its appeal. *South Park* additionally has a simplistic and rudimentary design based on the creators' original paper cutout designs. Whether conscious or unconscious, these designs are the antithesis of the pleasing styles of Disney, Warner Brothers, and Pixar, which have elegant proportions, simple pleasing lines with uniform and measured weights, and easily readable features and poses. Designs can be grotesque but still work well in animation. Simple and crude designs are also easier and faster to produce, with model considerations and formal design being left for overall story humor and laughs, which can be a good working trade-off, if the humor and story pack enough punch. If the humor isn't there, the story doesn't work, and the animation isn't visually pleasing or dynamic, then there's really nothing worth watching.

The Challenges of Photo Real

With CG, photo real and photo-real imagery is big business. Imagery that fools the eye into thinking that animation is actually filmed in reality has been one of the main goals of special effects since special effects began. Being able to create imagery that couldn't possibly exist is powerful illusion. Yet to the viewer's eye it does exist, unfolding before their eyes. It's real and it works seamlessly with the filmed elements it accompanies.

Most special effects, by their very nature, fail to some degree when someone notices that a special effect is occurring. Audiences want to be fooled and easily suspend their disbelief when an effect is visible. However, attempting to completely fool the eye has largely been elusive throughout the history of effects, because the human eye is so sensitive to motion that it can pick up millions of levels of slight color variations. The human eye, whether the owner can describe what they've seen or not, isn't easily fooled.

Stunt people have risked life and limb for years leaping from dizzying heights, only because everyone can instantly recognize a dummy or mannequin thrown from a building. No matter how sophisticated, people are attuned to watching and recognizing real-world movement and physics. It's hard to reproduce and if just one element is slightly off, the human eye will catch it and the viewer will know it is fake. Water and the ocean have a scale, and it's hard to reproduce; miniature ships and boats, regardless of their detail, always are betrayed by the water and its size. Special-effects people have tried adding chemicals to the water or having small motors create vibrations off camera, but in the end, miniature water just doesn't behave like the ocean. Even full-sized water tanks are hard to make look like the real thing. A stormy scene is often easier to do than a calm scene, because the surface of the water is hidden by white caps, driving rain, and wind.

Computer graphics have closed in on the completely CG actor, however, and CG characters that blend seamlessly with the filmed backgrounds are replacing stunt people in many shots. Unfortunately, they don't always blend seamlessly. Big movies that have tons of effects usually hire several animation or effects teams so they get mixed results because the quality changes from scene to scene.

Audience members passed out and ran screaming from the theater when the original *King Kong* was shown, which by today's standards is very dated in its animation and special-effects shots. Now it's easy for anyone to see that the motion is wrong, the lighting is wrong, and interaction doesn't happen as it would in reality. Yet at the time it worked, and the illusion sold millions of tickets, even though the star of the film was a tiny 15-inch puppet playing a 40-foot gorilla. Special effects have always been one step behind the sensitivity of the collective audiences' eye. When photo real is used in conjunction with a compelling and thought-out story, it is a powerful tool, but photo real and the illusion of reality aren't necessary for a compelling story and shouldn't be used as a substitution for story.

INSPIRATIONAL ART

Storyboards are often the first time that a character goes from the written page to a visible character. Long before storyboards begin, character design should be fleshed out in inspirational drawings, extreme poses, and if necessary finely tuned model sheets and turnarounds. There is no such thing as too much inspirational art, designs, or character studies; even images that are off the mark or going in the wrong direction can be useful as reminders of what wasn't working. Whether it's thumbnail scratches and five-second doodles or full-realized, colored, and even painted images, all these materials can inform the production about design, lighting, styles, character consistencies, and much more.

2D TO 3D

Going from 2D to 3D is a big jump. All the drawings in the world from every conceivable angle still can't solve every problem when a 2D drawing becomes a 3D model, whether it's a CG or stop-motion character. If a project is going to wind up with 3D characters, then the character cannot be evaluated completely until it moves into the 3D world. When making dimensional characters, it is often useful to create a maquette. If budget and time will allow, a maquette is an extremely useful tool.

A maquette is a sculpture of a character, usually solid and sometimes painted, that is 8 to 12 inches tall. When going from 2D drawings to stop motion and CG, maquettes can answer countless questions and solve visual problems from difficult angles. Maquettes aren't just for dimensional animation either. Cel animation also utilizes maquettes so that animators can use them for character consistency and difficult angles.

On large productions, maquettes are often molded and reproduced for animators. On commercials, maquettes serve many unique purposes as well. Often, clients are unable to visualize a character in 3D, and seeing the character in 3D for the first time on film or in a render can be a bit of a problem if they've never seen a 3D version before. Like storyboards and animatics, it's easier to change a maquette than to change a character in midproduction.

When working in commercial productions, maquettes are useful because clients are able to handle a tangible form of the character they had only seen in 2D. It also creates a comfort zone, and it becomes a likable entity when it exists in the real world and not just on paper or in the computer. In stop motion, maquettes can start out as solid "statues," but once approved, they can easily be turned into animatable puppets that look exactly like their statue counterparts. In 3D modeling, maquettes can be scanned with a number of scanning systems so that they translate exactly into the 3D CG character.

Figure 11.16 illustrates roughed-out sketches for a character that was ultimately stop motion. The process of model creation would be valuable in any animated medium that shows dimension either in models or in illustration, specifically when dealing with realistic-type characters with consistent volumes and sizes.

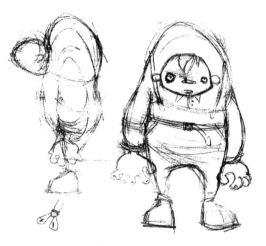

FIGURE 11.16   Two rough character sketches at two key angles. © 2004 Colin Batty. Reprinted with permission.

The maquette process is also valuable for CG, even though the characters are ultimately digitally created; being able to handle them and have a key reference is useful. From a technical standpoint, models can also be digitized or scanned to use directly with animation. However, when creating models for digitization, many specific considerations need to be made. Certain elements may need to be sculpted that are unattached to the character. If an item is going to move even slightly, it often must be created separately. A CG cowboy could be modeled with a cowboy hat, but if he's going to tip that hat or push it back on his forehead, then the hat will need to be separate. Certain areas like the facial features might require being scaled up in size so that enough detail exists to be digitized. Also, when modeling in clay for creating characters for digitizing, if the character is a semirealistic character and has a natural symmetry like most animals, then it's often quicker to sculpt on a mirror. This is because only half of the character actually needs to be digitized and can then be duplicated and flipped in the modeling program.

As the process of creating maquettes or as a model progresses, the drawings become cleaner, details are refined, and their locations are finalized. If the character is going to be moved into stop motion where it will become a stop-motion puppet, then many considerations about how the puppet is created, including costs and usability, must be addressed.

In stop motion, details can be painted or sculpted in. In the case of clothing, there can be actual miniature clothing. In CG, elements like buttons and clothing folds can be a combination of bump maps, texture maps, and geometry depending on the level of finish required. Characters in games often have many details baked in the surface maps to conserve geometry. A character that is going to be featured full-screen and close up in a feature film requires massive amounts of detail compared to game characters, depending on designs (see Figure 11.17).

FIGURE 11.17   A stop motion character further in the process, cleaned up with specific costume details in place. © 2004 Colin Batty. Reprinted with permission.

What makes the drawing in Figure 11.18 doubly useful is a standard for all model sheets, and that is a drawing from two distinct angles; the main two drawings are a profile drawing and a straight-on drawing as shown in Figure 11.18. In designing a character, creating the images from multiple angles has obvious benefits, but it is even more important when characters are extremely stylized. An issue also exists with a large dress like the character is wearing. If it's in cel or 2D applications, then it's probably not that much of a concern, because stylistically it could move either a little or a lot and would just be an element for the animator. In stop motion or CG, it's a different story, because it will have to be dealt with so that it looks like cloth and acts like cloth. Either stop motion or CG would require special rigging or motion plug-ins to animate such a large garment.

FIGURE 11.18   This illustration serves dual proposes. It illustrates both the body pose and potential design issues with the dress. © 2004 Colin Batty. Reprinted with permission.

Figure 11.19 shows the final 3D result of the drawings. The stylized character's details, such as the elongated nostrils, wouldn't be completely apparent with a simple straight-on drawing, making a profile and perhaps even a 3/4 drawing often necessary when creating a dimensional character from 2D art. Designer Colin Batty designed the characters and sculpted them, so he is keenly aware of volumes and can make his own 2D-to-3D extrapolations and decisions. When other artists are involved and images are passed off to others, there usually can't be too many drawings.

When creating characters, many elements that can influence the characters have to be simultaneously considered: design, functionality, cost, animatability, and overall consistency. The characters in Figure 11.19 are all of the same world, same style, and same coloring; they are ghoulish and dead looking. None of the characters looks remotely happy, and the one smiling character looks evil and malicious. All the characters have large eyes that have huge areas of white eyeball, but the pupil itself is small and pinpointing, making the eyes look mean and unsympathetic.

Maquettes, unlike animated puppets, aren't always painted. In fact, many modelers find paint distracting and prefer a neutral gray model for

FIGURE 11.19   The final culmination of all the drawings and sculptures. ©2004 Colin Batty. Reprinted with permission.

visual ease of studying angles. The character in Figure 11.20 is fully painted, and in this case it adds to the overall feel. The character is ghoulish and painted in gray tones and looks very unhealthy; his coloring is a large part of his design.

Often with maquettes, it's necessary to pose the character in an actual pose as is the case with Figure 11.20. A puppet that is set to move into stop motion or a design that moves into CG needs to have the standard "T" pose. This is a standard pose that allows for consistent modeling and casting. CG characters are often also posed this way, but unlike stop motion, the T isn't always the exact right choice, depending on the performance.

The monster in Figure 11.21 was drawn in the default "T" pose, because originally, a completely different purpose for the monster was in-

FIGURE 11.20   The original drawing and final maquettes of the hunchback character. ©2004 Colin Batty. Reprinted with permission.

FIGURE 11.21   From the film *Shards of Death*: one of the original designs for the monster character, in the "T" default pose. © 2004 Colin Batty. Reprinted with permission.

tended. The final version of *Shards of Death* was extremely different from the action story that had been developed earlier. Once production started, it became apparent to all the animators that the monster kept its arms out in front in every shot; pushing its arms and shoulders around was becoming problematic, causing strange folds and geometry intersections. Ideally, the monster would have been remodeled in a pose more central to its character of sitting and listening with its hands mostly at rest. In the end, some adjustments were made to the rig, and the animators pulled back on the animation and angled the character to hide strange texture intersections—a working solution but not the ideal situation. Knowing what the character is going to be doing will impact not only animation, but design, size, scale, and range of motions.

Figure 11.22 shows a dramatic moment for a very graphical monster. It's a great pose, but the designers must also consider how the monster would look in other poses, relaxed or knocked over, with such large claws. In considering the animation, a solution could be that the monster explodes into a pose such as in Figure 11.22, its claws are much smaller and more manageable. Animation can often solve many design challenges if the animation is stylized enough. Drawing or being aware of key poses, stances, and extremes is valuable to have explored long before sculpting or modeling begins.

Planning key poses is always valuable, even in a stop-motion production where the characters are physically sculpted. Good animators often draw key positions and facial expressions, not wanting to leave those decisions up in the air when all the other technical aspects of stop-motion

FIGURE 11.22 A stylized dramatic monster drawing.© 2004 Guy Burwell. Reprinted with permission.

filming have come into play. Making sketches from simple stick figures to fully realized illustrations all have inherent value because it forces more investment in the ideas, the concepts, and the performances.

Until *The Incredibles*, Pixar mostly avoided humans because as you start to cross into the realm of filmed work or "real life," audiences start to apply all the rules they have evolved with. Suddenly it becomes a slippery slope to creating an artificial person that looks 100% real. In their feature animated movies, Pixar, Blue Sky Studios, and Dreamworks were all clever in that all their productions skirted this problem. There are people in *Toy Story*, *Shrek*, and *Ice Age*, but they always stand out as the weak links in those films. This is due in part to that fact that as animated 3D films close in on reality, audiences start expecting people in the 3D environment to look as real as the lighting and perspective.

This expectation of reality goes back to evolution and to when we were all babies. We learned early on how to read facial expressions from the very overt to the very subtle. Most people immediately notice when someone has a speech impediment or affectation; we also notice glass eyes and other facial irregularities, because so much of our clues about how others feel come from their faces. We are tuned into what faces do, whether we are conscious of it or not. When someone watches *Shrek*, which uses the very real 3D world of CG, as well as the very real lighting and rendering down to the wind in the trees and the reflections on the water, people expect *Shrek* to be as real as the world. The audience now immersed in this real visual world will watch Shrek himself with all the tools they use to watch real people. So when Shrek forms certain mouth shapes, like Os and Us, audiences immediately recognize if something in the face isn't right; the muscles don't move the way a real person's do.

When a fish or a toy talks, audiences are more accepting because they don't have many precedents or expectations for talking toys. But, fortunately the reality of animation and CG keeps evolving. After many years of work, modelers, riggers, surfacers, and animators created the character of Gollum from *The Lord of the Rings* trilogy; it is arguably the best near-human CG character ever. For anyone who has ever worked on lip sync, Gollum is nearly perfect. However, the character comes at a huge cost and huge backlog of failed and strange attempts. Gollum is more than an animated character; he is essential to the story—is a character flawed with weaknesses that torture him and make him alive. The film *Final Fantasy: The Spirits Within* featured humans that looked very good, as long as they didn't perform. Colossal flops like *Final Fantasy* are both encouraging and discouraging, because it's obvious so much can be done better, but often is not.

The flip side is extreme characterization, and examples include *The Simpsons*, *Beavis and Butthead*, and *South Park*. In these cartoons, the animation is so far removed from reality that a stylized moving mouth just jumps from shape to shape, syncing up on large sounds. Lip sync is essentially not applicable, but it works, because the viewer isn't using the same set of criteria when looking at these talking characters. Again, there's no precedent for how these characters' mouths should look, so the viewer watches for a few seconds, accepts that movement, and gets into the story and the jokes without thinking about the facial muscle accuracy.

CG MODELING

When creating models for CG, whether fully developed dimensional characters like the characters in *Shards of Death* or simplified game characters, modelers have to do several tasks. Modeling for modeling's sake and exploring and "sketching" in 3D-like drawings can be a valid and viable way to create and design characters. However, when a production is underway and a modeler is handed drawings to reproduce and create in 3D, that modeler has to work more efficiently and can't simply explore the production. CG modelers often work as a clay sculptor would. Modelers deal with large simple shapes when modeling with metanurbs or with creating cages of polygons. Establishing the large shapes and working toward the finite details allows for checks and balances along the way to creating the final character. If a modeler is going to be handing off a model to be rigged by another technical director or rigger, then the modeler needs to set up a work flow with the rigger so that the model can go back and forth for adjustments and revisions. This flow often needs to remain in place well into the production, specifically when a CG character is called on to do something that requires a model and rig fix. Modelers also need to be aware of what the rigger or anyone else who will be touching the model is expecting. Storyboards and animatics are a great place for teams to go over what it is they'll be contributing to a given model.

Modeling for stop motion and CG are at separate ends of a short spectrum. In stop motion, great effort is put into making smooth models and avoiding irregular surfaces, seam lines, and other small details that can read as sloppy or rough. CG modeling is at the other end where objects are too smooth, too straight, and too sterile. Where stop-motion puppet sculptors spend hours trying to smooth our their models, CG modelers have to work hard to bring an organic feel to the character and overcome the boring, inherent, and stale nature of CG. To each sculptor or modeler, both in CG and stop motion, that extra effort fighting their respective medium is essential in creating characters that go beyond clay or CG.

Because so much CG is anchored in special effects, a majority of computer work is done that is realistic, but CG, like any other form of animation, responds well to stylization. Like the characterization of the old man back in Figure 11.4, the powerful traits of the horse in Figure 11.23 have been exaggerated. The model is a stylized iconic horse; its massive chest, huge hooves, curved neck, and smaller head all reinforce the idea of a powerful horse far beyond a reality, but it is still instantly recognizable as a horse. The important shapes and relationships that the eye expects when recognizing a horse are still there; all the stylistic cues came from the original drawing.

FIGURE 11.23   A modeled CG horse with its concept drawing.

© 2004 Amila and Patrik Puhala. Reprinted with permission.

The character in Figure 11.24 is a humanoid creature with stylized proportions and features. The creature has exaggerated feet, a head, and hands and muscle definition beyond a human's, not to mention pointed ears. Still the character has a realistic face and features that would be suitable for performance and acting, but physically the character design could also be part of an action game. In this figure, there are expression studies that the modeler could then use to begin to make blend shapes or morph targets that are in a consistent style with the character.

FIGURE 11.24   A side-by-side comparison of model sheets and the final CG model. © 2004 Don Flores. Reprinted with permission.

In cel and Flash, model sheets need to show as many angles as are being used. Simplistic or stylized Flash or 2D animation can be created where characters have only one or two poses, facing the camera or profile and often just quickly switching between the two. When creating full-dimensional characters and objects that will be moving around in 3D space, turnarounds are often useful and are rendered to evaluate volumes and relationships of 3D objects.

Turnarounds are characters that rotate 360 degrees and are easily created in CG 3D animation. Figure 11.25 shows a series of stills from a turnaround of a 3D character. With cel or drawn animation, drawings can manipulate the angle and can avoid specific awkward angles simply by not drawing them. Also with drawn animation or traditional cel, animators can cheat angles to play to the camera. CG is more literal because the objects are true 3D shapes, and their volumes need to be evaluated if they are going to move in 3D space. Whether for a character or an object, a turnaround is often necessary to study and finesse the final object.

ON THE CD

On the CD-ROM, the movies **Subturn1.mov** and **Subturn2.mov** are two turnarounds of a futuristic submersible vehicle in a lighting scheme close to underwater lighting. **Subturn2.mov** goes one step further by moving the vehicle in space as well, which is often useful in evaluating designs, sizes, and textures against the underwater environment.

FIGURE 11.25   A posed 3D character with images from various angles that make judging 3D volume easier. With characters that are beyond human it's important to judge every angle to see how it works in relation to other forms on the model. © 2004 Don Flores. Reprinted with permission.

STYLIZATION THAT FITS

We covered a lot of material in this chapter. To illustrate what we've covered take a look at *Shards of Death* again. In *Shards of Death*, the monster interviewer is modeled somewhat realistically, even though it is an extreme character with exaggerated volumes. The blue fairy creature is far more stylized, with cartoonish eyeballs instead of eyeballs that would grow out of a face. This creature is more childish and cartoonish. However, together the characters' differences and contrasts help to create tension in the telling of the story. The stylization still had to remain in a range because of the nature of the humor; both characters had to be in the same world for the kind of humor the story called for (see Figure 11.26).

FIGURE 11.26   The two characters from *Shards of Death*. Although one is more stylized than the other, the two are still able to work together.

As previously mentioned, stylization can be influenced by many factors, including the software or animation technique. Flash animation is often considered rudimentary because so much of what is seen in Flash is what is motion of simple objects, but stylization doesn't mean omitting details or compromising on a detailed look. Figure 11.27 is a frame from a Flash animation that looks much closer to full cel animation than tradi-

FIGURE 11.27   A Flash animation with high detail and well-created design that ultimately looks closer to cel than to what is usually thought of as Flash animation (see Color Plate 16). © 2004 Tracy Prescott MacGregor. Reprinted with permission.

tional Flash. As illustrated in this figure, with the proper use of color and design as well as time spent creating elements, amazingly complex results can develop. Flash is often viewed as a program that simply makes rough animation for the Internet, but that is completely inaccurate. This preconception exists because so much Flash animation isn't very well executed. A powerful feature of Flash and vector-based programs is that the vectors can be scaled in size with no loss, and a well-created Flash animation can easily be rastered (i.e., turned into actual pixels) at Academy film resolution or even higher.

An Example of Good Visual Planning

As discussed, the task of planning a production is really a plan that insures that the technical works in conjunction with the visuals and the basic underlying themes that tell the story. So let's take a look at a prime example of character and production design that works and is completely integrated—*Insect Poetry*, included on the CD-ROM under the file **Insect.mov.** The short film is a perfect example of an animated film that is well-planned on every level. *Insect Poetry* is a five-minute tale of insects having an intimate poetry-reading night. The insects include a weevil, a spider with a loose leg, and a beautiful female moth. The characters in *Insect Poetry*, as shown

ON THE CD

in Figure 11.28, are well developed and dynamic, with unique voices and individually unique performances. Ultimately it's also a simple and good story. It's not a story that starts with a standard beginning, but it's essentially a slice of life or a segment in time, is fascinating, and is a unique way of telling the story. The insects reading poetry is clever, and the film is purely animation. The insects in the film share a love of words and the words themselves take over for an elegant scene of calligraphy, which fits perfectly in a film about poetry and the written word.

FIGURE 11.28   The visually diverse characters from the stop-motion film *Insect Poetry.* © 2001 Marilyn Zornado. Reprinted with permission.

The film moves well both in visual pacing and in storytelling and also conveniently incorporates well-written poetry that the insects recite, so the film has several layers that the audience can connect with: compelling poetry, clever and well thought-out animation, and unique characters in an exotic setting. All of the film's layers are deliberately planned and executed and driven by the story.

Poetry and animation aren't strangers, and the standard presentation for animated poetry is a voice-over reading the poem that the animation then follows. *Insect Poetry* instead has created a unique and clever way to present the poetry, which allows, in a sense, two scenes to take place simultaneously: (1) the poetry the insects are reading, and (2) the how the insects read the poetry. A scenario where a narrator reads a poem and the animation follows along can be less dynamic because it has been done numerous times. *Insect Poetry* creates a totally new way to hear poetry—from insects (see Figure 11.29).

FIGURE 11.29   An animated graphical sequence is a perfect fit for a film about poetry. © 2001 Marilyn Zornado. Reprinted with permission.

The sheer fact that these insects are intellectual, well educated, and well spoken to the point of being almost highbrow is yet another underlying and interesting feature of the characters and the story. The story forms out of the characters. If the characters are complex, then the viewer can extrapolate that the characters' back story is complex as well, and the characters become that much more alive.

Stylistically, the three insects are complete opposites. The moth, as shown in Figures 11.30 and 11.31, is tall and elongated like a vertical rectangle that is soft and delicate. The weevil (see Figure 11.32) is short

FIGURE 11.30   The moth from *Insect Poetry* alongside the conceptual drawings. © 2001 Marilyn Zornado. Reprinted with permission.

FIGURE 11.31 The elaborate cloak of the moth. © 2001 Marilyn Zornado. Reprinted with permission.

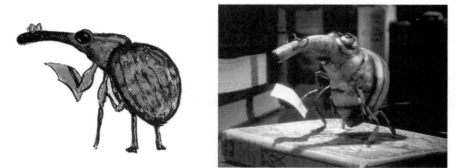

FIGURE 11.32 The weevil conceptual drawing alongside the final animation puppet (see Color Plate 15). © 2001 Marilyn Zornado. Reprinted with permission.

and round like a ball with a hard shell and short limbs. The spider is between them both, having long spindly legs and multiple eyes. The opposites work together in creating a pleasing and visual relationship. With all its other powerful traits, the film is still at a very basic level and is pleasing and fun to watch.

The moth character is tall and elegant, and like a real moth it is delicate. In the drawings the eyes were larger and closer to a true moth. On the animated character they're slightly smaller, which gives less of a cold look and makes the moth more feminine with heavy lids and lashes. The soft feathery material reads like a woman in elegant furs, and the delicate wings represent a luxurious gown, giving the idea that the moth is a classy creature. Her performance and voice are true to her being—an elegant character *and* a delicate moth.

The spider is also a very interesting character and a great choice for the film. Many people are afraid of spiders, but *Insect Poetry's* spider is aloof, comes across as sincere, and is a bit confused; he is a truly dynamic character. The spider loses a leg, which creates feelings of empathy and charm toward a creature that most people revile. The film plays on those feelings and just adds another layer of interest (see Figure 11.33).

FIGURE 11.33   The poetry-reciting, stop-motion spider's legs are just simply thin copper tubing inside one another. © 2001 Marilyn Zornado. Reprinted with permission.

Tips for Future Projects

The More Conceptual the Art, the Better

The reflex to make people look like people is acceptable, but animation and stylization can go so much further. In some stories, too much stylization can detract from the story, but designers need to find the perfect balance.

If Working in 3D, the Design Phase Must Include 3D

It seems obvious, but it isn't. The jump from 2D to 3D is a big one, and 3D models need ample development and testing. Often, because the actual modeling, or modeling in the case of stop motion, is so labor intensive, the transfer from 2D to 3D doesn't get the required adjustments, and the model suffers.

Push Designs as Far as Possible

Push designs, push exaggerations, and push colors. Create traits that aren't simply just exaggeration, but instead reinforce the character's personality, environment, and predicament. Designs can always be pulled back if pushed too far, but interesting discoveries often come from truly exploring what was perceived to work and not work.

The Environment and Visual Consistency

Backgrounds are the cycle of frames from the *Flintstones* cartoon that would cycle over and over, with the same lamp and chair going by again and again. Cycling worked OK with this cartoon, and it was done mostly out of economy, not style. The opposite is a background that brings as much to the production as the characters do, and isn't just a simple looped cycle. Good designers thrive on the idea of creating a whole world and everything that goes with that. Designers are also keenly aware of the relationship between characters and their worlds, with how they interact and look. Designers need to establish whether they're simply creating simple backgrounds, which are occasionally appropriate, or creating a world, because in reality they are both one in the same once combined.

There is a very apparent "gluing" that happens when scenes are finally watched on television or on a movie screen. The simple fact that elements are all joined in the final film or tape brings things together. When orchestrated correctly, even strange elements of different styles can be combined in interesting and compelling ways. Still, the glue of making a film doesn't ensure that designs will work together, and designers never trust filming or rendering to control the relationships of design.

Find Visual Inspiration

Like every aspect of animation and filmmaking, there is a huge history of good and bad work to learn from. Because animation is tied closer to visual arts, animation filmmakers have all of art history to learn from as well. Good visual designers often have a "morgue" of imagery that inspires them and that they use as references, from a few binders to giant collections of books, movies, and other artwork.

The Genius Is in the Details

Many have misconceptions about how the computer has made animation easy. Although it has made animation easier, character animation is still very hard. From modeling to design, every aspect of the animation really needs to be thought out.

INTERVIEW WITH TRACY PRESCOTT MACGREGOR

Tracy Prescott MacGregor is an experienced art director, master animator, and illustrator. MacGregor has worked in animation for many years and has worked on a variety of projects, from the *California Raisins* to *The PJs*. She was also the art director on the stop-motion comedy television show *Gary and Mike*. MacGregor is a skilled Flash animator who incorporates all of her talents in art direction, design, and animation into her work.

Wellins: What does it take to be a good animator?

MacGregor: Animation requires a combination of a good sense of physics and a really good sense of acting. It's a natural thing that some people have—the combination of those two things. You get your animators who know physics really well, but they really lack in the acting, and you get some people who are excellent actors or actresses, but their walk cycles aren't working and it looks really clunky because they just don't have the physics.

Wellins: Why do you think there's so much bad Flash animation?

MacGregor: There are a couple of things. I think it's part of the way that the program works. There are a lot of crutches that you can use, like for instance, there's a lot of tweening tools. A lot of it depends on how you use the program. If you use the tweening tools in a walk cycle you can get a slow, methodic, sort of lackluster walk cycle, whereas if you're going pose to pose, you can get it just right. If you use it just right, you can get some really nice punchy motion. A lot of it has to do with using it right, using the tools and knowing what you're using it for. Are you using it for streaming over broadband or are you using it for transfer to video? If you're using Flash for a final transfer to video, you have a lot more tools at your disposal, and if you're using it to stream over the Internet, then pose-to-pose [animation] is probably a much better way to do it.

Wellins: If you were going to go to broadcast, what would you do differently from if you were going to do streaming?

MacGregor: I think I would choose a style that accommodated streaming better, like pose to pose, and avoid using large bitmapped images, like BMPs, and instead use really nice vector art. Try to avoid using lots of points, and just stylistically try to make choices that are appropriate for the medium. With broadcast, the sky is the limit, because once you do your transfer to tape, then you're not worrying about bandwidth anymore—you're concentrating on other things. You can use BMPs or even high-resolution photographs for your backgrounds. You don't have to turn everything into a vector, and you don't have to make sure it's as tiny a file as possible.

Wellins: So if you're doing both?

MacGregor: Always go with the lowest common denominator. There's nothing more frustrating than being on the other end of that and trying to download something. I live out in the

$\rightarrow$

boonies and happen to have an Internet connection that's 26K, and there's nothing faster available, so I'm sitting there waiting for these things to download. You really want to accommodate the low-patience threshold of your viewer. You can think about it later, if you want to go to broadcast and you want to do something differently. You can make really cool art with vectors and fewer points. You can make cool, stylistic choices, really clever ones, and it doesn't have to have a lot of details and it doesn't have to look painterly.

Wellins: *Given those parameters, when you go into a job, can you describe the process? Somebody hands you a storyboard and says, "Animate this in Flash." What are you going to do?*

MacGregor: Sometimes people hand me a storyboard. Sometimes people hand me a concept with no illustrations or anything, so it depends on where the starting point is, but a lot of times it starts with a design. My latest Flash project was handed to me as storyboards, and in that case they handed me full-fledged drawings, and so ultimately that job was having me transfer their artwork into a Flash product that could be streamed over the Web. The designer of the job comes from a 2D art, drawn-line, cel background and did a lot of the preliminary animation. It was really quite fun, because I got to do all the backgrounds and I got to build the characters and use their animation, and then afterwards I would punch it up or move things around or exaggerate and add in things where they didn't have cycles and stuff like that. It was a real collaborative effort. I would take his drawings and do the animation for it on the backgrounds I had built. Then I would have to go back through, and this is very typical for a Flash project for streaming. I would go back through and optimize, which doesn't just include going down the optimize button and hitting optimize. It also means going in and finding leftover things in your library that you don't need or use. Checking all kinds of things like how many layers you've got going. Maybe you have a hidden layer somewhere. Say if you have a QuickTime reference of your animatic underneath everything and you forget about it. That could be several megs of memory, so there are a lot of little hidden things that you need to find.

Wellins: *If they had some background images that were JPEG or BMP, would you squish that down to its tiniest bit or would you just make your own no matter what? Just get rid of the BMPs?*

MacGregor: No, you can use BMPs—people often do. It really depends on how many you've got and how big they are. There are so many variables involved. You can vectorize some of that. You go down to "trace bitmap" and that can give you a really nice image in vector that's kind of painterly. In one project I worked on at Flying Rhino[ceros] studios, they used painted backgrounds. An illustrator had painted a book that they had to turn into a streamable Web product. So they took all the pictures, scanned them, then took them into Flash and then vectorized them. There are a number of factors in vector, and you have to mess with them a little bit and finally you get just the right amount, so it looks almost exactly like the painting but it's just broken into fewer pixels or vectors. It's much better to use it that way. Sometimes it breaks the colors a little bit incorrectly so you can go in and fix those things if you want to, but I don't think you have to necessarily. If you're going to use a lot of those high-resolution illustrations, JPEGs or whatever, then you might think about making at least some of them vectorized.

$\rightarrow$

Wellins: Is there a formula for if you want to stream broadband, or is it completely by the job?

MacGregor: I create what's called a SWF, which is basically a quick compression that shows you how it's going to stream and how it's going to play, and I take a look there and see how high, and it has a breakdown like what, a 56k modem, and you can play it on all those different things. It has a bar graph and you can kind of watch.

Wellins: How often do you go back and check?

MacGregor: Well, if I'm doing it for the Web, you should check it when you start to feel like it's getting kind of heavy or big. For the last job I did, for Wrigley's Gum, I checked it once or twice in two months, but it really wasn't up to me as much as the artist to do that. But I know where to check it if I need to. At one point it was 21 megs and I got it down to about 7.

Wellins: How long was the final piece?

MacGregor: I think it was a 30-second spot.

Wellins: What size?

MacGregor: I never got to see the finished product streamed over the Web, but I know they went back in and optimized even more after I did. They used a lot of alpha channels and had a bunch of camera moves where they wanted things to fade and dissolve, fade and dissolve, and that's always asking for trouble, especially for a background to fade and dissolve into another background that then also does a fade and dissolve. Then there were a bunch of crowd elements. I didn't feel that it was necessary or my place to really argue against using that, but it was too big. I watched it stream a couple times and it stuttered, especially right where those elements faded back and forth. It was obvious that it was chugging down, and the producer on it knew that it was going to chug down, but they wanted this real cinematic look and you just have to choose your battles when you're doing that. You're going to get some chunking and it makes your animation look like you don't quite know what you're doing, but that's the way it is.

Wellins: Say someone hands you a board and you're wide open, and it's going to do both—it's going to be broadcast or on tape and then it's also going to be streamed. What would be your process?

MacGregor: There're so many cool tricks you can do when it's broadcast that you can't do when it's streamed. Very often I'll work with three programs: Photoshop, Illustrator, and Flash. And I'll be working in Flash, but I'll go into Illustrator to do the text stuff, and then I'll import that in. Or I'll work in Photoshop and I'll create transparencies and things like that. I did an Eskimo character for the Oregon Museum of Science and Industry, and I wanted to make his cheeks kind of red, but I didn't want to have a hard outline—a red dot. So I went into Photoshop and I created a little red patch on a transparent background with the airbrush and saved it as a PNG, which is a pretty good trick. Then I moved it into Flash, and Flash reads the transparency [see Figure 11.34].

→

FIGURE 11.34   The result of the technique of using Photoshop to create the rosy cheeks on the Eskimo character (see Color Plate 17). © 2004 Tracy Prescott MacGregor. Reprinted with permission.

Wellins: Is that the function of a PNG?

MacGregor: It's one of the functions of a PNG. It's a little bit better than a JPEG. I think the bit depth is a little bit bigger, but I'm not sure. And I think you can do it with GIFs too, but GIFs are just not as good. But that's one way of incorporating those soft edges that vectors can't give you. Another thing, animation-wise, is I needed to make a blur, and there's no way in Flash to make a blur, except to make these elongated kind of graphic-looking shapes. So I went into Photoshop and in Photoshop of course there's that really nice motion blur tool; [I] created a few frames of that in varying levels, brought it into Flash, and I had my blur. It's on a transparency so your background shines right through, so you've got a character that's moving really quickly from one place to another, like taking off running. You do your anticipation and then you throw in your blur frame, and it works just like a cartoon, only better, in some ways. It's almost photographic. I take the Flash character and put it into Photoshop and create the transparency out of that, and then bring it back, so I'm always using those three programs together.

Wellins: What do you like better about Illustrator as opposed to just using the tools in Flash?

MacGregor: For a couple of projects, a bunch of the stuff was to be used in print as well as in animation for television, so it was really good to be able to convert the Flash files to Illustrator, and I was getting a lot of Illustrator files to put into Flash. Also, Illustrator has a lot more text control. I can manipulate things and tweak them. There are a lot more options you can use in

$\rightarrow$

Illustrator. The trick is that Flash and Illustrator don't always talk to each other exactly the same way. For instance, in Illustrator if you have one unclosed path and you import it into Flash, you're going to come up with some problems. It wants to see whole shapes. The other thing is that Illustrator defaults to CMYK because it's for print. One time I was doing a billboard and I did it in Flash and it was just gorgeous. The colors were all brilliant. I converted it into Illustrator and it had to be delivered right away, and every color was just dull. It looked like somebody had put a screen over the top of it. You can go back in and tweak those colors back up if you take the time, but you have to be aware of it.

Wellins: You went from a tiny Flash file up to a full-sized billboard, and because it was vectors, it scaled up?

MacGregor: Absolutely, yes. They scale up beautifully. That part was fine; it was the color that screwed me over.

Wellins: Why do you think so much Flash animation is so bad? A lot of people see Flash stuff and they think Flash animation always looks subpar.

MacGregor: Flash is just brilliant. They're not spending enough time on it. I think it's accessible to a lot of people who may not have the talent—I mean it's a $300 program. I think it's all those little crutches that are in there that if used correctly are great; they're brilliant. But it doesn't substitute for a good animator, and that's where you end up. Whereas things like Maya are so expensive and not just anybody can afford to learn on that, then you usually have to go through the ranks in order to get to the point to be able to study it.

Wellins: You have a huge background of art direction and art in general, especially stop motion. When you deal with Flash animation, how is that different from stop motion? How do you bring all your tools to bear?

MacGregor: One of the differences between stop motion and Flash is that with Flash, I can do it by myself. I can sit down at my computer and I've got all the tools right there that I need. Sometimes I have to go out and take some pictures or spend some time building a character, whereas with stop motion it's kind of like a live action thing. You have to have actors and cameras and lights—the actors being the puppets—and the table and there's a whole lot involved in construction and planning. With that being said, the animation itself is very different too. With stop motion, it's so instinctual, whereas with 2D you're doing a lot more measuring and using a lot of your squash and stretch, your traditional animation education.

Wellins: When you start out to animate a character in Flash, is it the same as it is in 3D programs like LightWave3D, where you can do one pass, block it through, and then go back and work on the hands and then the arms and . . . Say you built a character in Illustrator and then what?

MacGregor: Then I would transfer it into Flash. I would break down the body parts and give them hinges. You know: elbows, knees, neck, and feet. And sometimes you can use those body parts again—that was the style at Flying Rhino studios, which did a ton of educational

→

Flash, where you just build a whole bunch of body parts and pull them in. It's almost like constant replacement; your characters are built in each scene, piece by piece. What is more likely for me is as a solo animator I'm doing one project at a time, so I'm not doing these returning characters. I don't have to have a library that has 400 million body parts. So I'll build the standard body parts like profile, front, and most likely three quarter. And then I'll do the specialty body parts. So there'll be the extra long leg, like when he's running or sneaking.

Wellins: Then you've got it all built, and then what do you do?

MacGregor: Then I do my key frames and listen to the track. A lot of times, I'll put the animatic underneath everything, so I know the timings on everything. Then I'll start placing my key frames, and then fill in in-betweens. Key framing is an excellent way of getting exaggerated motion so you know where you can go, so you're not trying to just freeform it. Also it helps you keep your composition really good and it pushes you.

Wellins: How do you mean?

MacGregor: This is something that happens with stop motion that is different than 2D, and that is that on a piece of paper the sky is the limit. You can stretch and squash and make your characters just as wild as possible, and with animation if you moved around cartoon characters just like regular people, they look silly. They don't look like there's any reason that they've been animated. Why isn't this in live action if the motion is so realistic? In animation you have to really throw things way out of whack in order for them to even be funny or interesting in some way. So the key frames I use as a way to push me out that way. With stop motion you don't have that option as much. You have to build special parts to, say, give a character a really exaggerated facial expression. And you can't really do key frames in stop motion because it's a linear process. You're going from point A to point B and you can kind of plan it, but not nearly as well as you can if you're doing key frame animation. You say, "OK, I'm starting here and I want to go here and I want to just throw this character as far off as possible, or exaggerate that expression as much as I can." Then your in-betweens are all going toward that so you know that three frames before the end, you have to have it make sense, whether you're going to have it go really fast or you're going to slow into it or have a supercontraction or expansion or whatever.

Wellins: So of the two, what do you find the most rewarding?

MacGregor: I like them both. I could do either one forever. I'm one of those people who loves everything!

Wellins: Is the fact that you could do everything in the box (with Flash) an attraction to you, as opposed to having to go and get the lights and the set . . . ?

MacGregor: Ah, but there's something luxurious about stop motion that you can't get any other way. Not even 3-D . . . maybe eventually. There's something so incredibly spontaneous about it. It's like filmed takes and live action. It's so spur of the moment, and you're watching yourself slowing down time with this character, and these characters that you're holding in

→

your hand actually kind of come to life in that several hours. Maybe you're doing 200 frames in several hours and you're sitting there moving this character around and you're in that character's brain. It's like a living thing to me. In 2D I love having all the resources there, and also there's a lot of variety that you can get in 2D that you can't get otherwise. There's the style of cutout, and the [Bill] Plympton style of sketching and the Disney style of cel, just to name a few.

Wellins: *What do you think of the dimensional CG animation explosion?*

MacGregor: Personally, I'm just saturated with it. I'm sick of the look of CG generated 3D characters really. There's a quality they just cannot get away from. I love *Princess Mononoke*, and *Spirited Away* types—those are beautiful, like your *Grime Shoed Diaries*. It's really cel, but they're using the computer to enhance it, to build these little boxes of the houses so they can make them turn around, and I think that's a far better use of 3D than trying to exclusively use 3D as the solution. It all has the same look and I've seen so many of those 3D productions.

Wellins: *As an animator in all sorts of formats, you've worked with a lot of directors. How does that work, where you're working with a director who maybe has ideas that are different from what you're thinking?*

MacGregor: I've always credited myself for being able to work with just about anyone. One of the things you have to do is to eliminate yourself from the issues. The director is the person who has the vision, and you are part of creating that vision. That person has been hired as a visionary and whether you agree or disagree shouldn't come into the picture. It's more: is this possible or is this not possible? And that's the way I look at it. I try to get on the same wavelength as the director, and every director is different. Every director has different things that they like to focus on. That's one of things I really enjoy doing, is getting to know those directors, and getting to know their artistic styles and their aesthetic things that they want to see. So once I do that, I feel like I've gotten into their brains and I know kind of how to complement that vision, because that's my job. When I do that, the vision itself becomes stronger and that's what you want. You don't want everything designed by committee. It's more technical. First of all, the designs have to complement what they're thinking, and second, I have to make it possible for them to produce that piece, whatever it is.

Wellins: *So what if you really disagree? Will you just say it and move on?*

MacGregor: Oh, I always put in my opinion. I'm not afraid to put in my opinion. I get a sense for how they feel about it, because it's a collaborative process: Wouldn't it be cool if . . . ?, [or] Wouldn't this further the idea if . . . ? So I'm full of ideas. It's not like I just shut up and mind my own business. That's not true at all, but I'm not going to get into an argument over something that I disagree with. Another way to do it though is to look at it this way: maybe just because you disagree with something, doesn't mean you can't revisit it and take a look at it and see if you can't accommodate what they want, within the parameters of what you're disagreeing about, and come up with another solution. It's not a dead end. I really don't end up with too many dead ends like that, because there's always a way to figure out some kind of solution. And I don't want to say compromise, because art is not about compromising all the time. It

→

never should be. Art should be about creating solutions to define a vision. That's very important, and especially in commercials everybody has to get their two cents in, all the way from the producer to the director to the agency to the client. Commercials are some of the most powerful art of our day, and you can get some pretty wishy-washy looking commercials out there that look like a committee has designed them.

Wellins: *I've met a lot of directors who tortured or painfully abused their crew because they were trying to make some kind of personal artistic statement that went against what the client wanted, and they created a big fight over something that in a commercial doesn't really even apply.*

MacGregor: It's not a good venue at all. I don't recommend it for a director. To balance it, I have my own creative outlets. I think there are a lot of people like that. They are artists because that's what they are. And they're not just artists when they go to work. They're artists when they go home. That's what you do when you create one of your 137,000 films that you've been working on, and I go home and I'll paint or I'll build something. That's the time you can do the art that you own, so that when you go to work, you have that creative outlet already satisfied. A lot of people go into film and art and animation with the expectation that they're going to be the next Orson Wells or the next Tim Burton or whatever. The truth is that you can't live like that until you get there. I'll bet you dollars to donuts that Tim Burton goes home and he does his little drawings of the little matchstick girl or whatever, and he's doing that constantly. And I'm not convinced that everybody in the industry does that.

Wellins: *They should.*

MacGregor: Sure! The ones who actually make it are the ones who are artists because that's what they are, not because it's what they want to be. You always run across those folks.

Wellins: *I think people who get into this to make money are getting into it for the wrong reason. You're going to be up against people who love it, or at least have some fascination with it, and you'll never succeed because you don't like it.*

MacGregor: I think it's short sighted. Every artist who's ever made it has had passion. Passion is a huge part of it. In fact, passion is a huge part of anything. You can't have a technician mind to go in and feel things.

Wellins: *Is art an expression of passion?*

MacGregor: It's an expression of a passion that you have. And it's like you said, either you've got it or you don't. If it's not driving you, then what are you doing? Find something else! You see a lot of people who do things they're not passionate about, and I just feel so sorry for them because they end up doing things that are just expected of them.

Wellins: *What are we trying to do when we're creating?*

MacGregor: Control. It's my way of creating a world. It's my control over nature, where everything's up to me. I'm living in my fantasy all the time.

CHAPTER

LIGHTING

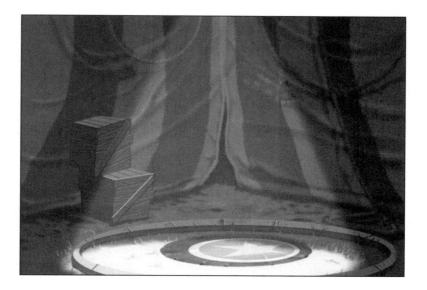

Lighting is the process where lights are placed in strategic locations to illuminate what's going on, so that the images can be recorded. Lighting is also a process that creates a visual tone. These two main functions of lighting are forever tied together—there cannot be one without the other. Without lights, there's nothing to film or render, and once a light is on, then a tone is immediately set. Whether it is a single candle, a raw lightbulb, a huge lighting rig, or the sun, an immediate feeling is created for the viewer, even if no thought went into the lighting design.

Lighting is a true art form, and calls for a truly critical eye that can recognize and understand color theory and composition in animation and live-action films. Lighting is unique in its ability to create mood, but the human eye is very sensitive to lighting when it comes to film or animation. What an audience expects regarding certain lighting in terms of defining certain types of stories is complex and has evolved and changed along with the audience's view of all film and animation. Lighting, even in animation, now leans more toward a "real" feel rather than a studio feel. Use lighting wisely, and always remember that in modern cinema and animation something that is overlit can be a much bigger disaster than something that is underlit.

ANIMATION LIGHTING

Animation is tied to lighting as closely as live action is, but in animation, lighting is far more flexible and can be manipulated in many ways. In live action, lighting falls under the domain of the director of photography, as do lenses and filters. However, even the most skilled director of photography has a certain amount of real-world lighting that must be dealt with, tolerated, or manipulated with great effort. Animation, on the other hand, is free to create any lighting scheme, which can be far more persuasive and emotional than dealing with light from the real world. Computer animation and stop motion have lighting starting points similar to live action, but in animation they go much further, especially in CG. Cel animation and 2D animation like Flash or Moho are completely unlimited and lighting is built into the artwork. In the instance of 2D, lighting goes back to the art director.

Figure 12.1 is a digital Photoshop backdrop from a circus-themed animation; the lighting effect and the glow of a perceived overhead light is all created traditionally into the backdrop. Creating lighting effects in the image is a technique as old as painting itself, but can be readily utilized in animation in various ways and to various levels. A slight depth of field is also worked into the image with background images slightly out of focus and de-saturated. The inner ring where the character would be focused is slightly over lit, enhancing the brightness of the perceived spotlight above. A simplified animation can have a very sophisticated look when the backgrounds are much more evolved than the characters. This has been true since the earliest cel animations, because it's often too laborious to recreate frame-by-frame animation with the detail that is given to the backgrounds. A backdrop like the one in Figure 12.1 could work well for a Flash-type animation and could combine the simplicity of Flash animation with a painterly background and a thick rich atmosphere.

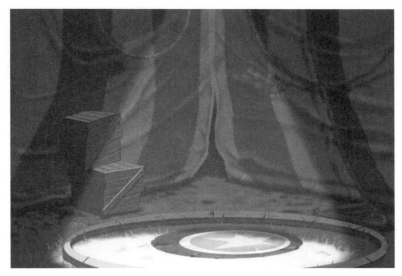

FIGURE 12.1   A backdrop of a circus animation, with lighting effects created in Photoshop (see Color Plate 18).

In Figure 12.2, the two simple characters come from a completely graphical and stylized animation-style film. The lighting is almost irrelevant in the traditional sense, for the scene is purely graphical and reads as brightly lit. In this brilliantly colored world, characters have no shadows of any kind, and the prevalent, thick graphical line removes it from the world of animated depth. However, the designs are so simple and iconic that it creates its own fun graphical reality, where lighting is built into the art and is more graphic art than dimensional film. Graphical, or stylized, animation has the capability to establish this type of look. At the other end of the spectrum, it's often disappointing that so much modern animation lighting is simply spent trying to mimic reality, when an unusual or dramatic lighting scheme, impossible in live action, would have further enhanced the story and add more visual appeal.

FIGURE 12.2   A scene from a purely graphical animated film. Lighting is inherent in the graphic design, instead of being lit with individual lights (see Color Plate 19). © 2004 Laura DiTrapani. Reprinted with permission.

LIGHTING BASICS

Basic lighting is three-point lighting, which has been the standard for still and motion. Three-point lighting uses (1) a key light, which is the brightest light; (2) a fill light, which is slightly less bright than the key light and fills in the shadows of the key light; and (3) a rim light, which is also bright and defines a rim on the outside edge of the photographed object. Three-point lighting is the simplest form of straightforward lighting, but in no way is there a standard or a formula. All lighting should come from the production design that comes from the idea of using lighting, shadow, and shade to reinforce whatever story is being told and to punctuate the visuals. The rim light is often useful in visually pulling a character off a backdrop and is a standard protocol for most filmmaking. However, there are scenarios where the character blends into the scene, so nothing fits every situation.

Figure 12.3 shows the various lights on a set of simple objects and a highly textured CG head. The very basic lighting is the key light, which is the brightest light source; a fill light that is set off from the key light; and then a rim light to define the shapes of the objects. From the figures, it's clear that less light makes scenes more dramatic. A director and director of photography (DP) must use darkness and the absence of light almost as much as they use light if the goal is to create a mood; a strong rim light reinforces the skull shape and the solid feeling of the human. Obviously, certain genre and types of film lend themselves to more dramatic lighting. Films or animations that would be considered light comedies don't usually work with a stark noir feeling. Bright scenes in comedies and romantic films have their own sense of darkness, and audiences expect a certain type of feel in a certain type of story. Night shots in horror movies often have dense blackness, or a large light source from off camera to mimic the moon, streetlights, or other sources. In comedies or light movies, the idea of "night" is a complete exaggeration, with lights completely lighting the scene well, but with a slight blue tint. When establishing and exploring a lighting mood or overall design, it is important that the DP never be afraid of the dark.

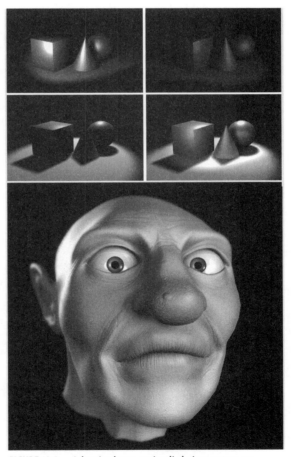

FIGURE 12.3   A basic three-point lighting setup on primitives as well as a human head. © 2004 Ben Neall.
Reprinted with permission.

DIFFUSION

Diffusion of light is also a powerful tool in creating visual dynamics. The simplest form all people know is the raw, sharp, undiffused light found on a bright white, cloudless summer day, where shadows are sharp and dark. The other end of the spectrum is a completely overcast day, where shadows are soft and faint. Diffused light scatters and shadows are softened and edges are blurred.

The six facets on the human face drove a great deal of the early film lighting that was designed to show the complex human face in a pleasing way. In Hollywood in the 1930s and 1940s, huge movie starlets would demand a specific DP who they felt lit them in the most beautiful light. The position of lights and their effect are nearly infinite; dark shadows from an overhead light can hide eyes and make some look sinister or mysterious, while lighting from beneath can create an equally menacing look. Modern lighting now often uses huge diffusion filter screens to soften everything, and the use of large black sheet material can draw light out of a scene giving dark values to a face or a scene. Animation can utilize any and all of these techniques. Animation also has more flexibility and almost infinite control over lighting and diffusion because a combination of shadows can be created. Background characters can be lit with soft shadows to keep them as background characters, while featured characters can have sharper shadows and lines to draw more attention. Diffusion also carries its own mood-effecting powers. Harsh and stark shadows aren't flattering to the human face. Harsh shadows and edges have a feeling of grittiness and starkness that makes facets sharp and unforgiving. Diffusion softens edges and smoothes out shapes, making scenes softer and more neutral (see Figure 12.4).

FIGURE 12.4   The difference between sharp and diffused lighting.

Lighting can be used to add great effect to a story. Lighting can mimic mood, lighting can change from scene to scene and build, or a lighting scenario can be consistent throughout an entire project. Pools of light can focus a viewer's attention on a performance or object, and shadows can direct the eye toward light. Light can also be allegorical, representing enlightenment, intelligence, or goodness.

Breaking up Light

Light can also be broken up as it often is in the real world. In creating scenes that hint of reality, lighting often passes through objects, like glass, leaves and trees, water, transparent objects, or those with holes, like fences or grates. Breaking up light creates dynamic shadows and interesting lighting patterns, but it also hints at other objects off camera. For example, dappled lighting that is broken up as it goes through tree branches and leaves enhances a scene in the forest.

MOOD AND ENVIRONMENT

Lighting is absolutely crucial, and must be informed by the story, the mood, and the scene. A prime example of lighting dictating a mood would be the television show *The X-Files*. The show was shot with the same fundamental tools with which the original *Star Trek* television series was shot; both used 35mm film. The key difference is that *Star Trek* was lit with a 1960s sensibility. The filmstock back in the 1960s had a slower speed, which means that it wasn't as sensitive to light as modern films, and required much more lighting to expose images correctly. Much more light had to be pumped onto the set, but it is more of a stylistic choice than a technical one. *Star Trek* was a TV show, not a movie, and it lived next to other television shows that all had the same feel. But now, almost 40 years after the first episode of *Star Trek* aired, audiences have become very accustomed to this visual medium of television and film, and are far more accepting of various lighting scenarios. Lighting has moved away from the Hollywood studio setting, and is closer to reality and to what the eye sees every day. When watching the original *Star Trek* series now, the lighting is almost silly, like a stage play. Today, a show like *Star Trek* would read as extremely overlit and less real. Many of today's television shows and feature movies still overlight scenes, and that can cause a serious disconnect. Intense dramas, thrillers, science fiction, fantasy, horror, and suspense all have a literal dark side. The idea is that the viewers' imagination fills in the blackness by creating images of what they think is hiding in darkness. Keeping areas in darkness, makes it so viewers don't know what's in the half-open closet, because they can't see in: it's a mystery. The closet may in fact be empty, and if the scene is overlit, then the audience will see the closet is empty and mystery is forfeited.

Imagine *The X-Files* with the lighting from the original *Star Trek*; it's almost laughable. *The X-Files* lighting is far more realistic and much closer to the lighting in movies. With the show's subject matter, darkness was an important part of the series' appeal and overall spooky mood.

However, that doesn't mean that scary and dark are 100 percent tied together. The opposite can also be true. A stark and extreme example would be a sterile mental institution. The idea of a mental institution is disturbing in its own right, and the bland flat fluorescent lighting adds to the feeling; the brightness is close to real and can have a creepy effect without using dark shadows and limited light. The human eye, whether the viewer is cognizant of it or not, is also very sensitive to visual "truth" in lighting animation and live action. When a great number of lights are added, each light creates its own shadow, and whether or not the viewer can recognize the lighting, the shadows do give away multiple light sources that can be distracting. In animated CG and cel, lights can be added that illuminate objects but do not cast shadows, which is very useful. Often a clean simple shadow helps "glue" an animated character to the floor, whereas multiple shadows might confuse the visual read.

Unique to lighting is the connection to what has been already established in collective film and animation. When establishing a lighting direction, it's important to consider the audience's perception of how lighting should appear for a particular genre. For example, a modern hospital that everyone knows and recognizes cannot be lit dark and scary. As a result, thrilling and frightening scenes often take place at night, or the plot allows for a power outage, which gives a hospital a reason for being lit in a horror-film style. Certain effects like caustics, where light bounces off water, are effective but are limited in their use. Bounced caustics in lighting work well when there's a swimming pool or a room is flooded. If there were no water in the rooms, the effect would be confusing instead of spooky.

The collective viewer has a clear idea of what a hospital is and what it isn't. If the goal of the film is to be "real," then there'd better be an explanation for the dim lighting, and if there's not, the lighting isn't working correctly. Like sappy music trying to make a sad scene sadder, inappropriate dramatic lighting has the same effect—audiences feel they are being pandered to. On the other end of the spectrum, poorly lit comedic scenes don't work well either, because it can be difficult to see subtle effects. In reality, standard rooms, houses, and kitchens usually have very simple, boring lighting. Art directors and DPs often choose to exaggerate windows or specific light sources, so that instead of a flat even lighting, there's a light source that picks out details and defines edges, even though in reality many lighting scenes are extremely flat. As more and more people become accustomed to real-world or available lighting, it has become more and more accepted in film and animation.

Still, many modern films suffer from the opposite: they are overly lit. A suspense or horror movie that is lit with near-perfect three-point lighting through almost the entire film for whatever reason can fall flat. When a feature film is lit, in the same manner as a drama television show, it can completely dull down any serious edge and weaken the mood that is inherent in real darkness and blackness. Audiences now demand a certain level of reality in their visual entertainment or storytelling. That sense of reality can also be genre specific, like *The X-Files*, or westerns, dramas, or situation comedies. For example, a sitcom like *Seinfeld* would never be lit like the *The X-Files*. Nothing visually reinforces or disconnects like lighting.

When a lighting director or DP builds a lighting rig or lights a set, assuming prelighting time allows, good lighting directors start with one or two key lights and work up slowly. Lighting directors put lights in, but they should also take lights out and do tests. They should also monitor how the lighting can look its best and do its part in giving the story lighting texture. Even though he is working with a DP, the director is still responsible for the overall look. At times the DP's job is to turn lights on, and the job of the director is to turn lights off, sometimes to the DP's chagrin.

COLOR AND FILTERS

Because of its level of control, animation has the ability to use color that live action isn't capable of using without looking odd or affected. The acceptance of animation as a reality also accepts unique color arrangements, color changes, and stylized lighting that seem at home in animation. Lighting is also forever tied to the color palette, and in all animation; the color combinations are limitless in creating a scene.

DPs need to know color theory intimately. Naturally warm colors come forward, while cool colors recede. Certain colors are complementary, while certain colors that are side by side almost vibrate and clash to the point of confusing the eye. When lighting a scene, a CG lighter or stop-motion DP needs to know as much if not more than the live-action DP. When a live-action DP puts gels on lights, he must know what it does to skin tones and the costumes. Although the tools are different, the CG or stop-motion DP must be able to know and control the same visuals.

The lighting combinations are compounded when colored lights are added to filters, and DPs have to make overall lighting decisions for continuity and lighting specifics to feature action and performance on a scene-by-scene basis. A DP also needs to know the emotional connection of colors.

Cold lighting sets a certain mood. A prison or modern-war movie, for example, is often tinted to a cold blue, so that black values are closer to a dark blue. Skin looks pale, and it gives a level of starkness and harshness. *The Lord of the Rings* starts in the Shire, which is warmly lit with vibrant colors: yellows, oranges, and bright greens. As the characters move away from the Shire, the color palette becomes more limited and stark, reinforcing the mood as it changes.

In live-action filmmaking, directors often talk about "the golden hour" for the most beautiful natural outdoor lighting. The golden hour is the hour right before sunset. The sun is low on the horizon, and the shadows are extremely long and perpendicular to the characters. The sunlight has usually changed color from passing through the sky. The sky is still bright blue so it fills in the shadow side with a pleasing ambient lighting, while the sun, which is often golden or orange, is a brilliant source of light. The golden hour is truly a dramatic lighting scheme, so much so that director Terrence Malick, director of *The Thin Red Line,* shot the exterior shots of his film *Days of Heaven* almost exclusively during the golden hour, making shooting only possible for one hour per day.

In CG, lights often default to white. In reality, there are very few instances where light is purely white and isn't affected by something else, such as other light sources, reflections, or atmosphere. Often, unappealing CG lighting reflects the sterile and blunt nature of default settings. Light and color also mix, and CG lighting often starts out far too pure when it needs to be mixed to take off the CG edge.

In live action, filters are frequently affixed to the camera lens to bring out different types of lighting. In animation, filters are usually moved to the postproduction, where overall treatments of color are added during color correcting or compositing. In stop motion, filters are nearly identical to live-action filming, but since all animation usually winds up being run through a computer, it gives another level of flexibility to shift overall filter-type effects to a postproduction treatment. Live action can also use specialty filters such as star filters or diffusion filters to soften an image. In stop motion and cel, diffusers and pro-mist filters are useful. Occasionally, imperfections in stop-motion puppets and artwork are visible in close-ups. Some of these imperfections include seams, fingerprints, and paint lines. Pro-mist type filters can help cover up these imperfections, but again, saving the filters and applying such treatments digitally adds more control. If a live-action or stop-motion scene is filmed with a diffusion or softening filter on the lens, and later it's decided that the diffusion is too much, it's virtually impossible to resharpen the image completely.

In the live-action black-and-white comedy *Paper Moon*, a red filter was used even though the film was in black and white. The red color changed the light so that the black and white was starker and more contrasting, which created the antique feel of the movie. Animators have far more flexibility than simple filters, whether using a postproduction treatment or a style that is incorporated from the start into the scene or artwork.

Figure 12.5 shows a night scene from the short film *Rat Trap*. The stylized animation is stylized on every level from design to color and models, so lighting should also find its own stylized place to enhance the charming feel of the film. Audiences are accustomed to shades of blue to indicate night lighting. In this situation, the blue is vibrant and a red ambient glow also fills the scene, creating a pleasing purple glow. Colors in live action of this intensity would have a very unrealistic effect, but in animation the color choice goes further to create the reality that *Rat Trap* has created.

FIGURE 12.5   Dramatic blue lighting fills the scene with an ethereal and pleasing version of nighttime (see Color Plate 20). © 2004 Gesine Krätzner. Reprinted with permission.

BASIC LIGHTING SCENARIOS

If a story is a comedy and is light and funny, it's usually well, evenly lit and simply shot to allow the character's performance to carry the humor. Comedies and romances are some of the last vestiges of the "studio lighting scheme." Audiences now have their own idea of what a specific type of lighting should be, and that image has grown to a level that is more realistic and reads closer to "available lighting." This real-world lighting feel has moved into almost every other genre. Even though lighting is still highly affected, it's now often designed to be less apparent and natural. If a story is somber and sad, the mood can be enhanced with cool lighting and a lack of color. Lars von Trier's *Breaking the Waves* is such a film, but also has a dark sense of humor that fits in well. *Paper Moon* is lit with stark lighting that fits into the production design that mimics a very conservative style indicative of old-period photographs.

INTERACTIVE LIGHTING AND ANIMATION

ON THE CD

Interactive lighting is a given in live action because light sources on a set affect objects near them. The same isn't true of animation, but interactive lighting is an excellent way to tie animation to its surroundings. DPs are always trying to exploit and exaggerate existing lighting to incorporate interactive lighting. The file **TVtest.mov** on the CD-ROM is a lighting test with exaggerated lighting coming from an implied television that is off screen, and its light is filling the room.

Stylistic interactive lighting is where the light is beyond just mimicking what is around it; instead, it involves exaggerating or having dynamic interactive lighting beyond what is normal. Being able to use interactive lighting for effect can give more texture and depth to an animated project. Flickering lights, fireplaces, torches, flashbulbs, and caustic reflections are all lighting sources that can work interactively to tie scenes together.

Interactive lighting doesn't need to be as dramatic as a roaring fire or water caustics in an indoor swimming pool. Lighting can exaggerate secondary light sources as well. A small green exit light that might not really provide much light can be amplified and used stylistically. Dashboard lights in a car are also often exaggerated to light a character's driving.

LIGHTING FOR DIGITAL

With the complexity of CG animation, there are also unlimited benefits from using the medium. The many tricks that CG can do with lighting can't happen anyplace else; if they are even doable in the real world, they are difficult and expensive to pull off. Often when working with CG and live action, a great deal of effort is expended getting shadow and reflection passes. Passes are individual filming or recording of elements that focus on a specific element. An example would be a shot that features a reflection that will be composited with other elements, and that reflection is filmed by itself, so it can be added and manipulated later and the final image can really be married to the background images. Those same tools and passes can be used stylistically with great effect and control that aren't possible in any other medium. The system of keeping elements separately animated isn't confined to postproduction. It can also be a powerful creative tool. For example, a character walks across the screen and is lit from the front, but its shadow is being cast from the back. Although this is impossible in real life, it can now be a stylistic design. The same can be done in cel, because everything is created. Creating separate shadow passes is relatively easy to pull off.

The main idea is to know that an element-by-element treatment is possible, if necessary. Again, rendering a pass for every single light and every single object obviously goes too far and takes too long. However, good CG lighting directors and technical directors know that they don't have to rely on the lighting the CG lights give to create shadows, for example.

Most CG 3D lighting packages will allow the use of negative light or putting a light into negative numbers, causing the render to decrease light from that source or to draw light out of a scene or area. Other programs allow lights that have no color or black lights (not fluorescent black light) that also draw light out of a scene.

All software packages also have ambient lighting, which is light that comes from everywhere, as if diffused in a fog bank, but without the fog being visible. Most default ambient lighting is too bright and too harsh, and waters down shadow edges and potentially drama. Ambient lighting is a powerful influence on the visual CG lighting and needs to be adjusted accordingly. Too much ambient lighting is indicative of poorly lit CG scenes. The uniformity of ambient lighting is very unrealistic and rings of computer rendering, because nothing else has that look of uniformity.

DEPTH OF FIELD AND RACK FOCUS

Depth of field is the area that remains in focus based on the given lens aperture setting. If focused on an object at a fixed depth, the depth of field dictates how much things are in or out of focus in the foreground or background.

For example, take a scene of someone looking for a crucial piece of evidence. The scene is a wide shot of a character ransacking a room; the story needs to show that piece of evidence to increase the anxiety of trying to find it. The shot could pan or cut to the object, but that might be spoon-feeding the audience like they did frequently in the series *Murder, She Wrote*. Instead the shot can have the evidence in the foreground, out of focus, and then the director slowly changes the focus plane. The viewer's eye follows the focus, as it moves across the disheveled room and finally focuses sharply on the evidence behind a book.

This way, the director doesn't have to interrupt the performance of the actor, who could be getting more maniacal as he searches for the item. When filming, the lower the f-stop, the shorter the depth of field, and when a shot lens focuses down very small, or when using a macro lens, the depth of field can be a fraction of an inch. The extreme other end of depth of field is the photography of great American photographers like Ansel Adams. Most of Adams' photographs were long exposures with an extremely small f-stop. In fact, he mostly used f.64, as small as the aperture would go, so that his depth of field was infinite. Whether it is rocks in the foreground, a few feet from the camera, or a mountain range 40 miles away, everything is in razor sharp focus. Depth of field is the physics of lenses bending light. It's an effective tool for a filmmaker or animator, and in animation, depth of field is far more easily controlled. Whereas film or video run at a specific rate, frame-by-frame animation isn't tied to a constant exposure time. This means that without blazing bright lights, stop-motion animators can have a flexible range of depth of field simply by closing down their lens and allowing a longer exposure per frame. It's even easier in CG or cel, because it has no real basis in physics. Still, many CG programs have interfaces that resemble a lens, including shutter angle, depth of field, and film aspect sizes, to mimic the film standards that filmmakers are used to.

Taking Advantage of Long Exposures in Stop Motion

Depending on whether you're using film or digital for stop motion, and depending on the capabilities of the camera, the fact that the camera or digital system doesn't have to run at live-action rate can be used to an animator's advantage. Since animation is simply just taking pictures sequentially, animators can use this to control lighting and depth of field. Live-action films run 24 fps and NTSC video runs at 29.97 fps; the exposure rate for each frame is about a 50th of a second and is constant and nonnegotiable without specialized equipment. Shutters can be adjusted to capture shorter exposures, but longer isn't possible if the rate is to run at a live-action speed. When shooting animation, however, long exposures can be utilized for a whole host of reasons. Most consumer video and DV cameras and single-frame film cameras don't have the flexibility to control the exposure speed, and often adjust automatically to a given lighting scenario. Animation film cameras that have computer controllers often do have exposure adjustments, including some higher-end digital cameras, which can be adapted to stop motion fairly easily. Being able to control the exposure time is an extremely valuable tool.

With numerous lights, the costs are obvious. Lights and bulbs are not cheap. Each light requires a stand or fitting plus many other peripherals, such as barn doors and filters, and many professional lights also draw a great deal of power. On a stop-motion set, a huge lighting scenario has tremendous impact; professional lights are hot, which is bad for the camera, film, set, animation puppets, and most importantly, the animator. By being able to set the camera to take longer exposures, the lights can be greatly reduced in wattage and can keep the set cool. It also enables the lights to be "split" with mirrors and reflection cards, making it easier to fill in lighting without having to keep adding actual lights.

If a short depth of field is a problem, namely with two characters, one upstage more than the other, and it is required that they both be in focus, instead of adding lights, the DP can slow down the exposure, allowing a higher f-stop that expands the focus plane. The opposite is also true; a faster exposure will allow a lower f-stop, contracting the focal plane and setting the background or foreground soft. This is an important aspect of "real" that works well with stop motion and all animation. Although it takes testing, having a background or other objects out of focus helps to aim the viewer's attention on where the focus is while reminding the viewer of the physical depth of the scene. Depth of field also helps miniature sets and models seem less miniature, because that feeling of depth of field is inherent in what we normally see at normal distances and sizes.

ATMOSPHERE, FOG, RADIOSITY, AND VOLUMETRICS

Air is often not as transparent as people would think. Between dust, haze, smoke, and fog, air can have a quality of its own, and that feeling of thick air, visible air, is very dramatic. Movies and television often rely on smoke machines that make soft blue smoke to add texture to a given scene. Animation again can make spectacular use of such textures from the simplicity of a beautifully rendered background image that has atmosphere built in to the image itself, to transparent layers that can be floated over scenes as mist and clouds. Transparency of almost any sort can be controlled in animation and have tremendous stylistic effect. Fog and mist are powerful diffusers of light. In thick fog, people and shapes can disappear and reappear, and keeping track of direction, even up and down, can be difficult. Audiences have an immediate reaction to fog and mist and other symbols of inclement weather, making these effects powerful story and mood points. Combined with lens flares, atmosphere creates hyperreality. Films like *Blade Runner* and *Close Encounters of the Third Kind* were early pioneers in using atmosphere and lens flares as cement to make special effects seem more real and filmed.

With modern CG tools, atmosphere can be pushed much further. Atmosphere isn't restricted to air, and can go even further when creating sequences underwater. Water can use ray tracing and caustics and subscattering of light to create rich textures; unless chasing reality, those types of textures can also become more stylized and influential, often without all the high-computation effects like caustics and subscattering. Figure 12.6 is a frame from a sequence from a work-in-progress film. The surface of the water is a 3D object, but the shafts of light are also 3D objects diffused with blurred edges and transparency falloffs. The animated sequence can be seen on the CD-ROM as **Sub.mov**.

FIGURE 12.6   A still from a cel- and computer-animated combination that uses geometry and fog to create a stylized underwater effect (see Color Plate 21).

Using geometry allowed for greater control and focus of a style. Avoiding caustics, ray tracing, and refraction was also a major consideration for rendering time as well as tweaking. Volumetrics, caustics, and special lighting techniques often require massive amounts of tweaking and finessing to create a simple effect. Ultimately, animators and film-makers know that eventually everything is flattened out into 2D via the television screen, computer screen, or movie screen. Game developers have long exploited the idea of "baking" complex textures into geometry, so that the illusion of lighting effects is actually created in 2D and worked into the geometry; often, complex setups that would utilize the caustics, ray tracing, and refraction can be created in surface and texture maps. Stylization usually makes such techniques easier, but in some cases, the full-blown high processor renders are the only solution for a specific look. No examples are better than Dreamworks' *A Shark's Tale* and Pixar's *Finding Nemo*; both films truly created a realistic and yet stylized undersea-scape. The movies used familiar images of water, both deep blue color and distortion of movement, to sell the feeling of underwater. In the case of *A Shark's Tale*, very human set ideas, such as bars, hair salons, and restaurants, were combined with an undersea world. Whereas *Finding*

Nemo was far more faithful to the true undersea look, because it was an adventure with real life and death peril, *A Shark's Tale* was attempting to be a zany comedy

Figure 12.7 uses several light sources to exemplify the air quality and the volumetrics, which are visible as long shafts of shadows that are visible when particles are in the air. On the CD-ROM is the animated sequence **Robotwalk.mov.** The scene makes great use of volumetric lighting, and a thick atmosphere is spread across a wide variety of lighting sources in the scene.

FIGURE 12.7   An example of volumetrics and a visible atmosphere. © 2004 Darrel Anderson. Reprinted with permission.

The short films contained on the CD-ROM are a testament to the uniqueness of lighting. *Shards of Death* has a neutral lighting, but with a dramatic light source and thick atmosphere. *Grime Shoed Diaries* is lit with a mixture of practical CG lights as well as lighting painted into the surfaces. The tone is reminiscent of film noir, but also features many bright colors, such as neon signs, which serve as a sharp contrast to the darkness and also modernize the film.

Unlike *Shards of Death*, there's plenty of darkness in *Grime Shoed Diaries*. The darkness allows for the character to move through it, for drama, and for the noir feel the film emulates while remaining graphical and flat like a comic book. *Insect Poetry* is lit for performance and mimics a desk, but also mimics a stage play; its recesses are dark and deep to give an idea of a full and old set. *107.6 Degrees* is a brightly lit film that pushes the idea of an intense sunlight that drives the entire film, which is the quest for shade. Lighting is unique for each and every individual project. For creative films and animations, no two lighting schemes are the same because no two stories are the same.

In animation, lighting often crosses boarders with art direction and character design. A Flash or cel animation rarely incorporates lights, and it has to be painted or designed into the animation. Animators who work in programs like Flash, Moho, and other 2D programs frequently need to wear all the hats of lighting design, performance, and art direction. Figure 12.8 is a purely cel- or Flash-type design of graphical animation. Dark shadows and a very dramatic side have been incorporated into the design, which fit with the futuristic sci-fi subject matter.

FIGURE 12.8   A graphical dramatic treatment of shadow incorporated into the artwork.

© 2004 Guy Burwell. Reprinted with permission.

Figure 12.9 is a potentially complicated scene that if not dealt with creatively could be epic in scale and profoundly time consuming to create. If the intent were to create a character for every visible child in the scene, the task would be huge, and the effect might become busy or cluttered. Instead, the use of lighting and color allows for a stylization that is more effective than attempting to render every single individual. A graphical version of a line of kids disappearing off into the distance carries more weight, and also allows the focus of the vivid colors on the foreground characters to carry the action.

FIGURE 12.9   A frame from a Flash animation that uses color and light to create distance and atmosphere. © 2004 Tracy Prescott MacGregor. Reprinted with permission.

Without a doubt, good lighting is essential to telling good visual stories. The possibilities of lighting in animation are almost endless, but the lighting schemes should be planned and selected wisely to set the proper mood and tone for the story.

Tips for Future Projects

Treat Lighting Like a Story Device First

Naturally, things will be lit so they are visible. In a broader scope, a DP looks at a given project and then tries to use light to help move the story along, create a mood, set a tone, and tie scenes and characters together. In some cases a DP even uses light as a metaphor for story ideas.

Don't Be Afraid of the Dark

Being overlit is a potentially bigger problem than being underlit. Allow the audience to fill in some of the blanks. In CG animation it's easy to keep adding multiple lights, but often too many lights begin to muddy colors and confuse or even remove essential shadows and shading. There is stylization in lighting, but because of its essential role in simply illuminating scenes it's often restricted to making sure the performance is readable and visible and clear.

Carefully Use Color for Effect

In CG, when trying to set a recognizable lighting mood or a lighting scenario that is familiar to known lighting scenarios, pure colored lights tend to give a plastic effect, because the colors are too pure compared to reality; add a gray or neutral value to colored lights for more atmosphere. Pure color doesn't mean to avoid vivid colors; pure colors mean absolutely pure, in one color shade, because it rarely ever occurs.

In animation, however, stylistically, there's always great and interesting reasons to use vivid and pure colors, and only animation can do so effectively. The images in Figure 12.2 are a perfect example of a vibrant and colorful style that uses almost nothing but bright colors, segmented by a thick design line. Animation is about creating its own reality, and lighting can be a strong instrument in creating new realities with new color schemes. The sky isn't always blue in animation. It can be any color depending on what feeling the story is trying to convey.

Tests and Experiments

Experiment with taking lights out as well as putting lights in. Whether on paper or in the actual software, try lighting schemes that are visually complementary but are also mindful of the mood of the scene and the emotions the scene is trying to convey. Don't accept face values or default settings on any light settings. Exploring unique lighting textures is valuable to establishing a lighting scheme that is connected to the mood of the story. In stop motion, lighting tests are crucial since rerendering isn't an option. Testing and making judgments from those tests is crucial to every step of the film and animation project, but nowhere is it more crucial than in lighting.

In stop-motion animation, a process using large 400-frame shots that could potentially take a week to shoot is very expensive from start to finish. For that reason, lighting and staging is tested often more than once to get the animator ready for the long shot. DPs, the director, and the art director watch those lighting tests and make comments and calls. If there is a move, then the character or a stand-in is popped through its positions, so that the lighting can be judged at every position. DPs always bracket the shot where they expose at least a few frames on virtually the entire spectrum of f-stops on the lens, from completely closed down to completely wide open. The DP also puts a card or a symbol in the shot that shows what he thinks is the perfect exposure. This helps him to keep a close watch on the light meters he's using and their relative calibration.

In many cases, even though the perfect exposure was at a given f-stop, the scene actually looked better a stop or two, under or over, for various reasons. If there were many shots in that scene, the DP would make this adjustment and then underexpose the following shots so that they matched the desired test shot earlier. Because of the potential disaster effect of film, lighting directors and cinematographers have created a series of checks and rechecks to make sure that if something goes wrong, it isn't on their end.

The goal isn't to make sure that it's lit and visible; the goal is to massage the lighting to help the mood: reflectors and mirrors are added to warm interesting props or signage, or to fill out the frame. Flags and dodges are used to restrict and mask light. These tools darken areas to either visually create a composition or to mentally drop out elements the story doesn't want to focus on.

With the use of motion-picture film, there is a serious do-or-die quality. Because the film must be processed, there are things that cannot be known until it is processed and viewed. As a result, there are numerous tests on the film that would eventually lead to a perfect exposure and lighting mood on the final scene. The idea is that testing is easily done, instead of reshooting a huge shot that takes a week, or compromising with lighting that is less than what was desired.

Digitally, however, that isn't true, but the mental process that professional directors and DPs use shouldn't change. Digital has an immediacy feel because it can be watched in real time. The time saved should still be split out on truly creating a lighting feel, an overall feel, and perhaps even an allegorical use of lighting as well.

Both overexposures and underexposures can give a feel: overexposed can be stark, bleak, and gritty, while underexposed can be mysterious or dense. Exposures combined with filters, whether practical or digital, can create a whole spectrum of feels and moods. Day for night is where a filter is added to the camera as well as being slightly underexposed; this can create a night feel that is shot during the day.

Yellows and oranges can be warm colors, but they can also make a scene feel aged, old, and worn. Because of the physics of lighting, however, some filters only work in front of the camera, such as a graduated filter that darkens as it goes up. In shooting against a bright sky, it's usually impossible to get proper exposure with the foreground elements and the sky without a ton of extra lighting. Instead, a graduated filter can be used to darken or tint the sky and create an overall exposure, so that the foreground elements and the sky and clouds are visible. Because of film's, and especially video's, inability to adjust exposure on two completely different lighting schemes, using a filter in front of the camera is often necessary. The filter should be one that is dark on the top and then gradually fades to transparent; this sets an exposure that both lights the foreground characters and objects correctly and also darkens to allow the sky to not be overlit.

Multiple passes can be shot digitally and combined in postproduction so that both elements are properly exposed. However, it can be complicated if characters are going to move behind other objects or cross in front of the sky, which could call for rotoing mattes to complete the shot.

PRODUCTION

ANIMATION

Animation at its simplest form is an object moving from one place to the next and is created frame by frame with images moving slightly in each frame to create motion. There are many different things referred to generally as animation, but lumping them together is far too broad. Although character animation, animation, and motion share movement and can borrow from each other, their designations are specific. There are always exceptions, and forms of animation are often combined, but three clear divisions exist in animation. First, is simple animation that is movement. Second, animation can be stylized or very mechanical, and can include anything from medical or forensic animation to flying logos. Third, animation can use the rules of gravity, and the principles like stretch and squash, anticipation, overlapping action, or it can be more stylized and mechanical. Character animation is making objects seem alive. Whether it's Shrek, Gollum, or a dancing credit card, character animation creates characters that appear to be living. Experimental animators often create animated films that have no characters but instead use animation as an artistic tool, instead of character acting. As experimental animation, the films move beyond telling a straightforward story, and instead create interesting visuals. Although experimental animators can forego the rigors of great character animation, their task isn't any easier. In fact, it can often be more difficult to create emotional connections from pure visuals and filmmaking alone.

Even though animation and character animation are usually lumped together, they are quite different in reality. Likewise, motion graphics often feature and utilize animation of text and type and imagery that stylistically moves from place to place, but it is different as well. With the many forms of visual imagery from motion graphics to experimental, animation can share the ability to use movement in unquiet ways. Often, there are no physics applied and the animation is pure stylized movement. In character animation, physics is usually a factor; gravity always exerts itself whether stylized or realistic. In motion graphics not only is physics not necessary, but it usually isn't really applicable and can distract from the design and graphical flow.

CHARACTER ANIMATION

Character animation usually has actual characters, people, creatures, and animals; it can cross over and make characters into inanimate objects like dancing soda bottles, talking flowers, and swaggering credit cards. Animation doesn't have to perform like a character to be interesting, surprising, or effective. It can create stylized movement and motion and morph, change, and create interesting abstract relationships, patterns, and designs instead of an acted-out story. Motion graphics are an example of extensive animation that is often rich and compelling with no characters.

Figure 13.1 is an animation that comes from a more artistic vein. The scene has a short depth with the figures and objects separated in a shallow box. The objects and characters move and change. Some are almost characterlike, while others are abstract shapes and designs, studies in color and relationships to motion and to each other; they are much closer to animated sculpture than to an animated cartoon, but effective in their own way. Other forms of animation that aren't character animation include pixilation, where actual people are animated frame by frame. Other animators use paint to animate, as well as clay painting. Even animators like Steve Segal create animations actually drawn on film itself, which is actually a camera-less animation.

FIGURE 13.1   A scene from an experimental stop-motion animated film that is more about interesting visuals and movement than acting. © 2004 Joanna Priestley. Reprinted with permission.

The difference between character animation and animation could be akin to the difference between a stage play and a ballet; both are very different types of animation but both are entertaining in their own right. A stage play focuses on acting, lines, and performance. A ballet might have no lines, but it can still tell a story, and the audience can still enjoy the form, movement, motion, and the relationship to music. In relation to animation and character animation, the difference would be experimental or motion graphics, as compared to full-up character animation. More detailed coverage of character animation will be covered in Chapter 14.

ANIMATION

Animation is an effective tool in showing how things progress and fit together. The educational use of animation is highly effective in a vast array of venues, far removed from entertainment- and art-like scientific modeling and simulations (see Figure 13.2). Still animation that shows processes and teaches doesn't have to be void of personality or character. The previously discussed Disney film, *Donald in Mathmagic Land,* combines character animation with more mechanical animation to great effect. In fact, *Powers of Ten,* the film from Charles and Ray Eames, also discussed earlier, has no character animation at all, and the animation in the film is quite minimal. Stories can be told with mechanical animation that is wildly popular and entertaining. Taking *Powers of Ten* to the next level, software designer Chris Laurel created a 3D version of *Powers of Ten,* a 3D model titled *Celestia.* Since it's a 3D model on the computer, the animation can send viewers, who have full control, on a real-time tour of the planets in which they can even fly out of the galaxy. The free software takes *Powers of Ten* to the next level known as interactivity, which is possible because of CG animation.

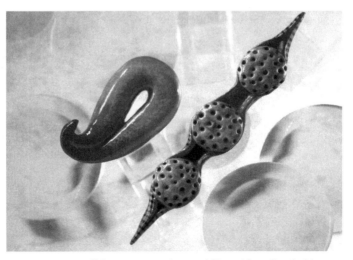

FIGURE 13.2 A still from an experimental film with stylized objects on a dimensional backdrop of real lenses and glass. © 2004 Joanna Priestley. Reprinted with permission.

MOTION GRAPHICS

Motion graphics are a prevalent form of animation from movie titles to logos to instructional animation. They are seen on every channel from weather graphics to sports intros and designs. Motion graphics can be graphical and treat the television screen or the movie screen as a flat shape. They can also incorporate dimension, as well as dimensional animation and even character animation.

Motion graphics can take advantage of designs and motions that have nothing to do with gravity or physics. They can follow abstract lines or interesting and complex designs they take from their graphical heritage. They can also mechanically move from one point to the next, without any anticipation, stretch, or squash. Incorporating the rules of physics and finessed character animation, motion graphics can also turn physics off and on when appropriate. Figure 13.3 is a 3D title sequence. In the sequence, the title letters and small globe follow a roller-coaster type movement and are influenced by the narrator as he annunciates specific words; the small earth then dots the "I" in the word *science*. Once the title is read, in comedic form, the gravity kicks in and the words fall out of frame. The actual title sequence is on the CD-ROM titled **Titlesequence.mov**.

ON THE CD

FIGURE 13.3   A title sequence that uses graphics and depth, but no gravity, as the words follow a roller coaster-type path.

Motion graphics can incorporate live-action footage, which is often the focus of many motion-graphic designs because they use elements of filmed footage or sequences of photographs. When using sequences of live action, motion graphics and editorial decisions have to be closely tied together, and often a motion-graphics designer is called on to become a footage editor as specific sequences tied to visuals appear on screen. *Flying chrome logos* is a term to describe the rash of 3D graphics that are easily created in any CG 3D package as near-button pushes. However, even though a sequence doesn't involve the rigors of character animatilon, motion-graphic designers are still responsible for creating dynamic and interesting designs that are surprising and inventive. While character animators concentrate on facial poses and body stances, motion-graphic designers concentrate on fonts, leading, palettes, and clever animations that will focus the viewers' attention on the pertinent elements.

In films, title sequences can be simple text that is overlaid with the underlying filmed footage. They can also be complex animation and stylistic designs that set the mood and the tone, and even stylistically set the story in motion. Graphically, or through texture, motion graphics do create emotions. Whether it's simply pleasing, cool, or over-the-top and zany, motion graphics like animation require development and serious attention to details. Object animation, moving from one place to another, can easily be created to look like motion, have vivid colors, and be flashy, but creating unusual, unique, and exciting motion and graphics is as complicated and involved as any art form.

Title sequences can also be full-blown character animation as well. One of the most famous is the title sequence for the original *The Pink Panther* movie that became its own animation franchise. A clever and suave pink-panther cat was a metaphor that represented the intrigue of the diamond named "the pink panther." The title and the character were so popular that the *Pink Panther* titles and animation carried on into subsequent movies, even though the actual diamond was never a plot point after the first film.

ROTOSCOPING

Rotoscoping is a form of animation, where the outline and form of live action are traced, and the motion is transferred to a 2D image frame to frame. Rotoscoping is a truly interesting technique because real motion and animation are usually distinctly different, but rotoscoping literally combines both. Rotoscoping isn't character animation. Instead, it's a masking over live action, because the physics of live action come through very clearly when comparing rotoscoping and good character animation. Rotoscoping is an animation by process, but on a very precise level. Figure 13.4 is a frame from an animated sequence incorporating rotoscoping. Seven black cats line a collaged wall overlooking a city, and the roto-scoping transfers the exact outline of the cats. The rotoscoping also stylis-tically creates a simplified read of the cats, with no features or color differences, which set well against the rich background.

FIGURE 13.4   An animated collage with seven black cats rotoscoped from live action and then composited together. © 2004 Laura DiTrapani. Reprinted with permission.

With Macromedia Flash and other digital tools it's now possible to create that same rotoscoped feeling by applying filters. Director Richard Linklater's *Waking Life* is a live-action feature film, treated with many dif-ferent and varied rotoscoping techniques. The film is a philosophical dis-cussion about the nature of reality in which the main character keeps waking up in a dream, over and over, knowing he can't really wake up.

Each waking segment features another type of this rotoscoping effect, where the digital filters take most of their cues on color and design from the live action film underneath. The technique in the form of a full-feature film is often interesting and even distracting, as the rotoscoping slips and slides from reality to surreal imagery. Animators of course can use as much or as little of the information that rotoscoping provides, but rotoscoping always looks like rotoscoping when following the live action. In CG animation, there's very little use for rotoscoping except stylistically, and capturing imagery for visual reference just becomes visual reference. In cel animation, rotoscoping was useful for creating "real" feeling images in character worlds. Walt Disney's Snow White character was in fact rotoscoped, and many female leads in Disney movies were rotoscoped because capturing subtle feminine movement and beauty was stylistically difficult. Disney also made use of rotoscoping complex scenes. In *101 Dalmatians*, the car crash between Cruella De Vil and a truck was rotoscoped because the straight lines and subtle perspective on a rigid object like cars and vehicles are difficult to animate, especially when trying to keep them looking more realistic than cartoonish. When Cruella's car crashes, it needs to look more real than cartoony to sell the seriousness of the accident. Rotoscoping is a fun place to create animation that takes its cues from reality but still has its own unique feel.

Tips for Future Projects

Develop Motivated Stylizations

Work to develop styles, techniques, and movement that are tied to the story or concept.

Doing animation that isn't character animation might seem easier because you don't need to work and crunch every pose, but animators doing nonphysics-driven animation have the same task when it comes to creating entertaining animation and visuals.

Without characters it is more challenging to keep viewers interested in visuals the longer the visuals continue. Visuals and animation then have to rely on other factors to remain interesting and compelling, so animators instead rely on surprise, dynamic, and pleasing movement, interesting designs, patterns, and movements through space. Often, noncharacter animation is tied to education and the relaying of information, like simulations and illustrations of processes, which in a very real sense is the story. All the rules that apply to film and character animation apply to experimental or any other kind of visual media. Whether making a short animation with found objects, animating and creating patterns and designs, or a character-driven feature, every aspect of the production should be considered: lighting, sound, angles, mood, tone, and all the other details covered in this book. Whether a viewer is sitting in a theater, playing a video game, or standing in an art gallery, they still expect to see something new, interesting, and engaging.

Pure Exploration

Creating art and animation means really corralling nearly infinite ideas to create compelling visuals and stories. Because the only criterion for animation is movement, anything can be moved for effect; discovering new and innovative ways to use animation is the supreme goal of artistic animators. Story does pack serious power, but a film that has a nonstory that works on a completely different level is no less valid or difficult. Film-makers have the flexibility of doing both or more. Some filmmakers and animators live in the world of mainstream stories. Others see animation as more of tool for creating truly compelling imagery. Neither form of noncharacter animation is done enough; animation as pure experimentation and animation as art has limitless possibilities, and only a dedicated few are creating truly new and amazing visuals as can be seen in Figures 13.5 through 13.8.

FIGURE 13.5   A simplified and stylized animation that incorporates both character animation as well as fanciful and design-based animation.
© 2004 Tracy Prescott MacGregor. Reprinted with permission.

FIGURE 13.6   A graphic design with a limited palette and a removed or rotoscoped outline of a person. The design is simplistic but has a big visual style, using the shoe product as an iconic shape of angle reinforced by the photo image behind that is a high-up angle. The composition is geometrical and graphical (see Color Plate 22).
© 2004 Toni Smith. Reprinted with permission.

FIGURE 13.7   A different design take on the theme, with a rotoscoped outline of a person as the running main element. This figure has more of an urban look, with the graffiti art and abstract imagery. © 2004 Toni Smith. Reprinted with permission.

FIGURE 13.8   A third take on the silhouetted person there, with live footage as a an element as well as animated type can be incorporated and combined with the imagery. © 2004 Toni Smith. Reprinted with permission.

For motion graphics, a sturdy foundation in graphic design is essential and almost every single frame becomes its own graphical composition. For graphic designers, pure exploration can be the opposite of rough sketches and can be defined, tight graphical compositions. The type of exploration needed is driven by the characters, the point of the story or idea, the medium, and the level of abstraction.

Experimental and art animation aren't done nearly enough, partly because it is so expensive. However, this type of filmmaking is invaluable and is a useful tool for the filmmaker or animator truly intent on learning and developing a style of visual storytelling and directing. The single best part, for most animators, is that such experimenting is also incredibly rewarding and fun.

Animation as Art

No book or volumes of books can begin to encapsulate what works and doesn't work in art, what is compelling and what falls flat, and what inspires a viewer or the artist himself. When creating animation as art, the end result can be dramatically different from mainstream animation. Art animators are free to discard stories, characters, and structures, but like a story-driven animation, the art animator still needs to have a point; he has to have things develop and try to create some connection with the viewer. Even repelling and shocking visuals create a feeling—pleasant or not. Without question, there are animated films in the traditional sense that do both: create a good story and are art as well.

CHARACTER ANIMATION

CREATING A LIVING CHARACTER

In certain productions, time isn't a luxury, so character animation sometimes begins long before anyone has given thought to what the character's personality will be. Developing what a character is all about, what their conflicts are, and what their purpose is in the story is known as characterization. As discussed in Chapter 11, some level of characterization should be known before an animator begins to make that character physically perform. Characterization for writers happens when they write the story, beginning with the first sentence about a character. Characterization also happens when an actor studies their script and determines how they will play their character. Likewise, character animation should be the culmination that reflects a character's personality, so deciding on very technical movements while still trying to develop a character's personality sells the story short. Before the mechanics of animation can begin, a personality that will drive the performance should be created, at least to some degree. In animation the script gives a lot of clues to the character, but doesn't normally give many details about physical performance, stature, or movement. For animation and live action alike, this detail usually comes from rehearsal or studies of many types: improvisation, studying performances, sketches, designs, and so forth.

CREATING A PERFORMANCE

Animators don't just make characters move, they make them act. By focusing the viewer's eyes on shapes, poses, and movements, animators make the character act frame by frame. Animators also know that animation is an exaggeration of reality, so they know when to push and pull their poses for effect.

Every single thing a character does should re-enforce their personality.

Every movement, motion, or reaction that is glossed over and not considered is a lost opportunity to improve the character and to better tell the story.

These are veryimportant ideas, but shouldn't be taken completely literally. For instance, sometimes a character sits and does nothing. Not everything is overanimated, and doing nothing often says more about a character than doing a million things. Either way, from a scene of intense sadness and agony to a simple scene of someone opening a door, every movement must be considered because unlike real actors, animation gives nothing; the animator has to make it all happen.

In a well-planned production, the character animation process begins after a whole bunch of other processes end. Storyboarding, character design, motion studies, and motion tests all contribute to deciding how things will be animated.

Knowing the story and motivation has connotations of having a connection to deep and complex thoughts and histories of characters that are far too literal. Some characters aren't deep at all. Although some have thin personalities, they are still motivated in someway that the animator must be in sync with. In *Shards of Death*, there's no deep motivation for either character. The green monster conducting the interview has motivation that is simple and mundane: suffer through his awkward job, perhaps not get fired, and perhaps just make it until 5:00 p.m.

The blue fairy creature (Figure 14.1) only wants to have a good interview, and once that doesn't happen, the fairy creature has no motivation at all. The creature isn't aware of being cute; it's not motivated to be cute; it just is cute. From the very outset, the creature is oblivious and doomed. What is the motivation for Beavis and Butthead? What is the motivation for Homer Simpson or Daffy Duck? Daffy is often an extreme character, so his motivation is to just stir things up and cause problems. Homer's motivation is far more human; he's motivated by food, laying on the couch, and just getting by.

In creating a performance for both characters in *Shards of Death*, several fundamental steps were followed. For example, to make the fairy creature

FIGURE 14.1   The blue fairy creature is unaware of its cuteness and can't help but act like the way the creature is.

perform, it is iconic of cute, as shown in Figure 14.1. It has large eyes that blink happily and hands that are clasped like a small child, gleefully clapping. The performance matches the nature and appearance of such a creature.

THE VOICE

If the character speaks or makes noises, the voice becomes an important element that should be recorded as early as possible. A quality voice actor will bring a level of performance to the character from which traits and qualities can be anchored. Voice actors are the closest animators come to having an actor act out scenes, and it is important to take advantage of this opportunity. With good voice actors and good voice and dialogue directors, performances can truly influence everything about a character, from design and movement to poses. An actor with big audible breathing and breaths could dictate a character's performance and use the breaths to pull large overly dramatic poses. A voice actor can also bring a cadence to a voice read that influences animation as well. So powerful is the voice or the sounds of a character that directors and dialogue directors need to specifically direct the actor for specific scenes; this often involves giving the actor information about what the situation and back story are, so that he can respond. Often, voice sessions do dozens and dozens of takes per line, massaging and pushing every word to get the best possible performance.

At this point in the production when character animation begins, it's assumed that the voice has been through a rigorous and successful design process. This is similar to the visual designing of characters. Instead of developing walks and postures, when establishing a voice, various voices, lines, and vocal ranges are tried. Once a final voice is established, then that voice or audio track is incorporated into the animatic and adjustments are made, allowing for story, timing, and movement. As a result, the voice that is ultimately animated to is the final, best voice possible.

PHYSICS

Unlike experimental animation that can flirt with physics or have none at all, when it comes to character animation, physics is the underlying principle that character animators learn. Once an animator understands physics, then it's no longer a process of figuring out each pose, because physics dictates how things move, for the most part. There are instances where extremely stylized character animation could avoid all the rules of physics, but for the most part, characters that live in a world with some sense of gravity are ruled by physics. Understanding the physics of movement is not only essential, but is truly a time-saving tool. For the majority of character animation, creatures are big bags of water on a hard frame, and a majority of character animation is dealing with that simple idea in a stylized form of gravity. Bags of water on a rigid frame, specifically people, trees, animals, and most organic creatures, will behave in a very specific and predictable way, where there is some form of gravity and inertia acting upon them. Even dinosaurs and characters we mentally think of as rigid still "slosh" around.

Because character animation is usually grounded in a similar reality to what the viewers know, the rules of physics always help to sell the characters' performance. This can range from near photo-real physics, like special-effects shots in *The Matrix* or *Terminator 3*, or Tex Avery physics, which is an exaggeration of physics that is mostly ruled by comedy and extremes. Characters have weight and bounce when they walk, but if necessary, they can float, jump, hang in mid-air, or stop on a dime. Their eyes can also pop to 20 times their body size when surprised. It is an important aspect of the character, because it ties the character to the world in which it lives.

Weight has to be considered with cel animation because it has to be drawn into every frame with stretch and squash, anticipation, and overlapping action. For example, as a large man walks down the street his head bobs along and his belly, affected by gravity, bounces up and down like a big water balloon. Although weight is another illusion in animation, it is an important one to convey, because a character must have weight to exist in a world. Even a bird that is just a couple of ounces of fluff and feathers has weight, which it shows ever so slightly when it lands: the head drops down, overlapping the body's movement forward before coming back up.

Real-life characters do real-life stuff, whether flailing around wildly or standing around daydreaming; characters do a host of autonomic things they aren't aware of, like sweating, breathing, panting, coughing, shivering. If a character breathes air, then a master animator can make the character breath through lip sync. This can be the clichéd big sigh, or one of the other versions of breathing that can be worked into animation.

All of these principles are governed and tied to their real-world counterparts, perception, and of course physics. If an animator understands how the physics of motion works, then any animation problem can be solved. Knowing physics is knowing how something should work even before it's animated; knowing physics saves having to figure the movement out on every single frame.

One of the fantastic attributes of animation is that there are infinite ways of stylization not just in character and design, but also in movement. There could easily be styles of animation that aren't bound by the physics of the world; they perform opposite gravity or any rules that the creator wants to apply. Impossible physics has always been the playground of animation. Examples include a character being able to pick itself up by its own tail, a tiny mouse being able to swing an elephant around like a big balloon, or Warner Brothers' Wile E. Coyote painting a one-dimensional image or a train tunnel on a mountain side, and then a train abruptly appears out of the tunnel and runs Wile E. down. Impossible gravity is a type of a gag, because it's surprising and unexpected. When trying to create characters that fall somewhere in the world we know, which corresponds closely to the physics on earth, it becomes important for the rules of physics to be consistent. This is especially the case when trying to tell a story that viewers can relate to beyond the visual gags.

If there are basic elements of ground and sky, and a character moves across this ground and has weight, then certain rules immediately come into play. Therefore, if the basic physics rules aren't visually met or aren't consistent, then the viewers will notice and disconnect.

A good example is a water drop. Whether it's a drop from a nozzle, spigot, or waterfall, a drop is shaped the same way world over. Liquid water performs with uniformity from the top of the tallest mountain to the depths of the deepest cave, and if it freezes, it freezes the same way. So if a drop splashes on the ground, regardless of its volume and regardless of the amount of stretch and squash that is added, it fundamentally has to read like a drop every step of the way or it won't look like a drop. Even a drop in very low gravity would do the same thing, except much slower and with much less effect.

In zero gravity, a drop would act like a drop, only with no forces acting on it, and it would form into a wobbly sphere. If a character bends to pick up a specific amount of weight, then the character naturally counter-balances with their arm, leg, or the rear. If it doesn't happen, then it robs the weight from the item being lifted, and it doesn't appear true to physics. If this is a stylistic choice for effect or absurdity, that's one thing, but if the idea is that the character is picking up something heavy, then there needs to be a counterweight. If a character leans too far over without putting out a limb as a counterbalance or doesn't hang onto something, then everything the viewers know tells them the character will fall over.

Dissecting animation down to the frame is essential, and for character animators nowhere else is the phrase "on the shoulders" more accurate. For frame-by-frame animation, the history has been a massive ongoing lesson in what works and doesn't when selling any action, move, or pose in animation. In order to learn about the truly specific culmination of that mastered art, there are no better books than *The Animator's Survival Kit* by Richard Williams, and the all-time bible of character animation,

The Illusion of Life, by Ollie Johnston and Frank Thomas. These books are invaluable for a character animator.

From the legends of the Disney Studios to Richard Williams' massive experience, these two volumes are the last word on the visual rules of character animation and the creation of living, animated characters with more personality than most real people. There is more than simply stating that a character has to act move in a way that is bigger and yet more concise than reality. The fact that the character has to act from pose to pose, delivering action and expressions that sell the emotion while being funny, clever, and often surprising is an easy doctrine to put forth. To pull it off frame by frame is another story, and the two books just mentioned clearly explain exactly how, from the first frame to the last.

Many of the rules that they explain so well are based on the laws of physics. A master animator, knowing these rules, should be able to figure out the movement of animation without having to reference books on every shot.

Gravity pulls on everything uniformly, and anything that is taller than it is wide is in a real sense balanced. When a person walks and raises one leg to take a step, automatically the character leans away from the leg that is being raised to counter being off balance for that frame; the bigger the step, the bigger the lean, until an arm starts to counter and stick out. In one sense, the physics of motion are mandatory, but they work both ways in that they can also reinforce stylized animation as well.

A stiff character with a limited walk cycle lifts it legs to walk, but if it's only the legs, then it might look like a march; using a bit of counterbalancing can reinforce the walk cycle. Still it's not to say that in every last instance, physics has to be used. Depending on the story, joke, gag, or animation style, it might be funnier or more in the overall mood if the character stays stiff and has no countering.

PERFORMANCE AND ACTING

In movie acting, the clichéd instruction directors give to actors is, "don't act, just be yourself." It is a Hollywood cliché, but it's also very true; in television and film, it's often not what you do, it's what you don't do. Overacted faces, expressions, and big-line presentations like acting for a stage play can look ridiculous in visual filmmaking because recording a performance has the capacity to record very subtle changes. Film and television are recording in the reality we exist in, so people watching people can pick up on subtle visual cues and expressions. Cameras can be placed and positioned in specific angles that most people don't ever or rarely experience in real life. For example, a human face projected on a giant screen 40 feet tall is something humans don't normally see. Only when people are extremely intimate, inches from someone's face, does a person see a human face so close and so precisely. Film and animation are both capable of that incredible intimacy, and being that close to a face, a viewer can easily recognize when someone is overacting. What would work to the viewer in the back row of a live theater would look like screaming and pantomime if filmed closeup.

"Be yourself" tends to encompass that idea to act as one would naturally; don't overdo anything beyond what a viewer would normally do. A subtle shift of the eyes or a solid stare can create a level of mystery that puts some of the work in figuring out the story square in the lap of the viewer, which helps draw the viewer into the story. "Be yourself" is an expression usually given to human actors, but it's just as valid in animation. Animation is at its very nucleus a puppeteer with infinite control, whether it's an animator acting through a character or a cel animator doing individual drawings. In animation with all its possibilities, "be yourself" could constitute the opposite of being subtle and instead of less equals more, more equals more. In cases of extreme animation, such as the characters Ren and Stimpy, Chuck Jones, and Tex Avery, being yourself means being extreme and over the top with distorted extreme frames ten times over where reality ends.

No one knows more about making a character act than Glen Keane, legendary Disney animator. Read the complete interview with Keane in Chapter 1, "Illusion of Cinema and Animation." In his interview, Keane describes his often-agonizing process in finding a link between himself and the character he's creating. For Glen, it is essential and he can't really know the character until he finds a very personal link. Whether it's a character in *Aladdin* or *Tarzan*, he must find a part of himself that is that character. Finding a part of yourself that is at the root of that character is a simple idea to put forth, but it isn't so easily accomplished and might just never happen on the same level for all animators. However, there's no arguing the mastery of Keane's characterizations. Whether trying to discover a personal link or at least the very heart of a character, there are many processes to use to discover that nature.

There are many modes of physicality that people and characters have. There are autonomic functions that people aren't aware of, such as breathing, and blinking, as mentioned earlier. A walking person swinging his arms is a natural aspect of balance. The line between autonomic and the person controlling it is very thin. A person can walk with a normal gate, and normal arms swinging, or he can deliberately swing his arms more, and it becomes obvious to the viewer that the person is deliberately swinging his arms, as if he is marching. In the case of swinging arms, the difference between an unconscious swing and a swing where the walker is trying to show something can be a matter of degrees of an arm that is just slightly stiffer and less relaxed.

As we've mentioned, human beings can recognize these subtle changes instantly because they are very in tune to body language and body posture, which is a key to animation. On the other end of the spectrum are people who can't read, or ignore, body language. The classic example is a self-absorbed person at a party, who despite the host's obvious yawning, folding his arms, rolling his eyes, and turning away, still doesn't pick up on the body language that he has overstayed his welcome.

When a person is truly surprised or startled, their reactions are usually an autonomic response, because their bodies react involuntarily before their brain does. A reflex is when an event evokes a response that bypasses the brain. Often when someone accidentally picks up a hot pan or pot, he will automatically fling or throw the pan without regard to where it will land, because the pain triggered a reaction that didn't require the brain. The pain signal only made it to the elbow, causing the muscles to seize up and throw the pot. Reflexes have evolved in people so that in dangerous and threatening situations, muscles intercept nerve signals and act; the pain signal doesn't need to go all the way to the brain to have the brain decide what to do, and then do it. In the split second it takes for the brain to process the pain it could make the difference between getting a first-degree burn or a third-degree burn. If an animated character were to pick up a hot pan, it would still have a slight if not major anticipation before the reaction, where in reality there often isn't anticipation. This is the difference between reality and character animation. Character animation isn't the duplicating of reality; it is superreality.

THE POWER TOOLS AND RULES OF CHARACTER ANIMATION

In *The Illusion of Life* and *The Animator's Survival Kit,* the animators stress the importance of the basics, and that remains unchanged. Animators, besides having to create good and fun poses, which requires them to understand acting, are also required to master the fundamentals of animation. Going back nearly 75 years or more, master animators have figured out the root of animation. All animators serious about creating performance through motion must master stretch and squash, anticipation, overlapping action, and arcs; they must also keep a critical eye on overall pleasing visual and clarity. The following sections are some of the crucial ideas that effective character animators must know and master. There is a dearth of information that follows in this chapter, and these next sections are a sampling of some of the truly powerful tools and techniques that can be used or must be considered when creating character animation.

Pose to Pose

Pose to pose is a form of animation that goes from pose to pose quickly. All these poses together are designed to reinforce whatever the character is expressing or feeling. Figure 14.2 is a classic pose to pose with physics of how a person would accomplish lifting such tremendous weight. To sell the weight, the poses must be reminiscent of reality but go even further in their extremes. Since the block is so heavy, changes from pose to pose happen quickly as the character wrestles with the weight. The rules of lifting something heavy are all respected in the sequence. The character is pushing against the object as it comes off the ground, counterbalancing the body like a spring. When the weight is at waist level, with legs

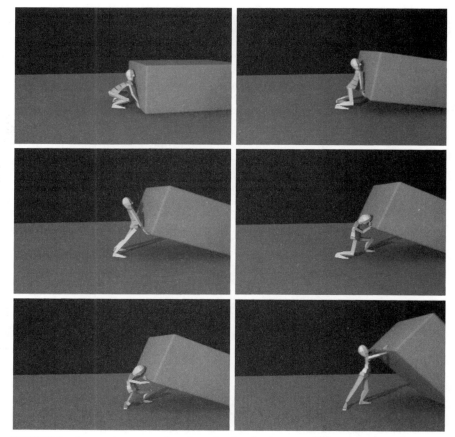

FIGURE 14.2   A pose-to-pose animation of a simple character lifting an extremely heavy object. That is the story of the quick action, and every pose the character does reinforces that weight. © 2004 John Hazzard. Reprinted with permission.

straight and locked at their strongest, the character pushes a leg for bracing under the cube, while putting the back and legs under the weight for the final lift and toss.

Poses can also be literal poses, if they serve the purpose of informing the character about what it is they are doing. Figure 14.3 isn't an autonomic pose or a physics pose, but instead it's a staged pose, meaning that the character is striking a pose like a magician or performer would. That type of pose is the literal interpretation; pose to pose means that all the emotions that the character goes through are defined by specific movements and pauses. Even as stylized as the drawing and the pose are, balance and counterbalance is still essential so that the character doesn't appear to be falling over, even with one leg so far extended. Pose to pose also applies to facial animation.

FIGURE 14.3   A stylized pose that is more self-conscious and deliberate, but also shows the character's personality in a more outgoing way. © 2004 Guy Burwell. Reprinted with permission.

Sketching and Drawing

Sketching and drawing poses work on many levels which is Glen Keane's main instrument for drawing out ideas from his brain. Drawings reveal what is working and not working and can direct the character in specific designs on a specific range of expressions. Going through the full range of emotions often reveals pleasing elements to the character or makes discoveries of types of movements. In cel animation where characters are drawn, the overall outline and cleanness of the outline are always considered. However, in CG and other forms, the outline is an afterthought. The overall outline and the readability of shapes are essential to clearly reading a character's movement, as shown in Figure 14.4.

FIGURE 14.4   A stylized character in silhouette, which is an effective way to judge outlines of characters.

© 2004 Guy Burwell. Reprinted with permission.

Video Reference

Animators often use video reference for physical performance and motion studies and to analyze motion and physics. Going one step further is acting scenes out, whether it's scenes from the script or even improvised scenes. Finding actors or improvisational groups to act out scenes when developing characters can have a wide range of influence; actors bring their own ideas to a character just as an animator does. When starting character animation, the same systems apply that apply when working on the production of a filmed scene: start from large movement and work down to smaller details. In CG and stop motion, characters are tested, bent, and broken to know their limits. In cel the process is similar in its own regard, and the testing comes from drawings and model sheets.

For animators, the sound track or voice track and the storyboards are the keys to getting a good performance out of the characters, so animators listen to the voice track over and over. They can also act the scene out in a mirror or videotape themselves or an actor doing their version of the line. The animator should also always be aware of what the character is trying to do, or what the character's motivation is, and distill the scene down to its fundamentals. Animators in cel often create a log of the words and sketch or thumbnail key expressions they want to use. Even if they don't refer to the log or the quick drawings, the time spent mentally thinking about and addressing the problem is time well spent in connecting with the character. In true stop motion, a scene that is long and has hundreds of frames with more than one character can take days, if not weeks, to shoot.

Using the stage-play analogy, CG animation starts with simple blocking. As actors rehearsing in a play simply walk from one mark to another, so do the CG characters. Blocking consists of moving the characters through their marks, as dictated by the shot's length, which were established in the animatic and by the audio track, if there is any. Blocking is another arena to iron out staging and movement issues, so that the largest moves from one place to the next all work out relative to action, flow, and hookups. If a character must interact with props or scenery or other characters, then that is blocked out as well. In CG, nothing else moves, and the characters slide like robotic chess pieces from mark to mark. The same would be true of 2D programs like Flash or Moho. In cel the process is slightly different, but its concept is the same: simple drawings or even rough sketches are done only at the big key frames, or big poses, and then are shot or scanned and tested to check if its a proper fit.

Stop motion is the exception when it comes to this process because stop motion is a "one-take or redo" type medium. All the movements large and small have to be incorporated into the one and only shot. Stop motion can do blocking or a "pop through," where the character or even a stand-in is moved through a crucial scene and is photographed but not animated. When testing effects, motion control, or other variables that aren't as certain as others, a pop through is a good idea. A pop through gives a clear test that is frame accurate and shows the motion or the potential special effects without having to commit huge amounts of time to an actual animated shot that needs to be redone when the motion control went too fast or too slow.

Once the blocking is done and all the large movements have been figured out, then character animation truly begins. Characters spend a great deal of time moving from one place to the next, making a walk cycle one of the early tests animators always do. The walk is figured out, or if the character isn't walking and is instead sitting, the big movements are figured out.

Walk Cycles

Walk cycles is a general term for a character moving from one place to the next. Often creatures don't walk, but most activity requires characters of all kinds to move from one point to the next. How that is accomplished should be a window into the character's personality.

Walk cycles are one of the first animations an animator works out when beginning an animation in any form. Its importance is pragmatic in that most creatures on land walk in some form; a few slither, many fly, but the majority walk. Whether people, ants, or giant monsters, most creatures move appendages of some kind to get around. Working out a walk cycle is important, but it's also important to consider a walk as another window into the personality of a character. Simply animating a person or creature from one place to another is fine, but designing a specific gait for a character is as almost as important as the character itself.

Another a cliché often tossed around with story characters is the "back story." It's used a bit broadly, but there is an essence of truth when applied in the right area. Whether it's revealed in a project or not, a back story can help define a character's actions. It can also give a character more depth, whether it's a photo-real person or an extremely stylized hand-drawn treatment.

Even if a character is a simple background character, a one-sentence description can give a back story that is visible. For example, a background man is an injured war veteran with a limp, but he is also proud and his walk shows it. A person raised with privileges thinks that he is better than others and walks with an air of superiority. In stylized version, the person can literally look down his nose at everyone else. Someone who is full of energy might not walk with the standard heel as his first step, but instead walks on the balls of his feet.

Quirky characters should have a walk that reflects them. A person who is beaten down might hang his head low; he walks purposely, dragging his feet with his shoulders rolled forward. A person who is suspicious or on the run might look similar to a beaten-down person, but he does different things. He doesn't walk aimlessly; his head is down, while looking around a lot and keeping its arms clinched. A beaten-down person's arms might hang limp or dangle in coat pockets. A carefree person would walk on his toes, with big swinging arms and his head held high, looking around for people to share his happiness with.

A cool person would walk slow like a beat-down person, but he would be purposeful in his walk. He would have an air about him that he doesn't care, but is keenly aware that others are watching him. He walks with a deliberate gate, hooking his arms in bravado with his nose high. His head turns slightly while scanning for others' eyes, or it even bobs slightly like he is moving to some internal music.

Obvious walks are people who are drunk, staggering and stepping out of line and trying to keep their head level. A romantically involved couple's walk can be much more subtle; they are light on their feet, and when distracted, they quickly turn and their arms flutter about. With a couple like this, the complexity of the animation compounds. If they aren't worried about others, they can lean and hang on each other. However, a more subtle walk would have these people trying, however poorly, to conceal their feelings.

A walk cycle can simply change over time. For example, a keyed-up hiker who is full of enthusiasm sets off on a hike. His back is straight, his head is held high, and arms and legs are stretched out to maximize energy. In just a few short hours, it becomes obvious that the hiker is out of shape, and the grade is grueling. Now the hiker's shoulders and feet drag, and the knees lift just enough to bring the feet forward. His head drops and his back curves, and if he becomes really winded, he puts his hands on his hips. A guard at a palace walks with deliberate stiffness. A young girl, snooping through a room, keeps her hands behind her back, even though her head pokes out as she scans for interesting items. Her head moves, but her body stays back, as she doesn't want to be caught. Changing walk cycles is dynamic in animation, and walk cycles that are opposites or change in mid-stride or mid-story can be a strong element.

Lip Sync/Facial Expression

Animating to the track specifically frame for frame is nonnegotiable when working on high-end, photo-real productions, such as with the characters Gollum or Shrek. However, it isn't completely necessary when working with more stylized types of animation that perhaps have a loose lip sync or none at all. What is an absolute is that the animator is creating a performance that mirrors the dialogue and reinforces what is being spoken through performance, regardless of the stylization or precision of the lip sync.

For animation, the voice is obviously important. Often reference video is filmed of the actor reading the lines and is recorded as a visual log of how he performed and the gestured while he was speaking.

Literally and mechanically using every mouth shape and position that the actor made when speaking doesn't translate to animation and looks very poppy and flapping. Animation needs more finessing and massaging of the animation to complete the idea that the animated character is talking. In *Shards of Death*, the conflict is the fairy creature trying to get a job scaring people which it's obviously incapable of. The more it tries to be frightening, the cuter it becomes. Another level of complexity is created by having the straight man, the green monster, be uncomfortable with the fairy creature's failure. If the monster had a low and deep growling monster voice, the cadence of concern, awkwardness, and the creature's sincerity would be harder to convey. There's also a practicality to being able to understand a voice that is too affected. It was essential the green monster be able to be subtle and modulate its voice into a soft whisper, which might prove difficult or forced if the voice was too rough or monsterlike. Hopefully, that creates another level of humor, making the monster a living conflict—a caring individual who looks horrifying.

And remember, pose to pose applies to all animation, not just body poses, but facial expressions as well (see Figure 14.5). Clear poses of expressions that go from one clear expression to the next are key.

Hands

Hands are great for secondary action, because they're usually heavy objects at the end of a long bone: the arm. They always settle and flop around according to physics. A huge mistake that is mostly a CG mistake is not finding realistic or believable hand poses, especially at rest. In cel it's easily drawn in a nice classical hand pose, but in CG this always seems to be a problem except for the very best animations. In part, CG characters are often modeled in the T-pose, with their arms outstretched, and most bought models of people, third-party models, and the like are always modeled this way; the hands follow suit, being flat out, with the fingers spread as if pushing up against an invisible sheet of glass. There always seems to be traces of this modeled pose in CG hands, which shows a clear lack of scrutiny between the animator and the director. Hands when relaxed are like cupping an invisible water balloon; when relaxed, or even in motion, hands rarely fan out like a CG model with huge spaces between all the fingers, and yet they always wind up looking that way. Even when someone is explaining with big gestures, the fingers still have

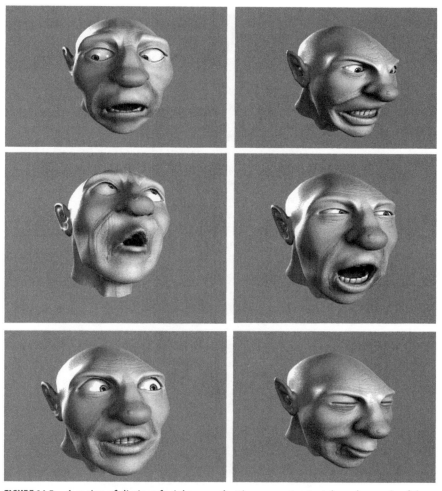

FIGURE 14.5   A series of distinct facial poses that incorporate stretch and squash of the features to create fleshiness and organic poses on top of the expression on the face.
© 2004 Ben Neal. Reprinted with permission.

a bit of curl. The only time they're ramrod straight, for example, is when a soldier is at attention (although his fingers are together), or if someone is pushing on a sheet of glass or flat surface.

Fingers are also stronger when they work together and that's often the case. Only in rare instances does a character fan out its fingers. Examples would include a character displaying extreme exclamation poses or clutching a basketball when making a free-throw shot. Hands also convey unconscious thoughts of characters as well. For example, someone who folds his hands and tucks them in can be shy, while someone who makes a fist can be angry. Tapping fingers and mindless hand play, although insignificant in real life, can add more dimension to the personality. Hands can also work as an opposite as well. A character that is brimming with rage sits at a table, and yet the hands sit calm and too uniform, perhaps taking the anger to another level.

Hands can also be overdone, with every word being punctuated by a huge gesture or an actual pantomime, which never really works. An example of an empty pantomime would be a character who says the following: "I woke up this morning, drove down to the lake, rowed out to the middle, and went fishing." While the character is talking, he rubs his eyes for waking up, mimics driving a steering wheel, mimics rowing a boat, and then mimics fishing with an invisible fishing rod. Not only is it a cliché, but it's tired and too obvious. It's also missing an opportunity for real performance and is visually redundant.

Pantomime can work if it is the opposite or unexpected. Someone talks on the phone while another person listens in. In *Shards of Death*, the blue fairy creature pantomimes what it would be doing if it got the job in the video game. In trying to be scary, the pantomime comes off as a silly attempt at fright and instead winds up being cuter (see Figure 14.6).

FIGURE 14.6   Pantomime is usually avoided, but if it is badly done it can be funny.

Giving animated characters something to do, whether hand props or an activity and depending on the story, can help ground the character in reality as well as reinforce the idea that the character has a working mind. Having characters just talk and gesture is fine for people, but even with people it's more interesting to have them doing something that informs the story reinforces the joke. For example, a man and woman argue about the man who is too fond of his car. There could be a humorous discussion about it, but if he's a car aficionado, then there's a perfect element to work into the scene. The scene could show the man working on the car, or the woman could try to have a conversation while he's under the car or under the hood. Using opposites like in *Shards of Death* is always good when they're unexpected or clever.

The illusion of thought is also a major tool. When a character thinks, the eyes become the key to the connection of a character. On the flip side, not being able to see eyes is a very powerful stylistic choice, because the audience gets no information from the character. Glasses and sunglasses are used to great effect in hiding the eyes. Walter Murch's book *In the Blink of an Eye* goes into great depth of the blink and its importance in film and perhaps perception. In animation, it's tenfold. In live action, you know that a person is alive by your experiences and by looking at them. The same is not true for animation, but blinking and eye movement can help create that illusion.

Eyes, Lids, and Brows

Eyes are the key to being alive. Eyes always look at something, unless someone deliberately gazes into space, but even then they look at an imaginary point. Eyes never move slowly and usually move from one focus point to the next in two or three frames. If the eyeball starts to move slowly, it starts to make the character seem tired or drunk. The way eye movement works is that it jumps from view to view; the eye moves and focuses, and almost never moves slowly. If eyes do move from side to side or go from one point to another slowly, it tells the viewer that the character is tired, drunk, has been drugged, or is on the verge of unconsciousness. In a few very rare cases, the eye tracks slow besides tired or drugged; this would occur when someone is watching something move slowly across his field of view. Usually even this is done more with following the object with the head and the eyes darting from point to point.

If a character has an incredibly tall stylistic forehead, it becomes easy with all that room for the animators to keep moving the eyebrows higher and higher because of all the space on the character's forehead. However, at a certain point, the eyebrows would be too far above the eye and would disconnect and not look like eyebrows anymore but like little worms. The eyebrow and the eyelid are essential to the expression on a face. They all work together, in very subtle increments. Going from the broad strokes of thinking about a story down to the minutiae of the eyes is a long road to follow, but there is a solid link because in animation the eyes are instrumental in performance.

The adjustment of the eyes for certain expressions is often slight, but also gives a huge range of expression with just a tiny move. An eyelid just covering the iris and the eye can look cool or sly. If the lid goes a few millimeters further and covers the pupil, then the viewer can recognize that the person's view is obscured and the person begins to look tired or even unconscious. Showing a great deal of white of the eyeball can show excitement, fear, or craziness.

Blinking is key to keeping animated characters' eyes alive. Blinking also allows for eyes to move during the time the eye is closed, so that when it opens again the eye is already focused on the next point. Blinks usually happen in a couple of frames, or they can go slow and feel like a deliberate blink. Lower lids can also get involved and create a whole range of expressions as well. Blinks can also pull in the face around it, with the brow and the cheeks pulling in, and behind a frame or two to reinforce the fleshiness of the skin. Blinks can also be organic and staggered, or the eyelids can stick together for a frame or two, giving a more organic feel.

Mechanical Techniques for Organic Animation

Animation is a technical and mechanical process that is often used to describe very organic movement and motions with arcs and curves. All the established tools of animation—stretch and squash, anticipation, overlapping, and secondary action—work to create organic movement and avoid straight lines. Creating interesting curves and placement are crucial. With computer animation, objects can be extremely straight and sterile, and poses can suffer from an unnatural geometry. Animators must therefore fight to create a sense of measured and composed poses that avoid flat compositions and instead create interesting visual balance.

Figure 14.7 shows two stills from *Shards of Death*. Even though each character is striking a clear pose, there is still variation in the hands and in the placement of the bodies. In the green monster's frame, the character leans its body back and tilts its head forward, creating a pleasing composition. The arms are also raised but aren't exactly mirroring each other, because living creatures often have a casualness about poses. The blue fairy creature is also in pose with arms that are in a similar pose, but also slightly different. The body is turned away slightly to give a more dynamic three-quarter feel, and the head is tilted so it's not precisely straight up. The eyelids and irises are all slightly staggered as well, which is far more visually pleasing than anything that is perfectly lined up straight.

FIGURE 14.7   Two poses that are organic compositions and avoid a flat sense of geometry.

Tips for Future Projects

There Is No Substitute for Animation

Being a great character animator requires being a great actor and animator; developing those skills only comes from immense amounts of practice. Even seasoned animators are always perfecting their craft, and after years of work, animators still struggle to find the best combination of acting and performance. In working on developing character animation styles and techniques, using simplified characters, such as seen back in Figure 14.2, is key because they are easily animated and manipulated and strip away all the other variables. If a character can act at such a simple level, then an animator knows he's on the right track; simple objects like the ones in Figure 14.2 are a CG animator's version of a cel animator's pencil test.

Log or Plan the Shot

Planning what a character is going to do before animating is always wise, whether in simple poses or gestures down to logged frames on a log sheet. Having a plan and a set timing helps focus animations, poses, and changes. Figure 14.8 shows a series of rapid-fire quick gestures that establish clean expressions and sharp and funny poses.

FIGURE 14.8   Rapid-fire quick gesture sketches are incredibly useful for establishing looks, moods, styles, and expressions. © 1999 Dean Wellins. Used with permission.

Preview as Much as Possible

ON THE CD

Stop motion is unique in that doing previews aren't possible in the way they are in pencil tests or blocking in CG. However, for cel, CG, or Flash, tests, previews of motions, and even simple cycles can help create a performance and a style. On the CD-ROM, the clip **charactertest.mov** shows simple pencil tests to develop a stylized chewing cycle for drawn characters eating pizza. Tests of motion and styles are essential, and all the still drawings in the world aren't going to give the information that even short bursts of motion and animation can.

INTERVIEW WITH ANDREW GORDON

Andrew Gordon has been an animator at Pixar for six years, and prior to that he worked at Warner Brothers digital animation. Gordon has worked on many of the Pixar features, including *The Incredibles, A Bug's Life, Toy Story 2,* and *Finding Nemo.* He was a lead animator of the character Mike on *Monsters, Inc.*

Wellins: *When you're animating, what is your process for when you get a scene? What's your mechanical process and what's your mental process?*

Gordon: When I get a scene usually what I do is to watch the storyboard reels and see what's been done. [I] look at the poses that the story guys have done because usually they've really put a lot of thought into thinking about the pose: the acting and the expressions. By looking at that, it gets me half the way there. Then after I get the storyboards I get the line, and I see where it fits into the story and write down a few notes: What is the point of the scene? Where's the entertainment value that I can milk out of it? What's the character thinking? . . . I just try to write down as many notes as I can about the scenario and what I want to do. Then if there are a bunch of scenes cut together, then I try to look at the sequence of shots and figure out where the highs and lows of the action might be.

Wellins: *And you're always somewhere between scenes, right?*

Gordon: So you want to look at your hookups, and see how it hooks up to your other shots and work with the other animators. Once I get that [I] track read the dialogue and break it down and really listen to it over and over. Then from there I take the dialogue and just go act it out, whether it's in front of a camera or in front of my desk. I try to look at my video reference on my computer and thumbnail from my video reference and try to push the poses that I'm getting. Once I do that, say I have a five-day shot, I try to spend at least a day doing the research, because then it really helps to do the actual work.

Wellins: *From a mechanical standpoint, how do you get ready for a scene?*

→

Gordon: I try to get a set of controls that has all the controls that I want to have in one little diagram. So I have the body, the blocking. My set of controls called blocking has my translates, rotates, and controls. If the character's got a chest, then it's got chests, the torso, the hips, and usually the legs. If it's a waist-up shot, then I have a control set that's all that plus the arms. If it's a full body shot, then I have legs and arms. I want every control up that I want to see, and then I start posing. I usually pose on fours; I'll do my different poses. So it's like pose . . . one, two, three, four . . . next pose. Then I'll start straight animating the scene.

Wellins: *When you block it, it'll take a day or a couple days to block, then they would cut that and you would render it and see the dailies?*

Gordon: No, they don't cut it in. I have the shots before and after. I'm the one who sets up the play list. And then I export that to the dailies.

Wellins: *So you never actually look at your blocking-in dailies?*

Gordon: No, we do look at the blocking-in dailies, and depending on how complex you want, some guys have more complex blocking. They may block in the body, the expression, all the hand poses. Some other guys might just do the basic blocking of the body plus a basic expression. Then they'll use some sort of a basic timing tool to go between those poses. So they'll hold the pose. Then once you get past blocking then you start figuring out how you're taking it from blocking to in-progress or finished animation. That's the part where you have to start overlapping body parts and you're thinking about your arcs: your head arcs, the way that the arms are moving, the poses on the arms, and the facial expressions.

Wellins: *Can you talk about your working habits during a typical day? One of the things I've noticed is that people don't run previews. They'll scrub and scrub and never play it at speed. They spend all day and then at the end of the day it looks weak because they never actually looked at it at speed.*

Gordon: I'm always doing recordings or previews, but that's the way the system is set up where I'm working. You work your scene out, and then you make a recording and it's live on another monitor, and you're constantly playing it at speed, all the time. The scrubbing happens from the actual recorded scene. Maya is different I think, you can actually scrub . . . It's a pretty close representation but I'm always doing recordings.

Wellins: *In the course of a day, how may previews or recordings would you do?*

Gordon: As many as I want coffee breaks. No, I just try to do as many as I can. I'll do detail cameras too. So I'll do the recording and then I'll set up another camera of just the face, or maybe I'll go way tight on the mouth so I'm getting really tight animation on the mouth. This stuff is going to film and film is very high resolution, so your animation needs to be totally polished to that level because it's going to be blown up huge with amazingly high resolution. So I try to do detail cams and render it out. A huge part of the process is bringing other people in. At

$\rightarrow$

some point you have five sets of eyes that you trust at the studio. There are five different people whom you would want to ask. This guy might be really good at doing mouth animation, so I'll ask him for tips on the mouth. Maybe I'll ask another guy about entertainment value. I'll talk to another guy about just global notes, and yet another guy on polish.

Wellins: So even though that's subjective, everyone has their own opinion, there is still value. You're going one way and they say, "I would have gone this way."

Gordon: You really do need other eyes on your animation because you start to not see what they're seeing. They may see something that sticks out right away that you may say, "Man, I didn't even think of that." And it's important to get people who know what they're doing to help you because they have a different sensibility. I can look at a shot and tell you where it needs to be polished. That's one of the things I like to look for, or expression pushed, or an acting thing. So someone might come to me and ask me, "Hey, can you look at the polish?," and I'll look at it and try to help them with that. Then I'll go to someone else and say, "Hey, can you help me with this idea?" or "What do you think of this physicality? Does this feel like it's physical?" and they'll say, "You might want to try this or overlap the chest-to-neck-to-head ratio." So it's really important to get other sets of eyes in to look at your work. It's a huge part of the process.

Wellins: In all the years you've worked at this, how have you developed a critical eye, where you can look at animation, see the problem, and then come up with a solution?

Gordon: Your eye starts to become trained. From looking at stuff for ten years in studios and dailies, seeing exactly what people are looking for, you start to develop an eye for what looks appealing, what looks physically correct: watching motion outdoors and learning about how things work in real life.

Wellins: Would you say that you're always observing? When you leave work, you don't stop looking at stuff.

Gordon: Well, obviously I'm not a complete nerd. I try to take a break, but you're always seeing something interesting like the way a flag ripples in the wind or the way a leaf falls to the ground. Noticing those things and even looking at video reference and single framing and doing action analysis is a big part of an animator's work. I think that animators should have a digital morgue of video clips from life and from movies and cartoons, and just from real life and the outdoors. By looking at those things, you build a library in your head, and if you have it digitally, you can always look at it.

Wellins: When you spend a couple of years on a movie, how do you keep your enthusiasm going?

Gordon: When you see other people's work that always keeps your enthusiasm up, especially when you see really good work. You think, "Damn, why didn't I think of that?" There's almost like a healthy competition between animators, and everyone's trying to, not really best some

→

body, but rather like, I really want to do good work, and I think that's really important in a healthy work environment.

Wellins: How about you personally, say you're a couple of months into it and . . .

Gordon: I think it's the research process. If the movie is about bugs, then I'm going to go look at videos of bugs. For *Finding Nemo*, I learned how to dive and tried to research fish and look at how fish move and figure out all the ins and outs of how fish locomote. That keeps me interested, and also a healthy amount of exercise. It's really important to get exercise. I know that sounds kind of progressive or whatever, but it really is important to go out and break a sweat and not sit behind the screen all the time. I really try to enjoy outside work as much as possible. Also, to be a good animator it also really helps to be a good actor. And then the other thing that separates a good animator, you have to have good ideas, because ideas are more important than anything. You could have somebody who is a genius animator, but has really boring canned acting, and you say, "I don't care about watching this." Then you watch something from somebody who has an amazing idea, and maybe it's not executed perfectly, but you're still more interested in watching that because the idea is so good.

Wellins: When you're working with high-profile directors, sometimes you pitch really strong ideas and you feel that it's a great scene and they say, "Eh, let's go this way." How do you deal with changing something that you thought was good?

Gordon: It's tough to go against what the director is saying. The directors are driving the movie, so it's ultimately their vision and you're kind of an actor in a sense. There are actor's directors who say, "Go to it. Do your stuff. I'm just trying to get you going the right way." It's a similar process with animating. There are certain directors who say, "I know exactly what I want," and they're down to the frame. They're doing every single frame and saying, "Push this pose here, put this expression there," because they are animators. Then there are other guys who give you a little more freedom, so I think it changes from movie to movie and that's an interesting part of it. I enjoy that change because you learn more, and you learn different things on each production.

Wellins: What's the most tedious part of your job?

Gordon: It used to be in the early days when I was starting out, that blocking was the hardest part because it was coming out with that idea, and the acting, and I would say, "I don't know how to do this." But now the hardest part of the job is keeping the ideas fresh and entertaining and pushing it far enough so that it's cartoony, so that it's more than normal. The tediousness of it doesn't bother me as much. I really enjoy polishing a shot because polishing a shot for me is like the finishing touches of crafting something. If you're sculpting something, it's like that sanding stage—you really get that nice shine on there. Polish is like a whole other art form. When I'm polishing stuff I'm looking for all kinds of things. I'm looking at the arcs of all the limbs and trying to figure out the slow ins and the slow outs of the corners of the mouth,

$\rightarrow$

and how the jaw is going up and down and the spacing between that. I'm looking at the arcs of the head and the physicality of the body and how it compresses. When a foot comes down I'm looking at how the foot squashes against the ground: the subtle overlapping elements of a character, the residual energy of when a character gestures and then his hand comes down from weight and how that sells the pose. All this minutiae that you have to do with CG because it's a medium of not only ones, but also it's so crisp. You see everything. I enjoy that part because that's really when it becomes a high level.

Wellins: If you understand how physics works, you don't have to figure these things out every time. If someone's got a big heavy head, you don't have to say, "Gee, I wonder how that's going to work?" You know that heavy things kind of drag real-world physics.

Gordon: Real-world physics are important. Obviously you don't need to know formulas, but the truth of a material is very important. John Lasseter is very interested in that, retaining the truth in objects' material, like a bowling ball wouldn't squash and stretch as much as a material that's say rubber or plastic. The thing about squash and stretch in CG is that you try to pepper it in so that you feel it more than you see it. Unless you're going for a really cartoony look, you want to feel a squash-and-stretch element rather than see it.

Wellins: There are a lot of things that happen faster than a frame.

Gordon: Physics is really important. Knowing how wind carries something, how a material like lace reacts, or how a fish swims through the viscosity of water. How a fish can carve through the water, how it feels to do that. That's the part when people say, "That looks real," because it always comes back to what people see on the screen. They say, "I believe that because it looks real." So many times you get people saying, "That human doesn't look right. It doesn't walk right." People have an amazing eye for what looks right with human beings and movements like that. So if something's animated incorrectly, people can't suspend their disbelief. They say, "This looks fake." Something doesn't look heavy enough or a character jumps in a weird way and you say, "Something's not right." You always see it in some effects films—a character will jump and they won't have the correct recoil. As an audience member you say, "That looks phony. There's something fake about that." As animators we're totally more into it.

Wellins: Glen Keane was saying that everything he does is on the shoulders of someone else. When he gets stuck, he goes and looks at Gustav Klimpt or Amedeo Modigliano or whoever. He always goes back to old masters or old films. Who are some of the people's shoulders you're on?

Gordon: I would say with a guy like Glen, I always find it amazing to hear what he has to say, so I tend to look at a Glen Keane scene. I'll look at some of the work he's done or a past talk that he gave to try to get reinspired, or if I have the opportunity, then maybe to ask somebody. I try to look at what's been done, or a good film—not animation. I always like to look at film that has good characters in them like *Dr. Strangelove*. I think about *Dr. Strangelove* and analyze some of the characters in that, George C. Scott and others. I like to look at the work of some of the great animators like Frank [Thomas] and Ollie [Johnston] and Glen Keane, and

→

even some of my peers' work, like Doug Sweetland and John Carr. Those guys are always doing inspiring work. I just try to keep my eyes open for everything. I wish I could say I could look at Picasso and it inspires me to do something. Yeah sure, sometimes, I can go to a museum I look at a Van Gogh. I'm usually very inspired by Rodin's work, because it looks like it's always in movement.

Wellins: *If you were just whipping by on a train and there's a bunch of animators standing there and you get to give them one piece of advice, what would it be?*

Gordon: To experience life as much as you can, before and during, being an animator so that you have a good base inside your head of things and characters. The old guy who sits on the side of the road who sits on the bench and has a funny attitude or . . . just pay attention to what's around you and be an observer. I also have another piece of advice: never stop being a student. Always be learning and never have an ego about what you do. Having no ego and always learning is so important. For one thing, there's no room for people with huge egos in this business, because people don't really want to work with them. Also there's always someone that's ten times better than you, and it's really good to get smacked down a lot and to realize that you're not that good. You have a lot to learn, and that's how you grow as an artist, as an animator, to always be a student. That's the one thing I love about teaching is by seeing other people's work. I'm like, man, I want to go back and do something like that. These guys are good. They're hotshots. I really enjoy teaching because it keeps me sharp and I really enjoy seeing students excel and grow.

Wellins: *What would be your dream project?*

Gordon: I must say I really have been just enjoying everything they've been throwing at me. I really enjoy the stories that we're doing at Pixar, so it's already kind of come true. I would actually like to do my own animated short film, and really just do it from start to finish and get some people to help me and try to get it around the festival circuit. I think that's the next thing I want to do is to start developing some characters for it. You get caught into doing work for other studios, which is great. It pays the bills and you get to work with the best people in the business, but it's always nice to do something that's your own. It's hard, because when you do animation from nine to seven every day, the last thing you want to do when you get home is get on that computer again and start animating, but one of these days, I'll do my own thing.

V

POSTPRODUCTION

EDITING

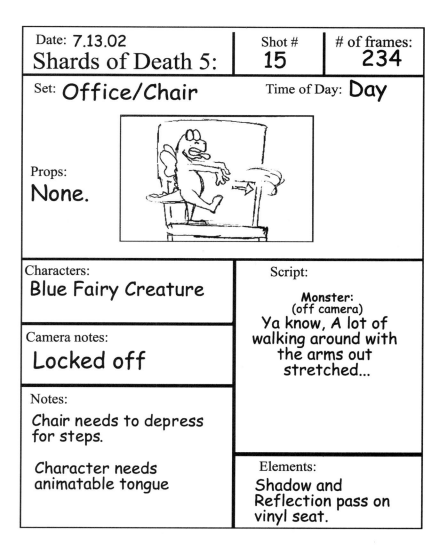

Date: 7.13.02	Shot #	# of frames:
Shards of Death 5:	15	234

Set: Office/Chair

Time of Day: Day

Props: None.

Characters: Blue Fairy Creature

Camera notes: Locked off

Notes:
Chair needs to depress for steps.

Character needs animatable tongue

Script:

Monster:
(off camera)
Ya know, A lot of walking around with the arms out stretched...

Elements:
Shadow and Reflection pass on vinyl seat.

Like many of the various aspects of film and animation, it's difficult to encapsulate editing in of itself because it is so intertwined with the project at every level. At its simplest, editing is the joining of scenes and images. At its most complex, it is the visual response to what has been filmed and how it should be put together to best tell the given story.

There are all sorts of superfluous language to describe cuts and cutting. A script may refer to "hard cut to" or "smash cut," but all cuts are really the same. A cut is a cut; it changes from one sequence of frames to another. Often what is meant by a hard cut or a smash cut is really a cut that focuses attention on two opposites changing, or the putting of two very different types of scenes back to back. It might also mean a cut that occurs in an unexpected point in a scene, such as an idea that abruptly interrupts the scene that is being watched.

For example, there is a scene in a film where a race car driver is consoling his concerned wife the night before the big race, saying that everything will be OK. The next scene cuts in, just as the driver's car crashes into the guardrail or explodes in a fireball. This smash cut has nothing to do with the physical act of editing. This is more a direction of the story, a jumping ahead in time, for a perhaps an ironic effect, which is a tried and true technique that is used a great deal in comedy. Consider the proverbial comedic version: a woman tries to coax a man to go out on a boat. The man replies, "There's nothing you can say that will make me set foot on that boat." And the next shot is the man with a beaten expression standing on deck as the boat pulls away. There are many of versions of this comedic reveal. Instead of seeing the man being dragged or cajoled onto the boat, the shot cuts immediately from his steadfast line to him obviously capitulating. Still, the change of ideas and scenes isn't editing. It's storytelling, and editing comes from a more specific point.

There would be no joke at all if you then saw the man being coaxed, getting on the boat, and finally sailing from the pier. The joke lies in the fact that the audience has skipped ahead in time to see the man saying the line, then immediately seeing the opposite. The fact that the man isn't in control or isn't able to do what he says creates the humor. The editing comes from how long the shot sits on the man after he says his line. If the shot lags too long on him before cutting, it would be obvious that something was going to happen. If the shot cut to close to his line, then the audience might not have time to mentally digest what has been said. When the film cuts to the next scene of the man on the boat, the same rules need to apply. The audience needs to be able to recognize what has happened.

The time that an audience takes to recognize a scene is brief, and audiences are so in tune with timing and pacing that even a few frames can have a powerful impact. For example, in a whodunit mystery, a detective is trying to solve a crime. A suspect explains that he knows nothing, and then the detective walks away. The final shot is the suspect watching the detective leave. If the shot is at a normal length, it would imply neutrality to the suspect, who simply watches the detective walk away. If the shot lingers on the suspect for too long, even a second or two, the linger starts to feel like it means something; the audience then starts to form ideas that perhaps the suspect isn't telling all he knows.

In the case of the comedic gag, there's a comic pacing that allows for the viewer to mentally digest what he's seen, and if it the shot sits too long, even for just a few frames, then the pacing is shifted off and the next shot is mentally late. The director only filmed the elements of the joke, and the editor put them together keeping in mind the pacing of the shots, scene, and overall production.

Editing can also take the visual flights of fancy that fill out the style and the mood of the story, but it also keeps the story grounded by showing standards of where things are. The animated feature *Akira* features a motorcycle chase through the futuristic city. The shots feature all sorts of low and cool angles, grimaces, and fists winding the throttle, but the action also periodically cuts to wide shots to show where the chase is and what position the bikes are in so that there is no confusion as to placement. This is often all worked out in the storyboarding and animatic phase, but it's often the job of the editor to create these "grounding" shots starting with the animatic. There is always the unpredictability of the final visuals, and editors have to have the eye to be able to feel that another establishing shot that shows relations in space is needed, and another establisher is cut in or shuffled around. The editor also has to keep the eye line in place so that the flow of motion doesn't become confused or flipped. Often when a line-of-sight issue occurs, it can be resolved by simply flipping images with editing tools and clarifying the line. This works unless there are letters or signage that would betray the trick of the picture being flipped, because words would then be in reverse.

Editing, like the shooting or animating, is closely tied to the entire project. Because of all the variables, editing becomes more fluid, and can take up the slack for other inflexible aspects such as scenes filmed that can't be refilmed or reanimated. This is by virtue of that fact that modern digital editing has a tool set that is designed to fix, modify, and improve what has already been delivered.

When doing an animated project of any length, editing can also dictate what must be reshot and what must be reanimated. If there ever were a shining example of the power of editing, then it's never clearer than when it goes wrong, and a common mistake is a jump cut. A *jump cut* is a cut that happens but nothing changes. Not enough new information has been given or revealed, and it becomes a cut that is completely out of place. A clear example is a medium shot of a person talking, then there is a cut, and the shot goes in a tiny bit further but doesn't really create anything new. This is a classic simple jump cut. If, however, the cut cuts into a close-up of the face, then it's no longer a jump cut, because the audience has a clear new angle and a new face to study. Many classic filmmakers argue there is no more interesting terrain than the human face.

Modern tools like desktop editing are truly revolutionary, but it is extremely important to know and respect the history of editing—the physical joining of film with tape or glue and the actual cutting of frames. The reality of doing analog editing currently is quickly becoming less and less relevant as time goes by. With factors such as speed, cost, and flexibility, digital editing from Avid's high-end editing system, Film Composer, to consumer desktop editing, is the now the range in which production is done.

Having a separate chapter on editing is somewhat deceptive. Editing is so infused with animation and film at every level, and is so dependent on the other aspects of the animation process that it can't exist without them. One of the best explanations and dissections of editing and emotional cutting is covered in the book *In the Blink of an Eye* by Walter Murch. In that book, Murch, one of the grand master editors, links emotional connections to the process of editing, illustrating how editing for emotion is the single most important aim of editing. Based on his lectures at University of California Los Angeles film school, Murch illustrates in a clear and concise manner, making his book indispensable to editors, animators, filmmakers, and directors alike.

Animation, being the hybrid that it is, can use editing techniques to an even greater extent than live action, making it even more powerful and useful than it is in standard filmmaking. The reason that editing can have more effect on animation than live action, is because there are techniques that can only be used in animation and would look wrong in live action. Animation can benefit from being able to duplicate, move, and repeat frames, an impossibility in live action that would look like visual stutters. Removing frames and duplicating frames is powerful tool. Theoretically, a film or animation is pretty frame accurate before animation begins, but there are always variables that just appear. Often a frame or two of a hold can seal a scene or punctuate an action, and even though it wasn't rendered or filmed that way, editors because of animation can duplicate and have frames "hang" for a beat or two, and it's often invisible that motion has stopped.

If working on a film, animation, game, or whatever, editors want to try to bring elements together as early on as possible, even roughed out or in a simple form. If an editor has a music score or sound effects, the story needs to at least consider their impact. It's rare, but it is possible to have a scene or entire animation scenes change because there was a music cue or a sound effect that worked so well with the story, concept, or gag. Cel animators often used to use a click track in the early days of animation invented by Ub Iwerks, a contemporary of Disney. It worked well for musical timing, like a metronome built into the sound track.

TRANSITIONS

Beyond cuts there's a whole host of transitions at an editor's fingertips. Dissolves were discussed in Chapter 9, "Animatics," as devices of transition, but it's often up to the editor and the director to decide when a dissolve is needed. Dissolves can jump through time, backwards in time, or from place to place. However, the dissolve in itself with one image fading to the next gives a sense of time, and it's up to the director to dictate how much has elapsed. Dissolves are strong effects, and long slow dissolves can go further in combining visual ideas as well as making a jump in time or space. The beginning to Francis Ford Coppola's *Apocalypse Now* has a multiple exposure with the jungle exploding with napalm, combined with helicopter blades and Martin Sheen's face, while mixing all the main ideas of the film (Vietnam and war) and the character at the heart of the story.

Editors also have fades to black or white or any other color, which also can be a jump in time or a punctuating end on a scene. Fades are incredibly powerful and can represent a strong stylistic choice or can simply end a scene or a day. The last light goes out in a window of a house and the scene fades to black. Fade to white can have an interesting effect as well depending on its use. It's stark, burns out, carries it own feel, and doesn't have the finality of a fade to black.

Although storytelling doesn't get much use out of 3D graphical transitions, transitions can still be a big part of the feel and mood of an edit. The classic spinning colors with the bat emblem was the standard transition for the *Batman* television show, and was part of the deliberate campiness of the show. Split screen can be very effective, and stylized comedies can have picture flips, wipes, and more. Some transitions go beyond editing and wind up being more of a special effect. For example, in a street scene in London a double-decker bus passes the camera, and as the bus passes it reveals a new scene. Transitions are tools to skip over less interesting or unimportant details and focus on elements that drive the story.

Creating interesting transitions can help add overall value to the story. The transition could be a simple dissolve or a shoot that had the transition built into it. For example, a shot of someone screaming and the camera diving into the darkness of his mouth to end a scene is a transition that would need to be rendered or filmed and would obviously have to be planned well in advance of editing.

LOGS AND SHOT SHEETS

Editors often create a log of all footage and reels, whether on tape, film, or hard drives. The log has frame numbers, ins and outs of scenes, various elements, and any notes for special considerations. Going one step further, when working on productions with numerous animators or production people, editorial departments can use the "locked" animatic to generate shot cards, which are cards that can be handed to anyone on the production. The cards contain every crucial piece of information on a scene-by-scene or shot-by-shot basis. For the animator, it often contains frame counts, the dialogue, the naming convention, special animation considerations, props, and more. For the art department, the shot card lists sets and characters and props that will be needed for each specific shot. For the camera or rendering crew, shot sheets can give crucial information for special effects, camera moves, or any other element that must be addressed.

Shot sheets are useful and can be made in any format, depending on the production. A shot sheet, as shown in Figure 15.1, contains all the pertinent information. For the editor in animation production with numerous people, the details get more and more complex. Editors often have to keep track of scenes that have several layers, with each layer potentially having its own cut. Editors often also work hand in hand with postprocesses, sending edit lists and fixes back and forth. Editors are also often required to push into the realm of engineer, and edit projects that have to go out to film or have to go to other standards, such as European phase alternation line (PAL) broadcast standards, and they are required to make those huge transfers of data and media management seamless.

Basic digital editing of basic footage shot on DV as live action has become incredibly easy with powerful desktop edit systems. Editing animation and keeping track of all the potential elements and their respective layers as well as effects, animatics, and versions, not to mention sound takes and sound effects, can be a true logistical challenge. When dealing with real-world production, updates and revisions are constantly being added. All of these different elements are expected to be seamlessly handled and managed by the editor and assistant editors.

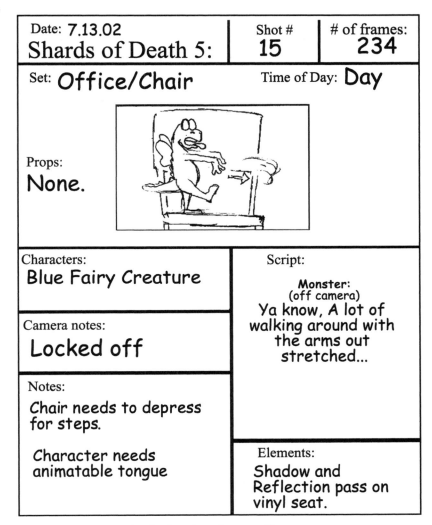

Date: 7.13.02 Shards of Death 5:	Shot # 15	# of frames: 234

Set: **Office/Chair**   Time of Day: **Day**

Props:
None.

Characters: **Blue Fairy Creature**	Script: **Monster:** **(off camera)** **Ya know, A lot of walking around with the arms out stretched...**
Camera notes: **Locked off**	
Notes: **Chair needs to depress for steps.** **Character needs animatable tongue**	
	Elements: **Shadow and Reflection pass on vinyl seat.**

FIGURE 15.1   An example of a shot sheet for a specific scene.

Before any project begins, if time and budget allow, good editors test the throughput of all their systems. If the final result of the edit is a 24-fps rendered film out, the editor would then do a test to sync up with the compositor as well as any production pipelines involved in supplying footage at that frame rate. The editor and the postproduction supervisor would also contact the film recording facility and establish any specific requirements that the film recording system needs.

Editors also benefit from a test on all avenues as to how the digital file will be stored, shipped, and then rendered to film. If the project is to go to digital tape or DVDs, then the throughput of that system should be tested as well. Quick tests and short discussions among the editor, the rendering technical director, the sound and audio mixer, and anyone else involved in handling or modifying the digital media can save hours of frustration later.

Tips for Future Projects

Always Make Motivated Cuts

If the editor is making his own decisions where he has the final call, then he has the monumental task of taking all the elements and putting them together in some form. The editor is now simultaneously looking for and pacing in what has been shot, and creating a pacing. He is also torn between what he feels and what he feels the audience will like. The editor assembles the project and hopes that he won't have to decide what he likes, or what the audience might like. Instead, he wants the solution to be so patently clear that there is no other solution. It can happen for a few scenes, a segment, or the entire film, but editors can feel it when the pieces fit together correctly; the rest of that is trying for the perfect connection for the next 50 scenes.

If the editor isn't making the final call, then he has to combine his ideas as well as incorporate the ideas of everyone else running the show. When a project is complicated and has lots of movement and angles, there seems to be countless ways that a production is going to fit together. There are so many ways that the editor can't begin to try them all—it would take years. Nor can it be said which way is better without seeing them side by side, because they just seem different; one is not obviously better than the other. The editor then often turns to the script, which is based on what he's working on, and the process begins.

Making the crucial decisions, whether it's the editor, studio, or director, is purely subject. Beyond the mechanical things that need to be seen, how everything is put together is totally based on personal experience and the implied mood, pace, and feeling. Obviously the director has filmed all the shots, but how they fit together is another huge complex system and an editor can feel and find the motivation to cut. Motivation is mechanical and expected. Someone speaks to another person, the other person replies, and then a cut is made.

Cutting just to cut isn't editing. Cuts should always be motivated; there should always be a reason to cut. Murch truly encapsulated the idea: cut for emotion as the first important driving force.

Make It Work in the Animatic First

There's a tendency to jump into animation because it's fun and powerful, but a lot of time and expense are wasted. Doing a working animatic dialed in is essential in almost any animated project that has multiple shots. Animatics aren't a hoop to jump through or a chore; they are creating a clear working schematic of the entire film or project. If something doesn't work in the animatic, animating it probably isn't really going to fix it. It might gloss over the problem, but flat pacing or rough timing is just flat.

Try Radically Different Versions

There is the old adage that if it works don't fix it, and that's true. When something is clearly working and is strong, it's recognizable and shouldn't be messed with or overanalyzed. Sometimes things do work out best on the first pass, and other times it's not so cut and dry. With the ease of editing, being able to try different versions or edits is often useful. The easiest place to do this is during the animatic phase, but it's not unheard of to continue to mess with versions up until the end of the project.

Organization Is Key to Editing

Organization is helpful in every aspect of animation. As an editor, it's indispensable, and a lack of organization can cause endless hours of frustration and the worst disaster—lost work.

POSTPRODUCTION

The overall concept of this entire book is to allow the story and basic motivations to help decide nearly every decision on an animated production. The story and the point are usually the reason why the project was originally created. Postproduction is a highly technical process, and to have true story problems going into postproduction is simply a bad place to be. Having a story that is flexible enough to be re-worked and be successful in postproduction is a tall order. It is said that films are ultimately made in editing. Another adage says, don't edit the film that was planned, but edit the film that was shot. There is a lot of truth to those sayings, but the difference between live action and anima-tion is where and how the energy of the project is spent. Animation spreads its production energy over the whole project. Live action has a huge burst while filming, and whatever is left over pieces the filmed per-formance together. To enter animation postproduction in the same posi-tion as a live-action postproduction would be a disaster waiting to happen. Nowhere does animation show its difficulty more than when there's not enough time allowed to do it. All the fussing in the world over a specific pose or misplaced element won't save a flat story.

Postproduction in live action is often defined after shooting has com-pleted. In animation, postproduction can and often should start when two final shots are being combined or edited, and as elements are com-pleted they can be put in place piece by piece. The idea of postproduction happening after animation as in live action doesn't really apply in the same way.

Once actual animation is completed, meaning the animators have finished animating in whatever form, technically postproduction begins for animation. In CG and in cel, animators can often be called back in for touchups, adjustments, and rerenders. Stop motion is more like live ac-tion, but because of the nature of the computer, CG and digital cel can create many versions, often hundreds, in the filmmaking process.

CG is more like a stage play in that it is run over and over. As actors in a play learn their lines and perfect their performance, the art department builds sets, the costumers create costumes, and the play is repeatedly re-hearsed under the watchful eye of the director, art director, choreogra-pher, and producer. CG is very similar, as blocking becomes precise and well-rehearsed scenes, and the analogy ends with final renders and finish-ing as the equivalent of a play's opening night.

CG now encompasses a wide variety of disciplines, from full 3D ani-mation like *Shards of Death* to digital cel like *DAE #3*, as well as Flash or similar programs. With 2D programs, render time is usually not a consid-eration, which allows for adjusting and tweaking literally until the job is delivered. In dimensional CG, rendering is often a complicated process with many layers, final effects, and textures turned on. Combined layers that incorporate all the essential elements, such as shadows, refraction, reflections, atmospheric effects, and many other processes, come to the final performance. Final resolution also has a huge impact on final renders. If working in a lower resolution during production, with an Academy-sized film frame for final finishing format, then render times and the number of processors to crunch the frames can become a major factor in timing.

If a project has a firm finish or delivery date, technical directors and postproduction supervisors have to be keenly aware of the final output size, as well as all the processes that are going to be added to the final render and their relation to rendering time as well. For maximum control, elements are often rendered separately; a character is rendered separately from its shadows, its background, and environmental effects. Having the control in a compositing program with separate layers is often necessary to dial each and every element and scene in relation to each other as well as the previous and following shots. However, time must be allowed for the rendering of separate layers as well as extra compositing time. Certain software can be scripted to render separate layers and elements as well as alpha channels and store them accordingly. The process needs to be established and time needs to be worked backwards so that whatever level of finish is to be accomplished can, given the amount of time, the number of processors, and the number of processor intensive effects.

Postproduction like live action is the last process in the production when all the final elements are brought together. Scratch tracks are replaced by final audio, final renders begin, and final composites are brought together. If a production is going well, the timings have been locked and animatics or earlier versions of specific elements are easily replaced by final images. Everyone is onboard, all the production pipelines have been established, naming convention is understood, and everyone knows exactly what he is doing: following the production plan and the shot sheets.

Often, postproduction is the opposite of ideal; animators are still animating, while compositors are composting and combining elements as they are created. This unfortunate situation usually is the result of the edit being changed, making shots longer or creating new shots or performances in an attempt to fix a variety of problems.

With the exception of small productions that have an unlimited budget, no overhead, and no time frame, animation often has many different people involved. As budgets grow, exponentially so do the number of people involved, and when that occurs, many opinions and directives can shape both a production and postproduction. It is a fact of animation that it's often expensive. It's also true that a lot of animation is for hire, and differences of opinion often come to a head in postproduction.

Working with layers always allows another level of control and flexibility. If working with clients, producers, or other artists, working with layers allows one to make adjustments on specific elements without having to rerender the entire frame. If it becomes complicated to composite, then the compositor's time needs to be measured in the equation. If the project is clientless, then rendering single frames may be faster, but not nearly as flexible as rendering elements separately.

LIVE ACTION COMBINED WITH ANIMATION

Live action and animation have been partners since the beginning of animation. The supreme goal is to create an illusion that the animated character is living in the same world with the film characters. Unlike standard animation, this idea is pass or fail. If the idea fails, then the illusion doesn't work, and the audience doesn't connect the animation with the live action. All sorts of elements contribute to that "gluing" together.

The pros of combining live action go all the way back to the earliest inspiration to create a special effect. CG animation can be seamlessly combined with live-action plates that completely fool the eye, creating impossibilities right before a viewer's eye. Special effects have always been of this world, and special effects have truly reached the pinnacle of the visual illusion. Films like *Forrest Gump, Terminator 2: Judgment Day, The Lord of the Rings, AVP: Alien vs. Predator, The Matrix*, and many other films before and after have spent hundreds of millions of dollars to create that complete illusion of reality, attempting to fool even the most critical eye completely.

The blockbuster special effects and subsequent animation is big business. Every element from digital set extensions and initial stuntmen to full-blown CG characters and complete realistic CG worlds is incorporated in almost every major movie.

The CG live-action combo is a true double-edged sword. If working with combining animation and film or video, there are many technical considerations. Video runs at 29.97 fps, which doesn't give clear frames to work with because the project is dealing with partial frames or video fields. As a result, the interpolated fields must be made into real frames or removed. When background plates begin on film that runs at 24 fps, then animation has to be done at 24 fps as well. This is not a problem for cel animators. In fact, it's a blessing and makes 6 frames per second less work for each second, which adds up extremely quick. However, in order to use 24 fps, the edit system must also be able to work at 24 fps if the shot is to stay in sync. Frame rates are just the beginning of challenges when it comes to combining live action with CG. Certain effects can be created that have no true interaction, and such details aren't necessary, such as a UFO being pasted on a night sky has no reference points, but once true interaction begins, frame rates become crucial for syncing.

In animating and compositing an animated character in a live-action scene, all the lighting, atmosphere, and reflections that exist in the scene now have to be recreated in CG. The details become more specific. For example, feet on characters have to be planted on the "real" ground, and the feet need shadows and falloff shadows that look exactly like all the shadows on real-world objects. Time can be saved by simply avoiding intersection shots with the ground. However, it's a true trade-off because the intersection shots are the shots that really sell the illusion that the character is in the scene.

Doing all the passes for shadows and reflections is tedious, but they are integral, just like the interaction of feet on floor, to selling the idea that the character is really completely in the scene. There are many ways of using foreground elements to help sandwich the animated character between live-action elements; depending on the scene, putting animated characters behind real-world objects always glues the illusion together. Nothing says depth in a scene like when animated characters go behind a chair or behind a plant or tree. This type of interaction is very visually effective, but also technically a challenge in that it usually means filming the plates with a green screen, or readying for a huge amount of hours hand-creating traveling mattes. Green screens must be lit correctly; it is yet another pass that must be dealt with in composting, but is almost a necessity in truly compositing characters into a filmed real world.

BACKGROUND PLATES FOR CG CHARACTERS

When combining live-action footage or filmed footage with animation, the live-action element is often referred to as a *plate*. When shooting film or video for live action, esthetically all the rules of composition apply, but animated plates need to go further to allow the character to exist in and interact with the plate. In most cases, the main goal or combining CG with live action is to create the illusion that the character is there in the scene. This is the job of the technical director. For the director and cinematographer, creating a scene that is ready for a character to be composited into is important. It's often more work to create that visual glue that seals the character in the scene, but it's always worth it. Having props interact with CG actors is a big part, such as chairs moving and a seat depressing when a CG character sits in it. All these practical technical effects are part of the process; they must often incorporate practical special-effects and art-department people to create interactive actions that are rigged with wires, or are designed so that whatever moves the object can be removed in postproduction. For such removal, clean plates must be gathered as well. A clean plate is a few frames or seconds of running film with nothing in the frame—there are no characters or objects that have to do with the animation. The idea is that if something is to be removed, the compositor needs something to remove to, and that is a clean plate of the shot. If the shot is a motion-control shot, then a clean plate or a clean pass is an absolute necessity for every different frame, unless hand-rotoscoping traveling mattes is understood and expected.

For the cinematographer composing for CG combined with live action, using the location, sets, and objects to reinforce the character's place in space is almost as crucial as getting a unique shot. Interactive lighting and reflective surfaces are elements that can give the animation side aspects to work with when combining the characters.

An example of a difficult shot is when a CG character walks behind a fish tank or climbs a tree. This is because a fish tank, with its real-world distortion and refraction of water and its subtlety and color, is incredibly challenging to nail in a photo-real sense. Trees and branches and mixed lighting and changing sources are hard to key out and to reproduce on CG objects, but when done correctly are extremely realistic. A moving camera is just that much more difficult and often requires green screens as well as extensive motion matching to combine the character with a loose camera. Tracking points are often required for rock-steady matching, and technical directors often also must include reference objects that are placed in the scene where the character stands to judge shadow projecting, ambient lighting, and any other environmental effect that is changing the light.

A motion-control system is useful in being able to repeat moves. With the right motion-control software as well as an interface to the CG software, the data from the motion control can be transferred to help in motion matching. Syncing up systems is a complicated and expensive process and can require highly trained engineers on both the mechanical side and CG side.

The human eye is still the most valuable tool in the animator's toolbox, and motion control and syncing systems aren't necessary when a skilled pair of eyes is willing to do the work. Motion matching can be and is done by a person going frame by frame and making adjustments. Motion matching can also be accomplished in software as well. In the process of combining live action and animation, creating plates correctly will ultimately lead to less confusion, less reworking, and a better end product. Since animation is either shot or rendered frame by frame, it is necessary to have a background plate that is consistent with the animation. If the shot is simply a plate, whereby the camera is locked off and doesn't move and no elements move, it isn't nearly as crucial. Once interaction begins with animated characters and filmed plates, then prepping plates correctly is extremely crucial.

Creating and finalizing plates moving or still require getting through the boards and animatic processes to create finite frame numbers as early as possible. If edits of scenes with CG characters in them keep changing in the edit cut, then it creates massive amounts of extra work for the animators.

WHENEVER POSSIBLE, USE FINAL PLATES AND ELEMENTS

In a project with a fixed amount of time that uses live-action plates, animators and compositors are often given temporary plates because the final edit hasn't been decided. It is always best to animate to the actual final plate that has been steadied and decided. It's often not possible, however, and often animation has to begin before the final plates are ready for composition because of a short time frame. Animators and production supervisors need to be aware that final plates can be different in slight ways, and matching action exactly to a temporary plate can be a waste of time if the plate is going to move or be edited or adjusted. Animators need to create animation and plan their work in a way as to stay productive on scenes and avoid true finessing if the plates are going to change enough that interaction or details would require being reanimated. Unlike live action and stop motion, reanimating scenes in CG is almost always a fact of life in creating good animation that is truly integrated into a live-action scene.

If working with compositing software and transferring live-action from film, separate transfer passes can be made from the same segment of film to digital frames. Making separate passes or adjustments from film or even tape can create the best exposure for the visual elements as well as a pass to get the best exposure for the green screen. Since picture and green screen are two distinct elements, it makes sense to make separate passes: one for characters or scenes and another for getting clean green screens.

If working with a specific compositor, postproduction supervisors should gather a list of what types of passes would be most useful for the compositor. It's also important early on, even before filming or shooting, that any special considerations for compositing be run past the compositor so that all the correct elements are filmed. Often, compositors can use a few frames of green screen with no characters or elements in front of the green so that they can pull mattes on any inconsistent chroma colors or deal with any anomalies or irregularities in the consistency of green.

When dealing with animated characters in a filmed or real environment, you take on a huge array of new challenges. With few exceptions, when an animated character is combined with live action, it is intended to create a grand illusion that the animated character is physically there with real people. If you move the camera, this entire problem becomes compounded because you must strictly adhere to the rules of the real world if you're going to pull off this complex illusion. There are ways to combine animation with live action where these harsh rules don't apply. If adding moving design elements, such as in a motion graphics, that are truly design elements, then interaction and that illusion aren't necessary. Even in motion graphics where animated or graphic elements move through a perceived 3D space, it's still far away from a CG character walking around in a filmed world convincingly. There are other various styles of animation that are independent of the world. This is a stylistic approach and is combing imagery, but isn't necessarily trying to trick the eye that the animated character is in the scene.

The visual compositing brings together all the elements. The staging in Figure 16.1 has a fun take on having fun and using imagination. The whole world isn't created, but instead the visual is a scene within the scene. The composition is "overshot," so that the audience can see off the stagelike set, viewing the back walls and the backstage. Unlike most animation being combined with live action, this scene is a live-action kid who is added to a very stylized and painterly scene. The focus is on the letter "B," the boat, the waves, and the girl as the sea captain. The set pieces beyond the boat set are limited in color and aren't exaggerated like the boat and the waves; the backstage feel is just muted and gives texture to the final shot, but doesn't compete with the central focus. The offstage props don't distract, but instead create texture that hints of a kid-made "after-school" feel. The scene is designed around the focal point of the girl, and the simplistic style with the simple colors and the girl appearing on the bright clouds completes the illusion. Bringing the elements together, making adjustments of placement as well as adjusting colors and brightness, is normal postprocess work.

The shadow and the lighting both in the real world and in the digital paintings are also correct, so that the design and the rules of compositing create a scene that is rich, yet simple, stylized enough to avoid reality and give it a fun feeling; all of the elements fit together perfectly as a composite. Because of the scene's artistic angle and the stylization, the viewer takes it at face value. This is unlike a CG character in a real-world special effect scenario, where the eye is far more critical because of the attempted illusion of a character that is actually in a real-world backdrop.

FIGURE 16.1   A very straight-on square composition for a *Sesame Street* episode, with a simple "school-play" depth (see Color Plate 23). © 2004 Laura DiTrapani. Reprinted with permission.

Figure 16.2 is a real-world CG combination of futuristic vehicles on a dramatic landscape and is stylistically chosen for aesthetic reasons, but also out of a deliberate design to enhance the visual idea. In this test, Figure 16.2 shows the first test render of two CG vehicles loosely dropped and rendered onto a filmed plate of an open vista. When creating elements, objects, or characters that will be combined with live action, the model and the plate need to be combined before too much work is done to see how objects and background plates fit together. Because the vehicles are off in the distance, it's not nearly as labor intensive as combining imagery convincingly in a close-up. Size hides details, and stylistically for this specific shot, which is a long shot photographed with a 300mm lens, size helps to create the first important part of a CG combination shot which is good, well thought out, and is composed on background plates.

ON THE CD   On the CD-ROM, the file **tanks.mov** is a motion test and the first time the two elements were combined. The rough matte or background plate is loose and hasn't been color corrected or steadied. The tanks obviously aren't intersecting with the ground precisely, but the point of the test is to judge size and speed; intersection is a given to be fixed. In the end, a layer of dust will be added to complete the scene along with film grain and more atmospheres. A simple render at this level is enough to

FIGURE 16.2 When creating elements, objects, or characters that will be combined with live action, the model and the plate need to be combined before too much work is done to see how objects and background plates visually fit together.

evaluate timings and movement of the machines. With dust and added atmosphere, the models potentially wouldn't require too much more texturing. If the vehicles were to be used in a close-up, then the whole list of requirements changes completely and dramatically.

SHADOWS

In creating live action and CG combinations, shadows are incredibly important for the characters in the CG world. The human eye can detect the slightest difference in shadows.

COLOR TIMING AND TAPE TO TAPE

Tape to tape, color correcting, and color timing are born out of necessity. The idea of tape to tape is becoming a bit antiquated because so many projects are being created all digitally, but the job is no less important. The idea of color timing or color correcting is to make final adjustments to create an entire cohesive color structure. The word "color timing" goes back to filmmaking, and it was an adjustment of the colors when the film was being printed. The simplest form is to balance the color from shot to shot. Often, shots are done on different film stocks or for reasons of production, shooting out of sequence or variances of time of day. Sequences, which could be done with in a few hours, a few months, or even a few years, often wind up being back to back on the edit line. In CG, each computer monitor, unless precisely calibrated, can have slightly different colors as well as levels of brightness and contrast.

The idea of color correcting is to adjust the colors so there is color continuity. The basics are along the lines of skin tone that stays the same throughout the production. For example, the sky is a uniform blue, and the grass is a uniform green. Beyond the basics, color timing can be a stylistic choice and can also work with a story or mood. Obvious adjustments are in a period epic, as in a western that is tinted brown or sepia toned, and all the green and blues are brought down. Another adjustment is a children's program or a vibrant animation where the colors are pushed to vivid levels. However, there are also more subtle adjustments. A scene filmed in winter might benefit from adjusting the color to a slight blue, giving a cool feeling. Stylistically, shadows can be sharp; the upper end of the spectrum light areas can be compressed to give a washed-out gritty feel. On the other end, darks and shadows can also be compressed to create a stark feeling with harsh edges.

A color correct can link one shot to the next so that the colors are balanced, but it can also slowly change over time, as the coming of night or other story elements. Film and video cameras with a raw lens were designed to reproduce the most accurate color, and perfect color doesn't always fit the story or the emotion. Color correction can also reinforce artificial lighting. For example, a rainstorm (or a rain machine) can be made to seem more dramatic when the color is bluer and vivid reds and greens are pulled out. Similarly, with the capabilities, a rain scene could feature a person in a yellow raincoat. A color balancing could diminish the background colors to reinforce the feeling of rain or inclement weather, but a fine tuning of color could keep the yellow slicker intact, and make it more of a visual focal point. Most digital editing systems have some color temperature and brightness adjustments; others, like Digital Fusion and Combustion and high-end flints, flames, infernos, and other high-end systems have extensive color-correction tools that can create matte channels to give even more distinct and very specific color control.

Color balancing and color correction are obvious for film, and extreme adjustments like a gritty war film or shooting day for night are used frequently, but subtle adjustments have their impact as well. The overall color correction on *Shards of Death* was to have a palette of near earth tones with the green monster and the office, which was subdued and a bit worn, trying to create a suggestion of a stuffy office. Since computer animation creates such striking and bright colors, it's often important to bring the colors into a more real world, especially when the mood is of a dusty office or something similarly worn down. Of course with CG animation, setting the lights and surfaces gets the color and lighting most of the way, but color correcting gives the artist another pass at control. In contrast to the dingy and dull office, the blue fairy creature was left bright blue with bright purple spots as well as an ethereal glow that was added in postproduction as stark contrast to its surroundings.

Adding overall adjustments is powerful. Most professional postproduction facilities that charge top dollar calibrate their monitors, so that the colors are consistent with the standard color bars. If a project is being color corrected on a desktop system and if calibration isn't possible, then it's always wise to make DVDs and tapes to evaluate color. However, without broadcast standards, every single television will look slightly different. Often, works in progress and tests and or dailies are saved or sent around to crew and clients via QuickTime or other digital media, which is a revolution in and of itself, as opposed to having to send actual videotapes for review.

Since it is easy to send QuickTime's or other clips as works in progress, this means that people involved in the production are viewing the work with laptops and other standard computers in any possible lighting scenario. It's an extremely bad idea to evaluate true color on something with as many variables as a laptop computer and a compressed QuickTime file. Color needs to be evaluated on the final format it is intended for, whether the Internet, DVD, broadcast, or film.

Tips for Future Projects

Preplan for Postproduction

In animation, postproduction should be considered when the entire project is planned out. It's potentially dangerous to get to postproduction without a plan of how all the pieces will be pulled together. The more complicated the project, the more important having a plan becomes. Having a plan can help determine who will do the work, the computer that the project will be performed on, and the project's cost.

Fix It in Post

The new adage, "we'll fix it in post," is often heard, but ultimately is it really fixed? There are very specific tasks that postproduction covers, such as rig removal, blue screen effects, compositing, conforming elements, and creating master projects. With digital control, postproduction tools are capable of much more. A good postproduction supervisor has to know all the complex elements of rendering and postproduction to decide whether a visual fix is cheaper to rerender or to fix digitally. Postproduction isn't as well suited to fix animation performance, and it is even less suited to fix a broken story. Never expect to fix a story in postproduction. A story can be enhanced and polished in an indirect way, but it's extremely rare that visual adjustments and timings are going to fix something with a serious story problem. The best rule is to not get into that situation.

Avoid Overthinking

Animation is unique in that the elements are always in flux until the end. This too is true with final audio, and dialogue doesn't have to be delivered until the picture is complete as well. For writers, this flexibility in being able to test dialogue lines as the animation develops is both good and bad. Often the changes are simply different because overscrutinized lines start to seem dull. If a project has a realistic lip sync, this can cause animation nightmares as animators try to keep up with revised dialogue or lip sync goes out the window, which is often the case. Because something like audio, lighting, and all the other animation tools are flexible doesn't mean everything has to be tried again and again. Good directors and producers often rely on instinct and experience.

Communication

In pragmatic terms, many of the ideas in this book revolve around clear communication. Whether communicating creative ideas, or creating budgets for specific processes, communicating with everyone involved in the project is essential. Reverse engineering postproduction can be valuable. An example would be a project that is going to be rendered to film. Establishing a flow of what the film-out system requires and working backwards will inform all the other processes. What resolution does the film out require? How are the files delivered, and what is the format? Working backwards, does the edit system allow for what the film out requires? If not, what is the interim system that will bridge the gap between the two?

Time and Money versus Artists and Feelings

Because postproduction is at the end of the production cycle, the project is often over budget before it begins. Budgets are usually created to the cent, and the entire project will spend every cent it gets; it is a simple fact of life that post production will often come up short. Budgets can be defined so that postproduction receives a specific amount of time, money, people, and equipment. Production can also have its own fixed amount, but production, while not overspending, can still create problems that are then shifted on postproduction, which hadn't been accounted for.

One of the grayest areas in production is figuring out how long it takes a person to do a specific task. Often when developing a character or a new process, no one can actually gauge how long something can take. A director and a designer can jockey back and forth, as they both try to zero in on some intangible idea. Still, everything must be accounted for, and it takes a truly knowledgeable producer to manage this. Good producers know everything about every aspect of production, including materials, services, and people's work habits. Producers also have to have an often realistic view on the overall project. A designer and a director can spend months perfecting one character, but how important are the character's specific traits to the project? Are they a waste of money and energy or are they important, with an end result like the incredible Gollum from *The Lord of the Rings*? Managing the intangible and having to put finite values on feelings is always hard, but good producers must develop systems to do exactly that.

17

TOOLS, TECHNIQUES, AND MODERN ANIMATION

Tools

Aside from the actual programs that create animation, such as 3D applications, Flash, Moho, etc., animation is now tied closely to digital. From creating DVD discs for distribution, to digital ink and paint and digital editing and compositing, almost all animation is going through a computer system at some point in the filmmaking process. The few purists, who do the entire project analog, are few and far between. For filmmakers with limited resources, film finishing, striking film prints in 16mm or 35mm, is just too cost prohibitive.

Combining 2D with 3D

ON THE CD

Mixing up styles of animation isn't new, but combining the traditional with the latest technology is. Many forms and combinations can be created, and benefits of one medium can be used to great effect. The submarine shots **Sub.mov** and **Sub_interior.mov** on the CD-ROM were created using 3D as a multiplane camera. The technique is exactly the same as *Grime Shoed Diaries*, creating drawings and applying them to polygons in LightWave3D and then using the 3D element to create a sense of depth. From the camera's point of view, the scene's depth is totally apparent and the confinement of the submarine is amplified by the pipes and structures. In addition, the background is set slightly out of focus, which is a combination of the depth of field in LightWave3D and slightly blurring the furthest back image in Photoshop.

This is similar to how an old multiplane camera would work. Instead of a real camera and the layers on glass separating cels, the camera is CG and moves through the layers that have been mapped on the polygons. It's a simple but effective technique. The appearance of a drawn style as opposed to a modeled 3D object moving in 3D space can set itself apart from traditional cel. If the model of the submarine was in pure 3D, then it would have a CG appearance. This two- and half-dimensional technique is a stylistic choice, looks more hand drawn than pure CG, and is economical in both time and creation. Ultimately, stylization creates a more cel-animated look and only takes days to create and set up a scene, instead of using a fully cel- or CG-animated scene that could take weeks to get to the same level.

Scanner Animation

The average scanner is a high-resolution camera. If working in CG or cel, animators have the beauty of bypassing expensive recording devices like cameras, film, or digital. Stop motion is still of that world, obviously, but digital cameras are now equal to film. Although the high resolutions are prohibitively expensive, that will quickly change.

With CG-, film-, or Flash-style vector animation, it's much easier to work at film resolution. Something that is drawn or cel-animated works easily at Academy resolutions, but the scope and the end format of the project must be examined. Is a project finishing for film? If the answer is no, then what is your final viewing source? If it's a film for the Internet or for festivals that will be submitted on video, then working at D-1 NTSC level is probably high enough.

Naturally, it's going to look better if animators can always work at film resolution, but cost, storage space, production, and rendering speed become serious factors. There are real-world issues with resolution, cost, and time. Film resolution and high definition mean that images are going to take that much longer to render, and also require drive space to store these bigger images as well as a system that can edit film resolution. There are a few film resolution systems for professional or home computers, but they are naturally more expensive and require fast and expensive drives.

At some point, the question has to be asked if cost will actually stop the production. If the goal is to produce something as opposed to not, then lower the resolution and do the work on an affordable system. A system or format doesn't decide the quality of an animation—it's the animation and, as always, the story.

Film recorders and film-out systems as well as tape-to-film and digital systems have had a quite a revolution. Various companies will scan images onto film from nearly any source or tape. Animation proves itself far more forgiving when transferred from tape to film than filmed images of the real world. If a film-out is a consideration, coming from tape source to film doesn't have the disappointing results it used to.

A realistic approach that many animators take is to render the film as high as possible given the time, money, and render speed. Save the rendered frames, convert the frames to a workable editing format (NTSC, Mini-DV, or a comparable format), edit the film at the resolution available, and most importantly finish the film.

If the film takes off, and the filmmaker or a distributor wants to foot the bill for a film-recording output session, then the original frames, uncompressed, are available and could easily be recorded to film. Even if the project were rendered at NTSC D1 resolution and was recorded off to D1 or D2 or Digibeta, the original frames would be the first choice for a film-out because the computer is capable of generating colors way beyond the legal limits of NTSC. When the frames are compiled and put onto tape, the colors are compressed to fit into the parameters of the NTSC television broadcast format. Using the original frames will allow the red, green, blue (RGB) colors that a computer is capable of to go straight through to the motion-picture film, which can also handle the full spectrum of RGB color, bypassing the NTSC color squeeze.

By saving the original frames and then editing on video, the best of both worlds is possible, safeguarding for a film-out at a later date, while still being able to edit and proceed with a video finish of the project. This holds true for all media: save the highest format available and burn it off to storable media as a safeguard. With CG animation, Flash, or any digital program, if the production is organized and creates clean backups and storage of scenes, then the option of rerendering the project at a higher resolution at a later date is possible. Rerendering is an impossibility with live-action video or stop motion. However, if the stop motion or cel or any other form of analog animation is shot on actual film, then the production does have the luxury of rescanning the film at higher resolutions by going back to the original shooting negatives.

Certain software programs are capable of doing proxy versions, working at a lower resolution so that its data and functions can go faster and smoother. Then once the edit is complete, the editor is able to go back and recomposite or reedit with high-resolution images.

Digital Stop Motion

Stop motion has a truly unique style, but with it comes tremendous cost and setup; the other forms of digital animation have outgrown stop motion. Stop motion is still viable and it too has benefited from the digital revolution. Anyone with a digital camera that can be hooked to a computer and software that can create movies of the frames is doing stop-motion animation. The digital revolution still didn't do too much to help the inherent problems that stop-motion animators have with puppet manufacturing, sets and buildings, consistent light, and all the other problems that come from the live-action world. With animation cameras and a good plan, there's no reason why animators can't occasionally edit in camera, either completely or in sections. Obviously, editing in camera is going to completely lock what's been done, giving little flexibility, but it still is a possibility.

Digital Frame Grabbers

In stop motion, there are now powerful previsualization tools when shooting side by side with motion-picture film. Frame grabbers make it possible to see what has been shot, and what frame is about to be shot. Completely digital systems are available that take frames several times the resolution of Academy, null and voiding the idea of having to have a grabber next to a film camera. With these systems, what you see is what you get, and stop motion or physical object animation becomes that much easier. Instead of motion-picture film, the image is recorded and then stored on a hard drive, or compressed into an AVI or other format, and then viewed. This is innovation that was dreamed of by animators for years and years, and now even basic editing programs will do time lapse or stop motion.

Many master stop-motion animators, before the completely digital system was available, when doing stop motion and ultimately filming their final product, would use more than one frame grabber and as many as three to do exactly what running a preview from multiple angles in CG would do. With multiple frame grabbers, animators could evaluate how the animation looked from the hero camera, overhead, and from the back or front depending on what they wanted to study.

In the days of Ray Harryhausen, surface calipers were used to judge distance and also did measurements; there were also strange projection systems where the animator could mark on glass, using measure marks, where they wanted the character to move to. The Video Lunchbox® is a system that is widely in use in stop motion, but a separate device like the Lunchbox has a short life expectancy as digital systems take over. The Lunchbox was designed for stop motion and works perfectly, but there's no arguing that entire digital systems will eventually take over because all digital can eliminate steps.

It used to be that the digital quality wasn't up to the resolution of a full 35-mm frame, but now cameras, scanners, and film recorders easily work at film resolutions, including super resolutions like IMAX. Now the entire film at film resolution can be digitized into the computer, edited, composited, and finally printed out to film or other release media.

QuickTime Professional

QuickTime Professional is a cheap and useful tool for all animation production. The small program is amazingly versatile in creating all sorts of different compression as well as tailor making QuickTimes of any kind. Except for the .01 percent of filmmakers still working completely in analog, cutting film for linear editing video, everyone else is finishing their projects on computers. QuickTime is fast becoming the clearest and most reliable system to view animation in progress or for presentation. Quick-Time Professional will accommodate older AVI files and even create AVI files, which is the standard for personal computers (PCs), although not nearly as reliable as QuickTime. In sending out clips of any size, the program can be tailored to the slowest Internet connection or be completely uncompressed with zero loss. For scrubbing animation, QuickTime is also quite helpful, although when it's crucial, all working animation should have its own window burn frame count running for true accuracy.

Standard AVI files are read by most PCs and are the standard. However, they are limited for animation and often scrubbing frame by frame with sound doesn't work, which an animator needs for accurate logging and tweaking. It's often a safe bet that software programs that originated on the Apple Macintosh are flexible and work well, including Premiere, Photoshop, After Effects, QuickTime, Final Cut Pro, and others.

LENS FLARES

This same acceptance of almost any form of visuals extends to strange peripherals. In the early days of cinema and well into the 1960s and 1970s, lens technicians and engineers struggled with the ongoing problem of lens flares. Lens flares occur when the direct sun or a bright light source hits the lens directly, creating a spherical aberration on the film. Often, huge shades are used to try to minimize lens flares, but when a raw light source shines in a lens, there is a flare of some kind. Now because viewers are so used to the lens' inevitably filmed visuals, special effects add lens flares back in to mimic the flaw of a camera in the real world. All comparable software has some lens flare feature to attach to lights to make them seem more real in the sense that they're in the collective mind's eye of something that has been filmed. Programs often even mimic specific lens flares like a lens flare for a Panavision lens, which because of the distortion of the anamorphic lens, lens flares tend to create streaks that run across the shot. It is a strange fact that a lens flare tells the average eye that something real has been filmed. It is, however, an effect often used too often in animation, because it is just a push of a button.

PHOTOSHOP AND DEEP PAINT 3D

One of the most useful tools in computer animation, whether it's CG, cel, or Flash, is Photoshop; it is an important tool that can be used in so many forms. Both *Shards of Death* and *Grime Shoed Diaries* were created in Photoshop and the program was used extensively on the surfaces. It's also an important tool when used in conjunction with programs like Deep Paint

3D. Deep Paint 3D and Photoshop were able to create the green monster's detailed surfaces and textures. Deep Paint 3D has a plug-in called right hemisphere that allows the Photoshop and Deep Paint 3D to work closely together. This is important because Deep Paint 3D, which allows an artist to actually surface a CG model in 3D, can also send the unwrapped UV maps into Photoshop. If the plug-in is set correctly, all the different aspects that Deep Paint 3D creates, namely bump maps, displacement maps, and color maps, can be flipped back and forth between Photoshop while keeping the separate maps intact. In *Grime Shoed Diaries*, Photoshop was excellent for cleanup, all the colorization, as well as creating mattes so that elements could float against each other. Short sequences were created in Photoshop and then looped to mimic blinking neon signs and other elements of the city. Current versions of Photoshop also have batch programming that can process series of images very quickly.

The process is as follows: Images are drawn on animation paper that is registered, registration bars are then attached to the scanner, and the images are scanned. Even the most basic scanner can do this, provided that it doesn't revert to a default setting automatically after each scan. To scan animation, the animator needs to be able to scan the images without any change so that they will continue to hold the registration they were drawn with.

ANIMATION IN THE REAL WORLD

Unfortunately, with the relative ease of animation production, not all animation is as well thought out as some of the true legendary films of animation. In some cases, now with animation's infusion into every aspect of society, including commercials, the Web, and education, animation is often viewed as a content provider and an expensive tool that makes money. Animation is now linked very closely with children, which is a huge market base. Every aspect of a child's life has the potential to have an animated character on it: diapers, bandages, food, drapes, bedspreads, clothes, lunch boxes, and almost everything. Marketing is big business around the world, and good or bad, its byproduct is a huge sea of poor animation that is little more than a sales tool. Animation and indeed all visuals at a basic level are driven by the imagination of the viewer, and children's imaginations are unmatched by any other age group.

Often these shows and products are created and truly have no back story, no depth, and often don't have any well-developed characters at all. There's a tendency to put arms and legs on potential characters, or worse yet, blindly sticking sunglasses and tennis shoes on any object, creature, or product. The creators believe that a viable dynamic animated character has been created, which isn't necessarily true. Moreover, because animation has its extremes of style, color, and motion, and overall illusion, it still actually works, even when things are poorly put together.

This is not to flatly imply that all commercial advertising is bad, and that all animation has to be fully evolved to be successful. Many standards and icons of animation, from holiday television specials to commercials, are truly enjoyed by young and old a like. Famous characters like The Pillsbury Doughboy®, Tony the Tiger™, and Hawaiian Punch's™ Punchy™ have all had long advertising careers and have become part of Americana and the western world. Advertising characters are often better known than countless other animated characters, simply because of massive exposure.

In the late 1960s up until the 1980s, Hanna-Barbera® churned out an endless lineup of poorly animated shows. The shows included knockoffs of live-action shows, such as *I Dream of Jeannie*, *The Harlem Globetrotters*, and *Star Trek*, and countless more of their own creation, including *Magilla Gorilla* and even *Scooby Doo*. Viewed with modern eyes, these shows were lifeless, poorly animated, and mostly not animated at all, with occasional bursts of activity. To the children who grew up watching shows like *Scooby Doo*, it made no difference; children aren't that discerning.

Perception is a curious thing and can vary from person to person and day to day; it can depend on an infinite number of factors. Animation is so new and vibrant, with strange characters with big eyes and weird voices; children don't need much for animation to completely grab their attention and hold it. Often, certain people can always tell when an effect shot happened in a movie when someone else thought it was seamless. Certain people with heightened senses of perception can pick up on all sorts of visuals others don't. For example, some people can always spot false teeth, glass eyes, and wigs or toupees, often to the chagrin of the owner. If asked how they can tell, they often can't put their finger on it, but instead they'll say, "It just doesn't look right." They can pick up on clues about the look of the glass eye: the wetness isn't right or the movement isn't right. False teeth are too uniform in color and size. Fake hair has a different sheen. There is something inorganic about the way it sits—for some it works and others it doesn't.

Disney has always gone to great lengths to develop animation completely from story to character performance. Now taking center stage are films like *The Incredibles* from Pixar, whose levels of animation performance consistency is almost unmatched in the world. Weta Studios did an incredible job with *The Lord of the Rings* trilogy, and *Ice Age* from Blue Sky Studios also had a well-executed story, characters, and animation. In citing good character animation and storytelling, Aardman Animations must be noted for continually excellent and consistent work on their shorts and as well as in their feature *Chicken Run*.

Shrek 2, the highest grossing animated film of all time, has animation far below the quality of the illustrious leaders just mentioned, but is a funny and clever film with brilliant lighting, texturing, surfacing, and rendering. The creators of *Shrek*, however, must have consciously decided to sacrifice the quality of the animation because to animation people, it's quite obviously not to the level of its peers. By its performance it is obvious that not all viewers notice or care about weak character poses, intermittent lip sync, and other animation imperfections. *Shrek 2* didn't become the biggest animated movie ever by appealing solely to children. Obviously, adults aren't discerning either, and the levels of appreciation and perception for good or mediocre animation is almost like any other genre in that respect. Levels of finish exist in every form of entertainment. For every A-list movie there are more B-list movies and even more made-for-TV and direct-to-DVD movies. It's a unique trait of films that feature animation that amazingly animated scenes can live side by side with a mediocre scene.

Genres exist and have existed in every form of entertainment, whether it's abstract art, pop art, classical art, jazz, classical music, rock, country and western, comedy, drama, romance, or documentaries. Genres represent specific tastes often driven by culture, age, and gender differences, and fans of one genre often have strong negative reactions to other genres. Animation is even broader because it has many sublevels such as comedy, children, and anime, but there are people who don't like any animation, just as some people don't like any classical music.

A difference in genres doesn't necessarily mean one is better than the next. Although genre fans may think so, it's all simply a matter of taste. Poor animation, weak designs, and weak production aren't a matter of taste—they're obvious. It's unrealistic to expect the best possible character animation, design, and storytelling from all animated films and projects. From a practical sense, it's expensive, tedious, and can be overkill, Children don't care if *Speed Racer* has incredibly stiff and almost nonexistent animation; they are still engrossed in the story and the action. In the end, truly amazing character animation might be most appreciated by true animators and animation fans.

ANIMATION AND COMMERCIAL PRODUCTION

The face of animation has changed so rapidly, that it is a completely different animation world since just a few years ago. Before the year 2000, most animated commercials were done by larger and well-known animation or production companies; budgets were quite high, and it wasn't unusual for high-end commercials to cost a half million dollars or more. But as desktop systems began to rival larger systems, it became easier for smaller companies that were traditionally hungry for work to underbid larger companies and grab the work.

This trend has driven the cost of commercials drastically down, and the prevalence of small companies made of small groups of talented individuals even furthered the idea of more for less. Now, animated commercials have drastically smaller budgets, and using programs like Flash and After Effects has knocked the price down on broadcast commercials to an all-time low; this is a mirror on the state of animation itself. True, there are more outlets for animation with cable shows, the Internet, and giant film and animation festivals that have become large money-making ventures, but disproportionately the number of talented animators and filmmakers has mushroomed. To add to this model is the fact that viewers are more fractured than ever before. With specialty channels and recording devices like TiVo™ and others, millions of potential viewers now only watch very specific genres. The fan base of animation is ever growing, but so are the animators and filmmakers. It is more important than ever for animators, animation houses, and filmmakers to create more polished and high-end work, because the competition is so incredibly stiff.

Student film festivals that used to be considered more open and featured more less-polished work now often contain films and animations that are as high quality and polished as the best animation studios can produce. No longer are second-rate or unfinished projects even considered against the flood of high-quality visuals. High-quality visuals don't always go hand in hand with good storytelling or truly effective character animation that creates an emotional response.

Cost is a big consideration for animators and filmmakers funding themselves, and there is a lot more work that can be done digitally than can be done on classic film because of the cameras and film costs. Still, there are projects where film would be the first choice regardless of the increased cost and hassle because that look is essential to telling the story. Examples of these film projects would include when filming plates for animation. For stop-motion, 16-mm film is still a great way to film animation or live plates and can be scanned to tape or even high definition with excellent results. Cameras like the Bolex, the Beaulieu, and even the Russian Krasnogorsk have single frame capabilities. With cel or drawn and stop-motion animation, it still may even be more economical to use digital cameras linked straight to a computer to capture frames or to use scanners instead of down shooters.

LEARN FROM ANIMATION HISTORY

The expression "on the shoulders" means that everything that is being done, created, or innovated is only because it's on the shoulders of someone who developed something earlier that enabled him to arrive at that point. This idea goes back for all human history, from creating fire to storytelling and the rules of perspective. Talented animators always refer to being on the shoulders of other classic animators because good animators and filmmakers are aware and have studied their predecessors and their favorite filmmakers. They've studied their work and have used their foundations from what they've learned from other experts. The whole of this book is on the shoulders of all the great artists, filmmakers, and animators who came before it. The same is true for all of visual media; artists always study other artists and adapt and modify what that artist was doing to develop their own artistic voice.

The idea of on the shoulders highlights the importance of knowing about the history of the media and of art itself, because everything learned prior has come from that history. History isn't merely 500 years ago—history is anything that isn't now. For filmmakers and animators, knowing the history, especially the history of innovations, is required. Good animators and filmmakers study their subject closely both as animators and as fans. With frame by frame on virtually any VCR or DVD, animators and filmmakers are always keen to unlock the secrets of their visual history.

SUMMARY: THE BIG IDEAS

Among the many ideas presented here, three major ideas stand out in importance in this book. These ideas—learning the fundamentals, experimenting through trial and error, and developing a critical eye—truly link all the various topics in the book. The importance of learning the basics can't be stated enough. It's always said over and over to learn the fundamentals, and that is so true when it comes to telling visual stories. Cinematography, lighting, character animation, and editing all have a language that the media-watching world speaks. These disciplines are vast and complicated in their own right, but knowing their fundamentals is a shortcut to mastering them. Fundamentals also go much further when it comes to creating any type of compelling visual story, because one of the basic rules about visual storytelling is that bringing all these concepts together is always different, depending on the story. There is no "one-size-fits-all" checklist for how to best tell every single type of story, but there is a system of processes flexible enough to accommodate any scenario. To use that system to create compelling animation and tell genuine stories arrives at another major theme of this book. Film and animation and all the digital aspects that go with them are complicated; it is time consuming to create even small bits of good work. It's a catch-22 because the key to learning anything is to constantly experiment. Akira Kurosawa was right: how can you get to know anything when you've only done it a handful of times? A feature film can take years to create and produce, so it's possible that a lifetime isn't long enough to really learn this stuff.

As difficult as animation and quality production are, it's pure luxury compared to the unforgiving rigors of traditional film editing. Filmmakers and animators who began in analog filmmaking and animation with cameras and film prints all have a special appreciation for the digital revolution. Today there have never been more accessible tools that are capable of doing high-quality video, animation, and storytelling. Digital nonlinear desktop editing and programs like Flash are a major revolution, but the task is still the same: use the tools to tell a story. Far too much animation and visuals are focused on showing what the tools can do—they are not just eye candy. For the true storyteller, who is trying to move people emotionally, falling in love with the tools is like a surgeon falling in love with his scalpel. There is a huge glut of media out in the world now, but there is always room for good stuff. There is no excuse for someone who is trying to learn any part or all of this to not be doing it all the time. Only through trial and error can one learn the fundamentals. The final idea that is perhaps most important in this book is the person who is telling the story, directing the film, or animating the shot.

The well-trained eye and the brain can instantly recognize good animation over bad, and stage beautiful shots or stark, foreboding shots. There are so many decisions that are involved, and because animation is the culmination of so many disciplines, the depth of knowledge is exponential. Like a doctor, a writer only has to know the human body and all its physiology, but the animation filmmaker or director is more like a veterinarian who has to know anything that comes through the door in detail. There is a remarkable amount of science involved in filmmaking, animation, and technology, and the best scientists diligently take notes.

"Either you have it, or you don't," is the pessimistic view held by some animators and filmmakers. They're referring to that innate talent to recognize visual relationships, feel pacing, catch visuals other's can't, be an amazing problem solver on creative levels, and be able to inject one's own sensibility while being cognizant of some larger future audience—all the innate things that can make someone truly exceptional. But the human brain is an incredible machine and for anyone exploring visual storytelling; as students or seasoned professionals, you have the luxury of seeing so much good work. So make use of these resources to help you develop a true critical eye. Being a truly compelling storyteller goes beyond having the job title. It must be a way of life. Filmmakers make films and animators animate. Although some people may make an occasional film, or do some animation, that doesn't make them animators. Treating animation like live action is a mistake. They are certainly similar, but the differences are massive. Likewise, treating animation like a job is a mistake. Animation, films, and visual storytelling in their most basic forms are an expression of self, a way of thinking. Some may see animation as a good job or a way to make good money, which is possible, and many may cringe at idea of living the life of an animator, filmmaker, or artist. It's a mistake to get into animation if you don't truly enjoy the process. The hours are long, and the work is difficult, complex, and laborious. In spite of these shortcomings, the true filmmakers, animators, and visual artists wouldn't have it any other way.

ABOUT THE CD-ROM

The CD-ROM accompanying *Storytelling Through Animation* contains many short films mentioned in the text, as well as all of the figures from the book, in full color.

CONTENT

Figures: Contains the figures from the book, in folders by chapter.
Movies: Contains the short films and animation sequences mentioned in the book.

SYSTEM REQUIREMENTS

PC

Windows 98/Me/2000/XP
Windows Pentium processor-based PC or compatible computer
At least 128 MB of RAM
Quicktime 5.0 or greater

Macintosh

Mac OS 8.0 to OS X
180 Mhz PowerPC 7300
At least 64 MB RAM
Quicktime 5.0 or greater

INDEX